NORTH INDIAN RIVER (

W9-BOJ-452

3 2902 00174 8473

MORE
FIXING ELECTIONS

"Steven Hill is making the case for real reform of America's decayed democracy—changes that will actually give weight to every vote cast and begin the hard process of convincing Americans of every persuasion that their votes really can matter."
—William Greider, National Correspondent, *The Nation*

"*Fixing Elections* is an eye-opener for anyone who still believes in such myths as 'one person, one vote' and 'majority rules.' As Hill superbly demonstrates, winner-take-all is 18th-century voting technology for the 21st century."
—Tom Brazaitis, National Syndicated Columnist, *Cleveland Plain Dealer*

"*Fixing Elections* is one of the most penetrating and devastating critiques of American electoral politics I have ever read." —Richard DeLeon, San Francisco State University, and author of *Left Coast City: Progressive Politics in San Francisco*

"*Fixing Elections* is a fascinating, well-written page-turner that describes how our political system evolved, why it is not working, and how we can fix it. *Fixing Elections* is a must-read on your road to real political empowerment."
—Phil Tajitsu Nash, *Asian Week*

"What's wrong with politics in America? What explains our abysmal voter turnouts — down, according to one international study, to 138th in the world, sandwiched between Botswana and Chad? Why are vast segments of the country political wastelands for one party or the other? Why are so many million voters "orphaned" in states where the candidates they prefer are likely never to win? Political analyst Steven Hill offers up a single answer in his new book, *Fixing Elections*—It's the winner-take-all system of elections."
—*Houston Chronicle*

"Hill says that the root cause of it all, the factor that has allowed our politics to deteriorate, is something that's rarely talked about: the winner-take-all system. He warns that a system "based exclusively on where you live, rather than what you think" will prove "increasingly disastrous in a diverse, pluralistic society like ours."
—Philadelphia Inquirer

Steven Hill is co-founder and Associate Director of the Center for Voting and Democracy, a nonprofit organization promoting election reform. He frequently appears on radio and TV to discuss political issues, and his articles have appeared in dozens of national newspapers and magazines including *The Nation, Salon, Ms., New York Daily News, Los Angeles Times, The Wall Street Journal, The American Prospect*, and *The Washington Post*. He is also co-author of the book *Whose Vote Counts?*

FIXING ELECTIONS

The Failure of America's Winner Take All Politics

STEVEN HILL

Routledge
New York and London

NORTH INDIAN RIVER COUNTY LIBRARY

Published in 2002 by
Routledge
29 West 35th Street
New York, NY 10001

Published in Great Britain by
Routledge
11 New Fetter Lane
London EC4P 4EE

Routledge is an imprint of the Taylor & Francis Group

Copyright © 2002 by Routledge

Printed in the United States of America on acid free paper.
10   9   8   7   6   5   4   3   2   1

All rights reserved. No part of this book may be reprinted or reproduced or utilized in any form or by any electronic, mechanical or other means, now known or hereafter invented, including photocopying and recording or in any information storage or retrieval system, without permission in writing from the publishers.

Library of Congress Cataloging-in-Publication Data .

Hill, Steven, 1958-
    Fixing elections : the failure of America's winner take all politics / Steven Hill.
    p. cm.
    Includes bibliographical references and index.
    ISBN 0-415-93193-2 (HB) — ISBN 0-415-93194-0 (PB)
    1. Elections—United States. 2. Voting—United States. 3. Representative government and representation—United States. I. Title.

JK1965 .H55 2002
324.6'3'0973—dc21   2001058921

CONTENTS

The Landscape of Post-Democracy

> It has been said that democracy is the worst form of government—
> except all those other forms that have been tried from time to
> time.
>
> —WINSTON CHURCHILL

The numbers would be comical if they weren't so alarming: only 5 percent voter turnout in a recent Dallas mayoral election. Six percent in Charlotte, 7.5 percent in San Antonio. Seven percent in Austin.[1] Seven percent in Tennessee's congressional primaries, 6 percent for a statewide gubernatorial primary in Kentucky,[2] 3 percent for a U.S. Senate primary in Texas, and 3 percent for a statewide runoff in North Carolina.[3] Several cities and towns in southeastern Massachusetts reported single-digit turnouts, with Rochester at 7 percent;[4] their 2000 state primary election drew less than 10 percent, a modern record low according to the Massachusetts Secretary of State.[5] Outside Detroit, turnout for several school board elections was in single digits, one as low as 1.1 percent of registered voters; in Ann Arbor, an area that has a reputation for emphasizing education, turnout for school board elections has been well under 6 percent for the past several years, with one election sinking as low as 4.4 percent of eligible voters.[6] In Virginia, the 1997 primary for attorney general, the state's top law enforcement official overseeing criminal as well as civil matters for the entire state, turned out 5 percent of registered voters, the lowest figure since 1949.[7] For the first time, we have been seeing an increase in *single-digit* voter turnout levels all across the nation.

In numerous other cities and states, turnout for local, state, and even congressional elections has fallen into the teens and twenties. In politically charged San Francisco, which some liken to a kind of Athens of American democracy, turnout for the 2001 runoff for city attorney plummeted to about 13 percent of eligible voters. In seven cities in Los Angeles County, California, elections for city council were *canceled* when no challengers emerged to contest against the safe-seat incumbents.[8] The 1996 presidential election produced the lowest voter turnout in America's premier election in the last seventy years, less than half of eligible voters; the 2000 election was barely an improvement.[9] For all the pyrotechnics surrounding the 2000 presidential election, it is easy to lose sight of the fact that nearly half of eligible voters once again sat it out. More people watched the Super Bowl or TV fad *Survivor* than cast ballots for either Gore or Bush.[10]

The 1998 midterm congressional elections dipped even further, to just over one-third of eligible voters, despite the first midterm use of motor voter laws, which greatly boosted voter registration rolls. The 2000 congressional elections clawed to a marginally higher level.[11] A week of *Who Wants to Be a Millionaire?* or O. J.'s freeway ride in his white Bronco drew a comparable audience.[12] Voter turnout in the world's lone remaining superpower has lurched to 138th in the world—sandwiched between Botswana and Chad.[13] Perhaps most disturbing, only 12 percent of eighteen- to twenty-four-year-olds and 8.5 percent of eighteen- to nineteen-year-olds voted in the 1998 congressional elections.[14] The future adults of America have tuned out and dropped out, electorally speaking, even more than their 1960s hippie counterparts.[15]

Rational choice theorists should instantly recognize the sanity of their reasons: for most people, voting doesn't matter anymore. The act of voting on the first Tuesday in November seems increasingly pointless and—particularly in the middle of a busy workday—a waste of precious time.[16] The "voting incentive" in recent years has seriously eroded, producing what Anthony Downs once called a "rationality crisis."[17] Washington, DC, has emerged as a kind of House of Horrors theme park, with much of what passes for politics today having degenerated into an obnoxiously partisan brew of bickering, spin, hype, petty scandal, name-calling, blaming, money-chasing, and pandering. Politics today certainly puts to the test that famous Churchill witticism, that democracy is the worst form of government—except for all the rest.

Americans, now the least exuberant participants in the established democratic world, have become used to diminished expectations. But in addition to our severe underparticipation—which amounts to nothing less than a political depression—recent national episodes have pulled back the curtain to reveal that, besides being a politically *depressed* nation, we appear to be a raucously *divided* nation as well. The impeachment debacle, the resignation of two House Speakers, piled on top of Elian, O. J., Monica, and various other deracinations now too numerous to list—and all of *that* capped by the astonishing UnElection 2000—have each in their national moment exposed critical fault lines and fissures simmering beneath the surface.

How deep these divisions go has been the subject of conflicting opinion and keen debate in venues ranging from the *New York Times* to Internet chat rooms, from the conservative *National Journal* to the liberal *Atlantic Monthly*.[18] Immediately following the November 2000 election, *USA Today* published a much-discussed red and blue map showing the counties all across the nation won by either George W. Bush or Al Gore. At the very least, what the map revealed in its huge swaths of fiery red (Bush counties) and royal blue (Gore counties), was that the national divide has a certain shape to it: it is partisan, of course, but that partisanship has a strong regional element, as well as a cultural and racial component. If nothing else, it was this potent combination of national divisions—partisan, cultural, racial, and regional—that raised the hairs on more than a few necks, for whenever that combination has emerged in our history it has been explosive. Think of the Civil War in 1865; the aftermath of Reconstruction that produced Jim Crow and the "solid South"; the disenfranchisement and terrorizing of the freed slaves and their descendants; the violent struggles for civil rights one hundred years later, and numerous conflicts in between and since.

Our national division has emerged like that volcano that suddenly arose in the middle of a Mexican cornfield, its orogenesis completely unannounced and unexpected, growing larger and its shadow looming ominously over the surrounding landscape. Moreover, Census 2000 has revealed the galloping pace of our nation's rapidly shifting diversity. Are our political institutions and practices ready for this? The 1990s began with the Rodney King riots that combusted South Central and other parts of Los Angeles; the decade ended and the new century began with a series of police shootings of unarmed black men in New York City; Washington, DC; Seattle; and elsewhere. In Cincinnati, a police shooting resulted in four days of the worst street fighting since the death of Martin Luther King. The 2000 presidential election displayed eye-opening levels of racially polarized voting, as did a statewide referendum in Mississippi in April 2001 that retained the use of Confederate symbols on their state flag.[19] There are ongoing and disturbing signs of national *frisson* on various horizons, and they seem loaded and capable of erupting without much notice if we don't deal with some of the precipitating factors.

But what are these precipitating factors? Obviously there are many complex interwoven social, political, historical, and economic elements. In this book, I tackle one element that I believe is fundamental to the rest, yet it has been overlooked in the past and will be overlooked again unless we pull it to center stage, and fully, carefully, examine it.

The central thesis of my examination is what is known as the Winner Take All voting system—Winner Take All for short. No, I'm not talking about voting *machines*, like the antiquated punch card voting machines known as Votomatics that burst upon the national scene during the botched 2000 presidential election. I'm not talking about chads, paper ballots or Internet voting, nor am I talking about the byzantine hodgepodge of voter registration or ballot access laws or even campaign finance laws enacted in the fifty states. While those are all undeniably important, and part of the many components of our "democracy technology" that operate to allow our republic to express and renew itself via periodic elections, I am talking about a type of "democracy technology" that is even more basic than those.

Rather, I'm talking about the rules and practices that determine how the votes of millions of American voters get translated into who wins and who loses elections, resulting in who gets to sit at the legislative table and make policy. I am talking about the voting system itself, the engine of a democracy. Voting systems are to a democracy what the "operating system" is to a computer—voting systems are the software that makes everything else possible. Like a computer's operating system, a voting system functions silently and largely invisibly in the background, and yet it has an enormous impact on the five defining dimensions of a democratic republic: representation, participation, political discourse and campaigns, legislative policy, and national unity.

What is a "voting system?" Popular reality TV shows like *Survivor* and *The Weakest Link* have been conspicuous in recent years in their use of elections. Remember when the Tribal Council voted for the final winner on *Survivor II: The Australian Outback?* The seven voters had to choose between the last two players, Tina and Colby; everyone had one vote, and the highest vote-getter won. Well, that was a type of voting system, and it even has a name—Winner Take All—because only one person, Tina or Colby, could win. The winner was going to get the million dollars, and the loser was going to get nothing (well, actually, the loser, Colby, got the consolation prize, $100,000). In fact, *Survivor* used the same selection method, that is, voting system, in each episode. For six weeks the highest vote-getter was voted off the show, whether that person had a majority of the votes or not.

The Winner Take All voting system—highest vote-getter wins—and variations of it, as well as other voting systems that are quite different, are used in thousands of elections all over the United States. Yet most people take for granted the voting system used by their town, state, or nation. It is invisible; just like a computer's operating system, we only notice it when it breaks down, when something goes awry like it did in Florida. But in fact there are different voting systems employed all over the United States, indeed, all over the world. For instance, we use one kind of voting system to elect the president that gives a state's Electoral College votes to whichever candidate wins the most votes, even if that candidate has less than a popular majority—that's Winner Take All again, just like on *Survivor*, but with a lot more voters. And the Machiavellian tactics used in our public elections aren't much different than on *Survivor,* either.

We *noticed* the voting system during UnElection 2000 because it broke down badly in various and unfortunate ways, well beyond malfunctioning voting machines, as we will see. Remember, Winner Take All is so named because the highest vote-getter wins everything, and all the other candidates win nothing. There was a lot at stake in the final official Florida vote for president, when George W. Bush won *all* of Florida's electoral votes even though he beat Al Gore—amid great controversy—by only a few hundred votes in the official count.

Many Americans think that this "highest vote-getter wins" method is the only way to hold an election because that method is so prevalent in the United States, but it isn't. *Survivor II,* for instance, could have required that the person "elected" for rejection in each round have a majority of the vote, instead of simply the "highest number of votes." The fact that they didn't created problems on Episode 7, when two players tied, one of them being Colby, an eventual final-ist. They resolved the tie by using votes in previous rounds as the tiebreaker, not a very elegant solution from a democratic point of view, since voters in previous rounds may have selected differently had they known the eventual stakes.

Similarly, each state could require, for instance, that the winner of their state's Electoral College votes must have majority support, and use a two-round runoff (which is used in many Southern states for state elections) or an "instant" runoff[20] to arrive at that majority. Those would be two other types of voting systems, both of which get rid of the problem of "spoilers" and allow fields of multiple candidates to compete, raising issues and presenting electoral options to voters, without fear of strange results like "split votes" and winners with less than a popular majority. Had we used a two-round runoff or instant runoff in the 2000 presidential election, we certainly would have avoided the five-week Florida fiasco, and probably ended up with a different winner besides. That's because voting systems *matter*; different voting systems can produce different results, and some primitive voting systems produce distorted results.

As this book demonstrates, our antiquated Winner Take All voting system is at the root of much of what is perplexing and polarizing about our politics today, not only in presidential elections but in legislative elections as well. Outside the brief display of "rally 'round the flag" domestic unity following the September 11 attacks, numerous pundits and commentators have observed that the general level of national division and partisan warfare has reached unsettling proportions not seen by our nation for many years. And even with the unifying stimulus of foreign aggression, by December 28, 2001 *USA Today* was running headlines like "Lawmakers Back at Each Other's Throats." But this hardly should be surprising, given how the "winner take all" nature of our electoral contests exacerbates the stakes, and hence the division and conflict.

Worse than antiquated, Winner Take All is downright *dangerous*. It distorts national policy, robs voters of representation, and pits partisan voters as well as racial, ethnic, and religious minorities against each other for a scarce commodi-ty—political representation. Americans are used to thinking of unstable democracy occurring in places like India, Italy, and Israel, where collapsing coalitions for parliamentary government can topple the government. But when a presidential candidate can win with less than a majority of votes, and with fewer votes than his main opponent, raising eyebrows as well as shouts of illegitimacy; or when one man, one Senator, Jim Jeffords from Vermont, can switch from Republican to independent and foment "a coup of one," throwing control of the U.S. Senate to the opposition party;[21] or when a small number of Senators representing a tiny fraction of the U.S. population consistently can torpedo legislation supported by the majority; or when one political party, the Republicans, can win less than a majority of congressional votes nationwide yet still end up with a majority of seats, as happened in 2000, those are clues that something is woefully amiss with our own democratic structures and practices.

This book analyzes the extent that the eighteenth-century "democracy technology" known as the Winner Take All voting system is affecting the five key dimensions of our democratic republic: representation, voter participation, campaigns and political discourse, legislative policy, and national unity. These five dimensions are like the sturdy poles of the great tent of the republic, of representative democracy,[22] holding it aloft. Winner Take All relies near exclusively on (1) geographic-based representation and/or (2) a two-choice/two-party political duopoly. From those two defining characteristics of Winner Take All other dynamics and tensions are unleashed that impact the five dimensions, often with unintended and damaging results.

This analysis finds that the impacts of Winner Take All are considerable; that the impacts are sweeping and, as we will see, decidedly troubling. Winner Take All is robbing voters of viable choices in the voting booth and is contributing to an entrenched decline in voter participation and engagement. As we will see, most voters have become bunkered down into "safe" one-party districts gerrymandered during a secretive redistricting process that guarantees reelection of incumbents. Winner Take All also is distorting representation of the majority as well as the minority, including millions of "orphaned" Democratic and Republican voters living in opposition legislative districts, as well as racial minorities, women, independents, and third-party supporters.

Moreover, Winner Take All's geographic-based paradigm is exacerbating national tensions that are turning entire geographic regions of the country into virtual wastelands for one political party or the other. It is producing "phantom representation" and "artificial majorities" where a minority of voters sometimes wins a majority of legislative seats and a disproportionate, exaggerated amount of political power. In short, as we will see, Winner Take All has produced a national legislature that does not look like "the people" it purports to represent, nor does it think like us or act as we wish it would. No, under the distortions of Winner Take All, the majority in the United States does *not* necessarily rule.

Winner Take All also underlies an alarming debasement of campaigns and political discourse, which have grown increasingly harsh, negative, and uninformative; it affects how political campaigns are conducted, as candidates and political consultants chase the infamous "swing voters," that small slice of fuzzy-headed and disengaged voters who determine the outcome of elections in a Winner Take All system. New campaigning technologies like polling and focus groups, it turns out, are *malignantly* suited to the Winner Take All system and its typical two-choice/two-party field, allowing the precise targeting of political spin and hack-attack sound bites to ever smaller slices of swing voters, while everybody else and the issues they care about are relegated to the political sidelines. The dynamics unleashed by Winner Take All also are affecting how much money is needed to run a viable campaign, how the media covers those campaigns, and how political ideas are debated and decided.

Finally, Winner Take All is draining the vitality out of well-meaning political reforms like campaign finance reform, the Voting Rights Act, term limits, and redistricting reform. Indeed, as we will see, the impact of Winner Take All is pandemic and indiscriminate, reaching into our communities and neighborhoods, into our psyches and attitudes toward government and elections, indeed into our very self-identity as a nation. Generally speaking, the pervasive impact of Winner Take All on participation, representation, campaigns and discourse, policy, and national unity is hurling us toward chronic national division and political depression.

In short, Winner Take All is making *losers* of us all. Even the apparent winners lose when our representative democracy is so sickly. This escalating combination of nagging national division and dispirited political depression is particularly perilous because each are mutually reinforcing of the other. As most players (i.e., voters) abandon the field in frustration, the game is left to be played by increasingly partisan careerists and professionals, and by the most zealous activists who seize center stage, further polarizing politics and policy. And as politics becomes more polarized, negative, and downright nasty, more and more people turn off and tune out.

One cannot help but wonder: what will be the political destiny of a nation that, on the one hand, has fewer and fewer voters and diminishing electoral engagement, but, on the other hand, is so rife with the heated passions of political division and acrimony, cleaved along the volatile lines of partisanship, regionalism, and racial and cultural polarization? It's a confounding and alarming paradox. Much like stagflation has bedeviled economists with the twin scourges of inflation *and* recession—theoretically impossible, the textbooks once informed us—our national politics is being squeezed between the Scylla and Charybdis of a passionless political depression intertwined with the torrid fervor of partisan obsession and divide. And our eighteenth-century Winner Take All system is at the root of the problem.

Despite the enormity of its impact, the Winner Take All voting system has been mostly overlooked or ignored by various political commentators, scholars, and reformers, much to the detriment of our national discussion and efforts at reform. Yet the gravity of the moment requires a new term to describe what is happening to the national consciousness: post-democracy—that is, a polarized, splintered nation, nominally democratic, but with fewer and fewer voters. A nation where many of our civil institutions are still vital and our individual rights reasonably well-protected, but where elections fail to inspire or mobilize, or to touch the issues most important in our lives, or to bind us as a nation. A nation where an emerging trend of regional balkanization—exacerbated by, as we will see, our Winner Take All practices—is alarmingly suggestive of the geographic-based polarization faced by other large

Winner Take All democracies like India and Canada. What are we to make of this fractured, voterless, post-democracy? Its onset is an alarming development in our nation's political history.

It is important to note that post-democracy will not be merely the latest stage of an old, familiar specimen; post-democracy is not the same as pre-democracy or proto-democracy. In fact, it will have transmogrified into a new and unexpected phyla of political life, a new evolutionary form without precedent in human history. Post-democracy is a type where huge numbers of citizens simply have given up. And they have given up because they don't think politics or elections matter in their lives. They have made a decision, conscious or unconscious, that political/electoral participation is a waste of time and that withdrawing makes more rational sense, despite its obvious perils. They have *chosen* to toss their political fate to the winds, keeping their fingers crossed that whatever emerges, or whatever faction is in control, won't screw them over. The specter of post-democracy unearths from the historical crypt Gaetano Mosca's disquieting theory of an elite ruling class, which asserted at the beginning of the twentieth century that "the history of all societies has been, is, and will be, the history of dominant minorities," contrary to any theories of majority rule.[23]

Post-democracy is a political iceberg of staggering proportions, and we are heading straight for it. Yet it is rarely talked about around American dinner tables, there is no presidential-sponsored national dialogue, there are no gavels pounding in Senate committee hearings or in august courtrooms. There are few opinion-page rants or *60 Minutes* documentaries attempting to galvanize public attention and mobilize the national brain trust, seeking a solution. Instead, all there is, is silence. A silence that is occasionally broken by a few well-meaning but misguided missives about the impact of private money in elections, or TV talking heads debating the passions of presidential ejaculatory stains on a dress—and now the vagaries of chad, Votomatics, and butterfly ballots. All the while the iceberg drifts, relentlessly closer, and practically nobody is talking about it. It's downright spooky.

*   *   *   *

The Framers and Founders of our nation prided themselves on being on the cutting edge of all manner of things.[24] Ben Franklin, besides being a statesman, philosopher, and author, was an inveterate tinkerer and inventor whose numerous scientific and practical innovations included the lightning rod, bifocal spectacles, and a stove. The equally brilliant and eclectic Jefferson, besides authoring the Declaration of Independence and serving as President and Secretary of State, was also an architect, designing his own elegant estate, Monticello, and buildings for the University of Virginia. Washington was a successful farmer who tried to keep abreast of the latest scientific advances, giving assiduous attention to the rotation of crops, fertilization of the soil, and the management of livestock.

Not surprisingly, the Framers also were on the cutting edge of "democracy technology." They paid close attention to the secular political theory of their times, and were well versed in the political practices and theories of the ancient Greeks as well as the Roman Republic (although, it must be said over and over, their "enlightened" politics was not so informed by what we know today as human rights, either seeing nothing wrong with or not being troubled enough by slavery and sexual inequality in their midst). Invoking a clock as the technological symbol of their Deist age, John Adams called the government "a complicated Piece of Machinery," requiring a "nice and exact Adjustment" of its "Spring Wheels and Weights."[25] Madison, Hamilton, and Jay, as coauthors of the *Federalist Papers,* presented a masterly exposition of the new federal system, as well as the burgeoning ideals of justice, the general welfare, and the rights of individuals. In *Federalist* No. 10, Madison weighed the causes and consequences of political factions; Washington, in his farewell address, warned—prophesied, actually—about the excesses of political parties. In *Federalist* No. 9, Hamilton wrote that

> the science of politics . . . like most other sciences has received great improvement. The efficacy of various principles is now understood, which were either not known at all, or imperfectly known to the ancients. The regular distribution of power into distinct departments—the introduction of legislative balances— . . . the representation of the people in the legislature by deputies of their own election—these are either wholly new discoveries or have made their principal progress towards perfection in modern times.

When we inherited our Winner Take All system from our eighteenth-century British colonizers, it was the cutting edge of democracy technology compared to the rule of a despotic king. As political scientist Robert Dahl and others have pointed out, the Winner Take All voting system was pretty much all that the Framers knew, since other voting systems like cumulative voting, choice voting, limited voting, proportional representation, instant runoff voting, and the like had not yet been invented. Nor would these other voting systems be invented until the middle of the nineteenth century or later, so, like the locomotive or the steam boat, we can hardly blame the Framers for not employing democracy technology that did not yet exist.

But today, just past the launch of the twenty-first century, Winner Take All is horse and buggy technology. It is akin to using DOS 1.0 rather than Windows XP or Mac OS X. More than simple, the eighteenth-century Winner Take All system is *primitive.* We will see how the internal mechanics of Winner Take All render it archaic and antiquated for the modern demands of representation, political discourse, and policy formation in an extremely mobile, pluralistic,

Internet-connected, multinational, multipartisan, multiracial, multireligious, multitasking, multi–World Wide Webbed and free trading mass society. Obviously the world today is a much different place that it was at the dawn of our nation. We should think carefully about the ramifications of using an eighteenth-century piece of democracy technology in the twenty-first century.

What Hamilton called the "science of politics" must continue to study and research our democracy technology with fresh eyes. This book presupposes, quite optimistically, that we can diagnose what ails our political system, that we can upgrade our political institutions and practices. I am quite certain that the Framers, being the enlightened rationalists that they were, would have applauded the effort to peer into the political fog and figure out the next step, or even the next ten steps, as their piece of handiwork continues to evolve into one that lives up to the lofty rhetoric and aspirations of their astonishing age.

To understand more fully how far we've fallen, consider the words of Alexis de Tocqueville, writing in his 1835 seminal work *Democracy in America*. Tocqueville had this to say about our political ancestors:

How happens it that in the United States, where the inhabitants arrived but as yesterday upon the soil which they now occupy, and brought neither customs nor traditions with them there; where they met each other for the first time with no previous acquaintance; where, in short, the instinctive love of country can scarcely exist;— how happens it that every one takes as zealous an interest in the affairs of the township, his county, and the whole State, as if they were his own? It is because every one, in his sphere, takes an active part in the government of society. . . . The citizen looks upon the fortune of the public as his own, and he labors for the good of the State. . . . The political activity that pervades the United States must be seen in order to be understood. No sooner do you set foot on American ground than you are stunned by a kind of tumult.[26]

The "tumult" of democracy, the animal spirits of popular sovereignty, have grown rather timeworn and tame in the United States today. The contrast between Tocqueville's description of that nineteenth-century democratic paragon and its deformed somnambular twenty-first-century descendant could not be more stark. So come, I invite you to fly over the terrain of the American political landscape, as we chart our descent into the twin black holes of political depression and national division, where an anxious future of post democracy awaits.

PART ONE
Geography Is Destiny

CHAPTER ONE

"A House Divided . . ."

A house divided against itself cannot stand.

—ABRAHAM LINCOLN

The Geographic Divide

On November 9, 2000, two days after the presidential election, as the nation was beginning to absorb the full extent of the five-week debacle that was about to ensue, *USA Today* published a map (similar to the one printed on the back cover of this book) that was portentous in its message. They say a picture is worth a thousand words, and this map was like flying in a spaceship high above the Earth, surveiling an aerial snapshot of the American political landscape.

What the map showed, specifically, was which candidate won the most presidential votes in each of the 3,111 counties in the fifty states. The Gore counties were in navy blue, the Bush counties in a fiery red. With such a close election and with so many counties in play, one might have expected to see a smattering of red and blue counties sprinkled all across the land. Not so. Instead, what one saw was solid blocs of red, engulfing entire states, starting about the Mississippi River and sweeping west. The Deep South was also nearly solid red, with scattered patches of blue. Huge chunks of the Appalachians moving north and west into Indiana and Ohio were also solid red. Most of the blue counties clung thinly to both coasts, thoroughly dominating there, and the blue also peppered various Midwest and Western pockets, but near-exclusively the urban areas of those regions. All told, the flaming Bush red formed a kind of Berlin Wall running north–south at the Mississippi River, fanning out in two directions to engulf most of the West and bending east near Missouri to embrace the southern areas stretching to Bull Run and Sherman's March to the Sea. It looked like the territory of two conflicting armies in a new kind of uncivil war.

George Bush's "army" captured an astounding amount of territory: 2,434 counties to Al Gore's 677, nearly 2.5 million square miles to Gore's 575,000 square miles. Yet Bush country was low-population and rural, while Gore's were the major population centers,[1] enough to give Gore over 500,000 more popular votes nationwide. Unquestionably, as the map revealed, ours is a divided nation—but there is a particular geography to the divide: a vast sea of fiery Republican red across the rural heartland, framed and trellised by bicoastal and urban patches of blue, the island outposts of Gore and the Democrats. If Al Gore had succeeded in winning the presidency, he would have been able to fly from Washington, DC, to the California border without passing over a single state that voted for him. The trend was unmistakable, and it has become more pronounced with each passing election. To view the aerial map was to feel a lump in one's throat, a creepy chill of the spine, north to south. There was no mistaking its alarming message, nor its ramifications—railing national division with a distinct *regional* axis.

But there was another axis to the national division. As illuminated by exit polls, the *cultural* differences between Bush's and Gore's voters were similarly striking. Bush attracted people who go to church more than once a week; who think it's more important that the president be a moral leader than a good government manager; who oppose stricter gun laws; and who believe that if a public school is failing, the government should pay for private school. In a throwback to the election of Jimmy Carter and the fallout from Watergate, Bush supporters believed honesty was the quality they valued most in a leader, followed by leadership and likeability. A great majority of Bush's rural voters felt government was stepping on their religious beliefs and out of step with their views on crime, abortion, and handguns. Nearly half of all voters across the country said the impeachment scandal was very or somewhat important in determining their vote, and three-quarters of them voted for Bush.[2] Voters with incomes over $100,000 also strongly preferred Bush.[3]

Gore drew heavy majorities of liberal and more secular voters who rarely or never attend church; who support stricter gun laws; and who say a public school should be fixed if it is failing. Their paramount value was experience, followed by competence to handle complex issues and caring about "people like me." Gore's more urban voters were defined by tolerance, progressive cultural views, and a fear that Christian conservatives want to impose their views on everyone. Union members went 63 percent to 32 percent for Gore;[4] low-income voters (making $30,000 or less) favored Gore, as did heavy majorities of gay and Jewish voters.[5]

Besides the stark regional and cultural divisions, the presidential exit polls revealed a third axis to our national division: *racial polarization*. Despite a relatively weak record by the Clinton–Gore administration on civil rights, affirmative action, racial profiling, sentencing disparities between crack and powder cocaine offenses, and welfare reform, an astonishing 90 percent of African Americans voted for Gore, as did 62 percent of Latinos and 55 percent of Asians (95 percent of blacks and over 60 percent of Latinos voted against Bush in his home state of Texas, a stunning rejection of the Texas governor's symbolic racial overtures and self-proclaimed "compassionate conservatism").[6] Combined, people of color accounted for an unprecedented 30 percent of Gore's total vote, and nearly 20 percent of all voters.

On the other hand, whites constituted almost 95 percent of Bush's total vote, with white men in particular preferring Bush, as did 80 percent of the white religious right.[7] More revealing, while women overall voted 54–43 for Gore, *white* women actually favored Bush by one point, 49–48. *Women of color* created the gender gap.[8] The same can be said of the poor: while 57 percent of voters with incomes under $15,000 voted for Gore, poor whites broke slightly for Bush. Moreover, of the demographic groups that had a fairly unified vote of 60 percent or more for one candidate—blacks, Latinos, Jews, union members, gays, residents of large cities, and white males—all but union members, gays and big-city residents were racial or ethnic groups. And the large numbers of people of color in big cities and unions (about 25 percent of the latter) largely accounted for the heavy Democratic vote of those demographic groups.[9]

These combined axes of division—regional, cultural, racial, and partisan—in essence defined the contested terrain between the two opposing camps. *USA Today* perhaps summed it up best: "Compassionate conservative Bush and New Democrat Gore tried broader appeals to change the color code of the presidential map. But ultimately, both wound up winning little more than their traditional political turfs."[10] The national fractures and fault lines revealed by UnElection 2000, then, were geographic, particularly city versus rural; they were regional, with the old Confederate South and the rural and Mountain West opposing the old Union states of the North and Northeast plus the West Coast, with New Mexico, Florida, New Hampshire, and the Midwest as toss-ups; they were heavily racial, with voting patterns starkly polarized along racial lines approaching that of South Africa's in its first post-apartheid elections; and they were somewhat gendered and income-based, but with an obvious racial component.

Visually, looking at the national map, it was red versus blue like two rival armies, each with their own geographic strongholds and legions of foot soldiers. And it solidified the suburbs and collar counties, particularly those in key battleground states, as the crucial swing districts for national politics. Suburbanites, so avidly stalked by both nominees via millions of dollars in obstreperous TV ads, tend to be a little more Republican than Democrat, and the candidate that wins this group tends to win the election. In the 2000 presidential election they split 50–50, with the suburbs casting well over 40 percent of the total vote. Fifty years ago, fewer than a quarter of Americans lived in the suburbs, now roughly half do; every ten years another ten members of Congress represent predominantly suburban districts.[11]

Taken as a whole, the emerging electoral demographic amounted to a stratagraphic mix kind of like Neapolitan ice cream—the vanilla rural layer and the chocolate urban layer sandwiching the mitigation of the tonier strawberry suburbs. This is the stratified political landscape for which the Winner Take All voting system, with it's zero-sum "if I win, you lose" calculations, is supposed to act as the political filter that translates votes into political power. As we will see, this augurs a worrisome national future.

The Geography of Division

> In America, there is more space where nobody is than where anybody is—that is what makes America what it is.
>
> —GERTRUDE STEIN

Flying high above the political landscape, one gets an urge to descend like a lunar rover and explore a bit of the terrain below to really get a feel for the mise-en-scène of national disunity. First, we touch down somewhere within that vast prairie of Bush red—the territory of Idaho. Idaho is a state some say was shaped like a logger's boot to reflect its rugged forests and mountain terrain, dominated by loggers and miners. Bordered to the east by the jagged teeth of the Continental Divide, with small and sparse towns meandering along the course of the Snake and other rivers, and with its interior subsumed by dark dense jungles such as the "No Return" Wilderness Area, Idaho provides some of the largest tracts of unspoiled primitive areas in the Lower 48. Legend has it that this is Bigfoot country, a vast canopied expanse where a gigantic and enigmatic ape-species can live undetected.

Idaho has been the terminus for all sorts of pioneers, wanderers, and vagabonds, including fur trappers, homesteaders, wild mustangs, the remarkable potato,[12] former Confederate soldiers (who settled here following the Civil War and dominated the legislature), vigilantes, Populist Party farmers, and tenacious trade unionists and miners.[13] More recent arrivals include racist skinheads, white Aryans, anti–United Nations separatists, ex-hippies, high-tech businesses fleeing California, radio talk show pull-yourself-up-by-your-bootstrappers, and anti-government back-to-the-landers like Randy Weaver, who fought off FBI and ATF agents for ten days at Ruby Ridge before surrendering after the shooting deaths of his wife, son, dog, and one agent. Yes, Idaho, which is smack in the heart of Bush country, has a little bit of everything—except elected officials who are liberal or Democrat. Those are practically extinct species, with sightings nearly as rare as Bigfoot.

For instance, the Idaho state House currently sits sixty-one Republicans and only nine Democrats, an astounding 87 percent Republican. The Senate is worse, with thirty-two Republicans and a lonely three Democrats. The handful of elected Democrats can be more properly described as political spectators rather than political players. Idaho's governor is Republican, as are both U.S. Senators. Elected Democrats are so rare in Idaho that the state's two seats for the U.S. House were won easily by Republicans in 2000 with landslide margins of 40 percentage points, on average; one seat was won by the Republican lieutenant governor, a fellow by the name of Butch Otter, despite a checkered past including a 1993 drunken driving conviction. He won the seat of retiring congresswoman Helen Chenoweth, herself the subject of a firestorm over a previous extramarital affair after her harsh condemnation of Clinton peccadilloes, particularly since she had been elected six years earlier partly by capitalizing on the admitted extramarital affair of her opponent.

As an indicator of how much Idaho had tilted Republican in recent years, in 1998 Idaho's former Democratic Congressman Richard Stallings tried to win back his old seat, which he had held from 1985 through 1993. Even though the seat had no incumbent and even though Stallings outspent his GOP opponent Mike Simpson, still he lost 53–45 percent. The state simply had changed too much. Thus, no matter how bad or kakistocratic the Republican candidate, Democrats and liberals in Idaho now have a hard time winning. Not that there aren't plenty of Democratic voters, especially in university towns like Boise and Pocatello; but they are effectively buried beneath the avalanche of Republicans, conservatives, Rush Limbaugh ditto heads, NRA Second Amendment fundamentalists, anti-government patriots, and Mormon communards. If people of color are the most consistent Democratic voter, it should be no surprise that Idaho is snowfield white.

The same is true in neighboring Utah. In November 2000, the Republican governor, Mike Leavitt, won his third term, and voters approved an initiative making English the official language of the state. Both its U.S. Senators are Republican, as are two-thirds of Utah's U.S. House seats and 69 percent of its state House and Senate seats. Ross Perot actually outpolled Bill Clinton in Utah during the 1992 presidential election, 27 percent versus 25 percent of the popular vote, with George H. W. Bush easily beating them both. In fact, the electoral outlook is so grim for Democrats in Utah that Democratic party leader Scott Howell has threatened the possibility of running no Democratic legislative candidates at all. The Democrats threatened this also in 1996, the point being, said Howell, to "make Utahans wake up to what local political life would be like with no alternative voice, no alternative power, to the majority Republicans. We have one-party rule in Utah."[14]

It's ironic hearing a Democrat bleat like this, given how hostile the national Democratic Party establishment was to Ralph Nader and his Green Party alternative. Yet Howell can sound positively vestal in making his case. "The Republicans give us no opportunities," he says. The GOP leadership, especially in the Senate, "crush[es] us at every turn." In the Utah Legislature, even motions that take two-thirds vote can fly through the House and Senate because Democrats don't have sufficient numbers of legislators to stop them. Thus, Howell maintains petulantly that the "No Democrats" alternative is viable. "The reality is we live in a one-party state. Maybe it's time to have no Democrats in the Legislature. Then let citizens see how they like that."[15]

Liberals and Democrats in the Western and Mountain states of Montana, Wyoming, Nevada, North and South Dakota, Colorado, Nebraska, Kansas, Oklahoma, and Arizona can bleat similar complaints. They too play more of a spectator role in state and local politics. That's a vast area of fiery red Bush country—for convenience of identification, let's call it Bushlandia—stretching from the Canadian to the Mexican borders, over 1 million square miles, the size of all of Western Europe including Scandinavia. If we add in Alaska, the region is practically the size of a continent. Bushlandia is its own nation of sorts, of over 26 million people, but sparsely settled with about the same population as the states of New York and Massachusetts—yet over five times the representation of New York and Massachusetts in the U.S. Senate, and nine more votes in the Electoral College.[16]

Although the denizens of Bushlandia have seen what must seem to them like a flood of immigrants in recent years, particularly Latino laborers, the region is still 85 percent white; Colorado, Arizona, and Nevada have seen the biggest influx, and without their numbers Bushlandia is 90 percent white.[17] Bushlandia has its own distinctive rural culture beyond the blandness of national TV culture, even its own distinctive art. Walking into an art gallery in, say, Jackson Hole, Wyoming, or Scottsdale, Arizona, is like visiting a temple to the myth of the Cowboy. Finely crafted paintings and bronze statuettes, replete with chaps, stirrups, lariats, rifles, six-shooters, and ten-gallon hats, have been sculpted into occupational poses and framed on the walls for the admiration of the customers and cowboy cognoscenti.[18]

Surprisingly, the southern United States, particularly the states of the Deep South, do not appear at first glance to be charter members of the nation of Bushlandia. Because of historical factors stretching as far back as the Civil War and Reconstruction, when the hostility of white Southerners toward Lincoln's slave-liberating Republican Party cemented their support for the Democratic Party, Democrats still win many elections in the formerly Confederate land. For instance, the states of Georgia, Alabama, Mississippi, and North Carolina all have Democratic majorities in both statehouses, as well as Democratic control of the governors' seats (a trifecta that was decisive for Democrats in these states during the recently concluded round of redistricting). In the states of Alabama, Louisiana, Mississippi, and Arkansas, Democrats still control a whopping average of 69 percent of state legislative seats, and George W. Bush's own state of Texas has a Democratic state House and a majority of Democrats in its congressional delegation.

But these are not necessarily Gore-blue types of Democrats; rather, most are fairly conservative, reflecting the schizophrenic history of the Democratic Party in the South, now as the civil rights party but previously as the party of segregation. Jim Crow, George Wallace, and now-Republican Strom Thurmond's States' Rights Democratic Party (the infamous Dixiecrats in 1948), which drew their strength from racially conservative working-class whites, are estranged stepbrothers of Lyndon Johnson, John Lewis, and the civil rights legislators of the post-1960s.[19] Truth be told, most white Southern Democratic elected officials would be *Republicans* above the Mason-Dixon line.[20]

Completing the Democratic Party profile in the South, more than half of all African Americans still live in the former Confederacy, and black voters, who are some of the most consistently liberal and Democratic voters in the country, have been able to take advantage of the Voting Rights Act of 1965 and subsequent amendments to elect a few of their own type of Democrat. This has woven an uneasy coalition in the Southern Democratic Party between conservative "Boll Weevil" or "Blue Dog" Democrats, with roots among those remaining working-class whites who have not defected to the Republican Party, and black Democrats who tend to be liberal.[21] Because of this historical freak circumstance, most national Democratic Party leaders—like Al Gore—are too liberal for most Southern Democratic voters (in fact, many *Northern Republican* legislators, such as Republican Senator Olympia Snowe of Maine, probably could not be elected south of the Mason-Dixon line in *either* party, since they would be seen as too liberal).[22]

So while the South may not be solidly Republican, it *is* solidly conservative, with the conservative vote generally pulling "R" for presidential and statewide offices and most U.S. House seats and "D" for many state legislative and a few U.S. House races, with island outposts of black and liberal Gore-blue electing some black Democrats. While one would have to place the core of Bushlandia in the Mountain and Prairie states, the conservative South contributes its own Confederate flavor to the mix. Together, these two regions form the solid geographic craton of the conservative movement. In the cowboy and formerly Confederate nation of Bushlandia, liberals and/or Democrats are effectively politically smothered, like a field of flowers snowed over by an avalanche.

The Land of New Goreia

A San Francisco Republican? What's a San Francisco Republican? That's a contradiction in terms.

—A DEMOCRATIC PARTY ACTIVIST IN SAN FRANCISCO

But let's not feel too badly for Democrats and liberals. Next we touch down in ... liberal San Francisco. Here, we overhear standing jokes about that rare and exotic bird, a San Francisco Republican. This species has zero representation at the city, state Assembly, Senate, or congressional levels. In fact, a Republican candidate hasn't won a local San Francisco election in decades. "In the San Francisco area, one of the wealthiest places in the country, there are now places where the Republican Party has all but disappeared," says one Republican strategist.[23] In California at large, where fully 12 percent of the nation's population resides, Democrats control the governor's seat, both U.S. Senate seats, all state executive offices except the Secretary of State, and over 60 percent of U.S. House, state Assembly, and state Senate seats. In the Assembly races the average margin of victory was nearly 35 percent.

Democratic gains in the U.S. House in 2000 were largely due to California, where shifting racial demographics combined with politically short-sighted, antiracial policies pursued by previous Republican Gov. Pete Wilson have made California a GOP wasteland. Even Republican bedrock Orange County now elects Latino Democrats due to the rapid Latinoization of that area, and state Republican leaders are scratching their heads over a viable strategy. Rather comically, an effort was made to draft Hollywood movie star Arnold Schwarzenegger as the white knight—or in this case the gubernatorial candidate for 2002—that might ride in and save the California Republicans from themselves. Ah-nold, after initially being flattered by the attention, declined the invitation.[24]

In Massachusetts, we discover a similar story. Democrats in Massachusetts have a complete monopoly on congressional representation; for the second election in a row, not a single Massachusetts Republican was elected to one of its ten U.S. House seats or to the Senate. Republican voters in the Bay State might as well not have showed up to the polls; they completely wasted their votes and their time. Of Massachusetts' ten Democratic House incumbents in 2000, five had no Republican opponent; of the other five incumbents, only two had opponents who had ever run for elective office.[25] In the Massachusetts state Senate, six lonely Republicans hold the ramparts against thirty-four Democrats, and in the state House Democrats hold 86 percent of the seats. Sixty-three percent of Massachusetts' state legislative races weren't even *contested,* mostly by Republicans, because they either couldn't find candidates or didn't want to waste resources fielding candidates in races where they didn't stand a chance (but hey, that was slightly better than 1998, when 70 percent of state races went uncontested). Of the remaining fifty-six contested seats, Democrats won thirty-nine of these—70 percent—by huge landslide margins.

The problems Massachusetts Republicans have in fielding credible candidates for elective offices have now become predictable, and its chances for changing in the near future are dismal. There is no better example of this than Massachusetts' senior senator, Ted Kennedy. Chappaquidick, personal family tragedy, infidelity, persistent bouts with alcoholism—none of these have been able to knock from the saddle a Kennedy in heavily Democratic Massachusetts. First elected to the Senate in 1962, Kennedy has never had a truly close contest. He won with 58 percent in 1994 even in the face of a big-spending challenge by Republican businessman Mitt Romney, even during the Republican national sweep. Kennedy's personal shortcomings would end the career of any Democrat in Bushlandia (although not the career of a Republican, like the aforementioned Butch Otter in Idaho, elected to the House), but in Massachusetts they are forgivable. It seems that, for Massachusetts voters, given a polar choice between any Republican and a scandal-plagued Democrat, the "D" trumps all else nearly every time.[26]

The outstanding exception has been the governor's seat from 1990 to the present, where the post-Dukakis era made Massachusetts ripe for a change—but to one of the more moderate GOP elected officials in the nation. Compared to many southern Democrats, Republican governor William Weld was so liberal that his later nomination by the Clinton administration to the ambassadorship of Mexico was blocked by Sen. Jesse Helms and hard core conservatives, who labeled Weld an "ardent advocate of abortion rights, promoter of the militant homosexual agenda, and champion of liberalized drug laws."[27] In other words, in liberal Massachusetts, successful Republicans are in step with their state's *voters*, not with their own national party.

Other states like Maryland and Rhode Island are similar Democratic Party strongholds. Both chambers of their state legislatures are at least 70 percent Democratic, and Republicans didn't bother contesting nearly 55 percent of the Rhode Island seats. All of Maryland's five highest profile statewide offices (governor, two U.S. Senators, lieutenant governor, and Attorney General) are held by Democrats, as are most of Rhode Island's. Major urban areas like Los Angeles, New York City, Seattle, Atlanta, Chicago, Detroit, Philadelphia, Newark, New Haven, Boston, Washington, DC, and others, where the population density is up to a thousand times greater than the sparse tundra of Bushlandia, are similar near-wastelands of GOP representation (and when Republicans do get elected—like New York City's last two mayors—almost always they are pro-choice, pro–affirmative action moderates who never could get elected in Bushlandia). In these areas, elected Republicans are, practically speaking, spectators in the legislatures. These bicoastal areas and urban strongholds of Democrats, combined with still-strong labor areas in the Midwest and scattered urban islands in the heart of Bushlandia red, comprise the latticework of blue Gore country—for convenience, let's call it New Goreia—that outlines and cross-hatches Bushlandia like a trellised picture frame.

New Goreia too is a nation of sorts, a shimmering urban peacock with nodal points of high population density, traffic jams, skyrocketing rents, and gritty crime; cities filled with a multiracial beat, jazzy Web sites, and a new demographic of affluent young dot.commers. Entire sections of cities today cling to the edge of livability, with ghastly extremes of poverty living in the shadows of sumptuous wealth, increasingly separated by castlelike gated condos and exclusive complexes, drawbridges pulled up. Nevertheless, when Election Day rolls around, most urban denizens are united—in the nation of New Goreia, conservatives and Republicans are effectively and politically smothered, just like Democrats and liberals are in Bushlandia.

Compounding the urban mosaic of New Goreia is a rapidly shifting racial demographic. For the first time in our nation's history since the early colonies, certain regions of New Goreia are galloping toward a demographic that will see whites eclipsed as a majority.[28] Minorities now make up roughly one-third of the nation's population, up from one-quarter in 1990. Those with Spanish surnames are increasing five times faster than the general population, and in Los Angeles, Houston, San Antonio, and Dallas, Latinos outnumber non-Hispanic whites. The 2000 U.S. Census reports that the Latino population, now 35.3 million nationwide, rose 58 percent over the past decade and now surpasses that of African Americans. Los Angeles has a Salvadoran population as large as San Salvador, and New York City has as many Puerto Ricans as San Juan and as many Dominicans as Santo Domingo. According to the Bureau of the Census, our largest state, California, no longer has a white majority, and our second largest state, Texas, will soon follow. By 2025, our third and fourth largest, New York and Florida, also will follow, and about one-fourth of the total U.S. population will be living in states where the racial "minority" population exceeds the white population. By 2050, Latinos will have supplied fully two-thirds of the nation's population growth, and U.S. Latinos will compose the third-largest Latino nation in the world, with only Brazil and Mexico having more Latinos.[29]

If Latinos are the slumbering giant of U.S. politics, Asians are keeping up the pace. The Asian population increased by 41 percent over the past decade, and it is projected that by the year 2025 Asians will comprise over 17 percent of California and 9 percent of New York State, most of this population growth centered in cities and 60 percent of Asian Americans being foreign born. While over a third of Asians live in California and New York, large communities now can be found in Georgia, Pennsylvania, Minnesota, and several other states. African Americans will hold at their present level, about 13 percent of the nation, most of that in the South where blacks now comprise 19 percent of the region's population. All told, nearly 40 percent of the U.S. population under age 18 is Hispanic, Asian, black, or another minority; minorities account for more than half of the non-adult population in five states—Arizona, California, Texas, New Mexico, and Hawaii.[30] Thus, the very terms "majority" and "minority" are being turned on their heads.[31] These are demographic shifts of epic proportions.

Viewed from the hinterlands of white Bushlandia, no doubt the salsa-rap-hip-hop beat and rainbow density of New Goreia must look like an "alien" nation, and possibly a hostile one, particularly as it becomes a launching pad for a Latino invasion of Bushlandia itself. In the 1990s, the white voting-age population rose by more than 22 percent in the Bushlandia states of Utah, Idaho, Nevada, Colorado, and Arizona, with most of the white migrants coming out of mongrelizing California. In the South, Georgia, North and South Carolina, and Tennessee also saw their white voting-age populations increase by more than twice the national average.[32] Nevertheless, by 2025 the Bushlandia states of Nevada and Arizona are projected to increase to over 40 percent minority, and Colorado and Oklahoma to over 25 percent minority; even the states of Idaho, Wyoming, Kansas, and Utah are projected to increase to over 15 percent minority within 25 years.[33] While the Hispanic population mostly is concentrated in major metropolitan areas, smaller cities and rural areas in the West, Midwest, South, and Northwest experienced the largest *percentage* increases, with states like Arkansas seeing an increase of 337 percent in its Hispanic population. Yes, the cowboy white nation of Bushlandia will be dramatically affected by the ongoing racial "coloring" of American society.[34]

One of the obvious ramifications of this demographic tide is that it is becoming increasingly difficult for a single representative to straddle the diverse constituencies residing in many of these districts. To paraphrase a rascal-turned-momentary-prophet, Rodney King, "How will all this diversity get along?" More importantly, *will* it get along? Or will pockets of demophobic white resistance spring up in Bushlandia and elsewhere, erecting legal and extra-legal barricades to try to hold back the tide?[35] Is America standing at the edge of an abyss, awaiting yet another anxious epoch of racial strife, turmoil, and violence? Bill McInturff, a Republican pollster, told the *Washington Post*: "We have two massive colliding forces. One is rural, Christian, religiously conservative. [The other] is socially tolerant, pro-choice, secular, living in New England and the Pacific coast."[36] Add the gun powder of race to this volatile brew, shake it a bit, and you may end up with a volatile cocktail that we are more accustomed to reading about in other large Winner Take All nations like Canada and India.

Between Bushlandia and New Goreia exist real differences of temperament, social values, and politics that appear to be, once again, muscularly implanted in regional geography, culture, and race. Whenever that combination—region, race, culture, and partisanship—has emerged in our nation's history, the impact usually has been explosive. Other previous episodes of fervent racialized sectionalism—the Civil War and Reconstruction, of course, but also the desegregation battles of the 1940s, 50s and 60s, which produced political factions in the South like Strom Thurmond's Dixiecrats and George Wallace's American Independent Party—inevitably were times of great political turmoil and violence. One study has found that presidential election results since the Reagan era most closely resemble the presidential election results from the two historical eras when the two parties were most polarized over racial issues: the antebellum period of the 1850s and the civil rights era of the 1960s. As it turns out, the "red states" taken by George W. Bush were much the same as those taken by James Buchanan in 1856, an alarming continuity separated by 144 years.[37]

As one recalls the bitter partisan battles of the past decade, capped by UnElection 2000 and the first one hundred days of the Bush administration which culminated in moderate Sen. Jim Jeffords bolting a rightwardly flailing Republican Party, one can't help but wonder about the future of our nation. The patriotic swell following the September 11 attacks postponed the bitter partisanship that had been building to a boil for the first eight months of 2001 (over, let us recall, wedge issues like tax cuts, a sudden deficit, arsenic levels in drinking water, national energy spikes, insider coziness among the Bush oil-men, and finally a looming budget battle). While the simmering lid was retamped under the weight of the collapsed Twin Towers, can there be any doubt that the underlying steam still is building pressure? It is, of course, always challenging to see far enough to know where we sit on the great wheel of history. Certainly opinions range about *how* deep is the Red America/Blue America divide. But in thinking about the level of recent national division, historian Robert Dalek has observed, "Maybe it's an overstatement on my part, but I have the scent of the Civil War in my nostrils. It reminds me of the tensions in Viet-nam during the 1960s. Now we are moving into a similar kind of moment."[38]

More to the point, as we will now see, these are the molten demographics that must be squeezed through the pinhole of the clunky eighteenth-century Winner Take All voting system. Winner Take All, it turns out, with its exclusive reliance on geographic-based representation and a two-choice/two-party duop-oly, is exacerbating greatly this national division, and is polarizing our politics along regional, racial, partisan, and cultural lines.

The New Berlin Wall

> Toto, we aren't in Kansas anymore.
>
> —DOROTHY, SOMEWHERE OVER THE RAINBOW

Because we use electoral practices that elect one representative per district, Democratic and/or liberal voters in Bushlandia and Republican and/or conser-vative voters in New Goreia are consistently and unsurprisingly outvoted for just about everything. For each individual contest, for each single-seat race, there are simply too many of one type of voter—Republicans in Idaho or Kansas, say, or Democrats in Massachusetts or California or in most cities—overwhelming the other type of voter. The resulting monopoly politics not only affects representation—to the point where elected opposition has become a nearly extinct species—but also creates a new classification of voters: "orphaned" voters.

Orphaned voters are those Democrats and Republicans who, like the sup-porters of third parties everywhere and most non-white voters, are *geographic* minorities in out-of-favor districts and states with little hope of electing a repre-sentative. Orphaned voters have no electoral or governmental outlet for their political sympathies or passions. Ironically, though, it's not as if there aren't mil-lions of Republican voters *living* in Democratic districts, and vice versa, all across the country. It's just that these orphaned voters—these geographic minorities—never win representation because, district after district, they don't have sufficient votes and are outvoted.

Using the presidential vote as an indicator of the numbers of Democratic and Republican voters in each state, we can estimate how badly—and unfairly—these orphaned voters are smothered. We can compare the disproportion between the presidential popular vote and the number of legislative seats won by each party to arrive at a vote-to-seats ratio (the presidential popular vote is used rather than the aggregate statewide vote for each party in state legislative races, since so many state legislative races are uncontested—41 percent in 2000—which serves to depress voter turnout totals for state legislative races).[39] So comparing the popular vote for Gore to the number of seats won by Democrats at the state legislative level, we find that the 29 percent of Idaho voters who pulled the Democratic tab for president in November 2000 ended up with only 13 percent of Democratic seats in the state House of Representatives. In essence, these voters won 16 percent less representation than their numbers would indicate they deserve. In Kansas, Democrats were similarly subsumed, winning 39 percent of the presidential vote but only 25 percent of state House seats. In Nebraska, Democratic voters didn't win a single seat in the U.S. House; just like Republicans in Massachusetts these voters have no representation at all.

This disproportionality works both ways, naturally, and in Rhode Island Republican voters accumulated about 34 percent of the presidential vote for Bush but ended up with only 16 percent of the state representation, a "representation ripoff" of 18 percent. In Maryland, 42 percent of voters pulled Bush—approaching a majority—but they ended up with only 25 percent of the Republican state House seats, a ripoff of 17 percent. In Massachusetts, 35 percent of voters pulling R in the presidential race won only 14 percent of state House seats, a huge representation ripoff of 21 percent.[40]

In all of these states and more, orphaned voters are smothered by the partisan avalanche that blankets the single-seat districts of their respective region or state. Consequently, the political cultures of these states and regions, which ideally should thrive on exchanges of ideas and robust public debate, have become political monocultures, lacking the most basic levels of political pluralism.[41] The bitter partisan divide gets exacerbated by the Representation Ripoff, as one side effectively wins more representation than they deserve, while the other side is frustrated and unfairly marginalized. Oftentimes these representation ripoffs produce undeserved veto-proof majorities that can ram through radical policies without a popular mandate. The resulting monopoly politics creates a dangerous tension—fenced off, district by district, into political turf where victorious majorities lord over vanquished minorities, it's nothing less than a new kind of political feudalism.

These sectional/regional schisms are becoming more and more cemented into the nation's bedrock—Bushlandia versus New Goreia. The politically schizophrenic South, which for years voted Republican for president but elected Democrats to the U.S. House, has all but disappeared. As recently as the beginning of Clinton's presidency, the breakdown of Southern House seats was 85–52 in favor of the Democrats; now it is 81–55 Republican (with one conservative independent). And the number of districts across the South that split Republican for president, Democrat for House, has plummeted from nearly seventy-five a decade ago to fourteen in 1996.[42]

This regional realignment in the South, as many observers have pointed out, has turned the politics of the South—and of the GOP congressional leadership on Capitol Hill—upside down. Since the civil rights era, the once-Democratic "Solid South" has shifted to predominantly Republican territory, leaving the Democratic Party more uniformly liberal and the GOP more solidly conservative—with the two sides more rabidly polarized than ever.[43] Moderates of either party are quietly but conspicuously disappearing—of the thirty-six U.S. House members in the Deep South, for instance, only six today could be described as moderate to conservative Democrats, and one or two as moderate Republicans, with the rest right-wing Republicans and a scattering of black liberal Democrats.

Gone also are most of the Democratic House seats in the Plains and Mountain states; Mike Mansfield-style prairie populism and Democratic congressional beachheads in this vast sector of the country are few and far between, buried beneath the Republican avalanche. The Northeast, meanwhile, has been moving in the opposite direction; moderate-to-liberal Rockefeller Republicans and New England congregationalists, once a granitic mainstay of Yankee politics, are now an endangered species.[44] Sarah Binder, a congressional scholar at the Brookings Institution, has charted the recent disappearance of centrists, estimating a decline from about one-quarter of all Members of Congress in 1980 to 10 percent in 1996.[45] Increasing numbers of liberal and conservative safe seats won by huge landslide margins of at least 40 percentage points make the political chasm once bridged by moderates implacably wide and deep.

"The divisions between the two parties are probably larger than they've been any time in the modern era," says Roger Davidson, a leading congressional scholar at the University of Maryland. On the full range of social and international issues, many experts observed that the House may be as polarized as at any time since Reconstruction in the late 1860s—the last time an American president was impeached.[46]

The Paralysis of the Two-Party System

Most portentous for the future, however, these schisms strongly reflect the degree to which national politics and partisan competition *still* are centered around appeals to culturally and racially conservative white voters, who *still* comprise the bulk of American voters. The University of Michigan's National Election Studies (NES), a series of public opinion polls taken over the last three decades, gives an interesting snapshot of political attitudes since the early 1970s. For a whole host of questions, including abortion, government intervention in the economy, the size of government, the amount of services government ought to provide, the desirability of a national health plan, and more, the general public has barely budged in its attitudes over the last three decades, even as both political parties have become more partisan in their platforms and their rhetoric. But in two areas the country indeed has become more conservative since the mid-1980s—the first, a decisive appetite for cutting government spending; and the second, decreasing government aid to blacks and minorities. And in the public mind these two are closely fused, half of the NES respondents now agreeing that "the government should not make any special effort to help blacks because they should help themselves," up from a third of the population in 1984.[47]

Another study of this attitudinal shift attempted to differentiate between Southern and Northern attitudes, and found that a link between Southern racial animosity and evangelical religion seemed to be fueling much of the shift toward conservative Republicanism among white Southerners. The old Confederacy, it turns out, "continues to be unique in generating great support for a conservative political party based distinctively on *racial* conservatism—just as it did in the years before the Civil War, and during the period of aggressive civil rights action in the 1960s."[48] This attitudinal shift once formed the basis of Richard Nixon's successful "Southern strategy" in the early 1970s, which used coded words and symbolic gestures and actions directed at white people in the South, particularly white men, to paint the Democratic Party as the party of racial minorities, rioting cities, and civil rights agendas.

Ronald Reagan continued the Nixon strategy, peeling off white Democrats, particularly in the South, with his attacks on race-based policies, government spending, and stereotyping of cities. George H. W. Bush used his infamous Willie Horton ads and coded language to finger Dukakis and the Democrats as the party of liberals, big spenders and, again, as being "soft on crime", that is, racial minorities. One study found evidence that the Jesse Jackson presidential bid in 1984 drove prejudiced Southern whites to the Republican Party.[49] New Democrat Clinton hoisted his finger in the air and, taking note of the political winds, tried to expropriate parts of the GOP strategy by taking high-profile steps to distance the Democratic Party from the racial tag. As the polarized voting patterns of the 2000 presidential election reveal, much of *current* U.S. politics still can be explained by the dynamics unleashed during this not-so-distant era by Nixon's politically shrewd yet racially reprehensible tactics.

Thus, in both acutely obvious and subtly subcutaneous ways, race still matters.[50] Today, while the portion of the national Democratic Party's agenda that speaks to broad-based economic security targets the white working class—the so-called Bubba vote—the association of the Democrats with urban areas, civil rights agendas, and racial minority groups alienates some of these same white working class voters.[51] Despite eight years of Clinton's racial-distancing, the Democrats now provide near-exclusive representation for the densely populated cities, the Republicans for the vast territory of sparse rural areas; the Democrats are now the "colored party," the party preferred by racial minorities,[52] while the GOP is the party of most whites, especially most white men who perceive that they have gotten next to nothing from governmental policy over the past generation and have been hurt by affirmative action and taxpayer-funded programs like welfare. Between 1979 and 1997, for instance, male workers with only a high school diploma saw a decline in real wages (after inflation) of 12 percent and high school dropouts saw a stunning 26 percent decline in pay. Their confidence in "government's willingness or ability to 'represent me' or 'get the job done' is at or near all-time lows."[53]

Given the rapidly shifting demographic picture, and the "if I win, you lose" calculations of a two-choice Winner Take All system, both political parties are tiptoeing as carefully as they can around the color line, strategizing as they go. Both parties try to attract white swing and suburban voters—but in qualitatively different ways. The Republican Party of George W. Bush appeals, ironically, by trying to appear less racist and more "compassionate," by softening the rhetoric and the harsh edges of the 1992–1998 Republican Party of Gingrich and Pat Buchanan, highlighting people of color at their nominating convention (raising charges of "minstrel show" tokenism), and appointing them to a few high-level positions in an effort to send a signal of reassurance to *white moderate suburbanites* that they intend to govern from the center, at least racially. And the Democratic Party of Clinton/Gore appeals by trying to appear less beholden to racial minorities, publicly distancing themselves from racially based policies (e.g., the 1992 version of Bill Clinton taking pains to distance himself from African Americans by dissing Sister Souljah and Jesse Jackson), in an effort to send a signal of reassurance to the *white working class and suburbanites* that they intend to govern from the center, at least racially, even as a prominent liberal segment of their party remains the only political bloc remotely interested in racially based solutions.

But if the Democrats bend too far toward conservative whites, they will lose the enthusiasm of racial minorities that handed Al Gore 30 percent of his overall vote. And if the Democrats are too vocal or visible in pushing race-based policies, they will alienate even more of the white swing vote. This is a real puzzle for the Democrats; it appears that for the time being they will have a hard time appealing to both racial minorities *and* white swing voters. No matter how hard they try, their national party and candidates cannot straddle that line and not suffer electorally. Even on the municipal level this dynamic raises problems for Democratic candidates, as was evident in the 2001 New York City mayoral race. The Democratic candidate, Mark Green, could not rally Democratic Hispanic voters after attacking their candidate Fernando Ferrer in the Democratic primary. Consequently, Green ended up blowing his lead and losing to a moderate Republican millionaire businessman, Michael Bloomberg.

The Republicans, on the other hand, are caught in a similar dilemma. They have been the obvious beneficiaries of the white vote migration since the Nixon presidency, particularly among white men. Yet in the longer term, facing an exploding racial demographic, the GOP has painted itself into a corner. At this point no amount of "compassionate conservatism" can easily erase the ghoulish site of Pat Buchanan at the podium during the 1992 Republican National Convention, nor the race-baiting rhetoric and policy of the Reagan-Bush-Gingrich era, nor the mean-spirited rollback policies of California's Republican Gov. Pete Wilson in the 1990s. Most racial minorities, both their leaders and their voters, can recognize the difference between a con job and a sincere effort at coalition-building. Certainly the racially polarized 2000 presidential election results indicate that the GOP has a long way to go in order to attract votes from the most rapidly expanding demographic in the nation—Latinos and, to a lesser extent, Asians.

Longer term, the shifting racial demographic can only hurt the Republican Party nationally, as it has in California, if their efforts at outreach to racial minorities don't go beyond symbolic overtures to actual substantive policy. But if they move too far in that direction, become too cloying or pandering with their "compassion," it will snap back on them in the form of Buchanan's "peasant army" abandoning them like Buchanan did. For perhaps the next ten years or so, the Republican Party as the incumbents perhaps will retain a leg up; but on the order of fifteen to twenty-five years, as the Latinoization of the United States proceeds in full swing, the GOP will be faced with the burden of its past and the dilemma of its future: whether to embrace racial minorities at the risk of alienating its base of white, racially conservative supporters. At that point, we may see the rumblings of another George Wallace–type party emerge, challenging the GOP for the white working class vote.

Thus, the two parties are pinned and wriggling between the twin horns of their Winner Take All dilemma. Given the regional splits and the shifting racial demographic, and with the two sides roughly tied nationally in terms of voters' sympathies, national politics is likely to career for some time from bumper to bumper like a frenetic pinball. As each side bunkers down in their foxholes of Bushlandia and New Goreia, calculating ways to triangulate into pockets of white swing voters, cross-partisanship and cross-fertilization of ideas have become increasingly difficult (except in campaign rhetoric around election time or when rallying around the flag following the September 11 attacks).

Curiously, most assessments of the future of Red and Blue America have concluded that the national divide, while evident in numerous polls and measures, is not all that deep or wide; that it is most vociferous in talk radio blather and during moments of crisis like UnElection 2000, but it soon subsides and life goes on. Author David Brooks wrote not long after September 11 in the pages of the liberal *Atlantic Monthly*, "although there are some real differences . . . there is no fundamental conflict. There may be cracks, but there is no chasm." Political journalist Michael Barone, opining in the conservative *National Journal,* concluded similarly, stating, "the two Americas face no revolution. ... The two nations with the different faiths will continue to live together, mostly peaceably ... often seeming to spin out of control, but ultimately stable—as two nations united by the politics that seems to divide us." Gertrude Himmelfarb in her book *One Nation, Two Cultures* and Alan Wolfe in his *One Nation, After All* arrived at approximately the same horizon.[54]

But there were two missing elements in their crystal ball gazing. For the most part, they limited their exegetic journey down the blue highways of the American divide to the axes of religion/morality or class. The question of race was given surprisingly little attention in their contemplations, despite its tide of influence stretching all the way back to Nixon's Southern strategy and beyond.

Moreover, these authors and others completely failed to gauge the prototypal impact of our Winner Take All political system, and how its zero-sum "If I win, you lose" dynamic exaggerates existing tensions and polarization. Only one side can win in a winner take all system, and under the helter-skelter imperatives of trying to win elections and legislative majorities under Winner Take All and the carving up of the political map into single-seat partisan fiefdoms, the two parties have ceased being vehicles for articulating a national course of fairness, equilibrium, or national unity. With the two parties effectively acting as proxies on geographic region, culture, and race, representing one side or the other of the divide, and with the Winner Take All calculations a tricky zero-sum game incapable of letting the steam off these mounting pressures, the racially conservative white vote and the multiracial burgeoning of our population are on a collision course.

CHAPTER TWO

Ex Uno Plures
"One System, Two Nations"

UnElection 2000: Paralysis in the Presidency

But the static of UnElection 2000 that hissed in the territories of Bushlandia and New Goreia was just a sideshow for the main event. In the state of Florida, stranger things occurred, courtesy of not only voting machines, but also our Winner Take All voting system.

Recall the taxonomy, so strange and exotic-sounding: Pregnant chad. Butterfly ballots. Dimpled punch cards. Votomatics. The new vernacular and vocabulary will no doubt redound in the national consciousness, history books, and TV game shows for years to come. Glued to our television sets, radios, and Web news pages, we watched the American republic spasming in crisis, as a presidential race hung in the balance in Florida. Ballot after ballot, lawsuit after lawsuit, the nation braced and we held our collective breath, as we lived through another breathlessly historical presidential moment.

The memory of the impeachment trial, which had carved a valley of shadow down the middle of the American soul, still throbbed in the not-so-distant-past. The ghosts of two expunged House Speakers, of relentless congressional investigations unmasked as political muggings, of "drive-by" confirmation hearings—all in all an unsettling decade of partisan civil war that the nation had wished to lay to rest—suddenly was stomping again around the national stage, refusing to die. We wondered if our political institutions, and some sense of our national comity, would survive intact. These kinds of thing aren't supposed to happen here, not to the American democratic paragon, not to the lone remaining superpower, not at this time with the nation enjoying its longest economic expansion in history. What had gone wrong?

The events in Florida were like a national Rorschach test—held up to the national gaze, a person could see anything she or he wanted to see. If you wanted to see Vice President Gore winning, you focused on 19,000 spoiled butterfly ballots in Palm Beach County, on antiquated punch card voting machines in Miami-Dade County that failed to count another 10,000 ballots, or on the fact that Gore won over 500,000 more votes nationwide than George W. Bush. If you wanted Bush to win, you focused on the vagaries of chad and the partisan leanings of Democratic Party county commissioners, holding disputed ballots to the divining light, searching for dispensation for their candidate. Despite being the world's lone remaining superpower, and the most technologically advanced nation in the history of the world, we were not up to the simple task of counting the ballots in our presidential election.[1] Bewilderingly, even after George W. Bush was declared the forty-third president, thousands of Florida ballots still sat in piles across the state, having never been tallied because the antiquated Votomatic punch card machines, for one reason or another, could not count them. The tragedy was that, as every pair of eyes quickly surmised, there could be no quick or clean resolution for partisans so bitterly at war.

The rest of the world watched our dilemma with utter and sardonic amusement. U.S. representatives and our proxies had poked our self-righteous noses into the electoral affairs of numerous nations with the sanctimony of Saint Peter at the Gates. But now the world was having a good laugh at our expense. "America today is a laughing stock," wrote the British tabloid *Mirror*. One British *Guardian* article included a reference to Stalin's famous quip that "it's not who votes that counts, but who counts the votes." The German daily *Die Welt* called the UnElection a "macabre spectacle." In a case of the sanctimonious shoe being on the other foot, the democratically flat-footed Italians, whose collapsing governments frequently have been the target of sneering missives from the *New York Times* and its syndicators, marked the occasion by lampooning us, Rome's daily newspaper *La Repubblica* leading with "A Day as a Banana Republic." American electoral turmoil gave the Chinese Foreign Ministry an unaccustomed glow of moral authority, as a spokesman pronounced, "Every country must decide which election method it should use according to local conditions." Mexicans drew eerie comparisons between Gov. Jeb Bush, the brother of the presidential nominee, and Raul Salinas, the brother of former Mexican President Carlos Salinas, who probably had stolen the 1988 Mexican election for his brother after a government-run computer system tallying the vote suspiciously crashed when early results showed the opposition candidate ahead.[2]

But truth be told, it wasn't only voting machine error, recount administration, screw-ups over ballot design, and ultimately a legally embarrassing Supreme Court decision that determined our forty-third president. So did the defects of the Winner Take All method we used for *electing* the president. For instance, as everyone knows, neither George W. Bush nor Al Gore won a majority (more than 50 percent) of popular votes across the nation; and as Gore supporters have pointed out endlessly, Gore ended up with more popular votes than the crowned winner, Bush. Yet if either the states of Florida or New Hampshire had required the winner of their state's electoral votes to win a popular majority—"majority rule," after all—and had used a two-round runoff (like that used in most Southern states for all nonpresidential elections or in France for its presidential election) or a ranked-ballot system known as instant runoff voting (used to elect the president of Ireland and the mayor of London)[3] to elect a majority winner, we probably would have a different president right now. Al Gore would have picked up enough "runoff" support from 100,000 Ralph Nader voters to surpass George W. Bush in Florida and perhaps New Hampshire for the popular and electoral college vote tally. More importantly, one candidate would have crossed the magic "majority" victory threshold, and we would have avoided the five-week Florida debacle and a presidency now tarnished by charges of illegitimacy.

Or, if we had used a "majority rules" provision in all fifty states, requiring a two-round runoff or instant runoff in each state so that the winner of each state's electors was favored by a popular majority, Al Gore likely would be president. Or, if we had used a national direct election of the president with a "majority rules" requirement for a national runoff (requiring a second election) or instant runoff (not requiring a second election) to reach the magic majority threshold, most likely Al Gore would be president, having picked up enough second-choice, "lesser of two evils" support from the nearly 3 million Nader voters to surpass the majority threshold.

But if we had used a direct national election of the president without a majority requirement, it is difficult to say which candidate would have won. The candidates would have campaigned differently nationwide, and the support for third-party candidates like Ralph Nader and Pat Buchanan was enough of a wildcard "spoiler" factor that their impact would have been impossible to predict. If each state had used a method of allocating electors by congressional district, such that a presidential candidate picked up an electoral vote for each congressional district won, allowing a state to split their electoral vote among competing candidates—like the states of Maine and Nebraska do now, which in the aftermath of Florida has been proposed in several states—George W. Bush would have won the presidency by an even wider margin in the Electoral College than with the current method. Bush won more congressional districts across the country, even though he had fewer national popular votes than Gore, due to the vagaries and distortions of single-seat districts created during the redistricting process.

Or, if each state had used what is known as a "proportional allocation" of electors, meaning that whatever percentage of the popular vote a candidate wins in a particular state they win the same corresponding percentage of electoral votes for that state, it is very possible that we would have a different president right now. With a proportional allocation, for example, if in California Gore had won 60 percent of the popular vote and Bush 40 percent, Gore would have won 60 percent—thirty-two—of California's fifty-four electoral votes, and Bush would have won twenty-two; in Florida, both candidates would have won about half of the state's electoral votes, matching their percentages of the popular vote (interestingly, both the Democratic and Republican parties use such a method for their presidential primaries, the Democrats in all states and the GOP for about one-third of the states).[4] In many respects, that would have been the method that comes closest to guaranteeing "majority rule" and better ensures that the Electoral College vote matches the national popular vote.[5]

What should be obvious from this exercise is that the exact *method* we used to elect our president in 2000—in addition to voting machine malfunction, election administration screw ups, and a bushwhacking Supreme Court—elected our forty-third president. You can take the same votes and count them using different voting methods and end up with completely different results. Summarizing, if we had used any kind of "majority rules" system, Al Gore probably would have won the presidential election because the "liberal/left-of-center" vote split itself between Gore and Nader. Together, they had a majority of the popular vote, more than all conservative/right-of-center candidates combined, including Bush and Pat Buchanan. In fact, their combined vote of 51.1 percent was the highest center-left total since Lyndon Johnson's 1964 landslide. With a split in the liberal/left-of-center support, Nader swiped enough votes that would in all likelihood have gone to Gore, allowing George W. Bush to eke out a slim victory in Florida and New Hampshire, and ultimately in the Electoral College. Thus, amid great controversy, Bush won the presidency with less than a majority of the popular vote and fewer national votes than Al Gore.

It didn't need to happen that way. We didn't need to end up as an international laughingstock. It is deeply ironic: we can send a man to the moon and map the human genome, yet we cannot adopt a method of electing our president that allows multiple candidates to run and guarantees that the winner will have support from a popular majority. That is ludicrous, a reflection of our lack of inventiveness and our clinging to outdated, outmoded methods. This is not rocket science, yet just like in the realm of voting *machines*, our eighteenth-century voting *system* is hopelessly backward compared to many other democratic nations. In democracies like France, Ireland, Australia, and to a lesser extent Great Britain, which tend to use either a two-round runoff or "instant" runoff to elect majority winners for offices like president, mayor, or district representatives, such an outcome as the UnElection 2000 is unthinkable, laughable even.

Allocation of electoral votes, whether by congressional district, proportional allocation, Winner Take All, or "majority rules by state," can be decided on a state-by-state basis without any changes to the U.S. Constitution. Only a proposal to abolish the Electoral College entirely would require a constitutional amendment; as the cases of Maine and Nebraska show, states are free to decide for themselves how to allocate their electoral votes. The fact is, the specific *method* we use for the Electoral College in forty-eight states, called "Winner Take All plurality by state"—*not* simply the Electoral College itself—produced a president with a minority of popular votes and fewer popular votes than his main opponent.

In the aftermath of the presidential election, particularly following the national outcry and mobilization following the September 11 attacks, that distortion seems to have been swallowed and digested by the media and most of the public, albeit like a chicken bone and not easily. Unfortunately, there were other troubling aspects of the 2000 presidential election related to our Winner Take All method that have not been as widely recognized or reported.

Affirmative Action for Conservatives

Because of the peculiar nature of the Electoral College, our presidential elections defy the fundamental principle of "one person, one vote" and create a bias toward conservative states over liberal states. That's because the Electoral College created by the Framers granted a "representation subsidy"—a form of affirmative action, if you will—to low-population states. California, our most populous state with 34 million people, has approximately sixty-nine times more people than Wyoming, our least populous state, with 494,000 people. If representation was based on the principle of "one person, one vote"—a democratic principle that we regularly export to the rest of the world—California would have sixty-nine times the number of electoral votes as Wyoming. Instead, in the 2000 election California had fifty-four electoral votes and Wyoming had three, a reduced ratio of 18 to 1.

In 1789, when General George Washington was the first president to take the oath of office, the ratio between the most populous state (Virginia) and the least populous one (Delaware) was only 11 to 1.[6] The Framers simply did not foresee such dramatic population imbalances two hundred years later (as we will see in Chapter 7, the Electoral College was a defective method from its inception, enacted by baffled, impatient Framers who debated and rejected several methods, finally selecting one of the rejected methods when the Constitutional Convention ran out of time). Consequently, the Electoral College formula they have saddled us with, which gives each state one electoral vote per each U.S. Senator (and one for each representative in the House) and gives each state two Senators regardless of population, has given the people of Wyoming nearly *four times* the per capita representation of Californians in the Electoral College.

Because of this affirmative action quota in the Electoral College bestowed by the Framers upon low-population states, there was a built-in bias toward conservative states in the 2000 election. Among the eighteen states (including the District of Columbia) with three, four, or five electoral votes, George W. Bush prevailed by a 42–26 electoral vote margin over Gore. That is, the Electoral College, because it awards every state two votes for its U.S. Senators regardless of its population size, padded Bush's slim total. Take that senatorial two out of each of the fifty state's electoral votes in the total electoral tally, and Gore would have won the Electoral College—even without Florida. The small-state padding explained the difference between the Electoral College vote, which went to Bush by a lean 271–267 margin, and the national popular vote, which Gore won by over a half million votes.[7]

Moreover, the Winner Take All structure of the Electoral College completely negated the votes of millions of racial minority voters. For example, 53 percent of all blacks live in the Southern states, where in 2000 they voted over 90 percent Democratic. However, because of extreme racially polarized voting, the more numerous white voters outvoted them in every Southern state and every Mason-Dixon border state except Maryland. While nationally whites voted 54–42 for Bush, Southern whites gave over 70 percent of their votes to him. Southern whites completely erased the massive Southern black turnout for Gore in that region.[8]

As a result, every single Electoral College vote from Mason-Dixon border and Southern states (except those of Maryland) was won by Bush. Since the Winner Take All allocation awards *all* electoral votes to whichever candidate wins the highest number of votes in each state (called a plurality, which is less than a majority), whether that plurality be by one vote or 1 million votes, the result was the same as if blacks and other people of color in the South had not voted at all. Despite an impressive $12 million get-out-the-vote effort by the NAACP, its ultimate impact was minimal, at least in the presidential election.[9] In Florida, black voters were disenfranchised not just by antiquated voting machines, long lines at the polling booth, or corrupted felon lists,[10] but also by the eighteenth-century Winner Take All voting system.

Similarly negated were the votes of millions of Latino voters who live in overwhelmingly white Republican states like Arizona, Nevada, Oklahoma, Utah, the Dakotas, Montana, and Texas. The white Republican vote of these areas overwhelmed the "multicolored" Democratic vote like an avalanche smothering a field of flowers. If each state, for instance, had used a proportional allocation of their electoral votes instead of Winner Take All, nearly everybody's vote, including that of blacks in the South and Republicans in heavily Democratic states like California and New York, would have counted toward *something* instead of *nothing*. We would have ended up with a national Electoral College vote that more closely reflected the national popular vote. And probably we would have ended up with a different president.

The Shrinking Battlefield

But the presidential vote revealed something else perhaps even more alarming—the partisan demographics of division have become so hardwired into our regional tectonics that most states now clearly tilt toward one party or the other. Under our geographic-based "Winner Take All plurality by state" method, the idea of a "competitive state" is narrowing down to an obvious few battleground states, making it easier for campaign strategists to carve up the political map. For instance, thirty-one states had monopoly representation in the 106th Congress' U.S. Senate, with eighteen states having two Republican senators and thirteen states having two Democratic senators. That's thirty-one states, including the largest like Texas, California, New York, Florida, Michigan, Ohio, and

Pennsylvania, where voters have no representation in the U.S. Senate if they are one of the unfortunate millions who supported the losing side.

On the presidential level, according to a study by the *National Journal*, fourteen states did not receive a single visit from either the Bush or the Gore campaign between April 1 and the election, including huge swaths of the Great Plains and Mountain states, because they were all locked-up states in the sub-nation of Bushlandia.[11] In contrast, the swing states were saturated: Ohio had twenty-one visits, Michigan twenty-nine, Florida thirty, and Pennsylvania thirty-nine. By late October 2000, the average person in Carbondale, Pennsylvania (or Scranton or Wilkes-Barre or Honesdale), had been bombarded with more presidential campaign spots than had television viewers anywhere else in the country. In addition, four of the nation's top eight media markets and largest population centers, Boston, Dallas, New York City, and Washington, DC—all comfortably ensconced in safe states for one party or the other—had a grand total of six presidential ads aired, while eight media markets in battleground states were carpet bombed by more than 6,500 presidential ads.[12] By mid-September, both the Gore and Bush campaigns had spent millions of dollars on advertising in key battleground states, even to some extent smaller states like New Mexico and Washington state, but in the safe-Gore state of California, where fully 12 percent of the American population resides, neither campaign spent a dime on advertising between the March primary and late September.[13]

As we will see in more detail in Chapters 9 and 11, this kind of targeted campaigning is contributing to a demobilization of tens of millions of voters in locked-up states. Voters in these states sit on the political sidelines watching the presidential campaign as if it is happening in another country. It is *not* happening in their town, or in their city or state, or even much on their television sets, with TV news broadcasters now spending considerably less time on election news coverage and an average of only sixty-four seconds per night where the candidates present their views, a mere eye-blink in an otherwise busy day.[14] Moreover, the specter of the targeted campaign is contributing to an astonishing loss of political ideas, as the issues important to a handful of swing voters in swing states become the de facto issues of the entire presidential sweepstakes. Thus, the presidential election ceases to be a national race at all, but instead the kind of regional contests with huge national ramifications that we expect to see in other geographically polarized, Winner Take All nations like India and Canada.

But if each state had used a proportional allocation of their electoral votes, instead of Winner Take All, no state would have been locked-up. Each candidate would have received the proportionate share of each state's electoral votes that matched their share of the popular vote, allowing states to split their electoral votes among competing candidates. All candidates would have had incentive to campaign in most states, competing for voters and taking fewer states for granted. Or if we had used a "majority rules" requirement to win the electoral votes of each state, the winning candidate would have had to appeal for voters' runoff votes (or second-choice ranking if using instant runoff voting), pushing candidates to build coalitions in battleground states and precipitating more unifying campaigns. Either way, the quality of presidential campaigns would be vastly improved, and voters might feel more like players on the stage, instead of snoozing audience members.

Perhaps most striking: a post-election study by the Center for Voting and Democracy estimated that an astonishing 436 out of 538 Electoral College votes now are considered safe or mostly leaning toward one party or the other in a competitive presidential race (148 safe electoral votes for Republicans, 168 for Democrats; 88 leaning electoral votes for Republicans, 32 for Democrats). That leaves only 102 electoral votes—*less than 20 percent*—in the nine states of Florida, Pennsylvania, Missouri, Iowa, Minnesota, New Hampshire, New Mexico, Oregon, and Wisconsin, as toss-ups in a nationally competitive race. Moreover, campaign appeals *within* these swing states will be targeted at the *10 to 15 percent of undecided voters*—a pitifully small slice of the electorate that will be deciding presidential elections.[15]

The numbers of safe and leaning electoral votes mark a sharp increase in partisan strongholds compared to previous presidential elections. Due to the geographic-based foundation of our presidential election method, each political party in 2000 essentially firmed up their base of support among states and regions, with the partisan divide very clearly cleaved along geographic, regional, cultural, and racial grounds—the areas of Bushlandia and New Goreia.

Defenders of the Electoral College method of electing the president typically boil their justifications down to two: (1) it means candidates cannot ignore less populous states, and (2) "it militates against regional parties" and requires "presidential candidates to build alliances across ideological and geographical lines," thereby achieves a national consensus.[16] But these reasons, which have a surprising amount of currency with many political scientists and the *New York Times* pundits, are demonstrably false. As we have seen, the political parties and their candidates are indeed breaking down regionally, with alarmingly balkanized voting patterns displayed by the red/blue electoral map of the 2000 presidential election that hardly achieved a national consensus. Moreover, even a cursory study of presidential campaigns shows that candidates in fact *do* ignore most low-population states, even though those states have a built-in representation subsidy. That's because most of these states already are locked up for one party or the other. In fact, as we have seen, presidential candidates today for the most part ignore *most* states, populous as well as less-populous, if they are locked-up states. And most states *are* locked-up, only about nine states are up for grabs. Yet even among the battleground states, the candidates spent far more time in the populous states of Pennsylvania, Michigan, and Florida than in sparse New Mexico, Iowa, or New Hampshire. It is just simple common sense if you are running a campaign, yet somehow that sense evades many political observers.

For the foreseeable future the hardwired regional balkanization means that Republicans start off with a clear and potentially decisive edge in the electoral college landscape, primarily due to the built-in affirmative action quota of the Electoral College that subsidizes low-population, conservative states, even as these locked-up states receive little attention or few presidential visits. Tallying the safe votes, state-by-state, shows that 236 electoral votes are safe or leaning Republican, compared to 200 safe or leaning Democrat (although this edge could be affected if either party nominates a mediocre candidate, or if extraordinary events like a war in the Middle East inflate or hurt a candidate's chances, or by competition from "spoiler" minor party candidates like Ralph Nader, as we saw in dramatic fashion in 2000). It's like holding a hundred-yard dash, and one sprinter is starting about five yards ahead of the other.

Despite this head start for the GOP candidate, what this all adds up to is latently alarming: based on the 2000 election results, there are strong indications of another razor-thin race in the 2004 presidential election. UnElection 2000 may have been merely Act I of an ongoing and ugly political drama, courtesy of the Framers' defective Winner Take All method of electing the president. While we had to wait 124 years between our last presidential drama and this recent one, we may have ringside seats to back-to-back epic productions. Hopefully by 2004 at least the nine battleground states will have had the sense to upgrade voting equipment to avoid another Florida-style embarrassment.

Pulling Back the Curtain on Domestic War

Voting systems matter. A different voting method other than the current "Winner Take All plurality by state" could have produced a presidential winner with majority support, prevented split votes and minor-party spoiling, and prevented certain states from being locked-up and receiving little attention from the candidates. In so doing, the votes of millions of voters, black, brown, and white, Democrat and Republican and more, would have counted toward something instead of nothing, particularly if each state had used a proportional allocation or some kind of runoff rather than a "Winner Take All plurality by state" allocation.

Instead, we ended up with the five-week debacle that ensued in Florida and the polarizing impact that event had on national unity. It would have been far better to have avoided it. For even more ominous than the Hollywood *noir* finish, UnElection 2000 pulled back the curtain to reveal a molten fissure seething just beneath the surface. As the political drama played out in Florida and across the nation, latent national divisions came to the fore, like subterranean fault lines suddenly revealed by the shaking of the earth above. Once again the howling partisans ran their banners, slogans, and accusations up the flag pole with the zeal of crusaders mounting a holy war. For those who think that national imbroglio already has passed into ancient history, let us recall for a moment how the hand counts and the headlines dragged on, rubbing salt into the previous wounds of bitter national controversy. A scary sense of insurrection permeated the air, at least in certain loud and powerful quarters.

Protesters in Florida wearing combat fatigues and black face eerily stood out, holding aloft signs saying things like "Bush or Revolution," with Revolution written in bloody scrawl. Other placards read "God Made Bush President," and threatening letters were mailed to judges, including one with an illustration of a skull and crossbones. Certain southern legislators, sounding like they had been possessed by the ghosts of John C. Calhoun and Jefferson Davis, spouted incendiary threats about defying the Florida courts. Bush campaign spokesman, former Montana governor Marc Racicot, employed rabble-rousing rhetoric over the controversy with military absentee ballots, charging that the Gore camp had "gone to war" in his judgment "against the men and women who serve in our Armed Forces."[17] As the drama wore on, positions hardened, moods turned ugly. We will never know how close we may have come to something even scarier, a modern-day "Bloody Kansas" played out in the temperatures of Florida.

Moreover, it wasn't just the presidential race that revealed the national fissure. After the dust had settled on UnElection 2000, the U.S. Senate also was precisely split in half for the first time in our nation's history, 50 Rs and 50 Ds, like Solomon's baby. The U.S. House was nearly as split, with the closest margin in five decades; during the last one hundred years only seven elections have produced congressional voting margins between Democrats and Republicans of less than 1 percent of the total votes cast for the U.S. House, and three of those seven have been the most recent.[18] Even the number of state legislatures under monopoly control by either of the two parties was a dead heat. The previous two presidential elections were similarly split, both of Bill Clinton's victories coming with less than a majority of the popular vote. Michael Barone, commentating for *U.S. News & World Report,* said that the same number—49 percent—keeps popping up over and over again, whether it's a congressional or presidential election, when we assess the percentage of votes won by the winners *and* the losers.

For the first time since the 1880s, the United States has gone without a dominant party for an entire decade.[19] For the first time in fifty years, since the Democrats started their decades-long domination of the Congress, we can categorically say that today there is no majority party in the United States. Instead what we have are two minority parties, approximately equal in strength and numbers, looking for any gamesman's advantage to gain a leg up on the competition. And it is the Winner Take All system, with its geographic-based, two-choice limitations and zero-sum "if I win, you lose" operational pyrotechnics, that is the electoral funnel through which these passions and partisanship will be squeezed. Not surprisingly, as the competition has increased, so have the passions of battle, the mercenary tactics, the name-calling, the internecine warfare.

After all was said and done, not only had our democracy played the unaccustomed role of international laughingstock over our primitive voting machines, electoral infrastructure, and feeble judiciary, but international observers also had quite a chuckle over the fact that, in the 2000 elections, the majority did not necessarily rule. Under our archaic Winner Take All rules, sometimes the minority can beat the majority, not only for the presidency, but also for control of the U.S. House and Senate. It also means that one side of the partisan divide can be overrepresented and the other side underrepresented, with impacts on policy and participation. Moreover, the division of the political map into the sub-nations of New Goreia and Bushlandia, where most districts and states are safe for one party or the other, means that millions of voters are bunkered down with meaningless votes that don't really count, even when the voting machines *don't* screw up. These voters may as well have stayed home on Election Day for all the difference their votes made.

Soon after the UnElection 2000, following the recriminations of the previous five weeks and beyond that of the previous eight years, predictable calls arose for a new across-the-aisles bipartisanship. In his brief victory speech, Bush used the word "bipartisanship" three times, not counting his comment that the country needs to move "beyond partisanship," as well as other buzzwords like "together" (used twelve times), "consensus" (three times), "cooperation" (twice), "shared" (twice), and "common goals" and "common ground" (once each).[20] No less than adversaries Newt Gingrich, busily refashioning himself for a future run at the national stage, and Al Gore, giving the performance of his life in his concession speech, turned positively warm and fuzzy, joining the off-key chorus of suddenly platonic voices. But with the country so evenly divided, with so much for each major political party to lose or gain, and with a clunky eighteenth-century Winner Take All system as the means for political discernment and verdict, how could it not be a surefire prescription for the continuation of a most uncivil war?

"Good fences make good neighbors . . ."

Fortunately, there are alternatives to the vagaries of Winner Take All. The poet Robert Frost, in his poem "The Mending Wall," after meditating over his neighbor's insistence that "good fences make good neighbors," wrote, "Spring is the mischief in me, and I wonder if I could put a notion in his head: 'Why do they make good neighbors?'" Similarly, in thinking about our bizarre and increasingly divisive "Winner Take All plurality by state" presidential election method, or the fenced-off feudalism of single-seat, geographic districts that are suffocating orphaned Republicans in New Goreia and orphaned Democrats in Bushlandia, and everyone else as well, a mischievous impulse wants to ask: *"Why?"* Why must these be the primary methods for electing our leaders? Is this the best we can do, dividing whole regions of the country into neofeudal Winner Take All fiefdoms of winners and losers? Are these the best electoral methods for ensuring that we remain good political neighbors?

We have already explored various ways we could change our presidential elections that, even without a constitutional amendment, would have provided distinct advantages over the current method. Now let's try a little thought experiment regarding our legislative elections. Let's play a game of *"What if . . . ?"* What if . . . we did not use single-seat district elections in monopoly politics states like Idaho, Utah, Kansas, Nebraska, Maryland, California, or Massachusetts? What if . . . instead we combined three adjoining one-seat districts into a three-seat district? And what if we elected these three-seat districts with a voting system known as cumulative voting, which is used by various cities, counties, and even various corporations to elect their boards of directors,[21] so that only slightly more than 25 percent of the vote is needed to elect one out of three of these representatives? Might that give the orphaned Democrats or Republicans and other geographic minorities in these states a chance to win their fair share of representation? Might that break up the edifice of monopoly politics that is walling us into a corner and exacerbating partisan, cultural, geographic and racial division, and allow a degree of cross-fertilization of politicians, ideology, and policy? And might that inspire orphaned voters everywhere to reengage in politics again?

As we saw with our presidential election method, sometimes the particular electoral rules and practices employed have a lot more to do with who wins and loses elections than we realize. One of the best-kept political secrets—in a land that seemingly has few left—is that our national division and depression are exacerbated, and sometimes caused and maintained, by our eighteenth-century electoral practices—in this case, the widespread use of geographic-based, single-seat districts.

Nationally, Democrats and Republicans coexist everywhere. Democrat Bill Clinton won at least 25 percent of the vote in every House district in the nation in 1996, and Republican Bob Dole slipped below 25 percent in only a handful of urban districts. But single-seat districts, whether in Illinois, South Carolina, Massachusetts, Idaho, Kansas, or California, bury this natural diversity beneath the partisan avalanche. This further exacerbates regional and racial tensions, dividing us and tearing the seam of our national fabric. Demographically, the multiracial coloring of American society is in full swing, and will intensify over the next two decades. How will our nation prosper when it employs a Winner Take All system with single-seat districts where only one side of the divide can win in district after district? How will we defuse this national tension when the Winner Take All system allows entire regions of the country to be "captured" by one side or the other of this partisan war?

Such a political landscape raises the alarming specter of extreme regional balkanization along the lines plaguing India, Canada, and Algeria, where single-seat districts and Winner Take All regions have produced a politics that is cleaved along volatile fault lines (religion, in the case of India and Algeria, and French Quebec separatism and western sectionalism in the case of Canada). In the United States, whole regions of our nation have become monolithic prefectures, except instead of religion or ethnic nationalism we have substituted political party, and the parties have become in the public perception a proxy for race and culture.[22] Following this trajectory to its logical extremes augurs a troubling future.

A case in point is the state of South Carolina, specifically its titanic struggle over Confederate symbols. Some have argued that the neofeudalism caused by single-seat districts has been the primary impediment to demasting the Confederate flag from atop South Carolina's state capitol dome. During the flag flap in the spring of 2000, public opinion polls showed a majority of South Carolinians favored moving the flag. On Martin Luther King's birthday in January 2000, over 45,000 residents marched on the capitol, raucously demanding its removal. The state Senate already had passed a bill to remove the flag (and voted several times for a Martin Luther King holiday), and the governor had promised to sign any deflagging bill delivered to his desk. In other words, South Carolinians were ready for the flag as a past echo of slavery and civil war to be retired to its rightful place—a history museum. But the problem was in the House.

In South Carolina, as in most states, lawmakers are elected in single-seat districts. As in most Southern states, certain districts have been drawn to encircle majority-black populations in sufficient numbers so that these districts likely will elect black legislators. In most Southern states that strategy has been successful in electing black legislators at local, state, and federal levels. But the inevitable result has been to create adjacent districts that were largely white—black voters have been, in effect, "bleached" out of those districts, rendering them more white. As an editorial from the state capital's leading daily newspaper said, "Although they've brought more African-Americans to the State House, race-based legislative districts have led many white lawmakers to believe they represent only white people and caused many black lawmakers to act as though they represent only black people. Thus, our Legislature often seems more racially divided than our state."[23] Were these polarized districts to blame, some South Carolinians wondered, for the House retaining the flag?

"We have trained a generation of legislators to think in terms of their constituents as either black or white, not both," wrote Brad Warthen, editor of *The State* daily newspaper in Columbia. "This is particularly true of many white Republicans, whose districts tend to be more racially homogenous than the 'safe black' seats. So I know where Rep. Jake Knotts is coming from when he looks out on the multitude demanding removal of the flag and doesn't see a reflection of his district, which contains 16,487 white voters and only 1622 black."[24]

A perceptive analysis by *St. Petersburg Times* columnist Martin Dyckman showed that, of South Carolina's forty-six state Senate districts, more than a majority showed at least 20 percent of their voters to be black, with twenty of those districts equaling or exceeding 27 percent black registration. That's a proportion that cannot be ignored, and is large enough to command attention and respect from white candidates. But in the House the concentration of black voters had been more severe.[25] The districts were smaller than those in the Senate, and constituencies were often exclusively white or black.[26] Numerous white districts had extremely low black populations because so many black voters had been "packed" into majority-black districts, draining their influence from the surrounding white districts. It was as if the black vote was a limited commodity, with not enough to spread around in the greater number of House districts, particularly when packed into districts drawn for racial representation. Thus, despite the tens of thousands who participated in the march on the capitol, the polarized nature of the districts made it unlikely that the throng would influence many white representatives. "These aren't their constituents," said one black House member pessimistically.[27]

On July 1, 2000, in a supposed compromise that appeased practically no one, the Confederate flag finally was removed from atop the capitol dome—only to be incorporated into a huge and conspicuous Confederate Memorial statue on the capitol grounds, where it now billows atop a thirty-foot pole, practically the first site a visitor sees when visiting the statehouse.[28] Once again, on Martin Luther King's birthday in 2001, thousands of protesters gathered and demanded that the flag be retired to a museum. So the single-seat conundrum continues to bedevil South Carolina, the flag controversy hardly resolved or diminished. The evidence in South Carolina is compelling: the use of single-seat districts in the House has blocked the natural opinion of South Carolinians from expressing itself at the ballot box and in the state legislature. In the process, it has perpetuated—unnecessarily—racial polarization and the flying of the Confederate flag.

But *what if?* we might ask ourselves. *What if* . . . instead of using Winner Take All single-seat districts, South Carolina used three-seat districts in the House, and a non–Winner Take All voting system known as choice voting whereby slightly more than 25 percent of the vote in a three-seat district wins one seat, so that candidates would have incentives to build cross-racial coalitions at the same time they appealed to self-defined minority constituencies in the larger districts? Might South Carolina remove this ancient thorn, once and for all?

Non–Winner Take All voting systems like cumulative voting and choice voting (the latter also known as preference voting or "single transferable vote") are designed to provide more opportunity for the electoral viability of orphaned voters—Democrats or Republicans, black or white, geographic minorities—than the traditional Winner Take All methods. Such a "full representation" system features elections using multiseat districts (also known as "at-large") rather than single-seat districts, but unlike the traditional Winner Take All at-large system, these alternative multiseat systems employ electoral rules of proportional representation designed to open up the political system and give a fair chance—fuller representation—to orphaned voting blocs of geographic minorities (for more explanation of these electoral rules of proportional representation, see the footnote).[29]

Fuller representation in the heartland

The state of Illinois used such a full-representation system for 110 years, until 1980, to elect its lower state House of Representatives. In 2001, former U.S. judge and Democratic Congressman Abner Mikva and former GOP Gov. Jim Edgar cochaired a high profile, blue-ribbon commission of seventy members that examined a return to this system.[30] The panel found that Illinois' use of cumulative voting in three-seat districts had a profound impact on Illinois politics that we will recognize as speaking directly to our twin national dilemmas of national division—regional, partisan, cultural, and racial balkanization—and a political depression that has led to the lowest voter turnout in the world among established democracies.

For instance, nearly every Illinois three-seat district had two-party representation. Democratic strongholds like Chicago elected some Republicans, and Republican strongholds like down-state DuPage County elected some Democrats.[31] Consequently, voters had more options because every three-seat district provided access to representatives in both major parties. For Democratic and Republican sympathizers there was no such thing as an "orphaned voter." Moreover, independent and maverick Democrats and Republicans who bucked their party leadership were able to win election, providing *intra*-party ideological diversity and more viable options for voters. Campaign finance reformers should take note of the fact that these candidates were able to run grassroots campaigns without the backing of their party machines' campaign coffers, yet win their 25 percent share of the vote and one of the three seats.

The *Chicago Tribune*'s political reporter Rick Pearson has written that the rolling coalitions that formed in the Illinois house "often helped lead to centrist pragmatic policies." But the return in 1980 to Winner Take All single-seat districts, Pearson wrote, "has centralized political power in the hands of the house leadership, who use the cudgel of the potential loss of campaign cash to dictate the issues to be considered and how a member should vote. The formation of a true bipartisan coalition is rare."[32]

In fact, Joseph Medill, Republican editor of the *Chicago Tribune*, pushed for the adoption of cumulative voting in 1870 as a way to bring the heavily divided state back together after the Civil War by ensuring that both parties were represented everywhere in the State. Crucial cross-fertilization of politicians and policies occurred under cumulative voting because both major parties had direct interest in serving the needs of all regions. Chicago's very urban needs had a voice in the all-important Republican Party caucus, and downstate's rural needs had representation in the Democratic Party caucus. Republicans from Chicago could stand up in the Republican caucus for mass transit, city schools, and public hospitals, while Democrats from rural areas and affluent suburbs could speak in their caucus for rural issues, farmers, and the needs of suburban and downstate school districts.

Abner Mikva, cochair of the commission and long-time Chicago Congressman, observed that fuller representation using three-seat districts and cumulative voting "helped us synthesize some of our differences, made us realize that even though we were different than the downstaters, different than the suburbanites, that we also had a lot in common that held us together as a single state." Former Republican Congressman John Porter has noted that in Illinois's three-seat districts "we operated in a less partisan environment because both parties represented the entire state." Illinois House Majority Leader Barbara Flynn Currie commented, "We had African-Americans representing majority white districts, and white representatives coming from districts that were predominantly African-American."[33] In fact, cumulative voting elected black Republicans, and now the Republican Party in Illinois—as in the rest of the nation—is virtually lily-white. The *Chicago Tribune* has opined, "[M]any partisans and political independents have looked back wistfully at the era of cumulative voting. They acknowledge that it produced some of the best and brightest in Illinois politics."[34] Chicago's other daily, the *Sun-Times*, also has editorialized in favor of returning to cumulative voting with three-seat districts.[35]

Other states today deviate slightly from the standard single-seat district, Winner Take All modus operandi. For instance, the state of Pennsylvania uses three-seat districts elected by a non–Winner Take All voting system called limited voting to elect most of their sixty-seven counties' commissioners. In the primaries, each party nominates two candidates to fill three seats. All voters then have a "limited" vote, casting only two votes for the three slots, and the three candidates with the most votes win. Because of this use of limited voting, the commissions almost always have bipartisan representation, two members from one party and one from the other party. As a point of comparison, it is interesting to note that the states of Washington, Maryland, Vermont, and North Carolina also use three- or two-seat districts for their state legislatures, but they use traditional Winner Take All rules instead of something like limited, choice, or cumulative voting. The result? Most of the multiseat districts elect representatives all from the same party. In other words, monopoly politics, courtesy of the Winner Take All system.

As we soar over our *USA Today* map, gazing down upon the great sea of Bushlandia red framed by borders of New Goreia blue and contemplating how to bridge the political divide between Americans and between the two major political parties, the Illinois and Pennsylvania experiences with three-seat districts and alternative voting schemes have a lot to lend. One of the alleged strengths of single-seat districts is representation of geographic interests. Yet when only one side of the political divide monopolizes a legislative district, region, or state, geographic representation becomes a zero-sum "If I win, you lose" game. Coherent policy for that region quickly becomes polarized. Without a balance of power, policy becomes subject to the whims of whichever party is in control. Single-seat districts greatly exacerbate this tendency toward polarization of representation and policy—and the polarization becomes the straw that stirs the brew of chronic division and political depression.

In a sense, then, we have reached a point where we need to promote institutional frameworks that will deflate the tensions of partisanship, region, culture, and race. But this is precisely what is so difficult under the architecture of Winner Take All. Winner Take All has produced narrow political parties that are deeply divided by region, culture, and race, and has promoted noncompetitive elections that often leave whole swathes of the electorate without any representation at all, election after election, with little hopes for the future.

Nothing in the U.S. Constitution requires single-seat districts for the U.S. House or the fifty state legislatures.[36] And nothing requires the forty-eight states besides Maine and Nebraska to use their current "Winner Takes All plurality by state" electoral allocation for presidential elections. *What if* . . . like Frost's protagonist, we examined with an open mind our eighteenth-century political institutions, electoral practices, and procedures? Might we discover that our current methods are actually contributing to, indeed causing, the current twin black holes of national division and political depression that are sucking the life out of our politics and launching us toward an uncertain future of post-democracy?

CHAPTER THREE

The Technology of Democracy

> Laws and constitutions must go hand in hand with the progress of the human mind. As that becomes more developed, more enlightened, as new discoveries are made, new truths discovered . . . institutions must advance also to keep pace with the times.
>
> —THOMAS JEFFERSON,
> WORDS ETCHED IN THE JEFFERSON MEMORIAL

The Pedigree of Winner Take All

The Winner Take All system possesses an internal logic that stems from two basic characteristics inherent to the system: (1) Winner Take All, for the most part, is a geographic-based political system; and (2) Winner Take All, for the most part, is a proxy for a two-choice/two-party system. From these two defining characteristics other dynamics flow that, as we will see in this chapter and other chapters, are particularly destructive in terms of the five sturdy poles holding aloft the big tent of the democratic republic: representation, participation, political discourse and campaigns, policy, and national unity.

Since Winner Take All's single-seat districts are based on geographic representation, they were well suited for an eighteenth-century rural society that was dotted with small communities and connected by slow modes of communication and transportation. The citizenry was no more than 4 million in 1790; in 1820 the U.S. population was over 90 percent rural, and still about 80 percent in 1860.[1] What neighbors thought about the important issues of the day was intimately connected to where they lived, who they lived next to, and their survival needs that arose from geographic exigencies. Winner Take All voting systems seemed a fitting vehicle for political representation and the policy demands of a small electorate of perhaps 200,000 propertied white males that excluded the poor, women, African slaves, and indentured servants from voting.[2]

The debate over how democracy technology, and voting systems in particular, affect representative democracy is not new in American politics. The Framers and Founders[3] and their early nineteenth-century political offspring understood and debated, sometimes with great passion, the impacts and consequences of voting systems. As far as the Framers knew there were two Winner Take All possibilities: either single-seat districts, or at-large/multiseat elections in which a plurality or the highest vote-getter wins (since alternatives like proportional voting systems would not be invented for nearly one hundred years).

Madison, Hamilton, and many of their peers regarded districts as preferable over an at-large method;[4] they were aware of the monopolistic "sweep effect" of the plurality at-large voting system (also known to them as the "general ticket"), whereby the electoral slate of one faction or political party with a bare majority or even the highest plurality could win *all* contested seats (see the footnote for a fuller explanation of the sweep effect).[5]

For instance, in 1790, Pennsylvania's general ticket/plurality at-large election led to a Federalist Party sweep of all eight House seats. Moreover, most of the eight elected Congressmen hailed from the eastern part of that state, so western Pennsylvanians pressured their legislature to adopt a single-seat district system that would more adequately reflect the state's regional differentiation.[6] Thus, it became widely understood during the founding years of our nation that, compared to the monopolistic general ticket voting system, district elections could help geographic minorities—kin to our "orphaned voters" from Chapter 1— overcome their statewide, numerical disadvantage by making them a majority within their own smaller subdivision, allowing the election of a representative sympathetic to their needs. Hence, district elections were viewed as the only way by which a state's partisan or regional minorities might gain adequate representation.

But true to their states' rightists sympathies, the Framers left it up to the states to decide the choice of voting system. Thus, when the first Congress was established in 1789, the voting systems used varied widely among the original thirteen states. Only five states elected all of their House representatives from districts, while six used the general ticket at-large system, and Georgia and Maryland used a combination of districts and at-large that permitted all citizens in the state to vote for each district representative.[7] The second Congress marked the beginning of a trend that would hold until 1842: large states opted to elect their U.S. House delegations by district elections, in a conscious attempt to give representation to geographic minorities; while low-population states chose the plurality at-large system in a conscious attempt to maximize their fewer votes in Congress by sending more politically unified delegations that result from the sweep effect. Given the propensity of Winner Take All at-large elections to cause glaring representational deficiencies due to this sweep effect, not surprisingly the congressional record from 1789 to 1839 reveals an unmistakable pattern in which one party consistently won a disproportionate share of the seats in these at-large states.[8]

In the early nineteenth century this debate did not go away; in fact it intensified.[9] Numerous attempts were made to enact a constitutional amendment that would mandate single-seat district elections for the U.S. House, with twenty-two states adopting districting resolutions from 1816 to 1826 and the amendment winning Senate approval three times. Reading the transcripts of the legislative debates from that era, one is struck how the discourse over how voting systems affect representative democracy was inherently tied to larger considerations of democratic goals and values—values like fairness, inclusion, and minority representation, but also passionate defenses of states' rights that only intensified as the decades progressed and the issue became linked to the much larger struggle between the states and the federal government that was to culminate in civil war. In the transcripts of the 1842 debates one can read thoughtful and fervent arguments for the representation of minorities, "minority" at that time meaning geographic and political minorities orphaned by the monopolistic sweep effect of Winner Take All at-large elections.[10]

Despite a tide of fierce opposition, the cause of minority representation trumped that of states' rights when Congress passed the Apportionment Act of 1842. This outcome illustrated how fundamental the concept of minority representation had become. But because these debates occurred in the context of a rural and agrarian society still mired in the slave-holding and sexist attitudes of the nineteenth century, the "minorities" needing representation were not racial minorities or women but geographic and political minorities—political partisans living in one part of the state being overwhelmed by the dominant majority from the rest of the state, much like the orphaned voters living today in Bushlandia and New Goreia. And in the mid-nineteenth century, Winner Take All districts were seen as the preferred democracy technology to promote the values of inclusiveness and broad representation.

Congress was to vacillate back and forth over the next century between requiring districts or allowing a state's right to use the Winner Take All plurality at-large system. As late as 1967, some states still were electing their state and federal representatives by an at-large system, at which time Congress passed a law mandating single-seat districts for U.S. House elections as a way of furthering the opportunities for racial minority representation.

The Mechanics of Winner Take All

Despite so many years spent pondering and debating the benefits and defects of the "operating system" of our political system, still it comes as a surprise to most people when they find out that you can take the same votes and count them using different voting systems—single-seat districts versus plurality at-large/multiseat districts versus choice voting versus Winner Take All versus instant runoffs versus proportional representation, and so on—and end up with *completely different electoral results.* Now, in the twenty-first century, we know that voting systems greatly affect our Big Five: who gets elected and who wins representation, how many voters will participate in the elections, the quality of political campaigns, the extent that money will affect representation and policy, regional balkanization, and, ultimately, what kind of policy will be passed. And we know that single-seat districts, while they usually are much better than plurality at-large elections in allowing geographic minorities to win representation, have numerous drawbacks that greatly impact our representative democracy. Particularly as society has changed so dramatically, and as we move into the twenty-first century, single-seat districts as well as the plurality at-large system reveal themselves to be outmoded eighteenth-century types of Winner Take All democracy technology.

The first important engineering principle of democracy technology is that *voting systems matter*. Just like voting machines can differ in quality, different voting systems also can give different results, and we have understood this, albeit not popularly, going all the way back to the Framers. In fact, when you select Winner Take All, or any voting system, for your local, state, or national elections, you are selecting a whole host of accompanying effects and results. In a sense you are selecting a set of *values* and a *philosophy* of government. Because of its fundamental importance, a voting system is nothing less than the foundation of the *whole* political system. The particular voting system used is so basic, so crucial, that it profoundly affects the five defining dimensions of our politics in such a way that you cannot study one of these factors in isolation from the other (although, to my consternation, that's exactly what most political scientists, journalists, and reformers do). They are all so intimately and dynamically interlaced that together they form a holistic unit, a hologram, where each part reveals a bit more about the whole. Consequently, more than talking about studying the Winner Take All voting system, it is more appropriate to talk about the Winner Take All *political* system.

Of course, we have been using the Winner Take All political system for more than two centuries. What is so different about today, one might ask, that should cause Winner Take All, which some would argue has served us well for so long, to suddenly go haywire? Why is Winner Take All leading to post-democracy now, instead of fifty years ago, or one hundred years ago?

While it is true that we are using the same basic geography-based and two-choice structures as those created by the Framers, in fact these structures are operating in a much different milieu today than in the eighteenth or nineteenth centuries, and one to which I argue they are particularly ill-suited. For one, we are an increasingly diverse society. As we saw in Chapter 1, our nation is galloping toward a multiracial society that will see whites eclipsed as a majority, particularly in certain regions and key states. The very terms "majority" and "minority" are being turned on their heads. Will our political institutions and practices be able to accommodate this horizon? Or will they increasingly pit different races, ethnicities, and partisans against each other for a scarce commodity—political representation? The Winner Take All system is designed to *overrepresent* geographic majorities and *underrepresent* geographic minorities/orphaned voters, whether racial or a political party. As we will see, this is not a matter of campaign finance inequities or who has better candidates or TV ads; it is simply a matter of how the Winner Take All system *works*. A political system based exclusively on geographic representation that creates such representational and policy distortions will prove increasingly disastrous in a diverse, pluralistic society like ours.

Second, like everything else in our society, politics is being transformed by technology in significant and alarming ways. For instance, how Winner Take All campaigns are conducted, and how they are covered by the media, have changed dramatically in the last twenty years because of the telecommunications revolution. New *political technologies*—computers used for redistricting; marketing technologies like polling, focus groups, and dial-meter groups, which now are used for targeting campaign spin and sound bites to sell political candidates like bars of soap; and media image manipulation packaged inside notorious thirty-second TV spots—all of these are *malignantly* suited for a two-choice/two-party system (these topics will be covered in great depth in Chapters 8–11).

Having been transformed by technology, the campaigns, campaign practitioners, political consultants, and corporate media in turn have transformed the Winner Take All game. While numerous commentators and pundits have remarked on the trajectory of campaigns fed by these new technologies, few of them have noticed how, as this book will demonstrate, the Winner Take All, two-choice and/or geographic-based system is so maliciously matched to these new technologies and campaign tactics.

Introducing: the Winner Take All gremlins

The Winner Take All system's geographic and two-choice paradigm begets a host of disruptive progeny that bedevils candidates, legislators, and voters alike. These mischievous gremlins often make political representation and policy formation into frustrating, confusing, and opaque exercises. Introducing, the Winner Take All gremlins: Phantom Representation, Artificial Majorities, Swing Voter Serenade, Two-Choice Tango, and the Winner Take All Conundrum.

The Winner Take All Conundrum

Under Winner Take All's two-choice structure, voters, candidates, and policy making are confronted by a relentless series of bipolar dilemmas and zero-sum decisions for which there are no easy solutions. It is not uncommon for Winner Take All participants to feel snagged between the prickly thorns of impossible choices. When this happens, you know you are in the haughty presence of the almighty Winner Take All conundrum.

The Winner Take All conundrum is in a league with other impossible paradoxes and binary riddles, like Arrow's Theorem and Heisenberg's Uncertainty Principle. It ensures that elections and policy making in a Winner Take All system will be a frustrating and disappointing exercise. Here are the operative principles:

If I win . . .	you lose
If I have representation . . .	you don't
If I vote for my favorite candidate, who has no chance of winning . . .	I'll help elect my least favorite candidate
Do I vote my hopes . . .	or do I vote my fears?
If we drive away voters from their candidate . . .	the only choice left is our candidate
If I run to the center to attract swing voters . . .	I will alienate my base
If I appeal to my base . . .	I'll drive away swing voters
If we're for it . . .	then they're against it
If we're against it . . .	then they're for it

The Winner Take All conundrum is a by-product of our two-choice system that turns so much of our politics into what is known as a zero-sum game: *if I win, you lose.* It pops up frequently, whether in political campaigns, in pundit conversation and speculation, in policy deliberations, in media coverage of the political horse race, and in voters' decisions over who vote to for. *If you have representation, then I don't.* It behooves us to learn to recognize it and name it, because it reveals so much about the underlying dynamics of what frustrates our politics today.

For instance, one of the defining characteristics of the Winner Take All conundrum is that it promotes pointlessly adversarial politics. On a whole host of issues it is painfully obvious that the overriding agenda of both major parties is not policy, principle, or ideology, but that each side stake out positions *contrary* to the other side. Each side hopes to benefit from the "if you lose, I win" dynamic of the Winner Take All conundrum. With minds never meeting and parallel lines that never cross, the Republicans and Democrats often engage in a level of partisan conflict that is shocking to most Americans.

So if a Democratic president is a hawk, as in Haiti, Iraq, Bosnia, or Kosovo, formerly Cold Warrior Republicans suddenly develop carefully nuanced, even dovish positions, questioning the president's military prerogative. If the Democratic president sets out to negotiate an anti–ballistic missile (ABM) treaty with the Russians, high-ranking Republican Senators block it and declare there will be "no photo ops for this president," even if that departs from traditional Republican positions on ABM treaties.[11] When Clinton moved to bail out Mexican creditors with a huge loan after the peso meltdown in 1995, the usually pro-business and pro-banking Republican Congress hemmed and hawed and sounded positively populist. When the nimble president embraced the welfare policies or the Star Wars initiatives of his GOP presidential predecessors, the Republicans accused the president of stealing their issues.

Such positioning and political gaming we can recognize as the Winner Take All conundrum at work. If one side says "up," the other is compelled to say "down," if one says "right" the other says "left." It is as reflexive as breathing. As Clinton drifted further to the right, this left Republican leaders in a bit of a quandary, groping for an agenda that the conservative Clinton wouldn't steal from them. Republicans tried to reorient themselves, completing acrobatic about-faces almost as fast as the nimble President. Finally, when there were few policies of their opponent to attack, because Clinton had tossed aside much of his own party's convictions and co-opted GOP policies, there was only one thing left to attack—Clinton himself, and his abundant personal shortcomings. So the Republican leadership used their majority status in various congressional committees to conduct a relentless series of investigations of their minority opponents. In a two-choice field it was a very effective strategy, because if you can drive voters away from your opponent there is only one choice left—yourself. But at times it resembled a pathetic version of a *Wayne's World* slapstick comedy routine, serving to further alienate an already disengaged and disgusted public.

In the post-Watergate era, Winner Take All has become synonymous with "take no prisoners." It often resembles a vicious state-of-siege where ethical and moral matters have become a weapon of political combat. The Senate's confirmation of presidential appointments has become a virtual morgue of partisan drive-bys and muggings, a minefield littered with past victims. The ghosts of Robert Bork, John Tower, Jim Wright, and Clarence Thomas have been joined by Lani Guinier, Bill Weld, Bill Lann Lee, Newt Gingrich, Bob Livingston, and finally President Clinton himself. In many ways, Monicagate was just the latest version of Whitewater, GOPAC, questionable book deals, Paula Jones, Gennifer Flowers, Travelgate, government shutdowns, "mediscare," and other attempts by both parties to toss political mud to see what sticks rather than debate the nominations on their merits.

But there's a reason why this has become the national tone—each of the two parties hopes to game the system and to gain a leg up in the relentless Winner Take All contest to beat the other side. And often they do this by carving out contrary positions based on the latest polling numbers. One of the driving dynamics of Winner Take All is that in a two-choice field neither political party has to watch their back much, since voters behind them don't have any other electoral place to go. You can more easily strip-mine your opponent's record, highlighting certain positions and ignoring others, without any third candidate intervening with conflicting messages. The ideological space is relatively wide open and undefined. This strategy extends into policy making and position taking, as the two parties play off each other to carve out their positions vis-à-vis their lone opponent.

Under the pressures of the Winner Take All conundrum, we can expect that such political gaming in the form of scandal and attack-style politics always will be excessively important because it is a way to demonize your lone opponent and carve out electoral space vis-à-vis that opponent in a close race. Americans understandably are disgusted by the pointlessly adversarial politics driven by partisan and campaign calculations rather than by the public interest. It affects the quality of campaigns as well as governance. With politicians and parties shuffling positions on certain issues faster than the dealer's hands in a game of Three-Card Monty, the transparency of national politics gets caught in the crossfire. But blaming the problem on "bad politicians" or on the lack of effective campaign finance reform instead of on the Winner Take All conundrum does not address the problem at its source.[12]

Phantom Representation

A subset of the Winner Take All conundrum and the two-choice system is something we shall call "phantom representation." It's ironic, but the thirteen original colonies rallied into a nation around the slogan, "No taxation without representation." Yet today, millions of voters cast votes for losers and, in the zero-sum game of Winner Take All politics, effectively end up with no representation. For instance, as we saw in Chapter 1, in the 2000 congressional elections not a single Republican in the state of Massachusetts or a single Democrat in the state of Nebraska cast a vote for a winner. Twelve more states have such monopoly representation by one party or the other, and eleven more states are only one representative shy of monopoly representation, a total of twenty-five states.[13] Many of these monopoly politics states overlap with the representation distortions in the sub-nations of Bushlandia and New Goreia, but not perfectly, meaning that well over half the states and their voters suffer from a substantial degree of monopoly politics.

All across the nation, millions of voters vote for losers and effectively have no representation. To disguise this appalling deformity of our democracy, and to obscure the disenfranchising nature of Winner Take All, it has been necessary to construct a truly odd notion that defies even second-grader logic: that a legislator represents you *just because he or she sits in the chair*—even if he or she is diametrically opposed to your point of view, and even if you in fact voted for someone else. Such a clever prevarication conjures truly absurd scenarios, like Newt Gingrich being "represented" by Bill Clinton or Al Gore by George W. Bush. As a citizen of New York State, Rudy Giuliani is "represented" by Hillary Clinton; former Senator Al D'Amato is "represented" by current Sen. Charles Schumer, with whom he fought a bitter campaign and lost. We can carry this logic to absurd *Twilight Zone* dimensions—like perhaps Louisiana blacks were somehow "represented" by former Klansman David Duke when he was elected as a state senator. Or perhaps the British Royalists should have been capable of representing the rebellious anti-tax colonists, and so, according to the logic of

Winner Take All, the entire basis for pitching the tea into Boston Harbor, indeed for the American Revolution itself, is null and void.

According to this canon, that is exactly how "representation" supposedly works, however much it defies common sense. It is representation defined in such a way as to be turned on its head and rendered meaningless, yet such a view has surprising staying power among academics, pundits, and otherwise thoughtful political commentators. If the loser in an election somehow is represented by the winner, then what's the point of holding elections anyway? Why not draw straws or rotate the office among the candidates? I call this "phantom" representation because it is a classic smoke-and-mirrors operation—it's representation that doesn't really exist.

From a perspective of democratic theory, geographic-based districts reward representation based exclusively on where you *live*, rather than what you *think*. That's fine for a jurisdiction like those in eighteenth-century rural America where most neighbors probably thought alike. But at the outset of the twenty-first century the United States finds itself an extremely diverse, polyglot nation, particularly compared to the eighteenth century of our Founders. There are numerous legislative districts where, for instance, a white Christian Republican lives next door to a Latino single mom Democrat who lives next door to an independent Korean small businessman who lives beside a Sierra Club member and Green Party supporter, and so on, ad infinitum. There are entire sub-regions of Bushlandia and New Goreia where orphaned voters/geographic minorities are swamped by the partisan avalanche that dominates their elections. Consequently, under geographic-based representation of single-seat districts, only a handful of voters ever win representation. Representation is turned into a frustratingly daunting zero-sum game, inherently so—"if I win, you lose." This in turn divides and polarizes the electorate along multiple fracture and fault lines.

The "representation voids" produced by Winner Take All's purely geographical representation are nearly unlimited in today's increasingly diverse world. Can farmers, construction workers, and blue-collar workers be "represented" by a bunch of lawyers and real estate and insurance professionals who comprised over 60 percent of the 1998 U.S. House?[14] Or Latinos by whites, or by blacks or Asians? Can internet-savvy entrepreneurs be represented by technologically illiterate politicians? Can Christian conservatives be represented by free-choice libertarians? Can New Deal Liberals be represented by fiscally moderate New Democrats? Can women, who still only compose 14 percent of the Congress, be represented by men? Opinions certainly range on these questions, but the Winner Take All system makes it nearly impossible to discover the answers since it artificially masks voters' true preferences behind a façade of phantom representation.

Thus, geographic-based representation via single-seat districts sorts voters into two unequal camps—winners and losers. Those who win representation and those who do not. But even many winning voters are stuck choosing the "lesser of two evils." Similarly, elected officials find themselves increasingly hard-pressed to provide representation for increasingly diverse constituencies. Asking a single representative to straddle the divide between so many perspectives has become impossible in most legislative districts.

No, phantom representation is merely a clumsy bit of propaganda to justify the fact that most people don't have representation, and *never will have it* under Winner Take All. Phantom representation is a way of placing the blame on the voter, instead of where it rightly belongs—on Winner Take All's geographic-based, single-seat representation scheme. It's a way to deflect blame away from Winner Take All, yet this peculiar view has remarkable acceptance and staying power among influential political scientists, pundits, and other political gatekeepers. Its proponents like to hold forth smugly with a little patronizing lecture that goes something like this: "If you would just get out there and work harder for your candidate, or for your political party; or if your party only ran better candidates; or if your candidate could only raise more money, and so on, ad infinitum—*then* you would win representation." But the paradox is that even if you do work harder or raise more money, and your candidate manages to win, then *somebody else* is now a loser and has no representation. That's the zero-sum paradox again—*if I win, you lose.* The zero-sum game *defines* Winner Take All; that's the sign of the Winner Take All conundrum at work.

On top of that, if you are an "orphaned" Democratic or Republican voter, or a racial or political minority, it is virtually impossible for you to win. Again, by *definition,* in the majoritarian Winner Take All system you simply don't have enough voters on your side, you are a geographic minority. For supporters of third parties or independent politics—more and more voters, in recent years— the Winner Take All system fundamentally is a disempowering zero-sum game, a long-shot gamble where the odds are lopsidedly stacked against you. The dwindling number of Winner Take All voters who still choose to participate on Election Day are confronted with barren choices, so most voters either stay home or are forced to vote their "lesser of two evils" fears, instead of their hopes—to keep someone *out* of office whom they truly dread, rather than vote for someone they really like, a demonstration of what playwright Arthur Miller has called a kind of "negative consent." That's the Winner Take All conundrum at work. Having to always choose between the "lesser of two evils" is very corrosive of the democratic spirit.

Instead of "no taxation without representation," the *real* slogan of our Winner Take All democracy should be: *"If I win representation, you lose."* That's the first operative principle of Winner Take All, and arguably the most potent. Once you have a political system founded on that principle, a whole host of undesirable dynamics kick into play. The redistricting process, the subject of

Chapters 5 and 6, becomes the decennial ritual where the Winner Take All leg-islative lines are carved up in a power grab to decide *in advance* who will be that highest vote-getter, and which voters will win representation and which will lose and be stuck with "phantom representation."

Artificial majorities that distort policy

One of the purported strengths of the Winner Take All system is that it comes closest to guaranteeing "majority rule." Yet nothing could be further from the truth. This point of view has gained widespread acceptance, both in the media and among academics, resulting partly from the highly influential theoretical work in the late 1950s of Anthony Downs.[15] Downs' theory will be analyzed more thoroughly in Chapter 12, but for now some rather obvious points can be made.

While it's true that a two-party system guarantees by default that one party must win a majority in the Legislature, it's also true that the governing majority hasn't necessarily been elected by a majority of the people. Consequently, the policy enacted may not be the policy preferred by a popular majority.

For instance, the current Republican majority in the U.S. House was voted in by less than *17 percent* of the eligible electorate—only one-third of the eligible electorate voted for either a Democratic or Republican winner (with the remaining two-thirds of the electorate either not voting or voting for losers). But among that successful third of the electorate, about half voted for Democrats and the other half Republicans. Even if you assume that most of the Republican voters who voted for losers receive adequate representation from those Repub-lican representatives elected from other districts and other states—not a perfect assumption, since some losing voters may have issues related to where they live that only a local representative can address—still you cannot be sure that a majority of voters elected a majority of representatives. Winner Take All sys-tems are legendary for producing disproportional results where the largest *minority* bloc of voters (called a "plurality") wins a majority of seats. Here are a few notorious yet underreported examples of wacky Winner Take All election results.

The British, as *The New Yorker*'s Hendrik Hertzberg has observed, have shoehorned three political parties into a Winner Take All habitat suited for two, ensuring that minority rule has become a way of life in Britain. For instance, in Britain's 2001 elections Tony Blair's Labor Party won barely 42 percent of the popular vote—hardly a mandate. But because of the vagaries of their geographic-based Winner Take All system (in Britain they call their voting system First Past the Post) in a three-party field, that translated into winning 63 percent of the seats in the House of Commons. The 1997 elections turned out nearly exactly the same, and characteristically for Winner Take All elections over 14 million of those Britons who voted—48 percent—elected *no one* with their votes.

But don't feel sorry for the losing Conservative Party—in the five previous British elections Margaret Thatcher and John Major's Conservative Party won substantial majorities of legislative seats despite never winning more than 45 percent of the popular vote—fewer popular votes than Michael Dukakis had when he lost to George Bush in 1988. In fact, the last time Britain had a peacetime government that represented a popular majority was 1935. The ones to feel sorry for, however, are supporters of the Liberal Democratic Party, a minor party that has been routinely ripped off by the distortions of Winner Take All. In 1992, their 18 percent share of the popular vote gained them only 3 percent of seats; in 2001 they did slightly better, with 18 percent of the vote winning 8 percent of seats.[16]

All of these daffy British goings-on, of course, rarely have been reported in the U.S. media. Instead, every victory has been bizarrely reported as a stunning landslide. That's because the American media and the pundits—including the flagships *New York Times* and *Washington Post*—are so fixated on the horse race aspects of campaigns. They are not particularly well-versed about the defects of Winner Take All, and consequently are blind to the problems of phantom representation and artificial majorities. After the Labor Party's victory in 1997, the *New York Times* headline blared, "Labor Wins Stunning Landslide Victory." A more accurate headline would have read, "Defects of Winner Take All Voting System Give Minority Labor Party a Lopsided Majority."

It's like having a great big elephant in the middle of the living room and pretending it's not there, hoping no one will notice. But in Britain people do notice, particularly after Margaret Thatcher's Conservative Party pursued a radical policy agenda that significantly restructured much of the British economy and society, all with the support of only a minority of its citizens. For over a decade, the anti-Conservative vote split itself between Labor and the Liberal Democrats, allowing the Thatcher juggernaut to roll along despite its unpopularity. This disconnect has fueled accelerating efforts in Britain to get rid of Winner Take All, resulting in the use of proportional representation for the regional parliaments of Scotland and Wales, the London City Council, and European Parliament elections, as well as instant runoff voting for the mayor of London. Many observers believe it's just a matter of time—and perhaps the specter of a Labor defeat—before the Winner Take All ways of the House of Commons are tossed onto the scrap heap of history.

In Canada's bizarre Winner Take All elections in 1997, the Liberal Party won a majority of the Parliament with only 38 percent of the national popular vote—less than Bob Dole's losing percentage in the 1996 presidential race. The Liberals were able to take 101 of 103 seats—98 percent—in Canada's biggest province, Ontario, with only 48 percent of votes in that province. The Reform Party benefited from Winner Take All in the west, where it won a lopsided 92 percent of Alberta's legislative seats with 54 percent of the vote and took three-fourths of seats in British Columbia with only 40 percent of the vote. The seces-sionist-minded Bloc Quebecois became the third largest party in Parliament, despite finishing fifth in the national popular vote and running no candidates outside of the province of Quebec! In Canada's 2000 elections the situation hardly improved. The Liberal Party won 59 percent of the seats nationwide with only 41 percent of the vote, and Canada's voter turnout plummeted to its lowest level since 1925.[17] All of these distortions in Canada, as in Britain, have been due primarily to the defects of single-seat Winner Take All districts. We will discover more about the mechanics of how this happens in later chapters.

Ah, those crazy Anglo cousins of ours, we Americans shake our heads. Thank goodness *our* Winner Take All elections don't exhibit such distortions in representation. Unfortunately, they do, although not quite as severely. And the pundits and political scientists don't bother either keeping track of it or telling us about it.

For example, in the 2000 elections for the U.S. House, the GOP majority won only 48.2 percent of the popular vote, yet ended up with 51 percent of the seats. Not a glaring disproportion on the order of the British or Canadians, yet still moderately troubling that a minority of the vote won a majority of seats. In fact, one could argue that the Democrats should be in the majority, since there were 371 U.S. House seats where both Democrats and Republicans fielded a candidate, and the Democrats won slightly more votes nationwide in those races, but because of the distortions of how the districts had been drawn the Republicans ended up with more of those seats, 191–179 (plus one independ-ent). But don't feel sorry for Democrats; during the last several decades, the Republican Party has been cheated consistently out of seats because of such distortions, losing as many as forty-three House seats in 1976, and an average of twenty-seven seats per congressional cycle from 1976 through 1988.[18] For most of the 1990s, Democrat and Republican vote totals for the U.S. House have been neck and neck, but as recently as 1992 the Democrats turned their bare majority (51 percent) of the nationwide popular vote in House races into a lop-sided 59 percent of seats.

Between 1945 and 1980, congressional elections produced artificial majori-ties 17 percent of the time, where one party or the other received less than 50 percent of the national vote yet ended up with more than 50 percent of the House seats.[19] Distortions are greatest in individual states, particularly at the state legislative level as we saw in Chapter 1, where the distortions of single-seat districts overrepresent the winning side and give them an exaggerated and sometimes veto-proof majority. Each congressional cycle, numerous states show distortions between the percentage of votes won and the percentage of House seats gained for that state's congressional delegation. For instance, in 1998 Democratic candidates in Mississippi for the U.S. House won a total of 48 percent of the statewide congressional vote, yet walked off with 60 percent of

Mississippi's U.S. House seats. In 2000, Republican candidates for the House in Ohio won a total of 49 percent of the vote but 58 percent of Ohio's 19 seats. Democratic candidates in Arkansas won approximately 45 percent of the statewide vote, yet after the dust had cleared held 75 percent of Arkansas' U.S. House seats. In 1994 in Texas, congressional districts gerrymandered by Democrats allowed them to win 63 percent of the congressional seats with only 42 percent of the popular votes. Now that's a gerrymander![20]

But the state of Washington holds a special place in the pantheon of wacky Winner Take All elections. The cornerstone state of the Northwest illustrates that, even when legislative district lines are drawn commendably to make district races more competitive, Winner Take All can create perplexing distortions. In 1992, the Democrats won eight of nine (89 percent) of Washington's congressional seats with only 56 percent of the popular vote. In 1994, the Republican revolution completely overturned that, and Republicans won seven of nine seats (78 percent) with only 51 percent of the popular vote—a swing of only seven percent of voters causing a dramatic shift of 67 percent in party representation. Two years later the Republicans lost ground, winning less than a majority of the popular vote (47 percent) but still managing to win six of nine (67 percent) seats, even though they had about the same share of the popular vote as in 1992 when they won only one seat. Two years later, completing the merry dance with Winner Take All eccentricity, the Democrats won back a majority of Washington's congressional seats.

Throughout the decade, displaying bizarrely distorted results that rival that of the Canadians and British, swings in Washington voters' support as small as 4 percent translated into lurches from left to right and back again. Washington State's dance with political oddity is even more pronounced in their state legislature. Washington elects three representatives per state legislative district, two to the House and one to the Senate, and thirty-four of forty-nine districts were represented by only one party in 1998. Winning voters have a monopoly of three representatives; losing voters have none.[21]

These representation distortions, which can greatly affect policy, are a product of two factors: (1) natural demographics of partisan strongholds, like we saw in Bushlandia and New Goreia, that overwhelm the opposition and win more representation in a Winner Take All system than their numbers deserve, thus *overrepresenting* the majority perspective or party and *underrepresenting* the minority; and (2) the decennial redistricting process whereby the geographic-based districts are gerrymandered to favor whatever political party is in control of the line-drawing which again can lead to overrepresentation of the majority party and underrepresentation of the minority party (we will delve more thoroughly into redistricting in Chapters 5 and 6). As we saw in Chapter 1, such votes-to-seats distortions can be quite severe in the numerous state legislatures of Bushlandia and New Goreia, creating "representation ripoffs" where the majority party wins far more seats than its vote totals should allow, an exaggerated majority with direct impacts on policy.

Despite such distortions and "representation ripoffs" that are rife throughout American elections, most political scientists who specialize in American politics don't bother keeping track of them or estimating their impact on policy, representation, or governance. It's not even on their radar screens. Journalists do not research it either, and the media does not report it. Thus, artificial majorities and exaggerated majorities are generating real-world impacts, but mostly remain unrecognized.

Swing voter serenade: the mighty roar of swing voters

In a Winner Take All system, swing voters are the mighty fulcrum that move politics. They are the Copernican center around which everything else turns, and the reason why is simple: how they vote determines who will win close elections. As a result, swing voters are extremely fortunate to have bestowed upon them vastly inflated influence in our Winner Take All system.

Given a choice between Democrats or Republicans, most voters know which party's candidates they will vote for. But in any given election, about 15 percent or fewer of voters, for various reasons, are fuzzy or unsure enough in their thinking that they cannot make up their minds. They are what Anthony Downs called the *baffleds,* the almighty swing voters.[22] One Democratic campaign consultant describes swing voters as those voters who "by definition are those least informed and interested in politics. . . . You motivate these people with fear, or 30-second sound bites that are simplified to make someone who is not interested or not informed take action. If you can't tell them in eight words or less why you are the better choice, you're probably going to lose."[23]

Ironically, these indecisive, baffled voters are the ones who politicians serenade the most in a Winner Take All system. Policy overtures are directed to them, campaign messages are fashioned for them. Millions of dollars are spent on focus groups and opinion polls to determine their opinions and then target those opinions back to them as slick TV ads and other campaign appeals. Every politician and political consultant knows in every fiber of their being that, without exaggeration, these baffle-headed swing voters determine elections.

But the shallowness of Winner Take All politics does not end there; no, it sinks deeper. Because swing *districts*—those handful of close races in legislative districts that are not safe for one party or the other—will determine which party will control the legislature. In any legislature that is closely divided between Democrats and Republicans—like the U.S. House—whichever party wins the swing districts will win a majority of the seats. Particularly today, with Democrats and Republicans across the country so evenly matched and the American people themselves so narrowly split along partisan lines, the handful of swing districts acquire exaggerated importance. As we saw in Chapter 2, this applies in presidential elections as well, where a handful of swing states determine which candidate wins the presidency.

Now, smash the two together—swing voters in swing districts and states—and you arrive at the utter pointlessness and absurdity of the Winner Take All system. A handful of muddle-headed, indecisive, and least-informed voters—those who are "best motivated by fear" and "30-second sound bites" and "need to be convinced in eight words or less"—stumbling to the polls in a handful of close races can determine which candidate wins the presidency or which party wins a majority in the Congress and in numerous state legislatures. By extension these voters influence national policy beyond the weight their minority numbers should warrant. Elections in 2000—all the hundreds of millions of dollars raised, all the strategies deployed—were predicated on this dynamic of our Winner Take All system.

This reality is a by-product of our geographic-based and two-choice system. Swing districts only exist because the political-geographic map has been carved up into single-seat districts. Most of these districts are gerrymandered to be safe seats that protect incumbents and/or the dominating political party, leaving a handful of competitive races that become the contested terrain of national and state politics. And the two-choice duopoly of our political system, when combined with the new campaign technologies, allows the targeting of ever-smaller slices of undecided voters. You simply craft your campaign messages to position yourself vis-à-vis your lone opponent.

Conversely, another category of swing voters that can have untoward influence over politics are the opposite of Downs' baffleds—those zealots who care passionately enough for a single issue or cause. A case in point is that of the Cuban boy Elian. That national travesty dramatically illustrated the power of swing voters in swing states under our Winner Take All system, in this case with respect to the 2000 UnElection. Because Florida is a big state in presidential politics—our fourth largest, with twenty-seven Electoral College votes—*and* because it is a swing state that might go to either political party, Florida is a big prize in the presidential sweepstakes. Florida is notably influenced by a particular group of swing voters—Cuban Americans. They are a cohesive, well-financed and vocal minority that has much greater impact than a group their size typically warrants. They can be zealots for their anti-Castro cause—in this case a little boy miraculously plucked from the sea, supposedly saved by divine dolphins, and nearly canonized by an idolatrous local crowd and Republican spin-meisters like former Reagan speechwriter Peggy Noonan.[24]

Make no mistake, if Elian had been Haitian, or had he popped up in electoral votes-poor Wyoming, or even a large state but one locked-up GOP or Democratic, he would have been given a one-way ticket back home in record time. But Elian was Cuban, and Florida was a valuable swing state on the path to a big prize, with a presidential election just around the corner. And we have a peculiar Winner Take All method of electing our president that allowed this small but influential group of swing voters to circumvent immigration law, defy the Attorney General for months, and grab national headlines.

And so Elian was courted like a visiting dignitary, given the golden key to Disney World and everything else a child from a poor country could want, and turned into a cause célèbre. Al Gore made a pandering pilgrimage to Florida, hoping to pick up votes, and the GOP—the "family values" party—strongly backed not returning the boy to his father. The media circus that sprung up outside the Little Havana home grew to "only in America" proportions: portable toilets lining the street, vendors hawking peanuts and snowcones, TV crew members lounging on lawn chairs until the house door swung open and they sprung into action. The TV crews called the anarchic scene "Camp Elian."[25]

But what the Elian debacle illustrated was that, under our Winner Take All system, if you are in the right state and in the right group of swing voters, you can bring powerful politicians and national policy to their knees. Surprising factors and events suddenly can acquire exaggerated importance, commanding national attention in the "all-or-nothing" atmosphere of our system. As we will see in the next chapter, similar "swing voter" dynamics—not campaign finance inequities—allow special interest groups like the National Rifle Association to thwart the majority national opinion demanding effective gun control.

It is deeply ironic—many defenders of Winner Take All criticize alternative voting systems of proportional representation because of the latter's propensity to elect minority parties that may hold the balance of power in a parliamentary government and cause the collapse of the government—the so-called "Italy and Israel effect." Yet under Winner Take All, small slices of the most uninformed and uninterested spectrum of the electorate, or conversely of the most fanatical parts of the electorate, also can acquire vastly exaggerated power, determine which party wins a majority, and thereby hold hostage any semblance of sane policy.

Two-Choice Tango

Another subset of the Winner Take All conundrum is the Two-Choice Tango. Nearly half a century ago, a French political scientist named Maurice Duverger proposed what became known to political scientists as Duverger's Law: Winner Take All voting systems tend to result in a two-choice/two-party political system.[26] This observation since has been seconded by American political scientists and theorists like Robert Dahl, Arendt Lijphart, Anthony Downs, Douglas Amy, and others.

In recent years, politicians and political consultants have figured something out: in a two-choice field, winning no longer requires issues. If the goal in Winner Take All is to win more votes than your lone opponent, you can game the system and win as easily by driving voters *away* from your opponent as by attracting voters to yourself. In fact, it's easier, all you have to do is find a good wedge issue or two or selectively strip-mine your opponent's voting record for votes on taxes, crime, or child pornography that you can distort out of all recognition. Even better is digging up your opponent's youthful indiscretions or some current smear or inflated sex scandal, and targeting a slickly-prepared campaign message to swing voters who determine the winner in a close race.

That's because under Winner Take All's two-choice system, *the last candidate standing wins.* In a one-on-one, *mano a mano* campaign, the dynamic inescapably boils down to a zero-sum choice: *"if you lose, I win."* If support for your opponent declines, your chances rise, a kind of teeter-totter effect, because voters don't have anywhere else to go. The optimal strategy, then, for a Winner Take All campaign in a two-choice race becomes mudslinging and vicious attack campaigning, and one of slicing and dicing the electorate and targeting your attacks on your opponent to the muddle-headed swing voters. Moreover, the new campaign technologies—polling, focus groups, thirty-second TV spots, direct mail, and more—are uniquely tailored to this task of gaming, spinning, hype, and targeting (this dynamic of Winner Take All campaigns will be explored more thoroughly in Chapters 8 and 9).

The two parties are trying to attract the same slice of undecided swing voters that decides who wins and loses close elections, as well as motivate their base of supporters, a delicate and often impossible balancing act that leaves the parties pinned on the twin horns of their dilemma. Under such electoral pressures, hack-attack politics—tearing down your opponent—becomes the primary means to distinguish yourself from your opponent and fulfill the dictates of the Winner Take All conundrum. Effective political attacks will allow a party or candidate both to mobilize their carnivorous base *and* to drive swing voters away from the opponent. You can game the system and not even have to talk about policy very much if you can effectively tear down your opponent. This dynamic becomes especially pronounced whenever the field has been reduced to two candidates, because that's when the Winner Take All conundrum is maximized.

Decades ago Anthony Downs' famous economic model of the Winner Take All system predicted that the two political parties will have incentive to take policy positions that are as ambiguous and equivocal as possible in order to maximize the numbers of voters you can appeal to, and hack-attack politics is a severe form of this. [27] Going negative on one's opponent is simply the most efficient and successful way to stay ambiguous and equivocal about policy. Unsurprisingly, one Danish visitor observing a U.S. political season commented that the campaigns resembled a mugging; a German observer compared them to the Wild West. With the specter of the modern "permanent campaign" that never ends and 24-7 media that never sleeps, these dynamics now extend past the elections and into the governance process as well.

The Two-Choice Tango effect was illustrated poignantly during the 2000 presidential primaries. The Democrats had a two-candidate presidential contest from the start and, unsurprisingly, were the first to go negative. When Bill Bradley began surging past him in the polls, Al Gore launched a full-frontal attack. Bradley at first refused to fight back, not wanting to be dragged into the mud. Some wondered whether Gore's attacks would generate a backlash like the kind Steve Forbes experienced when he attacked Bob Dole in the Republican primaries in 1996 but, as Democratic consultant Bill Carrick pointed out, a Gore backlash was unlikely because the Democratic primary, unlike the Republican primary in 1996, had only two candidates. Said Carrick, "That allows you to be aggressive and not suffer the consequences of potentially offending somebody who doesn't like negative campaigning, because they don't have anywhere else to go."[28] After being swamped in the Iowa caucuses and after not receiving any tangible benefits for taking the high ground, Bradley finally went after Gore. Their last debates were described in the *Washington Post* as "relentlessly negative."

On the Republican side, at first the nomination was a six-candidate field, with most observers believing only one candidate had a chance of winning. Frontrunner Bush and his sundry opponents for months pursued a generally positive, even gentlemanly, campaign. At one point, Bush even defended John McCain as "a good man." But Bush's waltz to the nomination effectively turned into a two-person battle royal after McCain's dramatic win in New Hampshire and the withdrawal of weaker candidates. Once the field was reduced to two, the nation was treated to a familiar sight—down-and-dirty, hack-attack politics.

The first casualty was comity. In South Carolina, Bush charged McCain with cozying up to special interests and betraying conservative values. McCain responded with ads attacking Bush's integrity and comparing him to Clinton, the lowest of all blows to flame-throwing Republicans. Bush continued to blanket the state with attacks and won the support of most voters making up their minds in the days before the vote. His success made the escalation of attacks by both campaigns in Michigan nearly inescapable. Thus, in both the Democratic and Republican primaries, once the field was reduced to two candidates the campaigns degenerated into slugfests of mudslinging and attack ads. The same was to happen in the presidential race during September and October.

Attack politics have become the modus operandi throughout our two-choice political system. Not only are campaigns relentlessly negative and invasive, but today attacks and wedge issue politicking continue throughout the governing process. What the Clinton impeachment debacle illustrated, as much as anything, is that two-choice, Winner Take All politics has degenerated into a type of gaming and manipulation for partisan advantage that has brought us the specter of the *permanent negative campaign*. Yet, despite all the national disgust and media attention over negative politicking, there has been surprisingly little discussion by pundits and political scientists about how the two-choice, Winner Take All system substantially *drives* attack-style tactics. In fact, it is *malignantly* suited for it.

Besides providing powerful incentives for attack-style campaigning and political gaming, the Two-Choice Tango also deprives voters of political choices, whether a range of political parties and candidates or a range of viewpoints and policy preferences. Despite a recent clamor by voters for more political choices, as evidenced by the successes of independent candidates like Ross Perot, Lowell Weicker (former governor of Connecticut), Angus King (governor of Maine) and Jesse Ventura, third parties have been notoriously unsuccessful in our Winner Take All system. Out of the more than 7,000 state senate and house seats scattered across the United States, five currently are held by third parties, all in Vermont (a fairly constant number, year after year, election after election).[29] Out of 535 Congressional and U.S. Senate seats, only two are held by an independent representative (one each from Vermont and Virginia), and none by third parties. It has always been that way in the United States (and to some degree other Winner Take All democracies as well, such as the aforementioned Great Britain). Out of the approximately 21,000 U.S. House races in the twentieth century, minor party and independent candidates won a mere one hundred times, plus another seven special elections, a total of 107 victories—or about 0.5 percent of the time.[30] Lightning strikes more often than that. The rate of third party success is as likely explained as a statistical fluke as much as any organic political momentum or alteration of the duopolistic landscape.

There have been over one thousand third parties in our nation's history, but only one has ever lasted—the Republican Party, which replaced in the 1850s one of the two major parties that had been riven apart over the issue of slavery.[31] Most third parties are only a distant memory now, for trivia junkies and TV game shows, but with a small but determined few still buzzing around the American political landscape against all odds. Third parties lose under Winner Take All not because they don't have good ideas or enough campaign resources but because they are a minority perspective competing in a majoritarian Winner Take All system that rewards the highest vote-getters, which, *by definition*, is not usually a minority. The prospect of wasting your vote on a third-party candidate who doesn't stand a chance or, even worse, voting for a third-party candidate like Ralph Nader who might spoil your "lesser of two evils" candidate and help elect your "greater evil," are powerful disincentives that have always knocked the legs out from under third parties.

The fact is, Winner Take All systems are notoriously hostile to the success and survival of third parties. Consequently, voters have fewer meaningful choices at the polls. Fewer viewpoints and policy options get debated during the campaigns, as the Two-Choice Tango "dumbs down" the quality of campaign debates by using extreme negative campaigning and by preselecting a narrow range of issues for political debate that will appeal to a narrow pool of swing voters in swing districts or swing states. It was telling during the 2000 presidential campaign, which was dominated by a handful of issues, including Medicare, Social Security, and prescription drug benefits for seniors, when one twenty-something commented, "I feel like if you aren't elderly or on Medicare or Social Security, these two candidates have nothing to say to you." As a result of the Two-Choice Tango and the use of the modern campaign technologies, most other policies and issues—and the constituencies interested in them—got left on the sidelines during the campaign.

Winner Take All—Does the "majority rule"?

Such are the roller-coaster vagaries and peculiarities of Winner Take All and its highly vaunted "majority rule." Unfortunately, these puzzling dilemmas and paradoxes confront voters, candidates, and legislators at every turn. Too often the majorities created by Winner Take All are "artificial" or "exaggerated" majorities plagued by phantom representation; and the successful party and their candidates use vicious mudslinging in a two-choice field to win by appealing to ill-informed and confused swing voters in swing districts. It is a majority by default in a two-party system where one party by definition *must* win a majority. But that's not necessarily a "representative" majority. And the policies they enact may not at all represent the true will of the majority, making politics feel to the average person like a bit of a crapshoot (Chapters 12 and 13 will explore the roller-coaster ride inherent to policy formation under Winner Take All).

While the surface structure for electing representatives under Winner Take All is simple—deceptively so, what could be more simple than "highest vote-getter wins"?—the underlying mechanics and the dynamics unleashed by the Winner Take All gremlins render it extremely complex and vexing. In fact, as we will see in this book, the Winner Take All gremlins create multiple opportunities for political professionals and technocrats to "game" the system—to take advantage of loopholes, technicalities, and peculiarities in order to win. Sometimes this political gaming—gambling, really—will allow a political party to win an undeserved majority of seats with only a minority of votes, or even fewer votes than their opponent; or it will allow a candidate to use modern propaganda techniques to precisely target their campaign spin and create multiple (and often conflicting) messages for different groups of voters, in effect speaking out of many sides of their mouth.

Other times the gaming will motivate party leaders to deploy redistricting techniques like "cracking" and "packing" to carve up the electorate, or to withhold candidates from running in non-competitive local or county races as a way to drive down overall voter turnout among their opponent's supporters in the more important statewide races; or to target millions of dollars in "soft money" to a handful of close races in specific legislative districts, overseeing the Winner

Take All map like military generals in the Pentagon's War Room. Winner Take All's gaming incentives prompt party leaders to live and die by opinion polls, focus groups and thirty-second TV spots, figuring out how to use "crafted talk" as a means to "simulate responsiveness," or to promote or kill legislative policy by gauging how it affects support in swing districts or swing states, in effect reducing national politics to the most provincial of considerations.

With all the political gaming, gambling, and manipulation going on, the *real* losers in the Winner Take All system are the voters. The constant calculations and bipolar dilemmas of the Winner Take All conundrum render campaigns and policy making into extremely opaque operations that are baffling to citizens trying to follow the process, or to find elucidation via stimulating political debate. The Winner Take All conundrum lays down a veritable minefield that may detonate at any moment, leaving voters feeling as if our legislatures are bizarre Halls of Mirrors, where little makes sense and where robbers are continually taking something from them—either their taxes, their dignity, or their comprehension of politics and representative government.

Considering the system as a whole, there is nothing simple or transparent about Winner Take All and its various calculations and paradoxes. Nor is there much "majoritarian" about it. Just because the highest vote-getter wins in individual races you cannot assume that this will lead to "majority rule." Often times, it does not. That opaqueness fools many observers, even the experts, political scientists, and reformers. What's the cause, and what's the effect? With Winner Take All, you can never be sure. There's no straightforward connect-the-dots, no map that gets us from here to there. With such distortions and discrepancies built into the Winner Take All system—courtesy of its disruptive gremlins, the Winner Take All conundrum, phantom representation, artificial majorities, the two-choice tango, and the influence of swing voters—it is inevitable that representation, participation, campaigns and political discourse, and legislative policy will become disjointed, distorted, and divorced from the desires of the nation.

PART TWO
The People's Congress?

CHAPTER FOUR

The People's House

You are the Rulers and the Ruled.
—FROM A CEILING FRESCO IN THE HALL OF CAPITALS,
U.S. CAPITOL BUILDING

Perhaps the best place from which to view the alarming erosion of our Winner Take All democracy is from inside the chambers of our most hallowed institution—the U.S. House of Representatives. The People's House. No single body better symbolizes the animating democratic spirit that swept through the American colonies in the mid- to late-eighteenth century. That Spirit of 1776 fomented a revolution that birthed, not without labor pains, a new nation, where it was held to be "self-evident" that "all men are created equal," and are endowed with "certain unalienable rights," as Jefferson and Co. so eloquently declared it before the eyes of a candid world.

The putative American revolutionaries had experience enough with chief executives and monarchs to tire of autocratic license invested in a single office. Washington, to his credit, had the sagacity and strength of character to resist the temptation thrust upon him by some who offered him the Presidency-for-Life. The constitutional Framers themselves regarded the new national legislature as the "first branch," enshrining it in the first Article of the Constitution.[1] No, it was the creation of a directly elected legislative body, roughly representative by capita and elected by the only known method at the time—Winner Take All, either districts or at-large—that was to become one of young America's most unique and enduring legacies.

The chamber of the People's House, when empty, is an impressive room. It's large and palatial, approximately the size of a high school gymnasium, and it is ringed amphitheater-like by a spectators' balcony from which the public and the media can watch the show below. The pit where House members sit is bedecked with the alternating regality of marble pilasters and a dark, rich walnut shine, walnut being the choice hardwood at the time of its last reconstruction. The finish work around the perimeter is gilted on the edges by a golden trim, a kind of fancy but not gaudy lace, like that of an elegant evening gown.

Semicircular rows of dark wooden benches for the 435 House members are arranged like church pews inside this cathedral to American democracy. The seals of the states and territories circle the ceiling in the order that they joined this new experiment in popular sovereignty, and over the gallery doors of the House chamber are twenty-three marble relief portraits depicting notable historic and legal figures: Hammurabi, Moses, Justinian I, Thomas Jefferson,

George Mason, Napoleon, and more. A large, full-length portrait of Washington hangs to the right of the Speaker's chair; plastered on the wall behind the Speaker stretches a large Old Glory framed by two pillarlike bronze representations of ancient *fasces,* invoking the authority of that republican war machine, the Romans. Thus, the patrilineal *imperium* of the American political system, and its simulacra of legitimacy, are well evoked inside this cathedral of the American republic.

The House chamber, when empty, echoes with history, tradition, and dissent. Here, the 35th Congress spent months of 1858 in heated debate over whether Kansas should be admitted as free or slave. "Every man on the floor of both Houses is armed with a revolver," observed one representative. When a Member accidentally dropped his weapon during a bitter eight-week struggle to elect a Speaker of the House, the uproar threatened to turn into mob violence.[2] Such were the centrifugal forces of slavery, argued in this very chamber.

Not far from the current House chamber is located the old Senate chamber, where one can almost hear Daniel Webster's pleas for Union "now and forever, one and inseparable"; or Calhoun's passionate retorts for states' rights; or back in the old House chamber, now called Statuary Hall, an elderly war horse in his final years, Quincy Adams, his snores in the back row still resounding. Some two hundred years later the senior senator from New Hampshire now sits at Webster's original desk, and the senior senator from South Carolina at Calhoun's; the senior senator from Mississippi occupies Jefferson Davis' desk and the senior senator from Kentucky Henry Clay's. The original desks—first made in 1819, and still showing carved initials of some of their former occupants—were moved to the current Senate chamber in 1859, just before the first cannon fire boomed at Fort Sumter.[3]

The corridors outside the House chamber, called Westward Expansion Hall, Statuary Hall, and The Great Experiment Hall, show colorful historical frescos and statues projecting hawklike visages of some of the statesmen (precious few women), saints and sinners who have paraded, grandstanded, and bluffed their ways through these halls. Like a never-ending tattoo, a kind of Illustrated Man of the national fable, the throat of hallways shows concatenated scenes: of Washington laying the Capitol building cornerstone; of the First Continental Congress and the Constitutional Convention; of the signing of the Mayflower Compact; of the British burning the Capitol; of the Capitol's Rotunda during the Civil War, with racks of war-wounded lining the perimeter; of Lewis and Clark standing on a bluff overlooking a native village; and of lustful gold prospectors and fur traders. At the bottom of the west staircase that ascends to the House chamber are two gorgeous ceiling murals of native peoples in their natural milieu, one of them showing the ominous presence of Columbus' death-ships, lurking offshore.

Flashing forward to 1913: President Woodrow Wilson visited the House chamber, becoming the first president since John Adams to address a Joint Session of Congress, initiating a ritual that subsequent presidents would follow. Four years later, Wilson addressed another Joint Session, announcing the severance of diplomatic relations with Germany—World War I was just around the corner. Winston Churchill addressed a Joint Session of Congress here after the Japanese attack on Pearl Harbor, predicting with his classic signature understatement a "long and hard war." Impeachment hearings have been held here for two presidents, one recently burned into the nation's memory cells; one other president, reading the handwriting on the wall, chose to resign. Sitting high up in the spectators' gallery ringing the House chamber, one would have to be a recrudescent syndicalist, a moderern-day Guy Fawkes[4] holding a match to the gun powder, not to be moved by the drama, the moment, the intersection of the past—the multiple pasts—that reside in this, our People's House.

Today, leaning over the House gallery's balcony, a spectator can watch as the chamber's current inhabitants—our elected representatives—trickle in and mill about, like so many molecules composing the whole. When the chamber is finally filled, say, just before an important vote, the first thing one might notice, gazing down from the gallery, is that this People's House doesn't look very much like "the people." There are a lot of white faces down there—86 percent in fact—and a lot of guys—about 87 percent.[5] There are also a lot of gray hairs and shiny pink pates down there—nobody that looks like, say, a regular at a local Midwest diner, or the waitress who serves her or him, or a Los Angeles bus-riding commuter, or a Bronx convenience store owner. Also, we know there's a lot of lawyers down there, and a lot of real estate, insurance, or finance specialists—taken together, over 60 percent of the House membership.[6] And there is a plurality of millionaires down there, in fact during the debate in April 2001 on the repeal of the estate tax, which sought to benefit a small affluent minority holding at least a half million dollars in wealth, it was estimated that 60–70 percent of the Congress would benefit by its repeal.

Indeed, it is rather shocking how little the face of this House of Representatives has changed since 1789, despite two hundred years of litigation, activism, protest, sacrifice, marches, sweat, blood, lynchings, and tears. No, the People's House still doesn't look like the people, hardly at all, and the U.S. Senate is even worse in that regard—there are no blacks or Latinos, even fewer women than in the House, and even greater income disparities between the Senators and their voters. A famous nineteenth-century aphorism said, "It is harder for a poor man to enter the United States Senate than for a rich man to enter Heaven," and things hardly seem different today. No, two hundred years into our history the United States Congress is still a fairly patrician body, more resembling the Roman Senate than a New England town meeting.

But this is what political scientists call "descriptive" or "mirror" representation. Descriptive representation is academic jargon for what some would label a kind of "political correctness," an apparently radical and disquieting notion that The People's representatives should mirror the demographics of the people they purport to represent, at least within some reasonable parameters. Like other matters PC, descriptive representation is not very popular today, either in the academy or in the mass media, ridiculed as government by bean-counters or affirmative action zealots. Which is ironic, because certainly the Founding Fathers understood that a monarchical and distant overseas British government didn't reflect *their* demographics, and they fought a war of independence to establish a principle that it *should*. John Adams, no Jefferson radical, wrote that "this representative assembly . . . should be in miniature an exact portrait of the people at large."[7] So let's just take note of the fact that, when we look in the mirror of the People's House, of this Winner Take All legislative body, the mirror doesn't reflect back, and then let that drop. For now.

The flip side of descriptive representation is what is called "substantive" representation. This is the more accepted notion that what is most important is not what our elected officeholders look like, but rather that they represent the best interests of their constituents and the nation. The corollary to this is that, while the inhabitants of the People's House may not look like the people, they at least *think* like the people; they share their opinions, or at least act as their constituents would have them do, and as a collective body duly represent the people's best interests. But is that really true? Do the current inhabitants of the People's House really think like the people or act as the people wish? Let's explore that notion a bit.

Once the great chambers of the House are full, and debate starts, other observations spring to mind. There are two sides in this chamber, a left and a right—Democrats on one side, Republicans on the other—with an aisle, a dividing line, down the middle. The People's House is divided into two partisan sections, like the line where the ocean meets the rocky shore, forever battering against each other. But surely the American people, with its vast array of ethnicities, religions, languages, geographic regions, political philosophies, Web sites, jazzy urban centers, and climate zones, are not so easily categorized. In fact, it's one of the great modern ironies that as consumers we can purchase at least fifteen different types of toothpastes, twenty-one different breakfast cereals, thirty-one flavors of ice cream, fifty-seven channels of cable, a dozen airlines, and a cornucopia of magazines, newspapers, TV shows, and Web sites—consumer choice being a mantra of the times—but in the political sphere we effectively have two choices (and as we will see in the next chapter, in nine out of ten legislative races we really only have *one* choice). The free marketplace has spread everywhere except to our politics. The American nation is a bright and splendid peacock, of dizzying colors and shimmering array, but the People's House is a rather drab, two-toned bird.

No, the People's House is the bastion of phantom representation, where

T-rex right-wingers like Tom DeLay and Dick Armey supposedly represent everyone in their districts, including the Democrats and liberals; and where fiery liberals Patrick Kennedy and Jesse Jackson Jr. represent even the Republicans and conservatives in their districts. This is the House of artificial majorities, where representatives who received less than a majority of popular votes nationwide nevertheless ended up with a majority of seats.[8] These are the 435 "chosen ones," those who currently reign over the semifeudal Winner Take All districts, the representatives of the two-choice tango. These proxies are supposed to represent "we the people," but they were the choices of surprising few numbers of voters—only a third of eligible voters actually cast votes for winning candidates. There is little inspiring about this leadership body, as evidenced by the numbers of voters who bothered to show up on Election Day, less than a majority (and in 1998 barely a third), the lowest in the world among established democracies.[9]

Needing an explanation for AWOL voters that can reinforce the legitimacy of our flaccid elections, the cavalry in the form of Official Rationalization has already arrived. One respected sociologist has proposed the radical notion that citizens participate in our modern society in a myriad of ways, and that voting and elections is just one of them, and not even necessarily the most important—so let's not get too worked up, presumably, over single-digit voter turnouts, disengaged young voters, or our spiraling national political depression.[10] George Will, ever the mischievous neo-con trying to burst liberal balloons, periodically tosses off the opinion that maybe people don't vote because they're satisfied—there are better things to do in a prosperous democracy, after all, than muddle through campaign sound bites and thirty-second TV ads.[11] But the Willian thesis conveniently ignores reams of hard evidence about who does and who does not vote: the voting electorate is overwhelmingly whiter, wealthier, older, and more educated than those who don't vote.[12] In other words, those who have *least* reason to be satisfied are those who have been no-shows on Election Day (in fact, it was a large and sudden influx of black voters to the Florida polls, many for the first time, that overwhelmed the unprepared poll workers. Knowing that many of their votes never were counted, it remains to be seen if these voters will lapse back into their previous standby mode). These voting demographics are one of the undeniable outlines, the shape of this place, wobbling toward post-democracy. And no amount of Willian sophistry can change that.

But back to the debate on the floor of the People's House. The deliberations are heated this particular day, uncustomarily so. Usually the debates are flaccid, quotidian even, as each representative stands and delivers with a rather perfunctory wind up, without much ceremony or fanfare. The Members usually don't listen to each other much, having heard each other's cant and rant a hundred times before. Rather, if they are present on the floor at all, they converse with their seat mates, or a page, or stroll around the chambers, smiling and waving at visiting constituents in the gallery like a major league baseball star hanging around the dugout.

But today the Members are rapt and riveted; Speaker of the House Hastert is having to bang his gavel and enforce decorum and civility more than usual. Rep. DeLay from Texas is a snarling Republican pit bull, rising on the House floor to deliver a series of elemental attacks, invoking God and nation and lancing his opponents with partisan barbs and opprobrium. Rep. Hyde is relentless, attacking his pet straw man, the entertainment industry, and tossing in sermons decrying "moral decay" for good measure. Democrats respond in kind; Speaker of the House–hopeful Gephardt accuses the Republicans of being beholden to certain special interests, of being out of touch with the American people, of leading a "do-nothing" Congress. Rep. Dingell from Michigan is appealing to his Democratic colleagues for crossover votes. Each side tries to score points in a governing process that in recent years has degenerated, sadly, into one long scorched-earth campaign filled with partisan rancor and legislative rope-a-dope.

And there are many points to score, because today the issue is—gun control. It's a particularly hot and muggy June 1999 in the nation's capital, and similarly the temperature in the House chamber this day is torrid. The level of vituperation and acrimony is palpable, the ripostes and sparring resound with the searing passion displayed previously in these chambers by abolitionists and states rightists, or Vietnam war hawks and doves, and manifest destiny mouthpieces who have plowed the way, come hell or high water. Not more than three weeks ago, two high school students in Littleton, Colorado, waltzed into their high school, each bearing more individual firepower than a GI storming the beaches of Normandy, and blasted away thirteen of their classmates and teachers and then committed suicide. This massacre is the latest tragedy in a string of suburban schoolyard shooting sprees, and before that a rash of drive-by shootings at urban schools, that has left the nation stymied about how to protect its children. According to the National Center for Health Statistics, ten children and adolescents in the United States are killed each and every day by gunfire—nearly 4,000 per year, 86 percent of the firearm deaths for children in the *entire world*[13]—a level of horror usually expected in death-squad dictatorships like El Salvador or Pinochet's Chile, or in the Taliban's Afghanistan.

Indeed, on this very June day, as the U.S. House of Representatives debates a change in gun-control policy, yet another armed student went berserk at a high school in Georgia, upping the ante as a restless nation looks toward their elected representatives for national leadership. National opinion polls clearly show an overwhelming majority of people favoring stricter gun controls.[14] This People's House, which doesn't look like the nation nor probably reflect the diversity of opinion encapsulated within it, is being asked to stand and deliver, in essence to show that, at the very least, they *think* like the people they purport to represent, or at least can *lead* the nation out of its current gun-slinging morass.

We all know how this one turned out. Congress punted the ball. If we wanted to look for a more fitting example of the trivialization of public opinion and national policy by what Winner Take All politics has become, we can hang a "Look No Further" sign here. Congress, asked by an anxious nation to do something about school safety and gun control, responded by passing a recommendation that the Ten Commandments be posted in the nation's public schools. Held hostage by certain Members elected from safe, one-party, Winner Take All districts and more interested in political posturing than effective policy, the gun debate degenerated into partisan screed blaming modern culture, including birth control, the theory of evolution, and daycare.[15] It was one of the most stunning congressional failures of policy formation in recent history. Washington, DC, once again revealed itself as a kind of *noir* movie without end, a horror flick that one cannot exit, where the hockey-masked assailant keeps rising again and again.

Make no mistake, the gun control measures being debated were milquetoast compared to the severity of the problem: closing the Magnum-sized loophole that allows people to buy firearms at gun shows without background checks or even a twenty-four-hour waiting period; child-proof trigger locks for handguns; and raising the federal minimum age from eighteen to twenty-one for those who can buy or possess a gun. The proposals weren't even comprehensive, in that they didn't cover sales by private gun owners which are responsible for millions of gun sales annually. In other words, these were not serious proposals if the goal was to join the ranks of other civilized democracies and curb rampant firearm proliferation in the United States—and still they failed.

Meanwhile, the General Accounting Office, Congress' investigative arm, had released a report claiming the U.S. military was selling old clips of .50 caliber armor-piercing bullets to a private contractor, who then refurbished the clips and sold them to private gun dealers all over the country. More than 100,000 rounds of ammunition designed to pierce tanks, bring down helicopters, and slice through buildings were refurbished and sold by Talon Manufacturing in 1998. The report showed that these shells and the weapons that fire them—long-range sniper weapons—can easily be purchased in gun shops and over the Internet. Indeed, there are fewer legal hurdles to buying sniper weapons than to buying a regular handgun. And while a person has to be eighteen or older to get this weapon from a licensed dealer—or sixteen to drive an automobile, eighteen to vote, or twenty-one to consume alcohol—there's no penalty whatsoever under federal law and most states' laws for a person who resells their gun secondhand to a kid of any age. The military also auctions off broken semiautomatic weapons to gun dealers and gunsmiths who then put them back together with replacement parts and sell them. M-1 carbines and M-1 Garands can be purchased easily by the average person on the street, who is free to resell them to kids or to people with criminal records.[16] Eric Harris, one of the teenage Littleton assailants, obtained his TEC-DC9 semiautomatic handgun from a friend of a coworker who was over twenty-one, perfectly legal under federal law (although a crime under Colorado law, which was later used to convict the supplier of the Columbine firearms).

No, reviewing our hodgepodge of firearms laws, one would conclude that we are a devout, even fundamentalist, Second Amendment society, with private individuals armed to levels exceeded only by countries like Milosevic's Serbia or the Taliban in Afghanistan. And we have a sorely unresponsive Winner Take All Congress to thank for it. Like our voting machine debacle, our gun-slinging culture has made the United States the butt of jokes around the world.[17] Instead of taking away the guns, our children have to deal with the concentration camp–like specter of metal detector gates at school entrances, video cameras panning the hallways, and flash searches and seizures like a village under siege by an occupying army. Walking into some urban schools today one is reminded of the heavily surveiled "model villages" in Guatemala during the worst years of its murderous regimes, no doubt an intimidating and thuggish atmosphere for an education.

Four years after Littleton, despite the Million Mom March and other attempts to mobilize during Election 2000 for gun control, little had changed on this front. Indeed, during the 2000 presidential campaign the adolescent carnage continued, one incident seeing six children wounded at the National Zoo during a gunfire feud between two groups of youths, and another incident in which an angry five-year-old loaded his mother's pistol and fired toward playmates, barely missing them.[18] Al Gore and his strategists, alarmed by a hemorrhaging of swing voters among pro-gun union members in battleground states like Michigan, Pennsylvania, Oregon, Florida, West Virginia, and Missouri, backpedaled away from his previously strong gun-control stance. Lamented a spokesperson for Coalition to Stop Gun Violence, "I'm worried that people are seeing this as just part of living in America."[19] Indeed, a national malaise has set in, and gun-control forces are in retreat, as a restless nation wrestles with how to keep its children safe in the absence of leadership from its national government.

But gun control is hardly the only issue where the current occupants of the People's House are badly out of touch with The People. In fact, it's just the tip of a rather large and ominous iceberg—the shipwrecker that the cruise ship of America's Winner Take All democracy is sailing directly toward. On a whole host of issues and policies, from Social Security to military appropriations to urban policy to health care to federalizing of airport safety in the aftermath of September 11, majority popular support does not necessarily lead to action in Congress. Surely the impeachment fiasco, where the public overwhelmingly supported its besieged President even as the tar and feathering proceeded apace, was agonizing evidence of a rogue Congress unrestrained by majoritarianism or the will of the people. No, the inhabitants of the People's House, as a collective body, not only don't look like the people but they also don't think like us either, or act like we wish they would.

Intensity versus preference in The People's House

How can there be such a radical disconnect between our elected representatives and those they purport to represent? How has our representative democracy become so—well—*unrepresentative*?

Many pundits and reformers say the answer is money. Specifically, the corrupting role that privately funded elections play in our electoral and legislative processes. They blame the failure of issues like gun control on organizations like the National Rifle Association (NRA) and its campaign cash and lobbying clout. After the Littleton carnage, full-page advertisements paid for by a campaign finance reform group, Public Campaign, popped up in daily newspapers across the nation with the bold headline, "Want Guns Out Of School? Get Gun Money Out Of Politics." A rash of statistics were released showing how the NRA and its allies outspent gun-control groups by a ratio of almost 27 to 1. "Money is a mighty fortress," intoned one news release.[20] These numbers appear persuasive, and undoubtedly political action committees (PACs) like the NRA spend their money for a reason. But, truth be told, money is of secondary importance for explaining the influence of groups like the NRA. A more accurate reading of the political landscape would have to account for the role of the Swing Voter Serenade and Two-Choice Tango.

The simple fact is that the NRA's money has power because there is a small but critical mass of passionate anti–gun control voters out there who are disproportionately swing voters. They often are classic Reagan Democrats, including some union members, who fear infringement on gun ownership. Others are Second Amendment zealots, passionate voters for their cause. Opponents of gun control fear infringement on gun ownership as much as civil libertarians fear encroachment on free speech, and are far more likely than most gun-control proponents to cast their vote based *solely* on this single issue. As NRA board member Grover Norquist has said, "The question is intensity versus preference. You can always get a certain percentage to say they are in favor of some gun controls. But are they going to vote on their 'control' position?"

Although most voters back gun control, says Norquist, their support doesn't move them to the polls. "But for that 4–5 percent who care about guns, they will vote on this."[21] Another NRA board member echoed that electoral wisdom: "Who cares about the mainstream? All we care about is who votes. Fear is a kick in the ass to every gun owner."[22] From the pro–gun control side, Rep. Barney Frank, a liberal Democrat from Massachusetts, succinctly summarized the political realities of NRA swing voters. "People on the left make the mistake of saying the NRA's power is big money. But votes beat money any day, and the NRA has votes."[23]

What the NRA has is a lot of members, several million by its own count (although that figure is disputed by NRA opponents). The NRA is able to coordinate with fifty-four affiliated groups in all fifty states, the District of Columbia, and Puerto Rico, and with scores of smaller state and local pro–Second Amendment organizations and hundreds of gun clubs nationwide.[24] According to Jim Vinopal, who heads the NRA-affiliated Illinois State Rifle Association's political action committee, his group has countywide branches organized in about half of Illinois's 102 counties. "We're organized all the way down to the local level, and most of the groups are affiliated with the NRA," he says. At a moment's notice, volunteers can be turned out to put up signs, ring doorbells, make phone calls, or visit the State Capitol.[25]

But what gives the NRA maximum bang for its buck and its votes is that its members and supporters seem to live disproportionately in swing districts and swing states, particularly in rural and suburban areas. A 4 to 5 percent swing of voters in a close race can spell the difference between victory or defeat, and this demographic reality of the Winner Take All system has allowed the NRA to game the system for advantage. As we will see in the next two chapters on redistricting, because 90 percent of legislative races are "safe seats" for one party or the other, special interest groups can more easily target money to the few close races that may tilt control of the Legislature. And few are more masterful at targeting—at gaming—than the NRA.

Moreover, because districts in the sub-nation of Bushlandia are safe for anti–gun control elected officials, the NRA is free to target its message and its resources to other parts of the nation, crucial terrain for determining presidential elections as well as legislative majorities in the U.S. House and in many of the fifty state legislatures which control redistricting. The task of the NRA then—to target their resources and try to alarm just enough swing voters and Democratic House members representing rural and swing districts to scuttle reform—is rendered much easier by the geographic-based political map of the Winner Take All system.

Some of the targeting is directed at precise constituencies—in particular, the NRA has been instrumental to the GOP because of their ability to appeal to pro-gun labor union members and pry them away from the Democratic Party in key swing districts and key swing states. The NRA claims that up to one-fifth of union members in those states are NRA members, which best explains why Al Gore began quickly backpedaling on his strong gun control position in the presidential campaign.[26] Union leaders were not afraid of the NRA's money—unions have plenty of their own—but they were afraid of the pro-gun side's support among union members in key swing districts and states.[27] In the aftermath of Election 2000, many Democrats now believe that Gore's earlier strong support for gun control may have cost him such heavily rural states as West Virginia, Missouri, Kentucky, Ohio, Arkansas, and his native state of Tennessee.[28] Indeed, Democratic Party leaders like House minority leader Dick Gephardt and Senator Charles Schumer also now have sidled away from their strong gun-control stands, talking instead about the evolving "political reality" around gun control. Wedge issues like gun control make policy formation under Winner Take All quite maddening.

The riveting reality is that the dynamics of Winner Take All allow gun control opponents to form a potent single-issue voting bloc that far outweighs their minority status. The NRA's influence has come from its capacity to move a relatively small number of swing voters in swing states and in swing districts—with fear and alarmist campaign messages, more than its money.[29] These kinds of political calculations are intricately connected to the dynamics of Winner Take All's geographic and two-choice structure. The NRA would not be nearly as effective if it weren't for the Winner Take All system, which allows the NRA to divide and conquer the 435 House geographic districts like squares on a checkerboard. And as the Democratic Party retreats from this issue, there is no viable electoral alternative such as a third party to hoist the pro–gun control flag.

The NRA's historic power can be better grasped by examining the strategic choices candidates must make in a swing district with a competitive race. The Winner Take All conundrum reveals itself best in such swing districts. For example, the third congressional district in southwest Washington State is a classic swing district. Its constituents vary greatly, from residents of the liberal university town and state capital of Olympia to those who live in socially conservative rural areas. The seat has changed parties in two of the last four elections. In 1988, Jolene Unsoeld, a liberal Democrat from Olympia, narrowly won the district and in 1990 faced the best financed challenger in the nation. Caught between the jaws of her conflicting liberal and conservative constituents, Rep. Unsoeld did what all smart politicians do when confronted by the Winner Take All conundrum: she listened to her pollster.

Consequently, during the campaign Unsoeld "came out" as a champion of the NRA, shocking many liberal supporters. The knee-jerk charge in the Seattle press and among many liberals, unaware of the realities of her district, was that she had sold out for the NRA's money, which indeed she received. In fact, Unsoeld always had voted against gun control, but her quiet opposition hadn't received much attention. But her liberalism on social and environmental issues had made her vulnerable against an aggressive GOP challenge for Reagan Democrats, union members, and timber workers in her district. Rep. Unsoeld made a dramatic and public bid for these swing voters' allegiance when Speaker of the House Tom Foley offered her a chance to sponsor major anti–gun control legislation. Knowing that her liberal voters feared her conservative opponent and had nowhere else to turn in a two-choice field, she accepted. During the campaign Rep. Unsoeld was free to highlight her pro-NRA views for the *votes* it won, not the cash. She went on to a relatively easy win, only to lose her seat during the Republican overthrow of the House in 1994.

In fact, an analysis of the House Democrats who voted against gun-control measures that sweltering June 1999 reveals that, as one would suspect given the dynamics of Winner Take All, most represented swing districts, primarily rural areas where constituents are more likely to embrace gun rights. The NRA is expert at targeting swing voters and anti–gun control zealots in these swing district. *Intensity versus preference.* For elected representatives from these districts, gun control is a critical issue that can cause them to lose their seats. Indeed, one Democrat who split his vote, voting both for and against various gun-control amendments, was Rep. Brian Baird, who recaptured Unsoeld's seat from the Republicans in 1998. In those swing districts, a small shift in the vote can cost you the election.

Awash in statistics and admirable zeal, many political pundits and reformers miss such subtleties about the realities of Winner Take All. They assume that you can establish in every case what the "right" vote for a representative should be—even one in a swing district, like Jolene Unsoeld—and then explain any deviation from that vote as proof of the influence of money. But that's too simplistic and overly deterministic. The fact of the matter is, Winner Take All dynamics allow well-organized minorities like the NRA to hold hostage important policy demands and have influence beyond its numbers, contributing toward gaming of the system and distortions in national policy. Media outlets like the *New York Times* often will portray parliamentary and proportional democracies like Israel and Italy as beholden to tiny political parties of electoral extremists who hold coalition governments hostage; yet seldom do they recognize how extremists like the NRA, Florida Cubans, and others work the Winner Take All turf to foist their radical agendas upon the mainstream. If we don't understand the complexity of how our system works, we will miss the mark when we try to improve it.

The disproportionate impact of swing voters in close Winner Take All district races has not only been frustrating and alienating to the public, but actually it has been *dangerous* to the nation's health. There was no greater evidence of this than the moving sight of watching the family members, friends, and loved ones placing flowers on the graves of the innocent victims of Columbine, mowed down by two disturbed high school students who were able to get their youthful hands on levels of firepower on a par with the Marines. Welcome to the wacky world of Winner Take All.

"My fellow Americans . . ."

What if the President of the United States were to go on television and announce to the nation that, starting tomorrow, the United States is switching to a new democracy technology and the results of this change will be the following:

- less than half, often only one-third, of eligible voters will participate in national elections;
- even fewer voters will participate in state and local elections;
- barely a third, often one-quarter, of all voters will cast a vote for a *winning* candidate;
- about three-quarters of U.S. House races regularly will be won by landslides (at least a 60 to 40 percent margin), and a full 90 percent of House races will be won by noncompetitive ten-point margins (at least 55 to 45 percent);
- state legislative races will be even less competitive than U.S. House races, with a whopping 40 percent of state legislative races typically *uncontested* by one of the two major parties;
- despite being primarily a two-party system, about 90 percent of voters will have only *one choice* of a candidate that has any chance of winning their district seat;
- at least 95 percent of incumbents will be reelected on a regular basis.

If the president announced these to be the results we could expect from this change in democracy technology, how do you think the nation might react? Or imagine if the CEOs of Microsoft or Cisco or any other Fortune 500 corporation announced organizational changes that would produce similar impacts on their bottom line—how do you think their stockholders and boards of directors might react? Most likely there would be an outcry. Yet this profile is exactly the prevailing snapshot of U.S. representative democracy using our antiquated Winner Take All methods and practices.

When you boil all the numbers down, the picture that emerges of Winner Take All elections to our national legislature is this: in the 2000 congressional elections, only about 5 percent of eligible voters had what we can call a *meaningful vote*. By meaningful vote, we mean a voter actually *voted*, they voted for a *winner*, and they lived in a district where the race was close enough that it *mattered whether they showed up* on Election Day or not. Those are the three conditions for a voter to have a meaningful vote, and unfortunately an appallingly small number of Americans possess it.

Even during America's most important election for President, 100 million voters sat it out. Another 30 million are no-shows during nonpresidential election years. Compare those figures to nations that use a different voting system such as the more modern ones that fall under the classification of proportional representation: voters have a range of political choices in a multiparty democracy, and generally we see an eligible voter turnout of 75 to 95 percent. About 90 percent of participating voters cast a vote for a winner, and approximately 70 percent of voters possess a meaningful vote. That "meaningful vote" statistic translates into real democracy. The absence of it leads to post-democracy. Votes in the United States have lost their value; using economic terms, political deflation has led to stagnation, and stagnation to political depression. For substantially this reason, nations using Winner Take All elections tend to place at the bottom of the barrel in terms of voter turnout, with the United States at the very bottom of the bottom of the barrel (see footnote for reports on voter turnout around the world).[30]

For millions of voters living in the vast numbers of noncompetitive districts, including "orphan" Democrats and Republicans who are a minority perspective in their districts, as well as the supporters of third parties, racial minorities, women, and independents everywhere, there are not a lot of viable choices when they step into the voters' booth. Instead, there are lots of opportunities for wasting your vote on losers and third-party spoilers, or holding your nose and voting for the "lesser of two evils." As we will see in the next chapter, while we are used to saying that we have a two-party system, in fact the frame of reference for most voters living in noncompetitive legislative districts is that of a *one-party* system—that is, only one party has a realistic chance of winning that district seat. Most voters are bunkered down in safe one-party districts, and most legislative races at state and federal levels—even most elections outside the regions of Bushlandia and New Goreia—are over long before election day.

The small number of Winner Take All voters who choose to participate on Election Day are confronted with barren choices, so most voters either stay home or are forced to vote for the "lesser of two evils"—which is the same as voting their fears, instead of their hopes, to keep someone *out* of office whom they truly dread, rather than to get someone in whom they really like. We do this out of necessity, not out of choice. There *is* no other choice. That's the Winner Take All conundrum at work. Having to always choose between the lesser of two evils is very corrosive of the democratic spirit. Most voters know something is wrong, but they don't know what to do about it. And most don't realize that they have to repair the operating system of this democracy—the voting system—in order to fix it.

Elections, ideally, should be the ultimate feedback mechanism in a representative democracy. On the first Tuesday in November our nation's citizens should trek out to the polls, do their electoral duty, and the results should constitute affirmation that representative government works, by God. Albeit imperfectly, yes, but that it actually is, well, *representative*. Yet this is hardly what happens on Election Day. Instead, what most voters are treated to is more akin to an electoral casino—maybe you win, maybe you lose, depending on whether you live in the right district or state or not. People are awash in a sea of too many elections—513,200 elective offices in the United States, from senator to sheriff[31]—and a declining pool of civic-minded voters continue to trudge off to the polls to do their dreary duty, like Boxer the faithful horse in Orwell's *Animal Farm*. What else is a good citizen to do?

But the dirty little secret is that, today, tens of millions of these citizens have been orphaned, left on the political sidelines, and either don't bother voting, vote for losers, or vote for "lesser of two evils" winners. While much has been made of the impact of campaign finance inequities on our elections, as we will see the impact of campaign funding in most legislative races is of secondary importance. Instead, the precipitating factor is the partisan leanings of the Winner Take All districts, which is largely determined during a backroom game of cards known as "redistricting" in which incumbent politicians and party bosses oversee the redrawing of the legislative district lines into safe, one-party fiefdoms.

The nightmarish specter of redistricting revisits us at the start of each decade like a recurring biblical plague. If Winner Take All is the operating system of our representative democracy, redistricting is part of the underlying computer code that makes the operating system work—or not work—as the case may be. If we are to understand our mudslide into a fractured, voterless post-democracy, the redistricting story is where our tour over the American political landscape must now proceed.

CHAPTER FIVE

Behind Closed Doors
The Recurring Plague of Redistricting

We are in the business of rigging elections.
— STATE SENATOR MARK MCDANIEL, NORTH CAROLINA

Since early 2001, a great tragedy has been occurring in American politics. It has been happening quietly, for the most part behind closed doors, and with minimal public input or oversight. The net result of this tragedy will be that most voters will have their vote rendered near meaningless, almost as if it had been stolen from them. Yet the stealing will have happened without a gun or a holdup, it's more like a silent burglar in the middle of the night, having his way, while American voters sleep. As a result of the theft, hallowed notions like "no taxation without representation" and "one person, one vote" will be drained of their vitality, reduced to empty slogans for armchair patriots.

And it is all legal.

Not only is it legal, but the two major political parties, their incumbents, their consultants, and even most political scientists and pundits consider it to be standard operating procedure, part of the everyday give-and-take—mostly take—of Winner Take All politics. It's just how the game is played. That's because most of these veterans are so much a part of the professional political class, so much a part of the institutional fabric that is robbing the American voter, that they have become inured to the crime being committed.

Consider this: following the 2000 Census, every legislative district in the United States—every city council district, every state legislative and U.S. House district—literally thousands and thousands of districts—automatically expired. By law these geographic districts must all be roughly equal in population, and so the decennial population and demographic shifts reflected by the new Census triggered the expiration of the existing districts. This means that every legislative district had to be redrawn before the next elections in 2002. This line-drawing occurs at the start of every decade, as certain as income taxes and death.

This line-drawing, in many respects, is the defining skirmish of the Winner Take All geographic-based system. Newt Gingrich once said "Redistricting is everything." That's because the impact of this line-drawing is to decide—in advance—the winners and losers of most legislative elections for the next ten years. And guess who is redrawing the lines? Is it panels of fair-minded citizens, making sure that the political and geographic boundaries of their neighborhoods are kept intact? Is it political scientists, armed with reams of data and computer tools to ensure that competition is maximized and that no single political party walks off with the prize? Is it learned judges or independent nonpartisan commissions, deliberating over objective and impartial criteria about what constitutes a fair redistricting? Will the process include public input of those whose votes and trust in government will be most affected?

The answer, in a word, is no.

In fact, contrary to all sense—except the type of sense that has been steeped in the defenses of the status quo—the lines usually are redrawn by none other than the politicians themselves. And these incumbent line-drawers generally are guided by no criteria other than two rather ambitious and self-serving goals: first, to guarantee their own reelection and that of their friends and colleagues; and second, to garner a majority of legislative seats for their political party or faction. When it comes to redistricting, the fox not only guards the hen house, the fox *salivates*.

The most recent redistricting has just concluded, with most districts redrawn by the primaries of 2002. The 2001–2002 redistricting plans in most states amounted to little better than incumbent protection plans, producing even fewer competitive districts than past efforts. The previous redistricting was in 1991–1992, and in a rare moment of candor the primary architect of Texas's 1991 redistricting plan admitted that the redistricting process "is not one of kindness, it is not one of sharing. It is a power grab."[1] One North Carolina legislator who sat on his state's redistricting committee had this fatalistic recommendation: "I would suggest that nobody be put on the redistricting committee who won't swear an oath that they won't run for Congress themselves."[2]

Obviously the political insiders know that a lot is at stake in redistricting.

The Incumbent Protection Racket

Every individual who participated in the redistricting process knew that incumbency protection was a critical factor in producing the bizarre lines. . . . Many of the oddest twists and turns of the Texas districts would never have been created if the Legislature had not been so intent on protecting party and incumbents.

—U.S. SUPREME COURT JUSTICE JOHN PAUL STEVENS,
BUSH V. VERA, JUNE 13, 1996

Forget what you've heard about Big Money buying elections—redistricting Winner Take All districts is the political class' slickest sleight of hand, and it descends upon us once a decade like a giant iceberg. Behind closed doors, incumbent politicians, their political parties, and their consultants conduct the decennial ritual of carving up their personal fiefdom, their legislative district. Collectively they jigsaw, jury-rig, and gerrymander their districts down to the neighborhood bloc level. They produce legislative districts whose shapes resemble, in the words of many observers, splattered spaghetti sauce, a squashed mosquito, meandering snakes, dumbbells, earmuffs, starfish, a gnawed wishbone, Bullwinkle the Moose, the "Z" mark of Zorro, and a host of other bewildering shapes that defy description or explanation other than the capricious acts of a powerful class of politicians looking to guarantee themselves lifetime employment and party preeminence.[3]

"The best example of how far you can push it is the California gerrymander from the 1980s," says Stanford Law Professor Pam Karlan. "[Congressman] Phil Burton, one of the architects, referred to it as 'my contribution to modern art.' It had districts that snaked all over the state, including the long-necked 'swan' district in eastern California, and the 'Jesus district,' so-called because you had to walk across water to get from one part of the district to the other."[4] One district designed to protect an incumbent Democrat in the San Fernando Valley was a ghastly looking, multi-headed, insect like polygon with 385 sides. In the 1984 elections following this redistricting the Democrats increased their take of California's house seats to 60 percent, even though the Republicans won a *majority* of the state's two-party vote. Now *that's* a gerrymander.[5]

Powerful politicians and their consultants often draw these districts according to highly personal and self-aggrandizing criteria. The *Los Angeles Times* reported that, in the 1991 redistricting, the ever-mercurial Speaker of the Assembly, Democrat Willie Brown, drew a particular Assembly district in West Los Angeles because Jewish voters "couldn't be counted on to vote for black representatives." Brown, characteristically blunt, said, "Because of the way in which [Jewish] people in that area [of West Los Angeles] vote, Gwen Moore [a black representative] would have to become Moorenstein in order to have an equal opportunity to win."[6] Other officials have jigsawed districts to pick up their favorite restaurants, amusement parks, professional sports stadiums, movie studios, hospitals, military bases, churches, country clubs, real estate developments, and, in one case, the cemetery where a particular legislator's parents were buried. At least some of the impetus is to add to one's district residential or commercial areas that are fund-raising motherlodes.[7]

Previous episodes have been marked by physical violence and near-death tragedies. In 1982, the Michigan Supreme Court imposed a redistricting plan on the state that was generally believed to favor Republicans. Knowing what potentially was at stake—namely, control of the state legislature, control over the line-drawing process for state and federal seats, and, consequently, not more than a few political careers—Michigan Democrats rallied the troops. At the time, the Democrats held a majority in both Michigan state houses, but according to the state constitution, their alternative redistricting measure, had to pass the legislature with a two-thirds vote, which would be difficult to achieve. The legislative session was due to expire, and time was running out. At the last minute, Democratic leaders tried to sneak through redistricting legislation by using one of the oldest parliamentary tricks in the book: they gutted the contents—but not the title—of an irrelevant bill and covertly inserted their redistricting legislation.

But the Republicans discovered the ploy. Furious, they launched their counterattack. Republican leaders used stall tactics and every legislative trick conceivable to try to halt the legislation. The situation grew extremely tense, with time growing short. Finally, in the heat of the long debate during a midnight session, a Democratic senator collapsed. Paramedics were called in, but the senator refused to leave the Senate floor before the vote. In a classic case of political hardball, a Republican senator used parliamentary procedure to delay the vote by insisting that the geographic boundaries of all 148 legislative districts be read into the record, apparently hoping the Democrat would die or be hauled off by paramedics. But the Democratic senator muscled up his partisan pluck and stayed through the entire reading. His party eventually won the vote and, hence, the redistricting battle.[8]

In Illinois, during another 1982 redistricting battle, a Republican state senate leader believed he had the crossover votes from enough Democrats to pass a GOP map in the Senate. During an exhausting Sunday legislative session the senator became outraged over the parliamentary stalling tactics employed by the Democratic president of the Senate. At one point the Republican senator charged the podium, seething with righteous fury, apparently with the intention of physically intimidating or even assaulting the Senate president. Before he could reach the president he was sucker-punched by a Democratic downstate senator, who connected with a right to the jaw. The place erupted, barely avoiding the type of dugout-clearing brawl you might expect to see in the seventh game of the World Series. According to one eyewitness from the *State Journal Register*, "for a moment it looked as though both benches were going to empty." With the television cameras rolling, the combatants finally were pulled apart. Later in the day, the senate president called back the remapping bill and with total party unity—the party no doubt rallying around its beleaguered leader—the Democrats passed their own redistricting bill (since the House previously had passed a Republican plan, this deadlocked the line drawing and handed the process over to a bipartisan redistricting commission, which itself became deadlocked, finally resulting in Illinois' redistricting plan being decided by *lottery*).[9]

John Gilligan, former governor of Ohio, tells the story about when he was a freshman Congressman in Ohio, after he and three other Democrats were swept into office on Lyndon Johnson's coattails in 1964. Democrats also took control of the Ohio House that year, so the Republican governor launched a preemptive strike—he called a special session of the Legislature two weeks after the election for the purpose of redistricting the state before any of the new Democratic legislators could take office. The result was that Gilligan suddenly was representing a heavily Republican district, and he lost reelection in 1966. "Myself and the other three Democrats were gerrymandered out of our seats before we were even sworn in," says Gov. Gilligan today, shaking his head. "It just shows you how idiotic the whole process can be."[10]

The 2001 redistricting in California, which was dominated by the Democratic Party, raised "incumbent protection plans" to a crass new level. According to Rep. Loretta Sanchez, she and thirty of the thirty-two Democratic U.S. House incumbents forked over $20,000 each to powerful consultant Michael Berman, who was overseeing the line-drawing. To hear Sanchez talk about it, the money was tantamount to a bribe, the type of "protection money" one might pay to a local mafia don to protect your turf. "Twenty thousand is nothing to keep your seat," said Sanchez. "I spend $2 million (campaigning) every election. If my colleagues are smart, they'll pay their $20,000, and Michael will draw the district they can win in. Those who have refused to pay? God help them."[11]

Yes indeed, the political insiders know that a lot is at stake in redistricting.[12] It's the public that doesn't know how much is at stake, and so the public doesn't pay attention—which is just fine by the politicians. They want this to remain a secretive insiders' game, an esoteric and inaccessible Delphic riddle that shuts out citizen involvement or even oversight. But if the curtain were pulled back on the wizards, what the public would see are some of the most unflattering moments of our Winner Take All ritual. This is "basic instinct" politics, nature raw, tooth and claw. So the process goes on behind closed doors, with technocrats hunched over computers remapping the most fundamental terrain of our Winner Take All democracy—the single-seat district. And the last thing on politicians' minds is the impact of redistricting on the public, on voters, on the health of our republic, or on national policy.

But the impacts are considerable. The impact of this line-drawing roulette is to decide—*in advance*—the winners and losers of most legislative elections for the following ten years. In Chapter 1, we saw how entire states and regions of the country—Bushlandia and New Goreia—suffer from political monocultures, monopoly politics, and unilateral policy because of the conglomeration of neo-feudal single-seat districts that drastically overrepresent the dominant party and exaggerate their legislative majority. Such distortions are largely because of natural partisan demographics—where people live, Democrats/liberals dominating in New Goreia, particularly in cities, and Republican/conservatives dominating in Bushlandia, particularly in rural areas and low-population states. But the hardwired realities of the map are compounded by how these partisan demographics are funneled through the Winner Take All system during the redistricting of single-seat districts. The dominant party controlling the line-drawing process can use various techniques like "packing" and "cracking"[13] to award themselves more districts—more representation—than their numbers warrant.

Incumbents and party leaders often have carte blanche to engage in redistricting shenanigans for personal and partisan gain.

Even outside the sub-nations of Bushlandia and New Goreia we can see similar effects, resulting from the partisan redistricting of the remaining districts. Depending on who is doing the line-drawing, most Democratic districts are carefully packed with enough registered Democratic voters, and Republican districts with Republican voters, to make it virtually impossible for anyone else to win. The redistricting of single-seat districts thus is a direct threat to key democratic values like electoral competition, representation, and choice for voters.

Monopoly Politics

Nothing Monica Lewinsky and Bill Clinton did together will ever have as much impact on election results as the partisan makeup of congressional districts around the country.
—ROB RICHIE, CENTER FOR VOTING AND DEMOCRACY

Research has shown that, as a result of Winner Take All and its redistricting roulette—*not* inequities in campaign finances—the vast majority of U.S. House races are so noncompetitive as to be done deals before voters even show up to the polls. To be precise, in the 2000 House elections 91 percent of races were won by comfortable victory margins greater than ten points, and 78 percent were won by landslide margins greater than twenty points (both of these figures include the sixty-five races that were uncontested by a major party). Only thirty-eight seats—less than 9 percent of all House seats—were won by competitive margins of fewer than ten points, the lowest figure in twelve years and second lowest in the past twenty. Like a Soviet-type Politburo, nearly 99 percent of incumbents won reelection, and most legislative elections were reduced to a meaningless charade.[14]

The 2001–2002 congressional redistricting made an egregious situation even worse. The political maps devised by the incumbents and party leaders in most states amounted to little more than "incumbent protection plans," deflating political competition and voter choice to disturbingly flat-line levels. Experts estimate that there will be fewer than 50 competitive races in 2002 compared with 121 ten years ago. Of those 50, only half really will be toss-ups, and that number likely will decrease as the decade progresses. That's a mere 25 or so races out of 435 where it will matter whether the voters show up to the polls or not. Redistricting—the gerrymandering of partisan districts—has become a glorified incumbent-protection racket.

State legislative elections are even worse. Astoundingly, of the thousands of state legislative races in 2000, a whopping 41 percent of these races were *uncontested* by one of the two major parties. Because the districts generally are so lopsided, it's a waste of campaign resources for the out-of-power party to contest for these seats.[15] That's two in five races where the only choice for voters was either to ratify the candidate of the dominant party, cast a hopeless vote for a third party candidate, or not vote at all.

In fact, in Election 2000 fourteen states had all of their U.S. House seats either uncontested or won by landslides; eleven more states had all but one of their U.S. House seats either uncontested or won by landslides.[16] Even the largest states were vastly uncompetitive, with New York having twenty-eight out of thirty-one of their U.S. House seats uncontested or won by landslides, Texas with twenty-six out of thirty seats, California with forty-one out of fifty-two, Florida with nineteen out of twenty-three, Ohio with sixteen out of nineteen, Pennsylvania with seventeen out of twenty-one, and Michigan with thirteen out of sixteen U.S. House seats uncontested or won by landslides, an average of 83 percent in these seven large states that together hold nearly half of all U.S. House seats.

In other words, there is not a lot of competition or viable choices for voters in the vast numbers of legislative races across the country, including in our largest states. Not only is it true that the "winner takes all" in our system, but usually the winner takes all without even much of a fight. These races are done deals before voters walk into the voting booth. That translates into uninspiring campaigns, if there are campaigns at all, for voters to get excited about. As will be demonstrated in the next chapter, the noncompetitive nature of most of these legislative races is not due to inequities in campaign spending, as many analysts have assumed. Instead, they are due to the natural partisan demographics of where people live, compounded by our geographic-based Winner Take All system and its gerrymandered districts that result from redistricting.

Most races are so predictable that the Center for Voting and Democracy (CVD), like handicappers at Suffolk Downs, was able to forecast the winners and their margins of victory in 84 percent of U.S. House races well over a year before the 2000 election *without knowing anything about inequities in campaign finance or candidate strategy.* The mainstay of CVD's technique is simply to estimate the partisan demographics of how the districts had been gerrymandered during the last redistricting and how incumbents had fared in the district. Of 237 House races that the Center predicted would be won by landslide margins of more than twenty points, fully 236 were correct (with the remaining race being won by "only" 19 percent). Fifteen percent of all races were uncontested, and 36 percent were won by huge margins where one candidate had more than 70 percent of the vote.[17] The overt partisanship of most legislative districts is so obvious that one political consultant boasted that "it is possible to predict with significant accuracy who will win most elections" simply by taking telephone polls and determining the overwhelming district partisanship.[18] We like to think of our Winner Take All system as a two-party/two-choice affair, but in fact the frame of reference for most voters in most elections, even those who are residents outside of Bushlandia or New Goreia, is that of a one-party system—the party that dominates their district.

In fact, when it comes to federal races, tens of millions of voters live in one-party *states*. As we saw in Chapter 2, thirty-one states have representation in the U.S. Senate from only one party, both Senators being either Democrats or Republicans, and forty-one states are locked-up in a competitive presidential election. And as we saw in Chapter 1, the 2000 U.S. House elections saw Massachusetts electing Democrats to all ten of its seats, and Nebraska electing Republicans to its three seats, all of them winning by huge landslide margins when they were contested at all. Voters voting for Senators from the losing party in those thirty-one states, or president in those forty-one states, along with Republican voters in Massachusetts and Democratic voters in Nebraska, wasted their votes. Not a single one helped elect someone. For them, the "monopoly politics" of their state meant that voting was a waste of time. To hammer the point further, twelve more states have such monopoly representation in the U.S. House, and eleven more states are only one representative shy of monopoly representation, a total of twenty-five states.[19] Adding it all up, well over half the states suffer from a substantial degree of monopoly politics and political monoculture in federal elections for the presidency, the U.S. Senate, the U.S. House, or their state legislatures.

Thus, Winner Take All strands most voters on a deserted electoral island, with little but uninspiring, choiceless elections to keep them company. For literally millions of voters across the United States, including those orphaned Democrats and Republicans living in Bushlandia and New Goreia, but also millions of citizens outside those regions who are political orphans living in the wrong districts, their votes did not count toward electing a representative at many levels of government. And they have few prospects of electing someone in the near future, in fact they can have more impact by writing a check and mailing it to a candidate in a more competitive race halfway across the country.

Ironically enough, the Framers expected originally that there would be a 50 percent turnover in the House following each election, creating an institution overflowing with new ideas and approaches. In fact, the Framers viewed "the people's house" as potentially so hyperresponsive and haphazardously attuned to a raucous popularity contest that they created the Senate in part to keep it in check. But, just like their erroneous estimations for how the Electoral College would work, the Framers were wildly off the mark. Congressional turnover is at an all-time low—only about 1 percent in each of the last two elections. Even the geriatric dinosaurs of the Soviet Politburo had more turnover than our House of Representatives. Perhaps our national legislature should be renamed the Congress Club, since it is more like a private exclusive organization with a select membership that admits very few new members, and mostly from a certain race and gender, with a 99 percent retention rate of old members.

To be sure, for a handful of congressional races the decennial redistricting process will shake things up a bit. A few incumbents whose districts change substantially will have to face many new voters; and for those states that lose seats during reapportionment a few incumbents may even face each other for reelection, which can make for extremely bitter party primaries as incumbents from the same party wage electoral war against each other. Redistricting can get quite personal, not just political, with vendettas being carried out within political parties.[20] And the districts usually are least competitive at the end of a decade right before redistricting, since by then districts have been "shaken out" of bad matches between incumbents and districts, and serious challengers wait to run and parties wait to invest big bucks on challengers until after redistricting when the change of lines may create a few more opportunities for upsets. But these are just footnotes to the real story, and the real story is this: the use of single-seat, Winner Take All districts with legislative lines redrawn by the incumbents and party leaders is a major factor contributing to the onset of post-democracy.

We condemn elections with one-party choice in places like Cuba and China; but for congressional and state legislative elections, Russian émigrés in most parts of the country must hardly notice a difference between their old and new home. We can pass all the campaign finance reform we want, but it will scarcely change this fundamental reality of our political landscape. With the redistricting of Winner Take All districts dividing the political map into winners and losers, any chance of a politics of inclusion and "representation for all" is immediately subverted. Redistricting is a time bomb hardwired into the Winner Take All system that detonates every ten years. The Redistricting Roulette quite rightly joins the swing voter serenade, the two-choice tango, phantom representation, artificial majorities, and the Winner Take All conundrum among the ranks of gremlin progenies that are frustrating and alienating to democratic participation, representation, campaigns and discourse, national unity, and policy formation.

The New Redistricting Technologies: "Politicians choosing their voters"

> This new [redistricting] plan basically does away with the need for elections.
>
> —TONY QUINN,
> GOP REDISTRICTING CONSULTANT IN CALIFORNIA[21]

Past redistrictings have never been models of fairness or exclamations of high democratic values. But this time around at least one new factor has raised the stakes of the redistricting roulette beyond anything previously experienced.

It will come as no surprise that, just like computers have impacted so many other areas of modern life, new computer technologies have dramatically altered the political game. The politicians and their consultants now have at their disposal extremely sophisticated computer hardware and software, combined with the latest Census, demographic, and polling data, to precisely gerrymander the political map. The days of plastic Mylar maps, magic markers, Elmer's glue, trial-and-error jigsaws, and cut-and-paste blueprints are over.

After the 1990 census, it took lots of money, computer equipment, and specialized personnel for states to draw legislative maps that reflected the new population data, as required by law. Now the job can be done on a laptop computer. Some of the new software comes with demographic data already keyed in, allowing users to easily outline new districts by layering statistics on race, party registration, population, and local voting patterns. During the April 2001 redistricting in New Jersey, for example (one of the few states to use a redistricting commission), when the five Republicans and five Democrats chosen by their parties couldn't agree on how to redraw the state's legislative boundaries, the state Supreme Court tapped Dr. Larry Bartels, a Princeton University professor, to break the impasse. After ten days locked away in a hotel with the two sides, Professor Bartels emerged with a resolution: an entire state redistricting map drawn on his laptop computer, using software that sells for $3,500.

In Texas, a GOP watchdog group called Texans Against Gerrymandering—which includes, rather ironically, U.S. House GOP Majority Leader Dick Armey and GOP Majority Whip Tom DeLay—bought ten copies of one software program to analyze plans at their convenience. Said GOP consultant Craig Murphy: "We wanted members to be able to draw their own lines and not have to make pilgrimages down to Austin."[22]

The software is more accurate and sophisticated than ever before, and the politicians and party leaders have greatly enhanced capacity to handpick their voters. Stanford's Prof. Karlan says, "The technology is so good, you can draw districts with absolutely equal numbers of people in them, and yet create virtually any kind of political breakdown between the districts that you want."[23] Adds Jeffrey Wice, an attorney for IMPAC 2000, the Democratic Party's redistricting program, "The ante has been upped immeasurably by changes in technology and the law. An excess of technology leads to a manic temptation where people try to connect the dots anyway they can."[24]

Previously, individuals and interest groups working on limited budgets often had to scribble on street maps with colored felt-tip markers. Now, the powerful and relatively affordable new computer software is allowing more people and organizations to offer alternative plans. Wider availability of redistricting technology is one small bright spot in a dismal landscape, but gaining the ear of powerful incumbents and party leaders who will decide which set of lines to use is as difficult as ever.

In fact, one can make a credible argument that, from now on, we will no longer choose our representatives—instead, the politicians will *choose us*. Every ten years when the district lines are redrawn, winners and losers will be decided for most legislative districts and that will entrench the dominant party for the rest of the decade. The choice of voters then will be simply to ratify the candidate from the dominant party awarded that district by the redistricting politicians some years before. From the voter's point of view, the candidate selection process, already an abject failure, has just gotten worse. Henceforth the political game will be played much differently than ever before, and these new redistricting technologies are crucial to the new paradigm.

Choiceless elections: Watching Your Vote Disappear

First they gerrymander us into one-party fiefs. Then they tell us they only care about the swing districts. Then they complain about voter apathy.

—GAIL COLLINS, NEW YORK TIMES COLUMNIST[25]

Amid all the headlines and statistics about partisan winners and losers, about record-shattering campaign spending, or about the Wild West contest over which party wins control of Congress, what gets buried is this: the real losers are the *voters*. Long before they vote, most voters in the United States have had their vote rendered impotent because they are bunkered down in safe, one-party districts where it doesn't matter whether they show up on Election Day. An effective redistricting, from the politician's point of view, will leave voters little choice each election but to ratify the candidate chosen *for them* by the party that dominates their district. At this point most federal and state legislative races have become choiceless elections, a pale farce of competition or accountability. Voters are starved for a political menu where *they* get to choose.

What happens to the power of your vote when 80–90 percent of U.S. House and state legislative races are so noncompetitive and lopsided that the winner is known by the media, voters and partisans alike, a year before the election? What impact does it have on the psychology of voters and their willingness to be engaged when as many incumbents have left office due to death than to defeat in party primaries since 1992? What happens to accountability when, in the 1998 party primaries, only one congressional incumbent failed to win—Rep. Jay Kim, who was unable to campaign because a judge had put him in an ankle bracelet and confined him to home detention after his conviction for accepting illegal campaign contributions? What is the impact on our democracy when 90 percent of voters either don't vote, vote consistently for losers, or live in a legislative district that is so lopsided that it doesn't matter if they show up to the polls or not? What role is the stark lack of choices playing in our plummeting voter turnout and in our national political depression?

Here is one indication of an answer: research has shown a strong correlation between voter turnout and competitiveness. For instance, in a study by the Center for Voting and Democracy of 1994 U.S. House elections, voter turnout dropped dramatically by as much as seventeen points as House races became less competitive. This correlation was duplicated for a study of the 2000 U.S. House elections, where voter turnout dropped by as much as nineteen points in contested elections, from the closest races to those won by huge landslides.[26] In the 2000 presidential election, voter turnout was highest in the key battleground states where the race was closest.[27] Most of the results of twenty studies stretching back to the early 1970s support the hypothesized relationship between electoral competitiveness and voter turnout, even when controlling for campaign spending, not only in United States elections but also in Canada, Great Britain, France, and Germany.[28]

Related to competitiveness is the likelihood that a voter can reasonably expect that his or her vote will make a difference in who wins. A recent study found that voter turnout among California's Latino and black communities was far higher in those congressional districts redistricted to give minority candidates a chance at winning representation. Latino and black voter participation was highest "in congressional districts where [Latino and black voters] are able to play prominent roles in deciding political outcomes" compared to white-majority districts where minority voters obviously could not elect a representative of their own race.[29] Moreover, political scientist Henry Milner has found that the competitiveness of a particular race has a profound impact on political behavior of candidates and parties, giving them stronger incentive to inform and mobilize supporters in close contests.

But these findings shouldn't be all that surprising. In the 2000 Republican presidential primaries John McCain's insurgent campaign caused record-highs for GOP turnout in most primaries until he was eliminated, as did Ross Perot's 1992 campaign and Jesse Ventura's 1998 gubernatorial campaign in Minnesota (Ventura in particular inspired a sizable bump in turnout among younger voters). When there are interesting or engaging choices on the ballot, or even a close race, voters often respond. Conversely, when there are no choices, or when it is known ahead of time which candidate will win, there is little incentive for voters to participate, even when the winner is from the voter's own party, because their vote is rendered superfluous. It's a classic Catch-22, pithily captured by *New York Times* columnist Gail Collins when she wrote: "First they gerrymander us into one-party fiefdoms. Then they tell us they only care about the swing districts. Then they complain about voter apathy."[30]

Public enthusiasm and participation wane when voters are bunkered down in noncompetitive districts where their only choice is to ratify the incumbent or party that controls the district, as determined some years before by a redistricting committee composed of or overseen by incumbent politicians and party leaders. Because of redistricting and the other Winner Take All gremlins, most voters have their vote rendered unessential, and the act of voting becomes one of dubious merit. Moreover, various studies have demonstrated that voter demoralization is replicated generationally: if your parents don't vote, chances are greater that you won't vote, and neither will your children, futher entrenching political depression. Voters instinctively know that most elections are virtually predetermined. In a real sense, the adjective "rigged"—the term used by North Carolina state Senator Mark McDaniel at the beginning of this chapter— is not too strong of a descriptor.

Surprisingly, the works of noted political scientists show an alarming acceptance of this state of affairs. Two authorities, Harvard professor Gary King and University of California–Berkeley professor Andrew Gelman, have written that "the decennial redistricting repeatedly injects the political system with a healthy dose of increased responsiveness. . . . The political turmoil created by legislative redistricting creates political renewal. Many of the goals sought by proponents of term limitations are solved by legislative redistricting. . . . Far from being a scourge on the political system in need of major reforms, legislative redistricting has invigorated American representative democracy."[31] The political science literature is rife with researchers and their redistricting studies, each one brandishing the latest data set and determined in an almost hypercompetitive way to disprove the previous studies and theories. The net conclusion of this sizable body of work is that there is no net conclusion about the impacts of redistricting—there are nearly as many opinions as there are researchers.[32]

Thus, Gelman and King's plaudits would be disarmingly reassuring if we did not contrast them with statements from the line-drawers themselves: "We can end up with four districts that are pretty safe Democratic and four that are pretty safe Republican and four that are swing . . . which is pretty fair," said one of the principals in the North Carolina redistricting. Or, "In general, an incumbent protection plan would create the least amount of change and would be the most acceptable plan to both sides," stated another, echoing their Senate colleague Mark McDaniel's comment about being in the business "of rigging elections."[33] Congressman Tom Davis, chairman of the GOP's 2000 congressional reelection efforts, warned, "[Redistricting] is all about raw political power. Don't let anybody kid you otherwise. This brings out the absolute worst of the political process."[34]

And Davis should know. For the 2000 redistricting in his Virginia, Davis reconnoitered with two colleagues—one Republican, one Democrat—representing districts to either side of his. Together they agreed on new boundaries for their districts that would make all three of their seats safe for years to come. The Democratic district would "stretch like a spoon" from Alexandria to Reston, with the spoon's handle only one-precinct thick in some places, and then widening in Reston to pick up three Democratic precincts that the Republican Davis "would happily do without." Congressman Davis was hardly worrying about "increased responsiveness" or "political renewal" when he told a *Washington Post* luncheon of editors and reporters, rather bluntly and without guile or tact: "None of us are endangered in these seats, even with the current districts. But obviously, you want to make yourself more comfortable."[35]

Nor was Congresswoman Loretta Sanchez and thirty of her California Democratic colleagues worried about "increased responsiveness" when they ponied up $20,000 each to buy themselves an "incumbent protection" insurance policy from the practitioners drawing California's legislative district lines. In Pennsylvania during the 2001 elections the GOP scored a trifecta (control of the governorship and both houses of the state legislature) which gave them absolute power over redistricting in their state.[36] Like an autocratic king, Pennsylvania's state House Majority Leader John Perzel waved his royal computer mouse and eliminated two Democratic-controlled districts and turned a third into a GOP seat in a state that Democrat Gore took in the presidential race. He was hardly thinking about "invigorating American representative democracy" when he said, quite candidly: "I am not going to lie to you. [The Democrats] losing three seats sounds like a pretty good plan. We want to maximize Republican seats. . . . We're not planning to do anything now the Democrats didn't do in 1990, when they cut two Republican seats."[37] The war stories of past redistrictings are filled with dozens of brazen quotes like this. Gelman and King and their colleagues, so stuck in viewing the political landscape from "inside the box," presumably find nothing troubling or incriminating about these statements.

But, like a Kafkaesque motif, the picture transmogrifies when we shift the point of view "out of the box"—from that of the political parties and incumbents—to the point of view of the voter. Voters in Winner Take All are truly stuck. For voters, all of the backroom goings-on occur like a cyclone descending from the gods on high. It is as if their votes have been drained of their influence and vitality, leaving most of them with choiceless legislative elections. And there's not much they can do about it short of devoting their lives to reforming the anachronisms of the Winner Take All system, truly a heavy burden simply to have your vote count for something.

No, Winner Take All's redistricting racket—or shall we say the "incumbent protection" racket—is hardly one that creates "political renewal," as asserted by Gelman and King; nor does it result in a "healthy dose of increased responsiveness." Instead the gerrymandering of Winner Take All districts, particularly when they are drawn by the incumbents, reinforces a political class of safe-seat politicians who have little to fear electorally because their rate of reelection is of Politburo-like dimensions. To be fair to Gelman and King, it certainly is true, as their research has shown, that district elections likely would be even *less* competitive if redistricting were never done at all. Yet with the line-drawing process and its effects so tumultuous and so much an insider's game, that's a strong indicator of how *defective* Winner Take All is. All defenders of Winner Take All can say is, "Sorry folks, but redistricting is the best we can offer, that's the best we can do"—safe, one-party fiefdoms, Politburo-like incumbents, dumbed-down campaigns, swing voter serenade, phantom representation, two-choice tango, and artificial majorities.

Thus, the slight benefits gained from redistricting as opposed to not redistricting are like shuffling the deck chairs on the Titanic. Damned if we redistrict, and damned if we don't, either way we lose under Winner Take All. The shenanigans that go on during redistricting are merely part of the symptoms, for at the end of the day the problem is Winner Take All itself, and its use of single-seat districts.

Redistricting, in short, is a proxy for Winner Take All's single-seat districts—you don't see one without the other. The paradoxes and zero-sum "if I win, you lose" dilemmas involved with redistricting are the defining quality, the very essence, of our Winner Take All system. With or without redistricting, most single-seat races always will be no-choice affairs, so is it all that surprising that the United States now has the lowest voter turnout in the world among established democracies? Most voters simply have given up, an unimpeachably sensible reaction.

Other Winner Take All nations like Great Britain and Australia, and even mixed proportional representation democracies like Germany that incorporate some single-seat districts, at least do not leave the important task of redistricting to the incumbents and party leaders. It doesn't make much sense to the citizens or leaders of these nations to leave the fox guarding the hen house. Instead, in those nations the task of "public interest" redistricting is turned over to nonpartisan, independent commissions using select criteria such as respect for geographic boundaries, compactness of districts, and enhancing competition. But in the United States, only a handful of states and cities use redistricting commissions (and even among those jurisdictions, unfortunately not all use democracy-enhancing criteria). Instead, in most states redistricting for federal, state, and local races is decided by the very politicians whose careers are most affected.

But even "public interest" redistricting in the hands of an independent commission guided by fair, nonpolitical criteria, while it would certainly introduce more competition into some congressional races, would still leave most districts with noncompetitive contests and safe-seat incumbents due to the natural partisan regional and demographic realities, i.e. Democrats dominating in urban areas/New Goreia and Republicans in rural areas/Bushlandia. Given the realities of the Winner Take All landscape, public interest redistricting is the best we can do. Yet in the grand scheme of things the slight benefits gained from public interest redistricting aren't much better than incumbent redistricting. For once again the problem, when all is said and done, is Winner Take All itself. Redistricting is merely a recurring and aggravated symptom of the larger problem.

At its best, then, the redistricting process is hardly an innocent one, nor are its outcomes best for American democracy or national policy, despite the claims of the professional political class. In fact, when closely examining the redistricting process in many states and localities, what emerges again and again is the realization that the last thing on anyone's mind, even that of noted political scientists, is the impact of redistricting on voters, on representation, on our democracy—indeed, on our national future. One of the most corrosive effects of Winner Take All and the gerrymandering of legislative districts is its understated impact on the psyche of voters, and whether each individual voter is imbued with an internalized sense that their vote is powerful. During the redistricting process most voters are plunked into safe, one-party districts, and at that moment their vote becomes either superfluous (if their party dominates the district) or impotent (if they are an orphaned voter/geographic minority). Either way, the act of voting becomes a waste of their time, and a cruel hoax to their democratic aspirations.

Moreover, as we will see in the next chapter, the hijinks unleashed by redistricting create numerous opportunities for party leaders and insiders to game the system. Only one side can win in Winner Take All, and both sides try rapaciously to manipulate the Winner Take All rules. The unsurprising results are "representation ripoffs" and "political power ripoffs" where one side gains unfairly as the bewildered public tries to follow along in what seems a House of Mirrors.

CHAPTER SIX

The Gravity of the Prize

Redistricting will determine the future control of Congress.
—KEVIN MACK,
DEMOCRATIC LEGISLATIVE CAMPAIGN COMMITTEE

Redistricting is the window through which we may view something
more profound and disturbing about our Winner Take All system.
Much as a comet brings to scientists periodic information from the
farflung reaches of the galaxy, the decennial line-drawings that
occurred in 1991–1992 and 2001–2002 afforded us an opportunity to glimpse
a rare insight into the workings of our clanking, antiquated, eighteenth-century
democracy technology. Taken in its totality, the madcap mayhem known as
redistricting raises even more general doubts about single-seat districts themselves, and about Winner Take All in general.

Virginia's November 1999 state legislative elections may have given us a
glimpse of our Winner Take All future, and it isn't pretty. In those elections,
Republicans pioneered a new tactic in carving up the political map that elevates
redistricting gaming and brinkmanship to an audacious, even disturbing level:
they purposefully withheld candidates from running in local races against popular Democratic incumbents, hoping to give Democratic voters in these regions
fewer reasons to go to the polls. The goal was to depress Democratic voter
turnout in specific geographic areas that overlapped closer state legislative
races. What's more, both Republicans and Democrats targeted a few pivotal
races for lavish spending while withdrawing candidates from many other races
where they didn't stand a chance. Consequently, an astounding three of five
state legislative races in Virginia had no candidate from one of the two major
parties. That's 60 percent of districts where voters had *no choice* other than to
ratify the lone major party candidate.[1] Helped by this tactic of slicing and dicing
the political map, Republicans were able to drive down Democratic voter participation and precisely target more money to the few close races. The result?
The Republican Party won control of the state legislature for the first time in
Virginia's history, even though the statewide vote two years later elected a
Democrat for governor. These trench warfare strategies were so successful in
Virginia that gleeful Republican leaders exported them to other states in time
for the 2000 elections.[2]

Following the Republican takeover of the statehouse, Virginia's Democratic
U.S. Senator Chuck Robb lamented that the Republicans now would "determine who gets elected to Virginia's General Assembly for the next 10 years," a

rather astonishing conclusion for a single election until you understand another little-known and quirky fact about our neofeudal single-seat district system. It is literally true that voters in 1998 and 2000 were determining representation for voters throughout the next decade—*they had more impact on who will win state and congressional elections in the year 2004 than voters in 2004*. That's because whichever party completes the trifecta of winning control of the governor's seat as well as the House and Senate of a particular state at the start of each decade wins the godlike power to redistrict their state's legislative district lines, not only for all their state's legislative seats but also for that state's U.S. House seats.

By using techniques like "packing," whereby the lines are drawn so that you pack as many as possible of your political opponents' voters into a few districts, and "cracking," where you split your opponent's supporters into two or more districts, those controlling the redistricting process can game the system, dramatically heightening their chances at winning the remaining districts. In Virginia, Republicans completed the trifecta and dominated redistricting in early 2001 (before the state elected a Democratic governor in late 2001); they were able to use these tactics to make their own congressional seats more safe and weaken one Democratic seat. In California, when Democrats regained control of the governor's seat in 1998 and completed the trifecta, they gained monopoly control over redrawing California's fifty-three U.S. House seats—12 percent of the national total—and 120 state legislative seats. The tactics of packing and cracking are so effective that Democrats gave abrupt notice that certain Republican Congressman could start looking for new work. "If James Rogan and Steve Horn are still in office after 2002, they will be representing districts in the Pacific Ocean," crowed one Democratic consultant (Rogan lost reelection in 2000, before his district was redrawn; Horn indeed was redistricted out of his seat, prompting his retirement from politics).[3]

Republican and Democratic analysts both say that control over the redistricting process gives a party such an advantage that the fifty state legislative and gubernatorial elections in 1998 and 2000—not the Congressional elections or the presidential election—determined who will hold a majority in the *federal* U.S. House of Representatives right through 2010. Jim Nicholson, chairman of the Republican National Committee, stated before the 2000 elections, "The winners [of the state legislatures] are going to determine the political landscape in at least the first decade of the next millennium, because they are the people who are going to preside over the process of reapportionment and redistricting of their respective states as a result of the 2000 census." In fact, numerous observers have stated that the outcome of the 1994 elections—when Republicans took control of Congress for the first time in forty years—was due in no small part to Republican gains made during the 1991–1992 redistricting. Morton Kondracke, writing for *Roll Call*, estimated that less than 12,000 voters nationwide—six-hundredths of 1 percent of the eligible voting population—swung the 1994 vote to the House Republicans.[4]

So the battle to complete or prevent the trifecta is fierce, and that's why, while the public's attention was riveted on the face-off between Al Gore and George W. Bush, the low-intensity conflict for control of the nation's statehouses was just as pivotal.[5] Despite the fundamental importance of these state legislative races at the end of each decade, for the most part they fly under the public's radar. But both parties were totally focused and engaged, committing unprecedented resources to end-of-the-decade legislative and gubernatorial races, targeting record-setting gobs of money to those few races where it would make a difference.[6] The trench warfare was fought state by state, district by district, in a handful of close races, the "Gettysburg" of our political landscape. In fact, the chance to draw districts that can screw your opponent is such a great prize that the Republicans and Democrats drove spending on *state* legislative elections past the billion-dollar mark for the first time in the 2000 elections.[7]

The numbers reflected the gravity of what was at stake: prior to the 2000 congressional elections, Democrats controlled both houses in nineteen state legislatures, Republicans in eighteen, and twelve were split (Nebraska's unicameral legislature is officially nonpartisan but leans conservative). In perhaps fifteen states, including some of our most populous states, the political balance was close enough that both parties had a chance at taking a majority in the November 2000 elections.[8] The races came down to raw numbers: thirty-three legislative chambers in twenty-three states; a crucial 250 or so legislative seats up for grabs out of over 7,000—a measly 3 percent of all seats.[9] At the time, given the wire-thin margin of the GOP's House majority—222 to 211 with two independents, the narrowest preelection edge since 1954—even a small shift could have had big implications for national politics. Swing states like Michigan, where party control of the state house has switched back and forth for the past three elections, was once again in play, just like it was for the presidential race. Other big swing states, including Texas, Ohio, Illinois, Pennsylvania, and Wisconsin, were battlegrounds in the winner-take-all-or-nothing game. Whichever party was ahead in the battle for state legislative seats at the end of the decade—not two years later in 2002, or two years earlier in 1998, but exactly following Election Day in November 2000—was going to win the grand prize.

What should be obvious from this reality of our political landscape is that, in a geographic-based system like Winner Take All, such gaming over the political map becomes an inevitable part of the strategic political tussle. The full force of this zero-sum dynamic is unleashed at the end of every decade when the incumbents and party leaders prepare to redraw their own district lines. The handful of competitive races become the contested terrain of partisan warfare, with much at stake because the "winner takes all," including control of the state legislatures and the U.S. House.

The Hidden National Election

This is a life-and-death struggle for survival. It just gets ugly.

—KEN KHACHIGIAN,
VETERAN GOP STRATEGIST IN CALIFORNIA

We're very opportunistic. You have to think of us as the great white shark.

—DARRY SRAGOW, POLITICAL CONSULTANT,
STRATEGIST FOR DEMOCRATIC CAMPAIGNS IN CALIFORNIA

Despite the high stakes, the role of the national parties in *state* legislative races goes largely unnoticed, deliberately hidden by the Washington, DC–based national party leaders' eagerness to avoid accusations of meddling in local and state affairs. Tim Storey from the National Conference of State Legislatures said of the national-level influence: "It's very, very difficult to get a handle on it. It's way behind the scenes, and it's hard to figure out what kind of money is being moved out to those [state legislative] campaigns. But it's a very sophisticated operation." Added Tom Hofeller, redistricting director for the Republican National Committee, "It's the hidden national election of 2000."[10]

The political skirmish of redistricting is often compared to Cold War espionage, in which the two "superpowers" are vying for tiny districts of strategic terrain, and half the game is trying to figure out what the other side is doing and where they are really putting their resources. The rest is trying to determine where the sneak attacks will be, with every move as much art as science, based more on instincts than information. And events large and small—like the impeachment gambit—can change everything.

For instance, in 1990 members of Congress pioneered a new ploy in the constant drive for incumbent protection during redistricting—they quietly dumped millions of dollars into the coffers of *state* legislative leaders and legislators, not only out of loyalty to help their party in the battle for control of the state legislature but also with the intent to influence the way the state lawmakers drew *their* new congressional districts.[11] It was raw Darwinian self-preservation, pure and simple. Occasionally incumbents from the same party will get drawn into the same district and pitted against each other, as personal vendettas get carried out between and even within parties. Not surprisingly, members of Congress always have eyed the statehouse anxiously in the first year of a new decade. "It makes it very disconcerting for members of Congress that their future rests in the hands of 400 to 500 state legislators that they don't know," said Kevin Mack, who headed the 2000 Democratic Legislative Campaign Committee.[12]

So the 1990 election saw money flow from Washington to state capitals in creative, unprecedented, and often unseen ways. State laws made the task easier, permitting contributions under state law that would have been illegal under federal law. The most conspicuous source of money was congressional members' own campaign committees. Some members of Congress formed their own state

PACs, and other members became adept at "bundling" contributions from their own wealthy contributors and federal committees to state legislative candidates and state campaign committees—so contributors to federal congressional campaigns in effect became contributors to state legislative campaigns, whether they knew it or liked it or not. What set the 1990 effort apart from previous efforts was its breadth and sophistication, according to party operatives. It was a financial strategy borrowed from the Washington lobbyists' handbook: give to get in the good graces of the decision makers—in this case, state legislators redrawing *congressional* districts. And make sure the important people know who is doing the giving.[13]

These tactics and manipulations were revived and refined for the 1998 and 2000 elections. For the 1998 election, the Republican National Committee and Democratic National Committee and other national committees of both parties transferred a combined $49 million in hard and soft dollars to the state parties and targeted state and local candidates. In 2000 they gave even more money.[14] Every advantage was explored and exploited because there is so little wiggle room between success and failure. As natural partisan demographics and regional divisions have become more rigidified in Bushlandia and New Goreia, and as the redistricting computer technology becomes ever more effective at carving up the districts to precise partisan specifications, there simply aren't that many competitive seats left up for grabs.

How important redistricting is to the national parties was demonstrated in Pennsylvania's special election in June 2000 to fill a single vacant state house seat that was predicted to be a close race. With the Pennsylvania house tied at one hundred seats for each party (with three vacancies), and with the GOP already in control of the state senate and the governor's mansion, Republicans were fighting to complete their trifecta and Democrats were fighting to prevent it. That lone seat in that special election very well might have determined the balance. The candidates spent millions of dollars, most of it raised from national campaign committees and outside sources. Vice President Gore campaigned in the district and President Clinton recorded radio spots for the Democratic candidate. GOP Governor Tom Ridge and national Republicans actively supported the Republican candidate. Meanwhile, ninety-one of Pennsylvania's house candidates (45 percent) faced *no major party opponent* in November 2000, as the two parties ignored districts they could not possibly hope to win.[15]

After the dust from the November 2000 election had settled all across the country, the Ds and Rs had dueled to a near-draw—the split in the U.S. House had crept a hair closer, 221–212, with two independents. The U.S. Senate was exactly split 50–50, and the presidential vote was a dead heat as well. At the sub-radar state legislative level, eighteen state legislatures stayed with the Republicans, and the Democrats lost control of three previously held, down to sixteen. The close breakdown reflected the nation's delicate political balance.[16]

"You've got two minority parties right now," said Ron Faucheux, a former Louisiana legislator and editor-in-chief at *Campaigns & Elections* magazine. "Neither party has a majority of the national electorate on their side."[17] Political journalist Michael Barone agreed, writing "The prospect ahead is for close elections, closely divided Congresses, and bitterly fought battles over issues and nominations."[18] The balance and the stakes drove up the costs—and the acrimony—of these elections, particularly in the closest races and in the overall drive to win control of the state legislatures and the U.S. House.

Climaxing a remarkable political decade for the GOP, for the first time since 1956 the GOP had won control of more state legislatures than the Democrats. After adjusting for seats added or subtracted to various states as a result of reapportionment, both Democrats and Republicans had complete control over redistricting one hundred U.S. House seats each.[19] In those states they mercilessly tried to carve back their opponent's share of congressional seats with the calculating nerve of cold-blooded executioners. In Michigan, a GOP trifecta created a congressional gerrymander that stuffed six Democratic incumbents into three seats; in Georgia, the Democrats drew a congressional map that buried four GOP incumbents into two districts.[20] Nevertheless, considering that the Republicans controlled the redrawing of only five seats following the 1990 census, the past decade marked a staggering reversal and a GOP ascension to power. Not since the 1920s have so many seats been under Republican control.[21] The Republican takeover of Congress in 1994 and the subsequent GOP victories in the 1996 and 1998 congressional elections marked the first time since the 1920s that the Republicans had maintained control of both the U.S. House and the Senate for more than a single two-year term.[22]

Not long after the 2000 elections Tim Storey, policy analyst and redistricting expert with the National Conference of State Legislatures, commented, "Both parties can claim victories by virtue of holding on to the status quo in some critical states. The redistricting wars will now begin in earnest."

The GOP Power Surge

> This is all about the Republicans from affluent parts of the state— the suburbs around Pittsburgh and Philadelphia—controlling the General Assembly. What they want to do is eliminate a Philadelphia seat or a Pittsburgh seat in exchange for a new seat in the wealthy suburbs. It's all about control.
>
> —ROBERT MELLOW,
> PENNSYLVANIA SENATE MINORITY LEADER, DEMOCRAT[23]

With the Democrats and Republicans so implacably close, naturally there has been much anxious speculation about how reapportionment and redistricting in 2001 ultimately will affect control of the U.S. House for the rest of the decade until 2010, as well as the Electoral College vote for president (since each state is granted one electoral vote per House seat). Of particular note, those districts previously drawn for racial representation that likely helped the GOP win control of the U.S. House in 1994 were unpacked to some degree in certain states during the 2001–2002 redistricting, which may allow Democrats to pick up a few more seats. Longer term, six of the eight states gaining seats have rapidly expanding, Democratic-friendly Latino populations. With the two sides so closely matched—only a six-seat difference in the House—the math gets complicated and highly speculative when trying to predict our congressional future.[24]

But what is most interesting—and no doubt alarming, if you are from the Democratic or liberal side of the aisle—is that if you look merely at voting margins between Democrats and Republicans, while there is a dead heat nationally for president, U.S. Senate, U.S. House, control over state legislatures, even the number of congressional seats in trifecta states, nevertheless the Winner Take All system has translated this dead heat into a *sweeping GOP triumph*. In fact, one could argue that the Democrats still retain a popular voting majority: in the 371 U.S. House seats where both Democrats and Republicans fielded a candidate, the Democrats actually won more votes, yet the distortions of the Winner Take All districts allowed the GOP to win disproportionately more of those seats, 191 to 179 (with one independent).[25] At any rate, the net result from Election 2000 was the first time since the 1920s that one party has held the presidency, the House of Representatives, the Senate (until moderate GOP Senator Jim Jeffords jumped to the independent ship), a functional majority on the Supreme Court, and a majority of both state houses and governors—even though both sides *essentially were tied* nationally in 2000, indeed for the last several election cycles. But the gaming and distortions of the Winner Take All system have allowed one side of the political divide to commandeer an astounding degree of power.

Moreover, when you add up all the gains and losses on both sides for the past two decades, perhaps the most startling fact is that the national vote differences between Republicans and Democrats changed relatively little throughout that era. From 1980 to 1992 Democrats won a nationwide average of 53 percent of aggregate votes for the U.S. House; from 1996 to 2000 the Democrats won an average of 48 percent (with the Republicans averaging also about 48 percent from 1996 to 2000)—a shift of only five percentage points. Nevertheless, due to the distortions and gaming of Winner Take All, that resulted in a *huge swing* in the Congress. Such are the roller-coaster vagaries of our geographic-based system, that a national swing of only five percentage points, spread out over the right districts and the right swing states with the legislative lines drawn just the right way, catapulted the opposition party into power, with dramatic impacts on national policy.

There is an arbitrariness to the swing of this pendulum that is rather unsettling. Recall Chapter 1, where we saw the Representation Ripoff in various states—one side winning more than its fair share of representation at the expense of the other side. But this is more like a Political Power Ripoff, where one side has risen to enormous heights of power at state, federal, presidential, and judicial levels, even though the national swing in voter affiliation was only 5 percent, and even though both partisan sides now essentially are tied. Yet due to the zero-sum nature of Winner Take All—"if I win, you lose"—and the way Winner Take All has expressed itself via the Monopoly board game of redistricting and in the regionally polarized sub-nations of Bushlandia and New Goreia, the thinnest of GOP gains has created a staggering consolidation of political power. But as we saw in Chapter 3 with Tony Blair's Labor Party and the Liberal Party in Canada, and also in other Winner Take All nations like India and France,[26] such vast discrepancies between votes won and heights of power attained is what we should expect from Winner Take All, particularly as our nation continues along its current trajectory of regional, racial, cultural, and partisan balkanization.[27]

Unquestionably, compared to before the 1991–1992 redistricting, the Democrats have been on the ropes, with the scrappy Republicans pressing the fight. The Democrats have tried to claw back to parity, regaining ground in the last three congressional elections. While the centrist Democrat Bill Clinton managed to hold onto the presidency for eight years, ultimately it was on his watch that the entire government, top to bottom, swung to the Republicans for the first time in decades. It was a historical watershed. Clinton's centrism, coupled with his considerable personal failings, could not prevent the conservative takeover and must be considered pivotal in any estimation of his historical legacy. But more importantly, the vagaries and gaming of Winner Take All have allowed a small shift in voter's party preferences to amplify into an exaggerated and dramatic coup d'etat. The palace wasn't exactly overrun by the opposing army; it's more like the insurrectionists crept in through a Trojan horse strategy, and in 1994 burst from hiding to smash down the front door with a vengeance.

Race and Redistricting: a Voting Rights Act at war with itself

> This is going to be the messiest redistricting—legally and politically—that we've ever seen.
>
> —PROFESSOR BERNARD GROFMAN,
> VOTING RIGHTS EXPERT[28]

With both sides so closely tied—a change in a mere six seats out of 435 in the U.S. House will cost the GOP their majority—each is searching for any opportunity, any advantage, to exploit. Under such a pressure-packed climate, the drawing of districts for racial representation moved front and center in both parties' strategies for winning a majority in the House. In the 2001 redistricting this led to some truly bizarre episodes in which the fate of racial minorities became a political football tossed from end zone to end zone. But more than that, the 2001 tug-of-war over racial redistricting underscored yet another absurd paradox of the Winner Take All conundrum, and once again illustrated the cynical ploys and manipulative gaming to which both Republicans and Democrats will stoop to win.

Plenty of states face voting rights issues for African Americans, Hispanics, and Asians—and with the sides so close, it is enough that the outcome of House districts' racial composition may be the single most exogenous factor outside partisan demographics that will determine which party will hold a legislative majority over the next decade. With so few of the 435 House districts competitive, and with only a few dozen swing districts up for grabs that will tip the balance of power, the share of racial minority voters in the swing districts is now pivotal.

A brief bit of recent history is helpful in understanding the high stakes. Following the startling GOP triumph in 1994, an insurgent challenger position emerged within the Democratic Party to its long-held voting rights loyalty. What this challenger position claimed was simple: that by achieving success through districts drawn to achieve racial representation,[29] racial minorities may have increased the number of minority faces in legislatures but actually caused a *decrease* in Democratic legislators. That was because racial minority voters, who are some of the most consistent Democratic voters, had been packed into fewer and fewer districts in order to maximize their chances of winning, and subsequently had decreased impact in the surrounding districts. Minorities had been, in effect, "bleached out" of the surrounding districts, creating more Republican districts.

Indeed, with neo-cons like George Will proclaiming that "racial gerrymandering is one reason that Newt Gingrich is Speaker,"[30] some Democrats scratched their heads in recalling how the 1991 Bush Administration's Justice Department had been such a vigorous enforcer of the Voting Rights Act, sharing data and redistricting software with voting rights organizations across the nation. It was odd, but while the ideological wing of the conservative movement had been using the courts to challenge any form of affirmative action, including in the voting rights area which resulted in a series of Supreme Court rulings overturning race-conscious districts throughout the 1990s,[31] another more pragmatic wing took a different tack. Led by Benjamin Ginsberg, then-Republican National Committee attorney and later George W. Bush's lead attorney during the Florida debacle, these Republicans seemingly had figured something out: by packing as many racial minorities, i.e., Democratic voters, as possible into minority-opportunity districts, they were electing more minorities but also making the districts around the race-conscious districts more Republican. Much of this clever GOP gambit went on beneath the radar screen in 1991, quietly and unceremoniously working with whatever voting rights advocates would let them in the door.[32]

The impacts were dramatic. For example, the state of Georgia's U.S. House delegation went from ten Democrats—one black—and one Republican in 1992 to eight Republicans and three Democrats—all three black—in 1994. While African-American representatives reached their highest numbers in history in the U.S. House, white moderate Democratic House members nearly disappeared from the South. Not coincidentally, insisted the challenger position within the Democratic Party, the Republicans captured Congress for the first time in forty years, plopping those minority congressional representatives in the middle of the most hostile Congress to race-conscious policies in modern times. So, the challenging theory asked, did we win the battle only to lose the war? Did we fulfill the goals of the Voting Rights Act, allowing more racial voters to elect their candidates of choice, only to end up with more right-leaning legislatures?

Here, then, was another zero-sum game of the Winner Take All conundrum: you could win more black or Latino faces in the legislatures, but seemingly at the price of electing more Republicans and more Republican-controlled legislatures. And, ironically, with fewer elected Democrats, there was less support for the traditional racial minority agenda. This debate raged throughout the 1990s and still nags today in Democratic Party circles, with different sides hauling out reams of statistics to back up their competing claims. Meanwhile, on the ground, things have gotten truly wacky, with various episodes in the 2001 redistricting revealing the utter absurdity that can arise when tweaking Winner Take All's majoritarian nature to do something it was never designed to do—elect representatives for a minority group.

The first line-drawing in the nation was in New Jersey in April 2001, and that episode announced with a cannon boom the new, bizarre parameters of the racial redistricting game: Republicans suddenly sounding like Democrats, *publicly* advocating for electoral justice and voting rights for racial minorities. Meanwhile, the Democratic Party backpedaled as incrementally as possible, the Democrats in New Jersey reversing their longstanding course and advocating the "unpacking" of minority districts, *with* the support of racial organizations like the NAACP. Their goal, they said, was to support voting rights, but only up to a point—they also wanted to prevent the packing of too many minority voters into racial districts and to place more minorities in the surrounding districts of white moderate to liberal Democrats, hoping to win more Democratic seats. As one Associated Press news story read, "In this strange year of redistricting, Republicans sound like Democrats, pushing for more minority districts and accusing their opponents of quashing the political hopes of blacks, Hispanics and others."[33]

In a tragicomic turn of events, Republicans in New Jersey went to court and filed their *own* voting rights lawsuit, charging that the unpacked districts of the prevailing Democratic redistricting plan violated the voting rights of racial minorities. During the subsequent court case both sides called black Democrats to testify in support of their position, an indicator of the controversy and divisiveness of the Democrat's new strategy. The "good Democrat" black witnesses said blacks would benefit by unpacking certain districts, saying blacks now have sufficient numbers to elect their preferred candidates without extreme packing. The "bad Democrat," that is, Republican, black witnesses asserted that the plan amounted to illegal dilution of the black vote. Two black civil rights leaders testified that black candidates historically stood little chance in districts that do not have a majority of blacks.[34]

Mischievous Republican leaders, sounding as if they had been possessed by the spirit of Martin Luther King Jr., pontificated effusively about racial justice and voting rights. The GOP leaders sounded so convincing that some began to wonder if the newly "compassionate conservative" Republicans, who had opposed every form of affirmative action and dismantled numerous strands of the civil rights tapestry, suddenly had "found God" in the form of a voting rights conversion. But others weren't buying the Republican Party's newfound holy conversion to voting rights. One Hispanic state representative in New Jersey said, "It's disingenuous. . . . Some of the most racist people I've heard get up and want to see more power for minorities. It sickens me."[35]

With the fate of racial representation hanging in the balance, the redistricting gaming proceeded apace. Battle lines emerged in many other states during 2001, especially those with large minority populations and lots of Congressional seats, such as Virginia, Texas, California, Massachusetts, New York, and Florida. In Texas, staunch conservative and fierce affirmative action opponent Rep. Tom DeLay cited the 1965 Voting Rights Act as he accused state Democrats of trying to destroy minority gains. In Georgia, former Christian Coalition leader and now GOP chair Ralph Reed suddenly was touched by the voting rights angel, declaring that the Democratic-drawn plan denied "minorities their legal rights under the Voting Rights Act." In Virginia, Republicans controlling redistricting packed superfluous numbers of black voters into the district of black Rep. Bobby Scott, Virginia's only black member of Congress, guaranteeing his seat but in the process helping white GOP Rep. Randy Forbes by draining away black voters from his district (where he had narrowly won a special election against black Democrat Louise Lucas).[36]

In Massachusetts, Republicans watched with glee as state House Speaker Thomas Finneran proposed a plan to create a new Hispanic district by uniting Hispanic communities in such a way as to wipe out the congressional district of Democratic Representative Martin Meehan. In the Los Angeles area, Democrats had to broker a peace agreement between Latinos and blacks as even longtime liberal Democratic representatives like Maxine Waters heard rumblings of a challenge from the insurgent Latino demographic in their districts. The Mexican American Legal Defense and Education Fund (MALDEF), the premier

Latino voting rights litigator in the United States, filed a lawsuit against the Democratic Party's redistricting plan in California, charging that the consultant drawing the lines had illegally diluted a potential Latino district in order to guarantee his brother—the white incumbent—a safe U.S. House seat. Democrats faced similar quandaries throughout the country, trying to answer Hispanic calls for greater representation while at the same time protecting white and black incumbents, including several who represented districts where a majority of residents now are Hispanic.[37] The gremlin called the Winner Take All conundrum was mischievously at work—"If I win, you lose"—but with a racial twist.

With so much at stake, experts are predicting more lawsuits over racial redistricting than ever before to continue throughout the decade of 2000. Said law professor Pam Karlan of Stanford University, "Because the Supreme Court has taken such a hands-off view on political redistricting, but such a finger-in-the-pie view of race, everyone has an incentive to claim that every *political* gerrymander is now a *racial* gerrymander. There's going to be a race to the courthouse. And so the redistricting process following 2000 is going to be more of a litigation-driven process than it was in the past."[38]

That's alarming news, considering that no less than forty-one states settled their legislative plans in court during the last redistricting. In the 1990s, the pockmarked legal minefield became unsettling to voters, voting rights advocates, and politicians alike and created truly bizarre—and expensive—scenarios. Consider Rep. Mel Watt's North Carolina district, which was drawn in 1991 in an attempt to elect a black representative in a state that was 22 percent black and that had not sent an African American to Washington since 1901. Watt's race-conscious district, which was tossed out in 1993 by the U.S. Supreme Court in the landmark reversal case *Shaw v. Reno*, was subjected to a bewildering aggiornamento known as *re*-redistricting. Over the course of the 1990s, Watt's district was tossed out by the courts and redrawn *four* times, following each successive round of legal sparring. Indeed, at the conclusion of the '90s, Watt's district—which originally had been drawn at the start of the decade—was once again in court.[39] Four times, thousands of North Carolina voters had their representative essentially swiped from them when the re-redistricted, then the re-re-redistricted, then the re-re-re-redistricted lines were arbitrarily moved, placing entire neighborhoods in another district. Thousands of voters went from having a Democratic representative to in some cases a hard-right Republican. With one omnipotent swipe of the computer mouse, these voters went from having a representative who thinks like them and represents their interests to one who in some cases was diametrically opposed.[40]

Events like those in North Carolina are doubly confusing, for voters and representatives alike. The bewildered public can only sit back and watch, waiting until the dust settles. Linda Meggers, redistricting chief for the Georgia state legislature, which had seen its own hair-raising version of re-redistricting, commented that "from the redistricting staff standpoint, [the 1990s have] sort of been the decade from hell." And yet, with the Democrats and Republicans so closely tied and trolling like sharks for any advantage, she can count on another decade at least as bad in the years to come. Meggers' office bunkered down for all possible eventualities, hiring court reporters to record hearings, bulking up databases, and crafting specific procedural guidelines.[41] In most states a tremendously costly investment of human and financial resources has been occurring, merely as a defense against what *might* happen in this Milton Bradley board game known as redistricting. One legal counselor to the Oklahoma House Redistricting Committee trenchantly advised her clients, as a way of covering themselves in case of litigation, "Don't write down anything that you wouldn't want on a billboard on the Northwest Expressway in Oklahoma City."[42]

Everyone knows that the decade of 2000 promises more such re-re-re-redistricting imbroglios like that in North Carolina, creating lots of business for lawyers and leaving voters and taxpayers scratching their heads. Following the initial line-drawing in early and mid-2001, multiple lawsuits ensued in numerous states. Most were quickly settled, but in many states the legal quagmire will drag on throughout the decade until the next redistricting in 2011.

All this confusion, of course, is a direct consequence of Winner Take All's geographic-based, two-party system. With control of the U.S. House up for grabs, racial redistricting suddenly became the jousting field of contested terrain between the D's and R's. Party leaders gamed the system, looking for any loophole or advantage to exploit. And unfortunately, given the fact that Winner Take All does not adequately represent geographic minorities/orphaned voters *unless* you can pack them into their own district, racial minorities have been caught in the crossfire. Their desire to elect their candidate of choice and to win "authentic" representation (rather than phantom representation) has been pitted against their desire for better race-based policies that have been decimated by GOP-dominated legislatures. The Voting Rights Act is at war with its reliance on Winner Take All's single-seat districts as the primary strategy for minority electoral empowerment. Which is to say that the Voting Rights Act is at war with *itself*, since suddenly it is being hamstrung by the very tool with which it previously had been so successful—single-seat districts.

While some Democratic Party loyalists expressed great dismay that voting rights allies had worked closely in 1991 with the GOP to win racial representation at great cost to the Democratic Party, it is important to be clear about one thing: race-conscious districting is not the fault of racial minorities for wanting political representation. It is the fault of a Winner Take All voting system that routinely excludes geographic minorities—racial or otherwise[43]—*unless* you can draw a district around an approximate majority of them. This has resulted in dogged efforts for the past thirty years to graft onto an inadequate Winner Take All voting system a hodgepodge of race-conscious districts to make up for that inherent defect. Voting rights advocates were pursuing, quite correctly, the only course available in a Winner Take All system in order to win authentic representation for their constituency.

Similarly, conservative opponents of voting rights remedies frequently have complained that racial minorities are being given special treatment, like other forms of affirmative action—but, again, that view conflates reality. It is really the Winner Take All system that gives "special treatment," but to *majority* constituencies. Geographic majorities are overrepresented by Winner Take All, as it excludes the remainder of geographic minorities/orphaned voters who don't somehow fit into the mushy artificial majority created by a lack of choice in the voting booth.

Winner Take All poses quite a challenge for those who care about representation for racial minorities. The barriers to creating representation opportunities for any geographic minority or group of orphaned voters in a Winner Take All system are daunting. The fact of the matter is, when we redistrict our Winner Take All, single-seat districts, only one race—or one political party, or one candidate, or one perspective—can win. By *definition* it's a zero-sum game—"If I win, you lose." The racial divide looms large in Winner Take All, never more so than during the decennial process of redistricting as all sides claw over a limited commodity—political representation. That inherent dilemma of Winner Take All has delivered us to this mad, mad moment, featuring pious "electoral justice" Republicans and coldly retrenching Democrats, who are prepared to wreak havoc over the landscape of "fair representation for all" in crass pursuit of partisan self-interest.

Thus, while the drawing of minority-opportunity districts the past thirty-five years designed to elect racial minorities has been essential to achieving electoral justice and more representative legislatures,[44] it has come at a price due to the more general drawbacks of Winner Take All. In the twenty-first century, multiracial cities like Los Angeles, New York City, Chicago, the San Francisco Bay Area, and Houston, spinning into megacities of a size, diversity, and complexity never before experienced, pose a vexing question: what political structures are necessary to create a more unified mosaic that, at the very least, will prevent social and racial conflagrations? With populations burgeoning and the racial demographic rapidly shifting, how can the turf wars be mitigated and a sense of "shared community" be promoted?

There are no easy answers to these questions, certainly. But what *is* certain is that the longtime voting rights remedy of Winner Take All districts in many ways will exacerbate the problem. Nothing magnifies the turf wars more than the decennial redistricting process of carving up racial districts in these cities. Nonpartisan forms of proportional representation and semi-proportional representation, which have demonstrated success in various American cities and counties in facilitating multiracial representation and coalitions that are not dependent on redistricting or residential segregation, clearly hold great promise for our collective political future.

The Undermining of Campaign Finance Reform

> Once you draw the district lines, you pretty much know who will win most races. And the amount of money spent on campaigns becomes nearly irrelevant. Most elections are over before they start.
>
> —STEVEN MULROY,
> FORMER ATTORNEY, U.S. DEPARTMENT OF JUSTICE[45]

The monopoly politics of Winner Take All also undermines campaign finance reform. New research is showing that most election results now correlate more closely with whether the gerrymandered districts lean Democrat or Republican than with inequities in campaign finance. As we saw in Chapter 4, in the anecdote about the National Rifle Association's ability to scuttle gun control legislation, the raw amount of money spent on candidates' races is not nearly as important as how well you target that money to the gerrymandered districts, specifically to swing voters in swing districts. This is a dramatic paradigm shift with which many pundits and reformers have not yet reckoned.

Using the presidential vote in each congressional district as an indicator of how strongly the voters in that district lean Democrat or Republican, we can make some enlightening observations about the relative impacts of partisan demographics versus campaign finance inequities on who wins elections. For instance, in reviewing "open-seat" elections—perhaps the best measure of money's impact since there is no incumbent in an open-seat race—over one-third of Republican winners in open-seat races in 1996 were outspent by their Democratic rivals. But not a single one of those Republican winners represented a district where Bill Clinton won a majority of votes cast. Where Bill Clinton ran poorly, Republicans won easily. Where he ran well, Democrats won easily. In districts where Clinton ran close to his national average, nearly every race was close. These results occurred no matter how much money candidates spent or how great the inequities in campaign spending.

If money were the biggest factor, one would expect that winners spending *more* money would win by *bigger* margins. But in open-seat districts the key determinant of victory margins was the presidential vote, not campaign spending inequities—the *strength of victory* more strongly correlated with how strongly Republican or Democratic that district was, rather than how much money was spent. For instance, in open seat districts that voted 40 percent or less for Clinton or 58 percent or more for Clinton—in other words, strongly conservative or liberal districts—no matter how much money was spent in each race, or how great or little the differences in spending between winners and losers, Democrats generally won an average of 66 percent of the vote in the liberal districts and Republicans won an average of 62 percent in the conservative districts. And the losers in these districts still won about 40 percent of the vote, regardless of whether they spent hardly any money, as much money, or even sometimes *more* money than the winner. There were conservative districts in which the Republican candidate actually was outspent, but still won the election walking away.

Similarly, when we look at districts that voted, for instance, 56 percent to 59 percent against Clinton, or 54 to 57 percent for Clinton—in other words, semi-conservative and semi-liberal districts—we see conservative winners averaging about 53 percent of the vote and liberal winners about 53 percent, *regardless of how much money winners and losers spent.* The close correlation between the presidential vote and party control continues in most House districts—winners and their victory margins more strongly correlate with how many Democratic or Republican voters are packed into those districts than with how much money is spent.

To check this demographic correlation, a multiple regression analysis was conducted by the Center for Voting and Democracy of the 340 contested House races from 1998. That analysis revealed that district partisanship and seniority were far more accurate predictors of House-winning percentages than inequities in campaign finance. The respected Cook Political Report has incorporated this type of partisan demographic analysis into its U.S. House predictions, and as a result was able to list a whopping 87 percent of House Republicans and 90 percent of House Democrats as easily winning reelection in 2000. Most of these Republican and Democratic safe seats were carved out of conservative and liberal areas of the country during the last redistricting.

Even when we look at close races in the 2000 U.S. House elections (where the winner received 55 percent or less of the popular vote), which are the races where money should matter most, we find a strange contradiction to the ubiquitous newspaper and reformer slogan, "Money Buys Elections." The sixteen Republican incumbents who won in these close races actually spent on average *less* than their Democratic challengers, $1,126,887 to $1,502,980, and the two Democratic incumbents who lost outspent their Republican challengers, $1,306,945 to $955,957.[46] Apparently somebody forgot to tell the voters that the candidate who spends the most money is supposed to win.[47]

The simple truth is that, in this new era of computer-driven, precisely gerrymandered districts, campaign contributors will *respond* to high incumbent reelection rates more than *cause* them. Donors will give to candidates they *know* will win because the district has been *drawn* to produce that result. Besides returning incumbents to office like the sea returns flotsam to the shore, gerrymandering trumps the impact of private money on most legislative elections, hands-down. It is this fact that has allowed the Center for Voting and Democracy to predict the winners in most legislative races eighteen months before the election, *without knowing anything about inequities in campaign finance,* primarily by correlating the partisan nature of how the districts had been drawn during the 1991–92 redistricting process. Using their partisan demographic method of analysis, the Center's executive director Rob Richie confidently predicted inthe early '90s, earlier than any other pundit or politico, "The Democrats' edge in House races in the post-New Deal era is over." And he was exactly right. Handicappers at the horse track should be so lucky as to have races as predictable as these.

This is a sea-level change of dramatic proportions, yet hardly anyone is talking about it. Certainly you would never know it by listening to the hype of many national pundits and reformers, still operating under the assumptions of the old paradigm. We still see countless headlines blaring "Money Buys Elections," and reports of the latest record-breaking campaign fundraising figures. For example, following the November 2000 elections, a press release from the Center for Responsive Politics, a leading campaign finance reform think tank, boldly announced: "MONEY WINS BIG IN 2000 ELECTIONS, TOP SPENDERS CAPTURE 9 OUT OF 10 RACES." A headline from a report by California Public Interest Research Group (PIRG), another leading campaign finance reform organization, blared "MONEY LARGELY DETERMINES ELECTION OUTCOMES."[48] Sure, the top spenders did in fact capture nine out of ten races, but these sorts of headlines confuse cause with effect: winners have more money to spend because donors know in advance which candidate is going to win. Most districts have been gerrymandered to produce that result. So donors are smartly placing their money on the winners. They are buying access, not elections—an important distinction.

While it is important to track information like relative campaign spending, this kind of hyperbole posing as analysis completely conflates reality and confuses the role that the Winner Take All system plays in creating safe, noncompetitive legislative districts. The intersection between money and votes is complex, but it can be understood best when you realize that incumbents are essentially CEOs of their own small businesses, dedicated to the expansion of their political fortunes. Yet unlike businesses in the free market, most incumbents have a monopoly on their market because *they* decide who their consumers, i.e., voters, will be, via the redistricting process. Once the district lines are set, the incumbents have a political monopoly over their political fortunes.

Under the new paradigm, where money will matter most is in the party primaries of the party that dominates each district. That will be the real battleground for deciding who wins and loses most legislative elections. But first the primaries need candidates—63 percent of incumbents' primaries were uncontested in 1998, presumably because the benefits of incumbency (widespread name recognition, contacts and "buddyship" with establishment leaders, editors, and the like, and the ability to raise gobs of money *if needed* for a close race) scare off challengers. In the handful of races for the primaries of open seats, better-financed candidates will have an advantage since voters won't have the benefit of party labels to guide them, and usually none of the candidates have sufficient name recognition. For the small number of contested races that are close, better-financed candidates may gain a few percentage points that could prove to be the margin of victory. But the number of close races is fewer and fewer every year—less than 9 percent of House races in the 2000 election.

So here is yet another befuddling paradox of our Winner Take All system: although most races are decidedly noncompetitive, often even uncontested, because of the lopsided partisan composition of the districts, the stakes each congressional cycle still can be huge because only a handful of races will determine which political party will win a majority in the U.S. House or many of the fifty state legislatures. With the major parties so evenly divided, hundreds of millions of dollars will be raised and spent as Democrats and Republicans joust for control, targeting the undecided swing voters in those districts with slick campaign mailers and thirty-second TV spots. Says Burdett Loomis, a political scientist at the University of Kansas, "A lot of money will flow to a relative handful of seats. In those seats, it's nuclear war. Twenty miles away, there's nothing."[49]

This paradox produces a certain schizophrenia in the national psyche. Voters see headline after headline screaming about all the hundreds of millions of dollars that are spent on our elections, about the Democrats and Republicans holding gold-plated fundraisers, raising money from the same corporate clients in the incessant drive to compete. Things certainly *sound* competitive, and politics certainly *appear* bought and sold by big money donors, even as most voters' experience is that of living in safe, one-party districts. From the individual voter's point of view, politics is a wash, a remote game that does not involve them, nor consequently interest them; but from the Democrats' and Republicans' points of view, every dollar and every *swing* voter count. The next section puts some meat on the bones of this paradox and illustrates more precisely where money does and does not matter in our puzzling and opaque Winner Take All political system.

The Captains of Cash and Soft Money Kings

> Redistricting makes the inequities in campaign financing even worse. Most elections are so non-competitive due to how the lines are drawn that big donors already know who's going to win. So they give to the likely winners to curry favor.
>
> —PROFESSOR DOUGLAS AMY, POLITICAL SCIENTIST[50]

We are used to headlines about politicians shaking down with near-religious fervor everyone from corporate CEOs and movie moguls to Christian PACs and Buddhist monks. But for the 2000 U.S. House elections Republican leaders set a new low standard—they shook down their fellow House members.

The Republican House leadership decided to hinge the reward of leadership positions and chairmanships of powerful committees to those incumbents who raised the most "soft money" for the party (money raised for a political party is called "soft money," as opposed to "hard money," which is raised directly for an individual candidate). Since committee chairs have near-dictatorial powers to set committee dockets, dole out pork, and establish the national agenda, this *quid pro quo* debased government to a whole new level of crassness and political patronage. What's more, the Republican leadership was able to do this because *most incumbents don't need a lot of money for their own reelections.* Most incumbents live in safe, noncompetitive districts where they have about as much chance of losing as a snowball melting at the North Pole.

So Speaker Dennis Hastert twisted the arms of these safe-seat Republicans to raise money they didn't need, demanding that they hand over the surplus cash to himself and other party leaders.[51] The leadership then was able to target this soft money like a laser to the three dozen close races that were about to decide control of the U.S. House and Senate. As *New York Times* columnist Gail Collins put it, "The Speaker of the House has already told Republican incumbents to raise money for those [vulnerable] candidates or risk being transferred to the Subcommittee on Toxic Waste."

As early as June 1999, seventeen months before the next congressional election, ultraconservative House Majority Whip Tom DeLay (R-Texas) had handed over $100,000 each to his party's ten most vulnerable House members.[52] DeLay is a prodigious fundraiser, raising millions of dollars for congressional elections, which is conspicuous not only because of the sheer size of his personal war chest but also because as a right-wing Republican representing an overwhelmingly conservative Texas district, he regularly wins with 70 percent of the vote. DeLay does not need to spend a dime to win reelection. But his safe seat allows him to raise millions and dispense it to colleagues, thereby gaining their support when the Republican caucus elects him to its coveted party Whip position, just two steps below the Speaker.

Not to be outdone, the Democrats engage in similar practices, with Democratic House leader Dick Gephardt and others paving the way. During the 2000 election cycle Gephardt personally raised $37 million for the Democratic Congressional Campaign Committee (DCCC), equaling the total the DCCC raised during the entire 1998 campaign. Gephardt also campaigned for sixty Democrats in thirty-five states, generating another $5.5 million for their campaigns. San Francisco Congresswoman Nancy Pelosi was conspicuous in raising millions of dollars for her congressional race to win an overwhelmingly liberal San Francisco district that she regularly wins with 80 percent of the vote. Pelosi is another of the many House members that do not need to spend a dime to win reelection, but Pelosi was visible on the other side of the aisle from DeLay, dispensing money to colleagues in tight races in a bid to buy their support when the Democratic Party caucus voted for party leadership positions.[53] As a "soft money queen," Pelosi managed to gain enough colleagues' support to win election to the powerful party whip position.

A new "soft money king" on the block is Rep. Patrick Kennedy (D-Rhode Island), famous Kennedy scion. He was made chair of the DCCC because he had become prodigious at trading off his family name and scaring Newt-hating liberals into ponying up big bucks. Kennedy brought the mystique and glitz of one of America's premier political families to the rough-and-tumble job of financing the party's drive to reclaim a House majority. He rewarded big donors with visits to the dynasty's fabled compound in Hyannis Port, Massachusetts, and entertained others at the grand oceanfront mansions of Newport, Rhode Island, that are part of his congressional district. He proudly invoked his legendary uncles, John and Robert, "to help pry open wallets in circles where the Kennedy name still sizzles."[54]

The DCCC and its GOP counterpart were the centers of action in the fight for the House, modern-day equivalents of the old-fashioned political machine. Both committees not only raised record sums of soft money, but they also targeted the money to the right districts and recruited candidates, even trying to anoint the party's nominees in certain contested party primaries. But while both parties regularly engage in such shenanigans, House Republicans in 1999 raised the bar and further debased politics by publicly and unapologetically hinging these fund-raising efforts to the awarding of leadership positions and committee chairs. The corruptive effects of such a crass *quid pro quo* on our democracy are obvious. Most legislative elections can't be bought because they already are too lopsided and noncompetitive because of redistricting and natural partisan demographics to even need to be bought. But the geographic basis of Winner Take All and its basic measuring unit, single-seat districts, allows safe-seat politicians to raise money far beyond their own needs, and then dole it out in such a way as to create their own political machines—yet another gaming of the system.

A comparison of congressional campaign spending trends from 1992 through 2000 reflects this change of strategy predicated on the tactical partition of the Winner Take All political map into competitive races versus noncompetitive races. As this strategy of targeting money away from safe incumbents and toward close races has taken hold, the median amount spent per race went from being greatest in incumbents' races to greatest in races for open seats. In fact, the median amount spent by incumbents rose only 25 percent throughout the 1990s—barely keeping pace with inflation, but it rose 140 percent—*nearly six times as much as incumbents' spending*—for open seat races.[55] Which makes sense, given the realities of the Winner Take All political landscape, where party leaders strategize over the political map like military generals, figuring out which will be the close races and where to sprinkle the most resources. The Soft Money Kings disproportionately pour money into the handful of close races.

This amounts to further confirmation that the role of money in politics is not as determinative as some make it out to be. If it were true that "money buys elections," the Republican leadership would not be able to shake down their Republican incumbents to steer money to the close races, nor would they want to, because these incumbents would need that money for their own reelections. That would be robbing Peter to elect Paul. But the reality is, no matter how much money opponents raise in these carefully crafted safe districts, their chances of beating the candidate from the dominant party are about as good as hitting the lottery.

Instead, the more complicated and nuanced reality of Winner Take All politics has created a fund-raising pecking order in which the "Captains of Cash" are rewarded for raising excess funds that are handed off to colleagues in closer races. This is how political machines and fiefdoms are created and maintained, with all their progenies of patronage, logrolling, and pork-doling. Such political juggernauts, rightly targeted for reform of soft money abuses by the McCain–Feingold legislation, are wholly a byproduct of the geographic-based Winner Take All system, and the dynamics unleashed by that system. The Captains of Cash and Soft Money Kings (and occasional Queens) sit atop the soft money pile, dispensing favors and collecting fealty, both within their own personal "safe" districts and within the legislature, and then sprinkle their booty around to targeted races, buying themselves higher ranking in the party pecking order.

Here then, is the explanation to the seeming paradox of thousands of noncompetitive safe seats swimming in a sea of soft money and campaign millions— the battle is not for reelection, since most legislators are easily reelected. The real war being waged is for control of the Legislature and for all the perks and power that come with it, such as control of legislative committees and personal clout for individual Members who are appointed chairs of committees and subcommittees. And for that effort party leaders raise gobs of soft money and sprinkle it around, calling the shots. The geographic-based nature of our Winner Take All system combined with the Redistricting Roulette *define* this pyramidal shape to our political landscape and permit this kind of gaming and manipulation to go on. The fundamental noncompetitive nature of most Winner Take All district races acts as a kind of lens that collects money from all over the country and focuses it on a few races where it can have overwhelming impact. This dynamic is much more distorting of our democracy than simply "money buying elections," since it concentrates and concatenates power in a small number of hands and Rolodexes.

Especially at a time when control of the U.S. House is likely to hang in the balance each election for the foreseeable future, it means that a handful of political leaders like DeLay, Armey, Gephardt, Frost, Pelosi, Kennedy, Hastert, and the like will be able to maintain their own well-oiled political machines, putting partisan and personality politics above sound policy and the national interest. It means that donors will be placing their bets with candidates they *know* will win, because the Winner Take All districts have been drawn to produce that result. Rather than buying elections, donors will be buying access to and influence of legislative leaders, and in some cases a chance to actually author important legislation—all pernicious practices that must be reformed, but it's not immediately obvious how some of the various campaign finance reform proposals currently floating around will achieve this.

Public financing of elections, for instance, shows promise as a means to introduce more competition into party primaries. There have been some encouraging results in Maine and Arizona's recent publicly financed state legislative elections.[56] Public financing also would give more candidates the resources to campaign and reach voters, thereby putting more information into the hands of voters about different political perspectives and policies, fostering a minimum of political debate even in noncompetitive races. This, in turn, would allow voters to make more informed choices about whom to vote for. One of the reasons I organized along with Common Cause a successful public financing ballot measure in San Francisco was that public financing will be able to slow down one of the most pernicious dynamics happening in Winner Take All politics today: the loss of political ideas (this will be explored in more depth in Chapter 11).

But without a McCain–Feingold type ban on soft money to crimp this targeting of surplus money by party bosses, much less a ban on all private financing of elections, the impact of voluntary public financing will be compromised. And even with full public financing of elections, most voters still will be locked down into safe, noncompetitive, Winner Take All districts, and except in a handful of close races public financing is not likely to change outcomes or greatly increase voters' ability to elect their favorite candidates or party. While debate will have been enhanced, representation will have been little affected.

In any case, all of these dynamics are unleashed by the geographic-based Winner Take All system, where whichever party, Democrat or Republican, dominates each particular district was decided some years before in a backroom game of cards in which incumbent politicians and party bosses supervised the redrawing of the district lines. The preponderance of safe seats leaves the handful of close races as the small postage stamp of political real estate where political war is waged, and where campaign ordnance is bombarded. In a nation so closely divided, whichever side wins more of these skirmishes for the swing districts will win the big prize—majority control of the various Legislatures, control over committees, subcommittees, and budget and tax policy, and control over redistricting in those states.

Dubious Democracy in the 21st Century

If we don't understand the full complexity of how our system is malfunctioning, we will miss the mark when we try to reform it. The shape of this pyramidal dynasty is all the more devastating because of a political landscape of geographic-based Winner Take All districts, where most districts have been gerrymandered to be noncompetitive safe seats. The party leaders' role starts resembling that of a mafioso *don*, dispensing favors and making decisions with "victory or defeat" ramifications for their party—to the victor belongs the turf *and* the spoils. While a slight partisan shift of 5 percentage points in partisan affiliation has occurred over the last two decades at the national level, to the point where the two political parties essentially are tied nationally, this slight shift was enough in the 1990s to allow the Republicans to outmaneuver the Democrats in the rollercoaster ride of Winner Take All politics. The Republicans were smarter and more strategic, used the emerging redistricting technologies better, were more clever in the drawing of race-conscious districts, and better targeted their resources to the right races. In short, they gamed the system better. In our bizarre Winner Take All system today, that was enough to ascend to the great heights of political power that had eluded the GOP for over four decades.

Redistricting and single-seat districts, then, are the Achilles' heel, the lynch pin, to understanding so many other dynamics of our geographic-based, Winner Take All system, and by extension of our political depression, national division, distortions of national policy—of our mudslide toward post-democracy. We have arrived at a stark yet seeming contradiction: on the one hand the competition *between* the two major political parties to control the various legislatures, the presidency, and appointments of the judiciary is as pointed, partisan, and acerbic as it has ever been; and the partisan contest is fought with all the tools and weapons of modern political warfare, for which party leaders must devise ever-new methods of skirting the hodgepodge of fund-raising regulations. Yet the competition for each *individual* race, thousands of them across the national landscape, is at low ebb, a virtual outbound tide of political melancholy. The battle for partisan control is waged like trench warfare over a diminishing number of races, ever smaller pieces of turf; and the point of reference for most voters *where they live* is that of safe, one-party districts where it hardly matters if they show up to vote or not.

It is a weird paradox in which most voters observe all the fire and brimstone between the two jousting parties as if they are mere spectators on the sidelines, viewing a strange kind of game on another planet, just one more TV channel to be surfed. Following the close call in Florida's presidential vote, various pundits, including President Clinton, proclaimed things like, "No American will ever be able to seriously say again, 'My vote doesn't count.'"[57] But the larger picture shows that such comments are fatuous and foolish: for the vast majority of voters, in the vast majority of elections, our votes *don't* count.

To sum up, in the last two chapters we have seen how the decennial redistricting of geographic-based, single-seat districts and its aftermath greatly define our political landscape. Incumbent legislators and party bosses of the two major political parties use sophisticated computers and comprehensive demographic and polling data to render 90 percent of single-seat districts into noncompetitive, essentially one-party fiefdoms, where most incumbent politicians and parties are virtually guaranteed victory, usually with landslide victory margins. The representation of millions of voters for the next decade rested in the hands of thousands of state legislators who decided redistricting, over 40 percent of whom ran uncontested—no challenger from the other major party—even as they received millions of dollars in donations that skirted federal law from congressional incumbents looking to protect their own seats. Party leaders—the Soft Money Kings and Queens—have created a pyramidal structure of political machines that raises tens of millions of dollars of surplus "soft money" that is steered to the few close races that, paradoxically, will decide which party wins control of many state legislatures and the Congress. From this brittle reality of the American political landscape, an assortment of twisted dynamics follow:

1. Legislative majorities get distorted, as one political side wins more representation and political power than it deserves (based on the numbers of votes received). This is especially pronounced in the balkanized regions of Bushlandia and New Goreia, which in turn impacts whether policy enacted corresponds to the "will of the majority."

2. Most voters' votes are rendered meaningless in the choiceless elections created by the Redistricting Roulette and by natural demographics of where Democrats and Republicans live, expressed via Winner Take All districts. Public enthusiasm and participation wane when voters are bunkered down in safe, one-party districts where their only viable choice is to ratify the incumbent or party that controls the district.

3. Millions of voters are geographic minorities or "orphaned voters" where they live, unable to cast a vote for a winning candidate who represents their viewpoints. Since voters and officeholders alike instinctively know that most election results are virtually predetermined, this depresses turnout and creates a weak connection between constituents and officeholders that undermines the accountability and legitimacy of government.

4. Recent court rulings overturning the strategy of race-conscious districting threaten racial representation and present a legal quagmire for future rounds of redistricting, even as the limitations of Winner Take All solutions become more apparent in our increasingly multiracial society. Democrats and Republicans alike have used racial redistricting as their pawn on the Winner Take All chessboard.

5. Redistricting contributes toward the freezing of policy debate and partisan

division, as districts become "locked up" as either Democrat or Republican, or as black or Latino or white, or as urban, suburban or rural, and so on, creating political monocultures that leave little political space for either counterconventional ideas or independent politics.

6. Goals of campaign finance reform—such as competitive elections, political debate, accountability, and more choice for voters—are undermined.

7. Winner Take All tends to produce adversarial government, where one side wins everything and the other side loses, so seeking a consensus between conflicting forces becomes nearly impossible. The incentives of Winner Take All do not promote consensual democracy.

No other single factor plays so large a role in defining our Winner Take All system as this redistricting of geographic-based, single-seat districts. And yet the entire process usually occurs with minimal public oversight. In fact, the process occurs behind closed doors, not necessarily in smoke-filled rooms but at computer terminals, party leaders huddling with technocrats and consultants over eerily glowing computer screens. The resulting electoral barrenness— produced by the ennui of predictability, the stark lack of competition, the utter lack of interesting or even viable candidacies and distortions of legislative majorities—is where voter capitulation and post-democracy begin.

If this isn't a bizarre way to run a democracy, then what is? But believe it or not, the fateful consequences of geographic-based representation can get even worse. As we will see in the next chapter, the Framers gave representation in the United States Senate to artificially created geographic entities called "states," rather than to people. Specifically, two senators were granted to each state regardless of the population of that state. This was the cause of considerable controversy and discord at the Constitutional Convention, particularly on the part of some of the young nation's most brilliant minds, such as James Madison and Alexander Hamilton. Nevertheless, under the pressures of nation-formation that sought to pacify low-population states and slaveholders, a wacky scheme of geographic malapportionment prevailed. Our democracy has been saddled with the U.S. Senate's considerable defects ever since.

CHAPTER SEVEN

Worse Than Winner Take All
Affirmative Action for Low-Population States

He thinks the civil rights movement was unnecessary. He still speaks fondly of brutal Latin American dictators like Chile's Pinochet. His favorite TV show is the propagandistically Christian *Touched By An Angel.* He hails from a sleepy Southern backwater where in his youth cotton wagons circled the courthouse, where flowers were put on the Confederate Memorial to honor Southern chivalry. He proudly displays in his office a letter from Spiro Agnew that thanks him for being "a truly wonderful friend."

Who is this man? If he were just your typical garden variety racist-next-door, a brash neighbor with a penchant for blurting out rude, offensive remarks that obviously amuse himself more than anyone else, perhaps you could ignore him over top the fence separating your yards. Unfortunately, he's more than that. Much much more.

He also has hanging on his office wall photos of himself pumping hands with presidents, foreign leaders, ambassadors, and celebrities and a framed copy of his floor speech during Clinton's impeachment trial. He has tormented American presidents and diplomats for twenty-nine years from his perch on the Senate Foreign Relations Committee. He has voted against so many bills—from food stamps to a Martin Luther King holiday to funding for the National Endowment for the Arts to practically every arms-control treaty—that friend and foe alike have nicknamed him "Senator No." As chair of the Senate Foreign Relations Committee he blocked so many nominees and treaties that he became a de facto Secretary of State. During one of his committee hearings, he had Capitol police toss out ten frustrated Congresswomen who had barged into his hearing room because he was single-handedly bottling up a United Nations treaty that urged countries to end discrimination against women. Senator No claimed that the treaty was the work of radical feminists, that it would legalize prostitution and abortion and outlaw Mother's Day, all demonstrably false claims.[1]

He is, of course, Jesse Helms, the Tyrannosaurus rex of the U.S. Senate. *Washington Post* columnist David Broder has called him "the last prominent unabashed white racist politician in this country."[2] Senator Helms, perhaps more than any other Senator, could serve as the poster child for an outdated sclerotic institution that is hastening our mudslide into a fractious, voterless post-democracy. The Senate is America's House of Lords, and Helms has been its King George.

Not too far away from Senator No, either in temperament or geography, and occupying the desk once superintended by antebellum states-rights Senator John C. Calhoun of South Carolina, is Senator Strom Thurmond. Thurmond, once the presidential candidate in 1948 of the States' Rights Democratic Party (also known as the Dixiecrats) that staunchly opposed desegregation and civil rights, first was elected to the Senate from South Carolina in 1954. Thurmond has set several longevity records, including once conducting the longest individual filibuster on record—twenty-four hours—as part of an attempt by Southern Senators to obstruct civil rights legislation. Thurmond is also the longest serving Senator; indeed, at ninety-nine years old, Thurmond by most accounts holds office in name only, appearing infrequently in public or on the Senate floor as a doddering artifact who must rely on aides and nurses for his cognizance.

While two Confederate war horses like Thurmond and Helms have long held sway in the United States Senate, there are no African Americans or Latinos in that powerful upper chamber. Only a handful of women have been elected to its privileged pontificate, and most of its members are millionaires.

Or think of it this way: if the Senate were chosen by lottery among all Americans, one-quarter of Senators likely would be black or Latino, and more than half would be women. But instead, two Senators are elected from each state using our antiquated Winner Take All methods. Given the stubborn patterns of racially polarized voting, that has translated into ninety-five out of ninety-six senators being white in the forty-eight states with white majorities (the one exception is a Native American Senator from Colorado). In the only two nonwhite majority states, Hawaii has elected two Japanese American senators, while voters in California, the other nonwhite majority state, elected two white women. Women generally lose out in the Senate, just as they do in most gubernatorial races; only thirteen women currently are Senators, yet that's the highest level in our history (completing the picture, only four out of fifty governors are women, and two out of fifty governors are nonwhite).

Many rebel against the notion of using race or gender as a factor in tracking representation, but the stark reality is that they *already are a factor*—the strong correlation in particular between the race of the majority and that of our representatives in most American elections is no accident. It is difficult to overlook—although some manage to do so with appalling aplomb—the fact that when the Senate undertakes such solemn constitutional duties as approving Supreme Court nominations, debating treaties, weighing the guilt of an impeached president, declaring war, or voting on matters of national significance, including policy related to women's and racial minority's health and livelihood, only thirteen women and not a single black or Latino is in attendance inside the chamber.

And there's great evidence that it matters. For instance, the presence of more women in the U.S. House has made a qualitative and quantitative difference in the types of legislation proposed and passed into law. Although outnumbered as much as 9 to 1, Congresswomen have been successful in gaining legislation long overlooked by their male colleagues, including gender equity in education, child support legislation, and laws for prevention of violence against women. It was Congress*women* who ensured that the offensive behavior of U.S. Senators Bob Packwood and Brock Adams, as well as Supreme Court nominee Clarence Thomas, were not swept under the "good ol' boy" carpet.

Back in 1993, the white jester himself, Jesse Helms, introduced a proposal to renew the United Daughters of the Confederacy's design patent on an insignia that featured the original flag of the Confederacy. Senator Carol Moseley Braun, the first black Senator since the 1970s, only the second since Reconstruction, and the first-ever black woman Senator, led the opposition to Helms' proposal. After Moseley-Braun argued in an impassioned speech that the Confederate flag was an emblem of slavery and brutality, the Senate, which had earlier approved the patent, reversed itself and voted 75 to 25 to reject it.

But in 1999, after Carol Moseley-Braun lost a close reelection bid the previous year, the once-again "no-blacks-inside" Senate rejected the nomination of a black nominee to the federal judiciary. Judge Ronnie White, a justice on the Missouri Supreme Court, was the first judicial nominee defeated on the Senate floor in more than a decade, and his confirmation process was tinged with racial acrimony. Would Judge White's nomination had been successful if there had been any black senators? Maybe yes, maybe no—but no question it would have been a different debate, with white senators having to justify their actions more clearly, just as when confronted by Moseley-Braun on the Confederate flag.

No, the Senate stands out rather ridiculously, like a Siberian's parka at the equator, for an obvious reason: if it were a private club, a member might need to *resign* before running for public office to avoid charges of belonging to an exclusive fraternity.

Big State versus Little State

But the lack of racial and gender representation in the U.S. Senate hardly sets it apart from the House, which is similarly, although not as drastically, unrepresentative, as we saw in previous chapters. What is unique about the unrepresentativeness of the U.S. Senate is that it bestows equal representation—two Senators—to all states no matter how small their population, drastically underrepresenting states with larger populations. The U.S. Senate was originally designed by the Framers as a compromise to settle the Big State versus Little State controversy, and the result was that low-population states like Thurmond's South Carolina have been handed a "representation quota," a kind of affirmative action for political representation. Which is ironic, considering that affirmative action for racial representation used in the House—the drawing of minority-opportunity districts—is under judicial and political siege.

Consider: more than one-quarter of the United States population now lives in three very large, rapidly growing states—California, Texas, and Florida, which also happen to be three of our most racially diverse states—yet they are represented by only six out of one hundred Senators. A mere 7 percent of the total United States population, on the other hand, resides in the seventeen least popular states and is represented by thirty-four Senators, sufficient to kill any treaties or constitutional amendments.[3] Texas, with 21 million people, has the same representation as Montana, with less than 1 million people. A Senator from Rhode Island represents 500,000 residents, while a Senator from New York represents over 9 million. California has sixty-eight times as many people as Wyoming, yet these states have the same representation in the U.S. Senate— Los Angeles County, with nearly 10 million people, has a higher population than forty-two states. According to author Michael Lind, today half of the Senate can be elected by 15 percent of the American people, and just over 10 percent can elect a filibuster-proof 41 percent of the Senate.[4] By filibustering, Senators representing little more than one-tenth of the nation can block reforms supported by the House, the President, and their fellow Senators, who represent the other 90 percent of the country.

Given current demographic and migration trends, by 2050 as few as *5 percent* of the population may have majority power in the Senate. Clearly this is a demographic meltdown in the making. By contrast, in 1789 when the first senators took the oath of office, the ratio between the most populous state (Virginia) and the least populous one (Delaware) was 11 to 1, and it took a minimum of 30 percent of the national population to assemble a Senate majority.[5] In Chapter 2 the point was made in regards to the Electoral College, and it applies here even more egregiously: the Founders and Framers simply did not foresee such dramatic population imbalances two hundred years later. The alarming trajectory is toward one of an ever more flagrant form of microminority rule. There is nothing "majoritarian" about the United States Senate. These are demographic changes that our two-hundred-year-old constitutional structures are ill prepared to handle. Indeed, the U.S. Senate is in the running for the least representative legislature among Western democracies, outside the aristocratic British House of Lords (which is in the process of being substantially reformed).

Political scientist Robert Dahl, with his usual gift for clarifying what others have made muddy, put it this way:

Imagine a situation in which your vote for your representative is counted as one while the vote of a friend in a neighboring town is counted as seventeen. Suppose that for some reason you and your friend each change your jobs and your residence. As a result of your new job, you move to your friend's town. For the same reason, your friend moves to your town. Presto! To your immense gratification you now discover that simply by moving, you have acquired sixteen more votes. Your friend, on the other hand, has lost sixteen votes. Pretty ridiculous, is it not? Yet that is about what would happen if you lived on the western shore of Lake Tahoe in California and moved less than 50 miles east to Carson City, Nevada, while a friend in Carson City moved to your community on Lake Tahoe.[6]

The eventual destination of this trajectory will be political bantustans where high-population and racially diverse states will have barely any representation in the nearly all-white, all-male Senate. Already the institutional favoritism shown toward low-population, white states is having real-world impacts.

Political scientists Francis Lee and Bruce Oppenheimer, in their ground-breaking work *Sizing Up the Senate: The Unequal Consequences of Equal Representation,* systematically demonstrate that the Senate's unique malapportionment scheme profoundly distorts policy and representation.[7] After first showing that, quite surprisingly given the peculiarity of its representation scheme, there has been little scholarly research or journalistic attention paid to the effects of the Senate, Lee and Oppenheimer demonstrate that the size of a state's population affects (1) the senator–constituent relationship; (2) the competitiveness, fund-raising, conduct, and partisan outcomes of Senate elections; (3) strategic behavior within the Senate; (4) leadership of the Senate; (5) policy decisions, and, ultimately, (6) the disproportionate allocation of federal dollars to low-population states.

Lee and Oppenheimer found that Senators from low-population states are in a number of ways strategically advantaged, compared to their populous-state colleagues. For instance, because they do not represent so many people, low-population Senators are able to establish closer relationships with their constituents and, in turn, earn higher job approval ratings than Senators from large-population states. Senators from small-population states on average win elections by wider margins and, accordingly, have more political leeway in office. Also, they tend to represent more homogeneous constituencies, and so they are not subject to the same interest-group pounding from all directions faced by their colleagues from large-population states on almost every issue. By contrast, senators from diverse, populous states are going to offend sizable segments of their constituency every time they cast a roll call vote.[8]

Lee and Oppenheimer also show that, because there are so many Senators from low-population states and so few from large-population states, the Senate designs policies in ways that distribute federal dollars disproportionately to the less populous states. Since a new dam or bridge makes a bigger splash in a small-population state, senators from those states tend to gravitate to pork-barrel committees where they are in a better position to do favors for the folks back home. "The over-representation of the citizens of the least populous states means that they receive more program funds per capita from the federal government than the citizens of the most populous states. One unanticipated consequence of the Great Compromise, then, is that it now creates a situation in which citizens are treated differently based on where they happen to reside."[9]

The authors also found that financing a reelection campaign is a far less arduous task for Senators from small-population states. Because their campaign costs are manageable, these Senators spend less time fund-raising, and they concentrate that activity in the final two years of their six-year terms. In the most populous states, where an incumbent Senator often raises more than $15 million to finance a reelection bid, there is no fund-raising break. Further, Senators from low-population states can depend on PACs to contribute a sizable percentage of overall campaign funds, while populous-state Senators must engage more heavily in the time-consuming process of prospecting and tapping individual donors. Is it any wonder, asked Oppenheimer in an op-ed piece, "that the most influential positions in the Senate, those of the party floor leaders, which were once dominated by large-state senators (Lucas of Illinois, Johnson of Texas, Taft of Ohio, Knowland of California, Dirksen of Illinois, and Scott of Pennsylvania) have in recent years been occupied by senators from [low-population states] West Virginia, Kansas, Maine, South Dakota, and Mississippi? Senators from the largest states no longer have the flexibility or time necessary to lead the Senate."[10]

Perhaps one of Lee and Oppenheimer's most puzzling findings was that, given the considerable impacts of the U.S. Senate's odd malapportionment, their political scientist colleagues in previous decades and in recent years had spent so little time collecting data and analyzing the Senate. "Ironically," they wrote, "the most intensely debated issue at the Constitutional Convention—how to apportion representation among states—has received very little attention since." They cite a long list of the many aspects of our democratic system that *have* been studied, and the political scientists that have studied them: separation of powers, checks and balances, length of legislative and presidential terms, legislative term limits, and, of course, ubiquitous studies on the impacts of campaign finance inequities. In the 1950s and 1960s there was a hefty amount of research into the effects of malapportionment at the *state* legislative level—especially the underrepresentation of urban areas and the overrepresentation of rural areas, which is ironic given even more extreme overrepresentation for low-population, rural states in the Senate. As Lee and Oppenheimer wrote, "almost every legislative body has received attention in this literature—the House of Representatives, state legislatures, city councils, and school boards—with one exception, the Senate. . . . Journalists, legal scholars, and political scientists have generally ignored the consequences of the Great Compromise and equal representation of states in the Senate."[11]

That's quite a glaring oversight—a research "blind spot" as large as the United States Senate! Certainly it calls into question the priorities, judgment, and perhaps even the objectivity of many generations of American political scientists and journalists, too steeped in the status quo.

"Affirmative Action" Quotas for Conservatives

Lee and Oppenheimer also demonstrated another curious factoid that potentially is the most explosive of all. Because low-population states tend to be rural, their Senators tend to lean conservative. According to data the authors have compiled since 1914, equal state representation in the U.S. Senate has served to augment the ranks of the minority party an astounding *85 percent* of the time, most often the GOP.[12] That "representation quota" has benefited the Republican Party in every election from 1958 through 1992, primarily due to Republican success in low-population states in the West and South[13]—that is, in the sub-nation of Bushlandia. For instance, if not for Senate malapportionment, President Ronald Reagan would have faced a Democratic Senate throughout his eight years in office; from 1980 to 1986 Republican senators as a group received fewer votes nationwide than Democratic senatorial candidates, yet they gained a majority in the Senate, with consequent impacts on policy, treaties, and judicial appointments.

This affirmative action for conservative, low-population states has continued into the 1990s. According to one report released by the Center for Voting and Democracy, the nine most conservative states with only 5 percent of the nation's population (and not coincidentally ensconced in the sub-nation of Bushlandia) control 18 percent of Senate seats, an overrepresentation in the Senate of three and a half times. Twenty-two of the least-populous twenty-eight states with less than 18 percent of the nation's population—all of them states in Bushlandia—have thirty-four Republicans senators, which means they have similar political values and attitudes about policy, culture, and race *and* enough Senators to hamstring any constitutional amendments or treaty ratifications. If that conservative Republican rump can draw seven more votes—an extremely likely prospect from other Republicans senators or even conservative Democratic senators—they control a filibuster-proof 41 votes, enough to block any Senate legislation or initiatives according to the Senate's arcane rules of filibuster.

Over the years, conservative senators from low-population states representing a small fragment of the nation's population have flexed their representation quota to slow down or thwart desegregation, campaign finance reform, healthcare reform, affirmative action, New Deal programs, gun control, even basketball programs for inner-city youth. They have wielded the deciding votes on the sale of AWAC radar planes to Saudi Arabia, the Clinton economic package in 1993, and the balanced budget constitutional amendment. In 1991, when the ostensibly Democratic-controlled Senate voted 52–48 to appoint Clarence Thomas to the Supreme Court, the Senators opposing Thomas (including those from California, New York, New Jersey, Ohio, and Texas) represented a clear majority of the American people—but found themselves in the minority in the Senate.[14]

Urban policy and assistance for inner cities have been bottled up by Senators representing conservative low-population rural states; Bill Clinton's domestic stimulus program, which was targeted at urban areas in megastates like California, was killed by conservative Senators from underpopulated states such as Oklahoma. Labor law reform, like a bill that would have prohibited permanent replacement of strikers, passed the House but could not muster the sixty votes necessary to break a Republican filibuster in the Senate. For years, until March 2001 and the McCain–Feingold reform bill, a similar fate always awaited campaign finance reform. The U.S. Senate plays a unique role in foreign policy, and with senators like Jesse Helms at the reins, it has been the command post of isolationism and bombastic anti–United Nations rhetoric.

Filibustering and legislative stalling by conservative Senators representing a minority of the population plagued our politics throughout the 1990s. In fact, purposeful gridlock in the 1990s became a Republican tool for winning elections and a congressional majority, and we can even point to its exact moment of origin: Election Night 1992. On that night, Senate Minority leader Bob Dole from low-population Kansas, presumptive Republican presidential candidate in waiting, declared that since Bill Clinton had been elected with less than half of the popular vote, Clinton was therefore not really President. And until the apparent accident of Clinton's election could be reversed, Dole promised he would take it upon himself to represent those Americans who had not voted for Clinton—to represent, that is, the majority. Not only that, Dole "hinted at the way his party planned to conduct itself in the months ahead: it would filibuster any significant legislation the new Democratic President proposed, forcing him to obtain 60 votes for Senate passage."[15] Under Dole's leadership, Senate Republicans representing a minority of the population launched a permanent campaign of gridlock as a political weapon for his own presidential ambitions in 1996, an election that was still four years away.

As soon as one campaign ends, the next one begins—partisans like Dole only pause long enough to reload the weapons—and the Republicans used their overrepresentation quota in the U.S. Senate to wage partisan war. In fact, when the McCain–Feingold bill for campaign finance reform finally was called up in the Senate in March 2001, numerous observers commented on a most refreshing change: an actual, serious, and substantive *debate* on the floor of the Senate. For the previous several years, what has been referred to as "the world's greatest deliberative body" had often seemed anything but, as lawmakers waged procedural warfare, gimmicks, and politically positioned gridlock to thwart the other side's legislative initiatives. GOP leaders in the Senate like Lott and Dole had used parliamentary rules and an overrepresentation of Republican senators from low-population, conservative states to stymie many of Clinton's policy initiatives, and Democrats not surprisingly had responded defensively in kind.[16]

As Michael Lind has pointed out, "the Senate has always functioned as the last bastion of white supremacy. The balance of slave states and free states in the Senate permitted the South to preserve slavery and weaken the federal government for a generation after its population had been surpassed by that of the North. In this century, Southern senators filibustered anti-lynching legislation, and later blocked civil rights reform. The gridlock they caused was one reason the federal courts eventually seized the initiative on desegregation." Even today, "the only Americans whose views are consistently magnified by Senate malapportionment are white, rural, right-wing isolationists. If you are nonwhite or of mixed race, if you live in a major metropolitan area, if you are liberal or centrist, if you support an internationalist foreign policy, or even if you are a conservative who lives in a populous state,"[17] you are being shortchanged by the representation quota—the affirmative action—bestowed upon low-population states in the U.S. Senate. Tom Geoghegan, commenting in a 1994 article in the *New Republic* about the Senate's proclivity to vote down progressive reforms, wrote, "We can't raise our wages. We can't get health insurance. No aid to the cities. And why? The Senate votes it down. By a weighted vote, for small-town whites in pickup trucks with gun racks all out there shooting these things down."[18]

It is deeply ironic that, for all the radical conservative philosophy oozing from the likes of Helms, Thurmond, Lott, Gramm, and their conservative Senate colleagues, low-population, conservative, and predominantly white states in the U.S. Senate have benefited from the most flagrant form of representational affirmative action. For a body that pejoratively tagged Department of Justice nominee Lani Guinier as a "quota queen" for some of her legal ideas regarding representation, the representation scheme for the U.S. Senate was *founded* on quotas—specifically, a representation quota, a subsidy, affirmative action, whatever you want to call it—for low-population states. And this subsidy, this affirmative action for low-population states, has disproportionately favored conservative and white-dominated states, and their Senators and majority-white voters, in the sub-nation of Bushlandia.

Moreover, this affirmative action has had dramatic impacts on national policy. Because of the Senate's unique constitutional role in screening executive and judicial appointees and approving treaties, this thoroughly unrepresentative body has a powerful influence on all three branches of government, as well as on foreign policy. The fact that the Republican Party has benefited since 1958 from this representation subsidy speaks volumes about why the U.S. Supreme Court has been so conservative for at least the past quarter century. Also, recall that Lee and Oppenheimer showed that Senators from low-population states, like Republican leader Trent Lott, tend to win elections by wider margins and to have more leeway in office, not only to take stronger partisan stands but also to pursue leadership positions in the Senate. So there has been a built-in conservative bias to Senate leadership as well. To make matters worse, the Senators' staggered six-year terms—originally intended by the Framers to insulate the "enlightened statesmen" of the upper house—have merely ensured that the Senate would be out of touch with the times, as well as out of touch with the American majority.

In Chapter 6 we saw how, even though both partisan sides now essentially are tied nationally in terms of voters' party allegiances, nevertheless the zero-sum nature of Winner Take All has fostered an astounding consolidation of GOP political power in the Congress, the presidency, the Supreme Court, and state legislatures; and that this, in turn, has produced a Political Power Ripoff, with one side winning more than its fair share of not only representation but also political power at the expense of the other side. This Political Power Ripoff is tremendously exacerbated by this affirmative action quota for low-population states, which is the indigenous basis for *both* the U.S. Senate and the Electoral College method of electing the President. Moreover, because U.S. Supreme Court Justices are nominated by the President and approved by the Senate, the third leg of our tripartite "separation of powers" naturally acquires a conservative cast as well. At this historical juncture, a bias toward conservative, low-population states in Bushlandia has been constitutionally hard-wired into all *three* branches of government.

Note that this condition applies even with the Democratic Party holding a slim one-vote majority in the U.S. Senate, after Senator Jeffords' walk to the middle aisle. The Democratic majority would be even *larger* if not for the Senate's affirmative action for low-population, conservative states. Moreover, since several Democratic Senators are conservatives elected from the low-population states of Montana, North Dakota, Nebraska, Louisiana, Nevada, and New Mexico, the senators often vote like their constituents, *not* like their party, further overtilting the Senate in favor of the conservative point of view.

Yet it wasn't that long ago that liberally leaning populist Democratic Senators like Frank Church (Idaho), Mike Mansfield (Montana), and Henry "Scoop" Jackson (Washington) wielded mighty legislative hammers that benefited their low-population states. So this is not an issue of conservatives versus liberals or Democrats versus Republicans—it's an issue of *fairness*. Isn't it time we revisit the question of affirmative action in the Senate for low-population states, to analyze whether this eighteenth-century quota still makes sense in the twenty-first century? Just as the Framers first elected the Senate by state legislatures instead of by direct popular election, necessitating the eventual passage of the Seventeenth Amendment in 1916, perhaps it is time to reconsider this other bizarre feature that we have inherited—a malapportioned Senate resulting from affirmative action quotas for low-population states.

As numerous comparative studies of other democracies have shown, some degree of unequal representation exists in most bicameral legislatures. Yet the degree of unequal representation in the U.S. Senate is by far one of the most extreme. In fact, among all federal systems around the world, including those in more newly democratized countries—a total of twelve countries—the degree of unequal representation in the U.S. Senate is exceeded only by that in Brazil and Argentina. As Robert Dahl suggests, it is time to re-ask a fundamental question: do people in low-population states possess additional rights or interests than the rest of the nation that make them entitled to protection from policies supported by the national majority? If so, what are they? And on what general principle can their special protection be justified? Considering that some of our poorest and most vulnerable citizens live in inner cities of high-population states, aren't they worthy of consideration as well? Is state-based geography really the best foundation for bestowing special rights and special constitutional protection?

Ironically, as the next section will show, these very questions vexed the Framers. The solutions they proposed and adopted, at least for the Senate and the Electoral College, vex us still.

What the Framers meant . . . or thought they meant

In 1963, the Supreme Court declared in *Gray v. Sanders* that "the conception of political equality from the Declaration of Independence to Lincoln's Gettysburg Address to the 15th, 17th, and 19th Amendments can mean only one thing—one person, one vote." In *Gray*, the Supreme Court determined that the structural principle underlying *state* senates (but not the *United States* Senate) at that time was unjust and unconstitutional.[19] Since that court decision, "one person, one vote" has been elevated to exalted status, practically a patriotic slogan one can hear bandied from the halls of Congress to radio talk-show hosts and their dittohead legions. Yet, in another display of our national democratic schizophrenia, both the United States Senate and the Electoral College method of electing our President completely violate this principle. The modern normative standard of "one person, one vote" has had a head-on collision with the original principles and institutions established by the Framers.

As political scientist Robert Dahl has narrated the story, when the delegates to the Constitutional Convention first gathered in May 1787, they had several solid points of agreement and others still to be hashed out. They knew their new republic needed roughly to be founded on a doctrine of "separation of powers" that would provide for stronger national government than the Articles of Confederation had allowed; they agreed that the new republic should include an independent judiciary, a legislature consisting of a popular house, perhaps some kind of second chamber to check the popular house, and an independent executive. But many of the details were fuzzy: how should the chief executive be selected, and what constitutional power should be assigned to the different branches? How independent of the Legislature should the executive be? And how long should be the executive's term of office? These were the types of questions with which the Framers grappled, with no relevant model of government to give them guidance. They pretty much were making it up as they went along, inventing their representative democracy whole-cloth. The British constitution was a helpful model in some respects, but particularly as a solution to the conundrum of the executive, it was completely lacking because a monarchy was out of the question for most citizens and leaders.[20]

So the Framers, at a momentous time in the world history of democracy, set sail without much of a shoreline or a lighthouse to guide them. They proposed and debated numerous methods for both the Senate and the presidency. According to Dahl, during the drafting of the Constitution the opponents of a representation quota for low-population states, that is, equal representation in the Senate, included three of the most illustrious members of the Convention: James Madison, Alexander Hamilton, and James Wilson. They opposed it not so much for its anti-democratic and unfair bias against *representation* but because of its impact on majoritarian *policy*.

Madison and Wilson in particular "bitterly opposed what seemed to them an arbitrary, unnecessary and unjustifiable limit on national majorities."[21] James Wilson asked at the Constitutional Convention, "Can we forget for whom we are forming a government? Is it for *men*, or for the imaginary beings called *States*?" Madison was equally dubious about the need to protect the interests of people in less-populous states. "Experience," he said, "suggests no danger. . . . Experience rather taught a contrary lesson. . . . [T]he states were divided into different interests not by their differences in size, but by other circumstances."[22] Hamilton identified equal representation of the states in the previous national government as one of the worst defects of the Articles of Confederation, writing in *Federalist* No. 22 that aligning representatives on the basis of statehood rather than population "contradicts the fundamental maxim of republican government, which requires that the sense of the majority should prevail." The larger states, he concluded, "would after a while revolt from the idea of receiving the law from the smaller."[23]

But the low-population states, particularly those where slaves would only be counted as three-fifths of a person, were not swayed by such arguments. The issue threatened to fragment the Constitutional Convention and the formation of the new nation. The national bond was saved by delegate Roger Sherman's famous "Connecticut Compromise," where each state, large and small, was awarded the same number of Senators without respect to population. In addition to equal representation designed to mollify the fears of less-populous states, Senators were to be chosen not by the people but by the legislatures, and for six years, with the intent that senators would be more sensitive to the needs of property holders, and less responsive to "popular majorities." The Senate, in other words, was designed to be a bulwark against "too much democracy" in the House and to protect the elite interests of wealth, particularly in the slave-holding states. As Dahl and others have pointed out, "although this arrangement failed to protect the fundamental rights and interests of the most deprived minorities [i.e., slaves], some strategically placed and highly privileged minorities—slaveholders, for example—gained disproportionate power over government policies at the expense of less privileged minorities."[24]

In fact, one can make a convincing argument that equal representation in the Senate—the overrepresentation for low-population states—perpetuated slavery for decades. Throughout the entire pre–Civil War period representation quotas in the Senate helped to protect the interests of slave owners. Until the 1850s equal representation in the Senate, as Barry Weingast has pointed out, gave "the South a veto over any policy affecting slavery." Between 1800 and 1860 eight anti-slavery measures passed the House, only to be killed in the Senate.[25] Nor did the Southern veto end with the Civil War. After the Civil War, Senators from other regions were compelled to accommodate the Southern veto in order to secure the adoption of their own policies. In this way, the Southern veto not only helped to bring about the end of Reconstruction and initiate the ugly national scar of Jim Crow laws, but for another century it also prevented the country from enacting federal laws to protect the most basic human rights of African Americans.[26] Other vulnerable constituencies similarly were abandoned by the Senate, such as migrant farm workers who were left out of the protections of the National Labor Relations Act in 1935 in order to win the support of conservative "Boll Weevil" Democratic Senators in the South.

So the considerable warts of the Senate's structure were apparent early on to some of the most brilliant minds at the Constitutional Convention. Still, faced with a refusal of the less-populous states to accept anything less than equal representation in the upper chamber, Madison, Wilson, Hamilton, and other opponents of equal representation finally accepted this compromise of principle as the price they had to pay to gain a nation. The solution of equal representation was not, then, a product of constitutional theory, high principle, or the Framers' brilliant design. It was nothing more than a practical outcome of a hard and difficult bargain. "The Framers were not philosophers searching for a description of an ideal system. . . . They were practical men, eager to achieve a stronger national government, and as practical men they made compromises."[27]

A similar path of constitutional trepidation was followed in the drafting of what we have come to know as the very strange beast called the Electoral College. The meandering trail of presidential election proposals entertained by the Constitutional Convention meeting in Philadelphia over the summer months of 1787 reveals a divided and confused body. Starting in mid-May, the delegates debated several different methods for months, and changed their minds incessantly, finding no consensus and little satisfaction with any particular method.

As reconstructed by Dahl, on three occasions during the month of July 1787 the delegates voted for the selection of the president by "the national legislature"—what we know today, roughly, as a parliamentary system. The first time the delegates, who voted as a bloc by state, voted unanimously to support this parliamentary-type method, the last time by a vote of six states in favor and three opposed.

But apparently this proposal did not fully satisfy, so over the torturous summer other proposals from subcommittees were thrust forward and defeated. But as late as August 24, despite mounting pressures to complete their work and adjourn, the delegates still had not settled upon a final proposal and had voted down every plausible alternative. On the last day of August the delegates turned the dilemma of choosing the president over to yet another committee. By September 4 this committee recommended, in contradiction to the recommendation of a previous committee, a solution the delegates had already rejected—that the executive be chosen by electors appointed by the state legislatures.

Two days later, with nine states in favor and only two opposed, the impatient and weary delegates, who had been meeting now for nearly four months away from hearth and kin and obviously lacking modern methods to "call home," adopted an apparent compromise, the now familiar language: "Each state shall appoint, *in such manner as the legislature thereof may direct,* a number of electors, equal to the whole number of Senators and representatives to which the State may be entitled in Congress." The key difference in the final language was that, instead of the state legislatures *automatically* appointing the electors, legislatures were to choose the *method* for selecting the electors, leaving open an important doorway that within twelve short years, under the burgeoning forces of popular democracy and political parties, would transform the Electoral College into something the Framers had never intended—a quasipopular election for the president. Ten days after they agreed on this provision, the Constitution was signed and the Convention adjourned.

To Dahl, what the strange meandering record of proposals and counterproposals suggests is a group of baffled, confused, even floundering men who considered several options, finally running out of alternatives before settling on a solution more out of desperation than confidence. Thus, like the formation of the Senate, our method of choosing the President was not founded on constitutional theory, high principle, or grand design. The Framers simply ran out of time and ideas. During the final debates over the Electoral College, delegate James Wilson commented: "This subject has greatly divided the House, and will also divide the people out of doors. It is in truth the most difficult of all on which we have had to decide."[28]

Like the Senate, which initially also was elected by state legislatures, not directly by popular vote, the Framers wanted to remove the choice of the President from the hands of popular majorities and place the responsibility in the hands of, as Hamilton put it, "men most capable of analyzing the qualities adapted to the station, and acting under circumstances favorable to deliberation."[29] In other words, men like them. Yet, as Dahl has written, "no part of the Constitution revealed the deficiencies in its design more quickly than the provision for the electoral college."[30] In fact, Dahl concludes, with the benefit of two centuries of hindsight we can see that the various "undemocratic aspects" that were built into the Constitution to guard against excesses of democracy grossly overestimated the dangers of popular majorities and underestimated the strength of the developing democratic commitment among Americans.[31] This democratic commitment began to subvert the Framers' undemocratic intentions from the very beginning.

Within a dozen years, the election of 1800 already had displayed two of the Electoral College's defects—the first, easily corrected, was a huge oversight by the Framers, who had failed to distinguish adequately between electing the President and electing the Vice President. They simply had not foreseen a tie between the top two candidates—duh! So much for the deified genius of the Framers and their ideas, so roundly quoted and extolled by modern patriots and strict constructionists of the Constitution. Amid all their collective and individual brilliance, the Framers were mere mortals, and the government structures they midwived were born with certain defects. The solution was obvious, resulting in the Twelfth Amendment, passed immediately, which required separate ballots for President and Vice President.

But the second defect, not so easily corrected, remains to this day. As originally conceived, the electors from each state would be a select body of wise, outstanding, and virtuous citizens willing to express their independent judgments. Thus, the Electoral College—in theory—was to serve as an independent body free of the supposed vices of popular majorities. But the election of 1800 shattered this elitist design, because already by then partisan politics had transformed the electors into agents of a political party, either the Federalists or Jefferson's Democratic-Republicans. Thus, the inevitable development of political parties and party loyalties "turned the elaborate machinery of the electoral college into little more than a way of counting votes"[32] cast by party loyalists.

In several crucial ways, then, the constitutional designs of the Framers never achieved their stated goals. Yet the Framers saddled future generations with their substantial miscues and malapportionments, and our nation has been paying the price ever since.

The Framers' Folly in the 21st Century

Dahl and others have identified several defects of the Electoral College as it has descended to us today. In a nation that believes that "the majority rules," our presidential election method utterly fails that test of democracy. For instance, in the 2000 presidential election, our peculiar presidential election method pitted the electoral vote against the popular vote, and by so doing confused and alienated an already disengaged public when they found out, as we did in Florida and in *Bush v. Gore*, that "we the people" don't even have a constitutional right to vote for the president. Ultimately, it turns out, it is completely up to the whim of the state legislatures to determine if a vote of the people or a vote of the legislators decides each states' electoral vote.

While such direct conflict between the electoral vote and the popular vote has occurred infrequently in our history, more commonly the presidential winner has failed to win a majority of popular votes. In fact, eighteen times—one out of three presidential contests—the United States has ended up with a winner who lacked a popular majority. Our last three presidential elections were won by candidates with less than a popular majority, as did Richard Nixon in 1968, and this trend may be accelerating. Far more states—75 percent—were won by a plurality in presidential elections in 1992–1996 than in any other two elections in the twentieth century.[33] That was because of the presence of third-party candidates who siphoned away votes from the two major party candidates, making this outcome more probable. Yet the third-party candidates rarely have enough votes to win for themselves any state's electoral votes—in 1992 Ross Perot, with 19 percent of the nationwide vote, failed to win a single Electoral College vote.

Today, forty-eight states allocate their electoral votes on a "Winner Take All by state" basis, meaning that the highest vote-getter in each state wins all electoral votes, even if they lack a majority of the popular vote (Maine and Nebraska allocate by congressional district, the candidate that wins the most votes in each congressional district winning one electoral vote per district). Like Winner Take All contests at the legislative level, the Winner Take All nature of each state's electoral contest overrewards winners and underrewards losers. Defenders of the Electoral College method insist that this Winner Take All padding provides the winner with a mandate to govern. But this is just another version of the Winner Take All gremlins of "artificial majority" and "phantom representation." The mandate won by the winner exists only by virtue of a kind of crude accounting trick. By having different ways of counting the numbers, by using a kind of funny math—presto!—the minority-supported winner ends up with a majority and a mandate. Such a ruse fails to satisfy, and is more transparent and alienating to the American public than its defenders realize.

For instance, the Center for Voting and Democracy sponsored a contest for youth ages sixteen to twenty-four that gave $1000 to the best answer to the question: "What changes in our electoral system would increase political participation by young people?" Nearly nine thousand entries from all fifty states weighed in on the subject, and one recurring theme was the shortcomings of the Electoral College. One typical essay, by Timothy J. Pearson, a high school student in Middleport, New York, read:

I can remember how surprised my U.S. History class was when we were taught about the Electoral College. We could hardly believe that many of the things that we believed to be undemocratic were used in our own presidential voting system. Learning about the Electoral College can be enough for most people to lose faith in presidential elections in this country. The drop in the number of young voters can be attributed to our lack of faith in the system that we are being asked to partake in.[34]

As we saw in Chapter 2, the "Winner Take All by state" Electoral College method employed for electing the President has tended to create a hodgepodge of a political map where candidates strategize their way to victory by winning the *right* states, without even thinking about winning a majority of the popular vote. This in turn has reduced the incentives of the presidential candidates to compete for votes in "safe" states that are clearly going to be won by the opposition, or to campaign in those safe states already in their own camp. As a consequence, it has increased the incentives of candidates to compete most heavily for voters in the handful of swing states, particularly the larger swing states like Florida, Michigan, and Pennsylvania, where so many electoral votes are up for grabs; conversely, locked-up states and smaller states receive hardly any attention. That means the issues that appeal to the narrow band of swing voters of these few large swing states will dominate presidential campaigns. And presidential elections will cease to be an occasion for mobilizing and engaging the greater national population in a political discussion about the future of our country or national policy, since most voters are neither swing voters nor live in swing states. Instead, most voters are left on the political sidelines, their issues and concerns unaddressed.

For all these reasons, as we saw in UnElection 2000, the majority does not necessarily rule in the most important election in our land.

The Ticking Time Bomb

The Electoral College and U.S. Senate are like ticking time bombs, waiting to explode. In our twenty-first century multiracial, multipartisan, and multicultural nation, the built-in representation quotas for low-population, conservative, and predominantly white states in both the Electoral College and the United States Senate point inevitably toward a constitutional and racial clash. The situation is very much like the British system in the eighteenth century, which became known as a "rotten borough" system because, in the absence of reapportionment, semi-abandoned rural towns continued to "elect" members of Parliament while newly burgeoning cities did not.[35] Similarly, European immigrants in crowded American cities during the nineteenth century were obstructed electorally by rural Anglo-Protestant "rotten boroughs" with sparse inhabitants who dominated malapportioned state legislatures.[36] Eventually the undemocratic nature of these statutory defects was uncovered and abolished.

But the "rotten-borough" U.S. Senate and Electoral College, and their malapportioned representation quotas for low-population states, remain largely unexamined, even as the inequality grows worse. Burgeoning Hispanic and Asian populations who tend to live in the largest states, as well as blacks also living in these states, will recognize how their votes are being diluted by the "rotten borough" of the Senate and Electoral College. With our nation evolving toward a multiracial amalgam without historical precedent, the Senate and presidency will continue to look like white rural America. Shifting demographics are colliding with antiquated, eighteenth-century, anti-democratic defects implanted into our constitutional institutions. Like I have said in other places in this book, almost sounding like a refrain: this is a demographic built to blow.

Looking ahead, the question is whether the Senate and our presidential election methods will enter the twentieth century sometime during the twenty-first. Most legislatures, not only in the U.S. but also around the world, base representation on population—that is, on some semblance of proportional representation, that a legislature should, in some fashion, represent and reflect "the people." This is a principle that many popular revolutions and struggles have fought and died for, wresting this sacred democratic principle from kings, dictators, and tyrants. It is a sound principle, and one that our American democracy proudly exported to the rest of the world, so many years ago. But in the United States, ironically, this principle still awaits fulfillment; today, it must be wrested from the special interests of low-population and predominantly conservative white states that benefit from the defective Senate and Electoral College established by the Framers.

Most alarmingly, given what is at stake, it will be very difficult to reform our antiquated practices. That is because the very states that benefit from this affirmative action essentially have veto power over constitutional amendments that require support from two-thirds of the Senate and three-fourths of the state legislatures. In addition, Article V of the U.S. Constitution says that individual states must give their *permission* to be deprived of equal representation in the Senate: "No State, without its Consent, shall be deprived of its equal suffrage in the Senate." And Article IV, Section 3, provides that no state can "be formed by the Junction of two or more States, or parts of States, without the Consent of the Legislatures of the States concerned as well as of the Congress." Not one, but two poison pill provisions, in addition to the difficulties of passing constitutional amendments.

It is deeply ironic—and more than a bit hypocritical—that those who oppose affirmative action based on race because of its alleged unfairness do not also suppose it based on low-population. It would seem that no one's special interest is more worthy of protection than one's own. If there is any hope, it is that the fundamental fairness of reform will carry the day, coupled with a bit of self-interest. There may be some convincing arguments for providing a representation subsidy for low-population rural areas—and perhaps our poorest citizens living in urban areas as well—but a subsidy that is less radical and less distorting of national majorities than what the Framers bequeathed to us. It would not be hard to work out a mathematical formula, based partly on population and partly on need, that could be reviewed every decade or two, providing fairer, more proportionate representation to all the various interests and constituencies than current methods. For instance, each state could be allocated two senators (like they have now) plus one additional senator for each 2 million in population. Using this formula, Wyoming still would have two senators, but California as our most populous state would have nineteen. California would still have less per capita representation than Wyoming, but the inequality would not be as severe as now. This would increase the size of the Senate, perhaps to 150, but that should not prove to be overly clumsy or onerous. The important thing to note is that such a solution will only be arrived at if *all* sides agree; which means it must come about through national dialogue, virtually none of which exists today.

And that dialogue will be difficult in the currently partisan and polarized climate. The close, rawboned margins in the U.S. Senate, U.S. House, presidential elections, the fifty state legislatures, for that matter in the Supreme Court, are not likely to resolve anytime soon. With the two sides so implacably coupled, nose to nose, eyeball to eyeball, winning margins will be decided by which side blinks first. Given the "all-or-nothing" quality of our Winner Take All system, that's not exactly the most fertile climate for national dialogue, and so the defective constitutional strictures of the U.S. Senate and Electoral College will continue to plague our closely divided, fractious, and alienated politics. Fasten your seat belts, because this is the shape of our political landscape as we plunge headlong into the twenty-first century.

PART THREE
The Death of Discourse

PART THREE
The Death of Discourse

CHAPTER EIGHT

Of Pollster-geists and Consultants
The Mad Science of Winner Take All Campaigns

> If I were a small-time congressional candidate looking for a con-
> sultant, I wouldn't hire one unless I had a metal detector and a
> polygraph on me. Frankly, I'm thinking of quitting and going into
> something legit—like dog track races.
> —MIKE MURPHY, POLITICAL CONSULTANT[1]

I f we could travel in a time machine back to colonial Virginia, where Washington, Jefferson, and Madison learned their politics, we would be struck
by at least this glaring political difference: elections were simple. An informal sounding of opinion among leading gentlemen of a community determined which of them should "stand"—no one "ran"—for office. Sociologist
Michael Schudson has written that "everyone knew that the reputation and
character of the candidates should be the basis for voting, not positions on
'issues.' When the white, property-owning males eligible to vote went to the
polls, they announced their choice to the sheriff before stepping over to the candidate they favored, who then may have offered a glass of rum punch."[2] Voting
was a quaint ritual that, for better or worse, reaffirmed the community's social
hierarchy. Naturally, white men lacking property, women, Indians, and slaves
were excluded from this transparent but elite process.[3]

Then, in the nineteenth century, Election Day belonged to political parties.
The advent of Jacksonian democracy observed by de Tocqueville was, depending on one's point of view, either a mess of political rabble and lumpenproletari-
at or a populist outpouring of the true democratic spirit. Despite warnings from
several of the Framers, including Washington and the younger Madison, against
the vices of parties and factions (although the older Madison later came to
embrace the role of political parties), political parties moved onto center stage,
organizing torchlight processions, pole raisings, and glee clubs to sing from the
party songbook. They hired burly men to rouse voters, bring them to the polls,
and distribute the party ticket—a printed form with the names of the party's
candidates. The voter had only to deposit the ticket in the ballot box, and partisan poll watchers could easily determine which party's ticket the voter held.
Simplicity defined, but lacking what we revere today as a secret ballot.[4]

In the late nineteenth and early twentieth centuries, political campaigns and
electioneering still retained a simple, down-home ambience. Historian Doris
Kearns Goodwin has written how, in the autumn of the 1896 presidential cam-

paign, 750,000 citizens converged on Canton, Ohio, where Republican presidential candidate William McKinley waited to receive them on his front porch. On McKinley's lawn, a handful of reporters gathered each day with pads and pencils to record his remarks for the stories they would send to their papers. "The atmosphere was relaxed, the pace was slow. McKinley never had to venture farther than his own front porch."[5]

As late as 1960, presidential campaigns were still relatively low-key, low-tech affairs. Veteran correspondent Jules Witcover wrote that

> in 1960, in my first exposure to a presidential primary campaign, I strolled down the Main Streets of small mining towns in West Virginia accompanying, with only three or four other reporters, Senator John F. Kennedy of Massachusetts as he canvassed for votes. He would pop into local stores, shake hands with storekeepers and customers, and somewhat deferentially identify himself as a candidate for the Democratic nomination, asking for their consideration on primary day.[6]

But late in that 1960 presidential campaign, something seminal happened that was to forever change political campaigns in the United States. Democratic candidate Kennedy debated Republican candidate Richard Nixon on national television. The first debate (out of three), watched by what was a huge audience, even by today's standards, of 60 million viewers, was decisive. Although listeners tuning in via *radio* considered the debate a draw or even slightly inclined in Nixon's favor, the TV camera showed something very different. While Kennedy appeared tanned and relaxed, Nixon looked pale. As Goodwin describes it, sweat appeared on Nixon's brow and cheeks, his facial muscles tensed as he answered questions, his lips seemed at times to form a disoriented smile completely unrelated to his words. To those who viewed the debate on television, Kennedy was the clear winner. "That night," *New York Times* columnist Russell Baker later wrote, "television replaced newspapers as the most important communications medium in American politics."[7]

As Goodwin has observed, rather self-evidently, "presidential campaigns are different now." In fact, political campaigns have changed perhaps more than any other single aspect of our Winner Take All politics, precisely because campaign technology—like all communications technology—has advanced so dramatically. And just as new redistricting computer technologies have changed that game, a toolbox of new campaign technologies is at the center of this transformation, lending itself in sinister ways to the "winner takes all, loser takes nothing" paradigm of our political system.

Now, people no longer come to the candidate's home, like they did in McKinley's day; instead, the candidate comes directly to the homes of the people—ubiquitously so—the candidate's face and message beamed into millions of living rooms, seemingly nonstop, whether we want to see him or her or not.

Political advertisements are plastered all over billboards, pre-recorded campaign messages harass our telephone answering machines, and gobs of targeted campaign mailers are dumped onto our doorsteps. But the invasive and ubiquitous nature of campaigns is not the only aspect that has changed.

Under Winner Take All's two-choice/two-party field, with the two warring sides so close in popularity (or unpopularity, as the case may be), and with so much to lose or win, every scintilla of opportunity and advantage is exploited. In a Winner Take All system where most races are completely noncompetitive, and where only a handful of swing voters and swing races will determine not only who wins and loses close elections but also perhaps the partisan majority of the Legislature—and where most pollsters and party leaders know in advance *which* races and voters these are likeliest to be—the game has come to be played differently. Oh so differently.

Meet Larry Preston Williams. Mr. Williams is a former police intelligence officer in New Orleans, now a private investigator. He makes his living by digging up dirt on people, particularly on political candidates. "There's not a garbage pail I won't get in, not an angle I won't aim a hidden camera," says Williams, who sends every statewide candidate in Louisiana an offer to dig up "white lies" and other information about their opponents. "I take cases from Republicans, Democrats, conservatives, liberals. It's all information."[8]

This kind of information is euphemistically called "opposition research." Feeding an almost insatiable bottom-feeder demand for negative information in today's world of bruising Winner Take All politics, the *New York Times* reported that private investigators are playing a larger—although mostly hidden—role in the public arena, digging up "opposition research" on everyone from regulators to elected national leaders to small-town officials.[9]

Probably no greater single factor defined the politics of the late 1980s and 1990s than the relentless drive in certain conservative quarters to dig up dirt on Democratic presidential candidates. In 1988, the Republican opposition research team, with over one hundred staffers and volunteers, worked around the clock and three shifts with a budget of $1.2 million to examine the life and career of Michael Dukakis. Republicans mounted an even more sophisticated $6 million opposition research effort in 1992 against Bill Clinton's past peccadilloes, with one bare-knuckle brawling opposition researcher declaring, "We're gonna strip the bark off the bastard."[10] Today, even candidates reluctant to get into the muck say they feel compelled to respond in kind. In a close race, digging up dirt about your opponent—whether salacious or simply a public record of untruthfulness or past indiscretion—can be so effective that many candidates today don't dare *not* do it, even if the information is painful and personal.[11]

Personal attacks have been part of political campaigns since before the Federalists and the Jeffersonians settled their slights with duels at ten paces.[12] But for most of this century unwritten rules kept opposition research within certain accepted bounds. It wasn't until 1988, when accusations of marital infidelity drove Gary Hart out of the race for President, that campaigns began snooping into nastier and more personal areas. Since then, professional investigators like Larry Preston Williams have replaced erstwhile amateurs such as a campaign worker or a moonlighting police officer who conducted rudimentary research.

"The number of cases has picked up in recent years," says Mr. Williams. "The aggressiveness has picked up. The willingness to use information publicly to simply obliterate the opposition forever has increased." Operating with little regulation or accountability, the detectives spy on opponents by posing as reporters or by sending in operatives who work as volunteers in the campaign. In a world where sensitive computer data can flow freely despite privacy laws, some routinely obtain protected information like phone records and medical histories. They track down ex-spouses and former associates and employees, often concealing the reason they are asking questions. They research a candidate's video rentals and dumpster-dive through trash from offices, campaign headquarters, and homes, looking for some tawdry bit of information that can be blown into a campaign "issue."

The series of events and investigations that culminated in the impeachment of President Clinton showed just how polarized and bitter the Winner Take All warfare can get. The "Sex Wars" sleaze reached some of its seediest and nuttiest moments during the impeachment debacle, when politics sunk to such a pathetically farcical level that Larry Flynt, publisher of smutty *Hustler* magazine, emerged as a key player in national politics. Flynt, having been recently lionized and bizarrely sanitized in a major motion picture as a defender of the First Amendment, went on a rampage against what he saw as conservative hypocrisy, spending his porn money and offering million-dollar bounties to "out" marital hypocrites and otherwise dig up sexual dirt on Republicans.[13]

With moral conservatives acting as a kind of sex police, proposing a virtual chastity belt for politicians—including that Congress members sign an oath proclaiming their marital fidelity[14]—it was only a matter of time before that backfired and the past peccadilloes of Capitol Hill Republicans also began surfacing. Revelations of past or current affairs by Clinton inquisitors Representatives Henry Hyde of Illinois, Dan Burton of Illinois, and Helen Chenoweth of Idaho, as well as two Speakers of the House, Newt Gingrich and his short-lived successor Bob Livingston of Louisiana, signaled the tenuous grip of the times. Carl Bernstein, the journalist of Watergate fame, aptly commented on CNN that America was experiencing "a moment of national madness."

For candidates wishing to defend themselves against the rapaciousness of opposition research, the challenge has given birth recently to its own bizarre antidote—hiring someone to investigate *yourself*. Called "vulnerability research," this latest trend is to contract with private investigators that are used defensively by candidates to identify dirt on themselves that opponents potentially could find, and then craft responses in advance. Richard Billmire, a vulnerability researcher in Virginia, assembles booklets for his clients that are designed to show just how bad the client can be made to look. Each page carries a bold headline like "Lacks Compassion" or "Hates Women," followed by a specific list of sins like "Consistently votes against reproductive rights" or "Voted to allow a proliferation of assault weapons." Some consultants even stage political crisis drills, posing as a reporter and calling a client's press secretary to confront the terrified staffer with a devastating accusation about the candidate, just to gauge the reaction.[15] While conservative opponents were busy prying into Clinton's sexual misadventures, the Clinton campaign paid private investigator Jack Palladino more than $100,000 in 1992 to probe into allegations and rumors of Clinton's *own* womanizing. Some two dozen women were targets of Palladino's damage-control inquiries.[16] Clinton's lawyers later hired investigators to dig up information on Paula Jones' sexual history.

With the "Sex Wars" and the "take no prisoners" tone of Winner Take All campaigns reaching banshee proportions, politicians everywhere now realize that no tidbit, however seamy or seemingly innocuous, is off-limits. Consequently, the 2000 campaigns were the first to seize on vulnerability studies. Defensive research of your own vulnerabilities has fast become an equally crucial component of running for office. One Democratic candidate involved in 2000 in a tight race for the U.S. Senate said, "It's not something I prefer spending money on. It is, unfortunately—because of the incredible negativism involved in politics today—just a necessity."[17]

The Winner Take All incentive

Yet such mudslinging, dumpster-diving, and attack campaigning are *exactly* what we should expect from our two-choice, Winner Take All system. It is Winner Take All taken to its logical trajectory. In a one-on-one campaign, the dynamic inescapably boils down to a zero-sum choice of "if you lose, I win": if support for your opponent declines, your chances rise. As we saw in Chapter 3's discussion of the Two-Party Tango, the process of "candidate definition" is much easier to do in a two-choice field because you can more easily strip-mine your opponent's record, highlighting certain positions and ignoring others to portray your opponent negatively, without any third candidate intervening with conflicting messages. The ideological space is relatively wide open and undefined in a two-choice field, leaving the candidates freer to transgress into each other's base of support by blurring certain policy and ideological lines. Winner Take All incentives lead to campaign sound bites that often substitute centrist *rhetoric* for actual centrist *policy*, reaching a point where even strong policy disagreements aren't discernable on the campaign trail. Consequently, the primary means to distinguish yourself from your opponent becomes the use of hack-attack politics—tearing down your opponent. The sight of our political leaders maliciously maligning and attacking each other and their policy proposals, particularly over what often seem like insignificant policy differences and details, can be maddening. But once the combatants are locked in a one-on-one, Winner Take All campaign in a close contest, the race to the bottom usually ensues due to the incentives of how you win elections in Winner Take All.

The zero-sum choice always has been a powerful incentive in any Winner Take All election, but now the new sophisticated campaign technologies have made these "divide and conquer strategies" so much more effective. Today campaigns are waged on the Internet, on the World Wide Web, and on twenty-four-hour TV, turning the lives of politicians into a kind of *Truman Show* fish bowl. Moreover, these technologies are *malignantly* suited for negative campaigning in a two-choice field. As we will explore in some detail in this chapter, the new computer technologies and forms of mass communication like polling, focus groups, thirty-second TV commercials, direct mail, and pre-recorded phone messages are uniquely equipped to allow ever more precise targeting of mudslinging and campaign spin to encourage turnout by some voters and discourage turnout by others, particularly of preselected constituencies of swing voters. Targeting in Winner Take All, consultant Matt Reese explains, "is a process of excluding people who are not 'profitable' to work."[18]

Much journalistic ink has been devoted in recent years to the degeneration of campaigns into mudslinging and scorch-the-earth sound bites. Yet there has been almost no analysis of how the peculiar incentives of the two-choice, Winner Take All system create this odious brand of sensationalist *Jerry Springer Show* politics. Campaigns provide serial opportunities for Winner Take All gaming, and curiously enough right there at the center of the game have been the mad scientists of Winner Take All campaigns, a peculiar species known today as "political consultant."

The Mad Scientists of Winner Take All Campaigns

Among the scalawags, tricksters, hustlers and sharks that inhabit the Earth, none is more devious than the species known as political consultants. And that is what their friends say about them.

—ROBERT GUNNISON, "CALIFORNIA INSIDER," SAN FRANCISCO CHRONICLE[19]

The role of the political consultant, and its celebrity practitioners like Carville, Morris, Rollins, Atwater, and others, has reached near-legendary status in the ramblings of the national punditry and in the national imagination. The number of political consultants has tripled in the last ten years, according to Political Resources, and their involvement in political campaigns, once confined to high-profile races, has spread infectiously to down-ballot races, ballot initiatives, and local elections.

Missing from all the commentary about the increasingly central role of political consultants, however, has been recognition of how consultants are precisely suited for the two-choice, Winner Take All game. The zero-sum of the Winner Take All conundrum inevitably devolves into a permanent negative campaign of partisan brinkmanship. In that milieu, consultants are experts at using modern campaign technologies like polling, focus groups, thirty-second TV spots, and direct mail to slice up the electorate into manageable bites, allowing the targeting of carefully crafted messages to the all-important swing voters and swing districts.

Political consultants have refined their craft of winning political campaigns to that of a cold, calculating quasi-science. In 1999, former President Gerald Ford bluntly characterized modern elections in an address to the Press Club as "candidates without ideas, hiring consultants without convictions, to run campaigns without content."[20] The Winner Take All game will be played much differently in the new millennium than ever before, and political consultants and their new technologies will be a major force driving the change.

But who exactly *are* these political consultants, waging these relentlessly negative, quasi-scientific games and campaigns? Upon reviewing the results of a recent survey of political consultants, we may discover that we don't want to know. The survey conducted by the Pew Research Center, the first ever conducted that solicited consultants' own attitudes, revealed the alarming *sociopathic* tendencies of these hired gunslingers. The survey found that the (mostly) men who run the nation's political campaigns were self-confident individuals who craved the "thrill" of a race, eagerly embraced scare tactics and negative advertising, but dismissed ethical questions as not their major worry. The problem with politics today is not them, they said—it's skeptical reporters, the public and, yes, their own clients, the candidates. Andrew Kohut, the director of the study which was appropriately entitled "Don't Blame Us," commented, "These are people who are really comfortable with what they do, irrespective of what other people are saying about them."[21] It is rather disquieting to think that such responsibility-avoiding imperviousness to what others think about you, or to whom you hurt with your tactics—the hallmark of your basic sociopathic personality—apparently is the psychological profile of the people who run Winner Take All campaigns.[22]

Under the gaming logic of Winner Take All, where the goal of winning is optimally secured by carving up the electorate, targeting your attack messages, and attracting swing voters, campaigns run by sociopathic political consultants who employ garbage pail snoopers like Larry Preston Williams make so much sense. These two characters—the Mad Scientist Political Consultant and the Garbage Pail Snooper—are quintessential figures of Winner Take All, two of the archetypes that define the very essence of the system, much like the faceless bureaucrat and the Soviet commissar defined the communist system. The internal logic of Winner Take All, following its path-of-least-resistance trajectory, makes the Mad Scientist Political Consultant and the Garbage Pail Snooper into inevitable players. It's not a matter of bad politicians, or sleazy consultants, or an onset of national moral decline; it's simply a matter of the *mechanics* of the Winner Take All system, of how that system *works*—or doesn't work, as the case may be.

The gaming incentives and disincentives of the two-choice system produce certain behavior and strategies; and those behavior/strategies replicate themselves in a Darwinian "survival of the fitness" fashion, a kind of political-cultural *meme,* with certain behavior/strategies proving successful, i.e. winning elections, and others proving to be failures.[23] These new technologies have become the steroids of politics—once one side is doing it and gains a competitive edge, you don't dare not do it. The new techniques and technologies are too powerful to ignore for candidates and party leaders salivating to win. And no amount of campaign finance reform or any other type of reform that leaves the Winner Take All system intact will be able to change this trajectory of our political landscape.

So when both sides are fully armed and ready for Winner Take All battle, we should not be surprised when things get extremely nasty. The 1998 U.S. Senator's race in New York between Democrat Charles Schumer and Republican incumbent Alfonse D'Amato was particularly instructive. Both sides, in an attempt to woo swing voters, dodged specific policy issues, selectively strip-mined each other's legislative voting record for the raw material of which negative campaigns are made, and resorted to a revolting brand of down-and-dirty, in-your-face campaigning.

So, according to the D'Amato campaign, Charles Schumer was soft on child pornographers, wanted less jail time for violent criminals, supported foreign aid for Mongolia, and was "a New York City liberal" who backed the three largest tax increases in American history. According to the Schumer campaign, D'Amato was a liar who cut Medicare, opposed federal funding for new police officers, raised property taxes, opposed a ban on *importing* child pornography, acted "just like a bully taking lunch money from hungry kids," and "doesn't really care about you or your family." New Yorkers experienced months of such vitriol, carpet-bombed into their living rooms via thirty-second TV spots.[24]

One D'Amato TV ad accused Schumer of being pro–tax increases, and used as proof a claim that Schumer cast the *deciding vote* for Clinton's tax increase (hint: the measure passed by one vote, leaving more than two hundred Democrats as well as a fair amount of Republicans vulnerable to this charge). Meanwhile, a pro-Schumer spot responded that he had voted to *cut taxes* for 2 million New York families (hint: by boosting the earned income tax credit). Ironically, both of these ads, one pro-Schumer the other anti-, drew their "facts" from Schumer's vote on the *same tax bill.* Each candidate highlighted what he wanted about Schumer's voting record on that bill to drive home their pro- or anti-tax message that polling and focus groups had told them would strike a chord with anti-tax swing voters.

D'Amato's accusation that Schumer was soft on child pornography stemmed from a 1977 measure in the New York state Assembly that was also opposed by libraries and publishers as too broad, and was supported by only 13 of 131 lawmakers. Schumer meanwhile got a lot of mileage out of D'Amato's vote against a 1994 crime bill that D'Amato claimed was laden with pork-barrel spending. Based on that vote, Schumer attacked D'Amato for opposing federal funding for 100,000 new police officers and for opposing a ban on importing child pornography, both of these provisions being part of the huge crime bill. Both candidates accused each other of lying about taxes, but in their eighteen-year careers both had voted for more than $250 billion in tax increases. While none of D'Amato's and Schumer's charges and countercharges were technically false, they were taken out of context and manipulated, misrepresenting procedural and other votes. Watching this kind of gaming, which amounted to little more than a political hazing, the *Washington Post*'s Howard Kurtz observed that "the most vituperative campaigns have turned into televised tennis matches" in which each contender lobs various charges at the other.[25]

Alienated voters and even politicians have expressed great alarm at the disquieting trajectory of our Wild West politics and our moments of "national madness." Yet these kinds of blood-lettings occur all over the country today during the "political hunting season." It is a despicable sight to watch, and a big turnoff to voters, but we should wholly expect this because of the gaming dynamics unleashed by the Winner Take All conundrum and the new campaign technologies in a two-choice race: "If I can drive voters away from you, the only candidate left is me."

Mutually Assured Destruction (MAD): the new weapons of (political) war

> Campaigns are like arms races. You didn't know you needed another battleship until the other country had one.
>
> —TREVOR POTTER, FORMER CHAIRMAN,
> FEDERAL ELECTIONS COMMISSION

The peculiar gaming incentives that arise under Winner Take All's two-choice, geographic-based system have given rise to a whole new tool box of ingenious campaigning technologies. These technologies allow the targeting of ever more precise slices of voters—most importantly, the crucial segment of swing voters. Keep in mind that swing voters tend to be those who are least informed or interested in politics, "best motivated by fear" and "30-second sound bites," and who "need to be convinced in eight words or less." Consequently, these technologies have been designed and adapted to identify these swing voters, and to identify the messages that will motivate them in a favorable direction, since whoever wins the swing voters wins the election in a close race. These campaigning technologies of polling, focus groups, dial-meter groups, push polls, pre-recorded messages, and thirty-second TV spots have reshaped dramatically the mise-en-scène of national politics, implanting themselves in the midst of our politics like so many weeds grabbing for the flower. Success breeds success, and so the cancer of Winner Take All campaigns spreads to the innocent and the unknowing, exacerbating tendencies toward political depression and national division.

Here is a rundown of some of the skills and tools that campaign practitioners utilize. Each tool, in its own way, reveals something disturbing about the trajectory of Winner Take All campaigns.

Polling

As Daniel S. Greenberg, editor of *Science and Government Report,* has written, "politics without polling has become as unthinkable as aviation without radar."[26] The techniques of polling were derived from the commercial and marketing sectors, and have resulted in politicians being marketed just like any other product that is up for sale. Today, "consumer testing" tells us what colors and shapes are most appealing, what slogan has the greatest believability, what images get a rise. Toothpaste and cars, Al Gore or George Bush—the selling process is identical.

The fully loaded campaign uses different types of polls with names like "benchmark survey," "trend survey," "dial meter analysis," and "tracking polls," all with slightly different techniques and uses that help candidates to form their campaign plan and their campaign message and then chart the progress of the message and the candidate throughout the campaign.[27] It is not unusual for telephones to ring in Michigan or Florida, with questions being read to respondents by interviewers in Kentucky or Iowa who are working from scripts prepared by a polling firm in California. The cutting edge of the polling profession is *instant information*. With current telephone and survey technology, polling data collected at 10 P.M. one night can be analyzed and delivered to the campaign the next morning.[28] With overnight information, a campaign can make quick decisions about advertising and about where to spend precious last-minute dollars, and can determine which ads, especially negative ads used against them, are working. Tracking via polls is so important that the Tarrance Group, a GOP polling firm, stays open twenty-four hours a day for the last six weeks of the campaign cycle, a kind of 7-Eleven convenience-store polling.[29]

Polling, however, despite what its boosters say, is still an inexact science, and results can vary widely. Besides completely missing the mark in calling the Florida vote for Al Gore originally, causing unnecessary national confusion and deserved embarrassment to the polling profession, who can forget the "poller-coaster" of the ubiquitous tracking polls throughout the 2000 presidential election? They swung wildly from week to week during the months of September and October, with first Gore up by ten points, then Bush, then back to Gore. According to the polling industry's own data, eight of the ten national polling organizations called the final national popular vote incorrectly, failing to accurately project Gore's popular vote victory. Only CBS News and Zogby/Reuters showed Gore beating Bush in the national popular vote, while the Harris poll had the race tied. The other seven – including Gallup/CNN/*USA Today*, ABC News/*Washington Post*, and NBC News/*Wall Street Journal*—had Bush winning the popular vote, with Battleground/Voter.com tallying a 5 percentage point Bush rout.

Nevertheless, the National Council on Public Polls, an industry trade group, released a post-election study that concluded, quite astonishingly, that the election polls of 2000 were among the most *accurate* of the last forty years. But as syndicated columnist Arianna Huffington tartly commented, "You'd think an 80 percent inaccuracy rate would be a source of great embarrassment, shame and regret. But apparently you've never dealt with pollsters—they can explain everything away with that *deus ex machina*, the margin of error. . . . This pretty much sums up the state of polling: 20-percent accuracy puts you in the Hall of Fame."[30]

Despite such a spotty record, polling has become the *sine qua non* of political campaigns—many politicians today don't make a move without first running it up the flag pole of public opinion and seeing how it flies. This new wave in politics can reach ridiculous dimensions. Bill Clinton took to polling like Barney takes to purple. He ran poll after poll to test policies, sound bites, and opponents. Clinton even polled which vacation spots would be politically popular. Tracking polls told the Clinton White House that Attorney General Janet Reno would be a credible voice after the Branch Davidian disaster in 1993, and later told Clinton policy makers that most Americans would support bombing of Iraq.[31] Clinton "polls as often as he breathes," observed his consultant Dick Morris.[32] Every State of the Union speech, every presidential address, and every major campaign announcement was pretested, topics were emphasized or disregarded, words and phrases were used or avoided, depending on what the polls said. Bill Clinton felt your pain "because he actually knew what your pain was."[33] Clinton embraced this technology as a means to figure out what people wanted to be told—and then he told it to them.

Focus groups

While opinion polls are used to measure *what* the public feels and *who* feels it, GOP political consultant Frank Luntz tells us that "focus groups are best used to explain 'why' the public feels the way it does. A properly constructed and administered focus group will draw out the 'motivational factors'" behind opinions, which is "critical to understanding what is driving public opinion," particularly among swing voters.[34] Focus groups are primarily concerned with *understanding* attitudes more than *measuring* them. Willing participants, usually anywhere from ten to fifteen people, are carefully selected to represent a typical swing voter demographic. Then they are stuffed into a room for several hours where they might watch a candidate's newly produced television commercials, followed by a barrage of open-ended questions about what they have seen. The goal of the moderator is to discover as much as possible about this particular swing voter audiences' attitudes, fears, and reactions to the TV spots before they actually air them.[35]

The focus group moderator works from a carefully prepared script, drawing out responses from participants in a variety of ways.[36] Questions first start with general and contextual concerns: in your everyday lives, what are you worried about, what are your big concerns in life? The entire session is video- and audiotaped for later review and analysis by the experts, almost a kind of "political group therapy" designed to unearth what makes this particular slice of swing voters tick. The next stage tests levels of political and issue awareness, probing levels of general knowledge about officeholders and issues. The following stage tests "image" information, by showing participants a campaign advertisement or a news clip of some relevant event and asking them to discuss it. The next stage solicits the participants' appraisal of the job performance of the incumbent or challenger candidate. Always the moderator is probing the participants, prodding for reactions and political reflexes from them like they are mice in a laboratory.

The final stage typically uses a set of what-if scenarios, presenting participants with a variety of hypotheticals that fit into the overall message and campaign strategies of the candidates. The skillful moderator elicits from them the details on their inchoate mumblings and half-baked thoughts. Participants are asked to comment on certain words or phrases in candidate speeches, or perhaps potential wording of referendum ballots or policy statements, their reactions carefully observed and gauged—again, not unlike lab rats—for meaningful information.

Luntz says that scientific studies completed in the past decade using focus group methodology have proven that "how it is said" and "what is heard" is more important than "what is said." For example, focus groups have alerted media consultants to the importance of "auditory stimuli" (that is, background music and sounds) to increase attention, recall, and persuasiveness.[37] The goal in any advertising effort is to activate "mental imagery"—the powerful and indelible mental images that the messages etch into consumer minds. In this way, it is believed that focus group research adds a qualitative dimension that cannot be matched by traditional polling methods.

But a little alarm bell goes off when the consultant "how-to" primer says that "focus groups most often are segregated by gender and by race." There is com-

mon agreement among practitioners that, if you want to find out what participants *really* feel, it is essential to get them to drop their guard, and "homogene-
ity appears to allow for a freer conversation." Frank Luntz writes, "Human
behavioral studies have consistently proven that people will reveal their inner-
most thoughts only to those they believe share a common bond. For example, if
your goal is to study the real, in-depth feelings of whites and blacks toward affirmative action, welfare, or crime, you cannot have an integrated focus group.
Similarly, women will not talk freely and emotionally about abortion if men
(including a male moderator) are present. This is just a fact of life."[38] The goal
then, is to foster a collective environment where participants will feel as unin-
hibited in a group of people as they are in the privacy of their own minds or in
the voting booth. That's when we find out what people *really* think.

Focus groups burst like a supernova on the political scene during the 1988
presidential campaign. A series of focus groups are credited with saving George
H. W. Bush's faltering presidential campaign and with giving the nation the
unseemly gift of the infamous Willie Horton ads. Michael Dukakis was sixteen
points ahead in the polls around Memorial Day and the Bush camp was panick-
ing. Lee Atwater, Bush's campaign strategist, conducted focus groups around
the country in swing states and districts. One such area was northern New Jersey, Paramus to be exact, where two sessions were held with conservative
Democrats who had supported Reagan in 1984 but were leaning toward
Dukakis. The moderator asked questions about Dukakis: what do you think if
Dukakis opposed capital punishment? If he vetoed legislation as governor that
would allow teachers to lead the pledge of allegiance in classrooms? If he permitted murderers to have weekend passes from prison?

The reactions were strong and fierce. According to Bush campaign pollster
Fred Steeper, "majorities favoring Dukakis became majorities opposing and, he
was fingered as a liberal." Lee Atwater concluded, "I realized right there that we
had the wherewithal to win . . . and that the sky was the limit on Dukakis' nega-
tives."[39] Bush was shown the videotapes of the Paramus focus groups and given
a choice by Atwater: attack Dukakis now, or attack him later. Bush chose now,
and one of the ugliest presidential media campaigns in modern political history
soon was under way. Willie Horton became a national icon as the campaign targeted swing voters like Reagan Democrats with the charge that Dukakis was a
liberal who was soft on black crime.[40] Frank Luntz writes that the Paramus
focus group "has reached legendary stature, and deservedly so, for that single
gathering may have changed American history."

To a certain degree, focus groups can be credited with the GOP takeover of
the Congress in 1994. As former consultant now professor Dennis Johnson
reports, it is not widely known that Newt Gingrich and the House Republicans'
ten-point "Contract with America" was fashioned using focus groups. Republican pollster Ed Goeas conducted three focus groups showing participants eight

television ads that had been prepared. Words and phrases were tested in the focus groups and later by Luntz. According to Dennis Johnson, who interviewed Goeas, the word *contract* in "Contract with America" came from observations of focus group participants. The term *empowerment* was scrapped because participants did not understand it and was replaced with the phrase *individual choice*. The term *citizen legislator* was used to explain the concept of term limits, and even the word *Republican* was avoided because of negative reaction from focus group participants.[41] It turns out that the Republicans, who prided themselves on being the "party of principle," derived at least some of their principles via the tools of expediency. Like Clinton, they figured out what key groups of voters wanted to hear, and then repackaged it and gave it back to them.

In a very real sense, focus group participants willingly cooperate in a process that will be used *against* them and their fellow citizens, as the mad scientist consultants and pollster-geists scientifically craft messages that will be *aimed back* to the public. The laboratory mice, in a sense, have become willing subjects, somnambularly submitting to the experimenter's shocks as the practitioners scientifically dissect them in an effort to figure out what spin, what pack of "lies,"[42] will motivate people just like them and win elections. And the politicians, supposedly the leaders of our nation, have redefined leadership to mean that they spend a lot of money finding out what specific words, phrases, and images get a rise out of people—and then regurgitating it back to them.

Dial meter groups

If focus groups are the barometer of what gets people hot and why, then dial meter groups—also called *electronic* focus groups, instant-reaction meter groups, or people-meter groups—are their Orwellian apotheosis. The participants in dial meter groups are carefully selected to meet certain demographic and political criteria. They often sit in an auditorium, watch videotape or television, speeches or commercials, and critique what they see.

But now each participant holds a "perception analyzer," essentially a dial that can be moved left to right, from 0 to 100, with 50 as the starting point; if a participant agrees wholeheartedly with what is said or seen on the television screen, she or he moves the dial toward 100; with total disagreement, the dial is moved down to zero. Each dial meter is hooked up to a computer that instantly graphs the responses of the participants, displaying their collective reactions, showing spikes of approval or flat lines of disinterest and boredom. Several test sites can be linked together to a central computer, recording the reactions of participants in, for example, Seattle, Dallas, Denver, Buffalo, and Atlanta instantaneously. A presidential campaign can find out from dial meter sites across the country which phrases are instigating a reaction from the laboratory mice, i.e. voters, and which are falling flat.

Dial meter groups now are a standard feature in virtually every presidential and statewide race, and are moving broadly into ballot initiatives and other races. Analysis from dial meter groups is far less subtle and more crude—yes or no, up or down—than that of traditional focus groups, but it has the advantage of *instantaneous* reaction from a far broader audience.

At the 1996 Republican National Convention, in a cavernous hideaway room beneath the convention floor unbeknown to the swarming faithful delegates above or the media covering the convention, campaign operatives carefully monitored the reactions of dial meter groups. A bank of computers tracked viewers' reactions to the speeches of Colin Powell, Nancy Reagan's tribute to her ailing husband, Elizabeth Dole's talk-show-friendly stroll among the delegates, and Bob Dole's acceptance speech. The computers tracked the reactions of participants in electronic focus groups in Atlanta and Denver, participants watching the televised speeches and cranking their dials. Words and phrases were carefully monitored to see which caught the imagination and reaction of the individual participants.[43]

It's a bizarre and frightening spectacle, this notion of wired humans cooperating in the fashioning of campaign missiles that will be aimed right back at them. It is a kind of Orwellian group-think that is being expertly crafted and staged to induce maximum emotional peaks from viewers, trying to attain a kind of visceral script that will prod and poke them. This, tragically, appears to be the trajectory of our Winner Take All campaigns, particularly in the gaming environment that seeks to manipulate and exploit idiosyncrasies of the two-choice, geographic-based system.

The 30-Second TV Spot

Thirty seconds. Think about it. What can you really say in only thirty seconds? The answer is: not much, and certainly not much of substance. Why then, has the thirty-second spot become the dominant form of political communication in America? The answer is disturbing, and it reflects another deficit of Winner Take All in the modern era: in a two-choice system, where you're carving up the electorate in such a way as to attract the most uncommitted, uninformed, muddle-headed swing voters, politics no longer requires either discourse or substance. All it requires is *image*. And for that, the thirty-second spot is the most potent vehicle.

Ronald Reagan's team was perhaps the first to perfect this twisted art form. In 1984, CBS News correspondent Lesley Stahl put together a story for the evening news on the "orchestration of television coverage" in the Reagan campaign. While the piece showed images of Reagan handing out medals to handicapped athletes and cutting the ribbon on a new nursing home, surrounded by the American flag and by cheering crowds, the voice-over pointed out that the Reagan administration had consistently cut budgets for the disabled and for nursing home construction. Stahl worried that her piece was so tough on Reagan that she might be frozen out of the White House. But after it ran, Reagan aide Richard Darman called her and complimented her on a great story. "Didn't you hear what I said?" a perplexed Stahl asked. Darman replied: "Nobody heard what you said. You guys in television-land haven't figured it out, have you? When the pictures are powerful and emotional, they override if not completely drown out the sound. Lesley, I mean it, nobody heard you."[44]

Thus, the thirty-second television spot is the tool of cynicism. It is the triumph of image over words, even over ideas. And it dominates our two-choice, Winner Take All politics today by constructing powerful images designed to attract swing voters with precise campaign messages that have been devised using polling and focus groups. In a Winner Take All, two-choice field, the thirty-second spot is perfectly suited for gaming the system via hack-attack campaigning.

"Negative information travels farther than positive information," says Michael Murphy, a Republican consultant. "What's really happened is that some campaigns have started to really lie on television, and they get away with it. There really is very little consequence, it seems, for highly misleading TV ads. There is no cop out there. It's the Wild West. That's disturbing."[45]

Clinton took the tool of the thirty-second TV spot that Reagan had used so effectively and added a new twist: nearly a year and a half before his 1996 reelection, he unleashed a *seventeen-month* barrage of commercials attempting to define, early on, the issues and the race. He spent freely (a record $18 million of soft money in TV advertising in 1995 alone), and he spent strategically.[46] Clinton's ads helped to redefine him in the eyes of the narrow segment of the public without which, his consultant and pollster Dick Morris and Mark Penn had determined, he could not win reelection (Morris and Penn also had identified those voters staunchly in his camp whom Clinton could safely ignore).

So instead of a broad-based campaign that might woo all Democratic voters, Clinton tailored himself and his message to appeal directly to the voters he needed. In forty strategically targeted television markets mostly in the Midwest and California, the Clinton campaign hammered home its message. First, the Dole campaign was linked whenever possible with the unpopular Newt Gingrich. Second, Clinton jettisoned any old-school Democratic language that smacked of class warfare, as in "the rich Republicans against the middle-class Democrats." Indeed, Clinton's advertising stressed duties and values, school uniforms and V-chips for TV sets, even when talking about traditional Democratic Party issues such as Medicare. Voters living in the targeted areas saw thousands of thirty-second spots; voters in Chicago, Boston, Minneapolis, Baltimore, and New York, which were in locked-up states and therefore outside the targeted areas, probably wondered if an election were happening. Dennis Johnson noted that "no other presidential campaign had spent so much money in a sustained effort . . . this far in advance of election day." According to political scientist Steven Schier, since Clinton's 1996 reelection campaign the new campaign and targeting technologies have dominated American political life—policy making as well as campaigns—as never before.

Furthermore, today with sophisticated digital technology any image can be manipulated. Digital image enhancing of candidates can provide makeovers that nature never could, including weight loss, adding hair, adding healthy facial coloring or rosy cheeks—anything is possible. Also, unflattering shots of opponents can be touched up, shown in grainy black and white, shown with scowls, eye bags, and goofy looks. With digital technology now widely available, there will be great temptation to alter reality in search of the potent image, the thirty-second spot, that corners your opponent and nails down your swing voters. A study from the 1996 presidential campaign found that 28 percent of the 188 commercials examined contained questionable use of technology: news conferences that were never held, debates that never took place, use of audio or video tricks to stereotype or ridicule opponents—more games and tricks in the Winner Take All funhouse of mirrors.[47]

Targeted direct mail and pre-recorded phone messages

So much of the new technologies are about targeting your message, and direct mail and phone messages are the most effective and precise ways to do this. Targeted direct mail and telemarketing can send out specific messages to a variety of select audiences, with each message tailored to that constituencies' interests: thirty-five-year-old, pink-collar female voters; white, high school graduated male independent voters; northeastern Pennsylvania members of the National Rifle Association; conservative Democratic homeowners in western San Francisco's Sunset district. The possibilities are endless, limited only by your access to mailing lists and demographic data. U.S. Census Bureau data offer a wealth of information based on census blocks of approximately eight hundred households each, measuring between thirty and fifty economic, family, ethnic, employment, and neighborhood characteristics. This information, coupled with voting data and geodemographic information integrated into nine-digit ZIP codes, gives a mind-boggling amount of information for targeting purposes.

One mailing list firm—appropriately enough called I Rent America—advertises some 220 million names on computer lists.[48] Clients can read the names of the 266,302 active donors to Handgun Control, the 154,551 alumni of Outward Bound, the 338,424 American millionaires (or the 14,632 multimillionaires), the 748,213 persons over age sixty-five living in Illinois, or the 345,895 subscribers to *Vegetarian Times* magazine.[49] One mailing list management firm, catering to pro-life, conservative candidates and causes, includes the following among thirty-five lists available: Born Again Doctors Who Vote, Check Writing Evangelical Activists, Texas Christian Activists, and California Evangelical Political Givers. Another mailing list company rents a list entitled America's

High Income Donors, including Conservative Wealthy Arts Donors, Spanish-Speaking Donors, and Cream of the Crop Jewish Donors.⁵⁰ Previously, targeting techniques sorted the 36,000 ZIP codes into forty "lifestyle clusters" given clever names like Furs and Station Wagons, Golden Ponds, and Norma Rae-Ville. We are talking *extreme* targeting.

The net result is that, instead of a single campaign with one overriding theme that unifies a candidate's supporters, parallel campaigns emerge, each articulating themes narrow enough to appeal to the peculiar characteristics of each sub-constituency. And so the candidate ends up standing for practically nothing. In one California Assembly campaign, for example, married Catholic homeowners learned that the candidate supported *family values*, while single Jewish women under age forty found the same candidate had been consistently *pro-choice*.⁵¹ This mirrors the political variant of niche marketing found throughout the American economy. Virtually every citizen has been sliced, diced, and categorized into some demographic category, or an overlap of various categories, based on previous purchases and consumption patterns, voting patterns, U.S. Census Data, and residential demographics.

Aristotle Publishing maintains a voter database of all 138 million registered U.S. voters. Campaigns can purchase access to the names, addresses, and phone numbers of every registered voter in a geographic-legislative district and, using CD-ROM software, can select and sort registered voters by party, vote history, age, district, and twenty-five other criteria. An advertisement on the World Wide Web for new sophisticated computer software called GeoVoter brags that it can "graphically pinpoint the people you need to reach for every aspect of your campaign, from voters to contributors to volunteers." A typical ad for GeoVoter reads: "When people say the NRA has an unfair political advantage, they're absolutely right. The NRA has GeoVoter!" GeoVoter lets you run virtual elections, analyzing the effects of unlimited "what if" scenarios on any segment of the voting population, and allows you to use vast amounts of data to sort desirable from undesirable voters—right down to the individual household level. The cost of the software for a single congressional campaign is $6,900. Brags GeoVoter: "Give Yourself The *Unfair* Political Advantage!"⁵²

The most recent innovations use statistical analysis and predictive technologies to aid in targeting voters. One firm created a statistical technology called CHAID (Chi-Square Automatic Interaction Detection), which analyzes how different variables may predict voting behavior. The CHAID program builds "trees" of voters contacted, dividing up voters into branches of Democrats, Republicans, and Independents, then sub-branches like education levels, percentage of children in the neighborhood, ethnicity, and many other variables. In one 1996 Senate campaign in Oregon, the CHAID software was able to probe down the targeting tree and discover that "younger Independents who lived in neighborhoods with less education and many children" were undecided voters at a rate nearly double that of the Independent group as a whole.[53] Such targeting, like all the new campaign technologies, is as expensive as it is sophisticated, and the technologies give a huge leg up on the competition to the campaigns and candidates that can afford them.

Usually these targeting techniques are used to contact supporters, either to raise money or to ask for their vote. But not always. Sometimes they are used to drive *down* participation, especially among the opponent's supporters. For instance, the Jesse Helms Reelection Campaign in 1990 and the North Carolina Republican Party illegally violated the civil rights of the state's African American voters by mailing 125,000 postcards to registered voters in eighty-six predominantly black precincts informing them that *they were not eligible to vote.* Furthermore, the postcard warned them, quite outrageously, that they could face criminal prosecution if they tried to vote. These voters would have voted in large numbers for Helms' opponent Harvey Gantt, who was African American. The campaign maintained that it had no knowledge of the mailings, but accepted responsibility and agreed to pay a $25,000 fine for violations of federal election laws. But for the Helms campaign, which spent millions of dollars on reelection, the fine was just another campaign expense, and not even a very large one, on its way to gaming the system to win six more years in the Senate.[54]

Push-polling

Perhaps the most effective gaming technique for maligning your opponent is really a stealth campaign, and it probably trumps all others for sneakiness and underhandedness. It is called push-polling, and it is used in the waning hours of a campaign as one final attempt to spread negative information about your opponent and suppress turnout among wavering voters likely to vote for your opponent. Under the guise of a legitimate poll being conducted by official-sounding organizations like the "National Research Council" or "National Market Research," telephone callers feed damaging or misleading information about a candidate to the person answering the telephone. These surveys are not conducted to *measure* public opinion, but to *influence* it.

In Colorado in 1994, a push-poll designed to hurt the campaign of Governor Roy Romer asked leading questions like, would you be more or less likely to support Romer if you knew "there have been nearly 1,300 murders in Colorado since Romer was elected and not one murderer has been put to death?" Or, would you vote for Romer if you knew that the state parole board had "granted early release to an average of four convicted felons per day, every day since Romer has been governor?" Push-polling hones in on an opponent's record, strip-mining it and often distorting or exaggerating it.

During the 1996 presidential primaries Bob Dole's presidential campaign paid over $1 million to a telemarketing and phone bank firm to run a push-poll against GOP opponent Steve Forbes. In Iowa, an estimated ten thousand to thirty thousand anti-Forbes calls were made to Iowa farmers by a phone bank operation located in a strip mall in another state. The caller, supposedly calling with a message from "Iowa's farm families," relayed the information that "Iowa's farm bureau" had adopted a resolution opposing Steve Forbes' flat tax. Yet the real Iowa Farm Bureau never passed such a resolution, and the callers never revealed that they were working on behalf of Dole's campaign, not a non-existent group called Iowa Farm Families.[55]

As Robert Dreyfuss has written, what's important about such voter suppression efforts is that they combine the power of negative advertising commonly used on television and radio—with its proven ability to erode support for the candidate under attack—with the power of personalized and precisely targeted voter contact, often connecting with hot-button issues that move small but important segments of the electorate. Instead of GOTV for "Get out the Vote," Dreyfuss calls it SOTV, for "Stamp Out the Vote," since you are trying to suppress turnout among swing voters most likely to vote for your opponent.[56] Voter suppression operations like these are hard to detect and almost impossible to prevent. As one consultant has said, vote suppression campaigns "come in with the fog in the last couple of days and then disappear."[57] Media consultant Bill Hillsman, who created Jesse Ventura's and Paul Wellstone's TV ads for their successful runs for governor and U.S. Senator from Minnesota, calls push-polling "basically lying."

The future of targeting and campaigning technology

As television merges with the World Wide Web, newer technologies will make it possible to target television ads the way consultants now target direct mail and pre-recorded phone messages. The prospect of these two powerful campaign techniques merging is chilling. Web TV will be able to deliver to you—and to other viewers like you—television ads that are specifically groomed to your interests and tastes. Political campaigns will be able to do this as well. Consultants and media specialists will spin precise messages to targeted voters, just like they do now with direct mail and phone messages, except the messages will be delivered using the more powerful, multisensory medium of television. We will see a proliferation of Web TV ads beamed at us in the comfort of our living rooms, targeted at specific demographics and dumped on our "cyber doorsteps," much the way political mailers are dumped on our doorsteps now. Campaigns of the future will be able to send out daily doses of spam, the electronic equivalent of political junk mail, to targeted audiences, but with 3-D pictures, sound, and interactive capabilities.

Polling also is due for a makeover, particularly as more and more people, constantly harangued by telemarketers during their evenings and on weekends, hang up the telephone or don't answer at all. To get a more responsive sample, a Silicon Valley start-up initiated by two Stanford University political scientists-turned-entrepreneurs raised $42 million in venture capital to create a *permanent panel* of 100,000 people in 40,000 households from all fifty states and the District of Columbia, representative of the entire population. These "volunteers" have been given a free $249 WebTV box made by Microsoft that connects to the television and free Internet service valued at $25 per month. The company also offers occasional drawings for cash and other prizes. In return, the participants respond to Web surveys about their preferences for the four Cs—cars, clothing, computers, and candidates. By doing this, this company can guarantee a response rate twice as high as traditional methods of polling. They also use "metering" software to track where panel members go on the Internet, what they watch on TV, and what they buy at the supermarket.

"We are going beyond surveys to get information on people who are a microcosm of the country," said one of the political scientists. One of his large clients, CBS, hired his firm for instant polling of TV viewers' responses to President Clinton's last State of the Union address, the final episode of *Survivor*, and the three presidential debates in October 2000. CBS used this firm's newly developed "Public Pulse" technology to instantly gauge how 493 viewers of the debates felt about the candidates *at the very moment* the candidates answered questions, interrupted each other, or used certain words or phrases. The participants reacted positively or negatively, simply by moving the right and left arrows on their remote-control devices. CBS discovered that independent i.e. swing voters, reacted positively when Bush talked about morality and education. They liked what Gore had to say on the economy and healthcare, and they disliked personal attacks.

It was the height of irony, however, when, following the debates, one of the inventors of this new technology commented that presidential campaigning in the 2000 election seemed "very scripted."[58] Even the gamesters at times recoil from the artificiality and lethargy that result from their gaming.

"Simulated responsiveness" and "crafted talk"

Such "brave new world" technology will further isolate us into our own partisan ghettos, magnifying monomania and monoculture and contributing to national division. But that is the trajectory, the tragic logic, of Winner Take All—target, target, target, game, game, game. These technologies are hugely expensive to employ, and more than any other single factor are responsible for the escalating costs of running for office, particularly in close and high-profile races. A political candidate is at the center of a huge dramatic opera, yet she or he often knows the least about what is going on behind the scenes where the professionals are pulling the strings. To reach their goal of winning, Winner Take All candidates must rely on the mad scientist consultants, the pollster-geists, the garbage pail snoopers, and their Orwellian laboratory of tricks. The candidate only knows their lines, and come November they will know the thrill of victory or the agony of defeat.

But most disturbing perhaps is the Machiavellian ends to which these new campaign technologies are applied. There have been some pundits and politicos who have made the claim that, while the growing influence of the new campaign technologies has increased pandering by politicians, on a positive note the new technologies also have increased politicians' *responsiveness* to the public—pandering, after all, is a form of responsiveness, is it not? With polling and focus groups, politicians can more accurately discover the wishes and desires of the public and can strive to meet that need; at least that is what some claim, especially pollsters and consultants. But political scientists Lawrence Jacobs and Robert Shapiro, in their recent book *Politicians Don't Pander*, have largely debunked this notion.

Jacobs and Shapiro collected an impressive body of documentation to show that, while politicians rely heavily on the new campaign technologies and therefore appear pseudoresponsive, in fact they use those technologies not so much to pander (except around election time) but instead to *hoodwink* voters—to find words and phrases to manipulate and mislead them. This "crafted talk," as the researchers called it, is designed to "simulate responsiveness"—to deceive voters about the politician's true intentions and policies and to free themselves to pursue their own partisan agendas that the majority of voters would reject if they were clearer about what the politicians actually were up to.[59] In other words, politicians are busy with their own agendas that have little to do with what the majority of voters want, and use the "crafted talk" and "simulated responsiveness" to sell their agendas like a used car salesman trying to foist a lemon onto a customer.

Jesse Ventura's media consultant Bill Hillsman, characteristically blunt, says, "Candidates are parroting back to voters what polls say voters want to hear." It is politics reduced to the type of niche marketing found throughout the American economy. Indeed, McCampaigns have become little more than sales pitches and advertising jingles, using "crafted talk" and "simulated responsiveness" to sell political products *and* to mask the true quality of those products. Such a sinister dynamic becomes all the more possible under Winner Take All's two-choice/two-party system, where each side can position themselves vis-à-vis their lone opponent, strip-mining their opponent's record for the fodder of which political campaigns are constructed today.

The immediate and long-term outlook for Winner Take All campaigns is troubling, since the internal logic of the system will continue to exacerbate existing tendencies. Consultants, pollsters, and politicians know too much about how to use these steroidal technologies, and how effective they can be in a two-choice, Winner Take All system to fashion "crafted talk" and "simulated responsiveness" in order to win elections. The uniquely malignant incentives of Winner Take All, unfortunately, are powering this hellbound trajectory of political campaigns.

Winner Take All: making most people losers

While we can be impressed by the cleverness of the technologists and practitioners who have developed these advanced methods, we can't help but also feel mortified by their impacts. Winner Take All campaigning with the new technologies is contributing to an alarming erosion of political discourse and representative democracy in numerous ways. Besides those already discussed, the following are additional impacts of Winner Take All campaigning.

Decline in voter turnout and activism

The new campaign methods and gaming techniques undermine and bias voter turnout by failing to communicate with all but the most *likely* voters. Says Ron Faucheux, the publisher and editor of *Campaigns & Elections*, a magazine for political consultants, "It's not unusual for campaigns to concentrate on as little as 5 percent of voters."[60] This denies all other voters the information and motivation they need in order to *get interested* and participate—particularly voters at the lower end of the socioeconomic spectrum. Not surprisingly, in late October of Election 2000 undecided voters disproportionately included minorities, younger voters, and those with lower incomes and less education. Since so few of the message missiles of both the Bush and Gore campaigns were targeted at them, these undecided voters said they "saw little difference between Bush and Gore" and that they didn't "believe the election will have much impact on their lives."[61]

Studies like those of political scientist Ray Wolfinger have verified that people are most likely to respond to other people, yet the new campaign technologies turn campaigns into aerial media wars, with little personal contact on the ground. Without that contact, voter response and motivation have significantly declined.[62] Consequently, Winner Take All campaigning is contributing to the decline in voter turnout and political activism.

Inhibiting the formation of political opinion

The new technologies and diminished voter contact have produced a "dumbing down" of politics in recent years and have inhibited the formation of political opinion. One poll by the Vanishing Voter Project showed that in the closing days of Election 2000, there was only one policy position—Al Gore's stand on prescription drugs—that half or more of the respondents could accurately identify as a candidate's stand. Seventy-five percent said candidates "will say almost anything to get themselves elected."[63] Michael Murphy, a GOP consultant, says, "I think voters are highly intelligent, but we have trained them to act a little irresponsibly. We tell them what they want to hear, [so] they vote for it. . . . We take polls and find out that if we offer them chocolate ice cream, then they say they're for chocolate ice cream. So we only run on chocolate ice cream."[64] It is a vicious cycle, and unfortunately in the process we are losing political *ideas*, which are vital to our collective future.

Weakening of civil society

It is not an exaggeration to say that Winner Take All campaigns have led to the weakening of civil society. As Marshall Ganz has written, the new campaign technologies have "undercut broad-based democratic organizations through which individual citizens have traditionally participated in public life."[65] Traditional intermediary and mass organizations which rely heavily on volunteers once served as important "schools for democracy," where citizens acquired resources, skills, and motivation for active political participation. These organizations—political parties, unions, political clubs, churches, and civic groups—helped formulate political choices and provide organizational mechanisms to encourage voting.

But the atrophy of these associations as grassroots political vehicles and the rise of Washington, DC–based lobbies and nongovernmental organizations that are little more than a letterhead, a P.O. Box, and a Web site soliciting members' money through direct mail, both reflect and reinforce the declining importance of citizen participation. The "scientifically professionalized" campaign has made activists and campaign volunteers practically superfluous, furthering alienating potential supporters and depressing participation. As journalist and best-selling author William Greider has written, "The marketing culture has swallowed not just parties, politicians and voters but also a vast array of mediating institutions, from TV and newspapers to most organizations that ostensibly speak to and for their members. Every major outfit does focus groups and polling now—it's less time-consuming than talking with their members."[66]

No, the genie is out of the bottle, and it can't be stuffed back in. Its enticements are too powerful to ignore. Mad scientist consultants and pollster-geists have learned too well how to play this Winner Take All game. The specter of substance-less, faked campaigns prompted playwright Arthur Miller to comment about the 2000 presidential election that "one is surrounded by such a roiling mass of consciously contrived performances, it gets harder and harder to locate reality."[67] Perhaps the gravest indictment of the consultants' craft and the new campaign technologies is that, as Marshall McLuhan warned three decades ago, "the medium has become the message." In the next chapter we will see how "the medium" dominated "the message" in the 2000 presidential election. A clear and chilling trajectory of Winner Take All campaigns over time is now evident, starting with Ronald Reagan, passing to George H. W. Bush, and then to Bill Clinton. Ironically, as we will see, Clinton's most apt pupil was not Al Gore, but George W. Bush.

CHAPTER NINE

The Wizards behind the Curtain

Pay no attention to that little man behind the curtain . . . I AM THE
GREAT AND POWERFUL OZ.

The sinisterly effective use of targeting and campaign technologies in
Winner Take All contests began in earnest under Reagan. Ronald Reagan, a former actor and radio broadcaster, utilized his understanding of
the television medium and a well-honed "aw-shucks" act to reach voters with powerful TV imagery. His campaign and administration adopted
"Morning in America" icons to project a sunny disposition melded to a John
Wayne–like "get tough" persona. Reagan, it has been said, constituted the
"apogee of style over substance."[1] No wonder the Reagan administration sometimes seemed like one long movie—in a very real sense, it was.

George H. W. Bush, as we have seen, in 1988 effectively used the Paramus
focus group and thirty-second Willie Horton and Boston Harbor ads to devastating effect, fingering Dukakis as a liberal and crushing the Democrat's presidential campaign. In 1992, the Bush reelection campaign used electronic focus
groups to test-market campaign themes. During his State of the Union speech
in January 1992, the Bush campaign assembled an electronic focus group of
targeted swing voters from Chicago suburbs who voted for Bush in 1988 but
were undecided in early 1992. Bush apparatchiks observing the Chicago electronic focus group were distressed, since none of his speech's themes were resonating: not his paean to winning the Cold War, nor creating more jobs via
NAFTA. Not until the last few minutes of his speech did the needles finally
leap into the high-approval zone: when Bush said, "This government is too big
and spends too much." The campaign had found its theme, and the very next
day they filmed a new commercial in the Oval Office for use in the New Hampshire primary.[2]

But no one embraced these modern campaign technologies like Bill Clinton.
Clinton adapted to the accelerated news cycle of the contemporary age and is
considered by some like Yale professor Jonathan Koppell to be "the father of
the permanent campaign."[3] Clinton advanced the Winner Take All technologies to their next logical step. Political scientist Steven Schier has written that
Clinton's success with targeting, what Schier calls a "ruthlessly pragmatic
means of winning votes," could be Clinton's "most significant contribution to
the American electoral process."[4] Liberals have complained that Clinton
endorsed many conservative programs like welfare reform, free trade, and environmental rollbacks, which Reagan/Bush never had been able to push through

the Congress. But just as wantonly, Clinton and his collaborators also advanced the targeting and campaign technologies that the Reagan forces had initiated.

On the roller-coaster ride of Winner Take All, Clinton used polling to follow every bump and dip of public opinion, lurching from one bloc of swing voters to another as the psychodrama of his presidency imploded. More than his predecessors, Clinton's 1996 reelection effort also paved the way for the "soft money" spending explosion—an infusion of lucre that the expensive, addictive new technologies craved—with Democrats arguing that as long as issue ads financed by soft money did not expressly advocate his election, they passed legal muster. Republicans soon followed the path that Clinton blazed. Clinton transformed—probably forever, and not for the better—how Winner Take All campaigns are waged.

Clinton employed all of the techniques of polling, focus groups, dial meter groups, thirty-second TV spots, and then some. Numerous White House sources disclosed that Clinton governed by polls. If Nancy Reagan had her astrologer and Czar Nicholas II his wild-eyed soothsayer Rasputin, Clinton had his divining pollster-geists. When polls told him that teenage smoking was unpopular, Clinton called a press conference and, standing before the television cameras and looking very presidential, he signed an executive order that accomplished approximately nothing—except, of course, score points with the public. During his nightmare anguishing over how to handle his sexual affair with Monica Lewinsky, Clinton had consultant Dick Morris conduct a poll to find out if he might clear up the mess by apologizing to the public. When Morris came back a few days later and told Clinton the public would forgive him his sexual excesses but not perjury, Clinton's course became clear, and the rest was, as they say, history.[5]

According to GOP consultant Frank Luntz, no one in political history had a greater commitment to focus group research than Bill Clinton. During the 1992 campaign, the strategies for dealing with Gennifer Flowers, a draft-dodging charge, and the other moral challenges that faced his campaign in the primaries were developed through focus group research. And then the technique followed him into the Oval Office. "In President Clinton's first year alone, his pollster conducted more focus groups than were conducted in all four years of the Bush presidency," maintains Luntz.[6]

By 1998, in the era of Clinton, targeting with the modern campaign technologies was widespread; for the 1998 congressional elections, the two major parties, still in the polarizing throes of impeachment hearings, focused on turning out their core supporters around emotionally partisan themes, and largely ignored the rest of the voters. Not too surprisingly, voter turnout dropped to less than 33 percent—the lowest for any midterm congressional election since 1942. A few weeks before that election, one Republican consultant summed up the underlying logic of targeting: "Who cares what every adult thinks? It's totally not germane to this election," he told the *Washington Post*.[7]

What was seminal about Clinton's use of the new technologies was not just that he targeted his message like a laser, but how he morphed that message—and by extension the message of the Democratic Party—to the point where the Democratic Party of today is virtually unrecognizable compared to even eleven years ago. In his effort to make the Democratic Party more appealing to certain groups of swing voters, especially working-class whites, Clinton jettisoned much liberal baggage. Affirmative action, welfare, demilitarization, the drug war, opposition to free trade and the death penalty, all of these traditionally Democratic Party positions were downgraded by Clinton and his conservative Democratic Leadership Council. In place of an unequivocal pledge of health insurance for all Americans, which was the holy grail for Democrats from Harry Truman to Clinton himself in 1992, the Democratic Party platform under Clinton shrank the cause of healthcare reform to a single timid paragraph. In a more central place the 1996 platform boasted, "Because of the success of the Clinton-Gore administration, a debt-free America is within reach." As *USA Today* columnist Walter Shapiro noted, in 1990 only a few right-wing economic cranks talked seriously about paying off the entire national debt, and now it was central to Clinton-Goreism, which had triangulated toward that position to woo Perot's economically conservative swing voters. Reflecting on the drift of Clinton's Democratic Party, Shapiro commented that Clinton's brand of targeting and campaigning had replaced "unabashed liberalism with poll-tested blandness."[8]

Many have marveled at Clinton's political instincts and penchant for survival, calling him the "greatest politician of our times" (followed by the inevitable disclaimers about his personal failings and trysts in the Oval Office). His liberal critics, on the other hand, argue that he traded their once-cherished beliefs for the elixir of power. But more to the point, Clinton was only gaming the Winner Take All system better than the rest. As a Winner Take All politician, Clinton was a master at what we saw in the last chapter, namely Jacobs and Shapiro's "crafted talk" designed to "simulate responsiveness." He skillfully used these techniques to target the swing voters he needed to triumph in Winner Take All elections, and ultimately to finish his term with one of the highest popularity ratings of any president despite the sexual psychodrama of his presidency. That was quite an accomplishment, and the Winner Take All technologies and their practitioners like Dick Morris were at the center of Clinton's "success." But in the process, Clinton redefined campaigns and leadership, accelerating a perilous trajectory that bodes ill for our democratic future.[9]

Now fully deployed, the new campaign tools of electoral warfare will prove to be impossible to revoke. In a competitive Winner Take All milieu neither side will disarm; instead, both sides of this domestic uncivil war ratchet up the arsenal, the steroids of politics, the full metal jacket, not daring to be the side to let down its guard. Campaigns will never be the same. Even the strategists behind George W. Bush, as we will see, tore more than a few pages from the

Clinton playbook. And then they ratcheted up the new technologies another notch, another logical step along the Orwellian trajectory of Winner Take All campaigns.

Election 2000: a case study of the ill-fated future of Winner Take All campaigns

> Even though viewership habits change, the requirements for politicians to reach half the audience doesn't. Politicians are no different from Coke and Nike.
>
> —JOHN HUTCHENS, MEDIA CONSULTANT,
> MEDIA STRATEGIES & RESEARCH

Clinton's understudy, Al Gore, similarly embraced the new technologies, methods, and strategies in his 2000 presidential campaign. But he was quite a bit more clumsy than the nimble Clinton. His campaign tried several attempts at reinvention and makeover, even going so far as to change his wardrobe and alpha-maleness, which only brought him heaps of national ridicule. In the heat of the campaign he backpedaled on his previous aggressive anti-gun stance because it was hurting him with swing voters and union members in important swing states. In the campaign's sprint to the finish, the author of the ecological homage *Earth in the Balance* proposed to tap 30 million barrels of oil from the Strategic Petroleum Reserve to lower fuel prices during an unexpected spike at the pump. During the Elian debacle he trekked to Florida and expressed a sympathetic line toward the Miami relatives, undercutting the Clinton administration and Attorney General Janet Reno, which nevertheless didn't gain him much support with Florida's heavily Republican Cuban population and padded his already considerable reputation of pandering and "saying anything to get elected." As *Slate* political pundit Jacob Weisberg later wrote, "the Gore campaign seemed like an experiment designed to answer the question . . . is it possible for a presidential candidate to pander too much?"[10]

But the more accurate explanation of Gore's half-starts and missteps was that his campaign was having difficulty figuring out who exactly the key constituency of swing voters were in Election 2000; they were unsure *who* to target in order to triumph in this Winner Take All contest. Carving up the electorate, even when done by expert consultants and pollster-geists as scientifically as possible with the new technologies, can be tricky business.

In 1996 Clinton had targeted suburbanites a few rungs up on the economic scale, with a prosperity-celebrating message that promised help for people trying to pay for education and balance the demands of work and family. But according to several senior Democrats both within and outside the campaign, Gore's strategists apparently believed that the 2000 election would be won a couple rungs lower—among lower middle-class voters, particularly women, who had little to celebrate in the new economy and felt victimized by obstacles they were confronting in daily life. If anything, Gore's 2000 election strategy most resembled the Clinton strategy of *1992*, rather than 1996. The similarities perhaps were not coincidental, with Clinton's 1992 pollster, Stanley Greenberg, taking on an increasingly important advisory role to Gore. Eight years before, Clinton had mixed populist rhetoric—including denunciations of high executive pay and his "it's the economy, stupid" rant—with a traditional values message that was aimed squarely at the working class.

It was to these voters that Gore spoke directly in his Los Angeles acceptance speech when he said he sympathized with how "so often powerful forces and powerful interests stand in your way and the odds seem stacked against you." Later in the speech he gave those forces names—"Big Tobacco, Big Oil, the big polluters, the pharmaceutical companies, the HMOs"—and pledged that as president, "sometimes you have to be willing to stand up and say no, so families can have a better life."

There was considerable anxiety in Democratic circles, and some arguments inside Gore's campaign, as he began striking this populist tone. Al From, head of the centrist Democratic Leadership Council (DLC), said "there's a big debate about who the swing voters are" in 2000. The DLC believed they were more likely to be educated New Economy suburbanites, and that "it's better to have a positive politics than a negative politics" to reach these voters. Clinton himself, according to Democrats who spoke with him, expressed concern that Gore risked overdoing it with rhetoric that sought to tap resentment rather than the essential optimism and desire for political consensus he believed most Americans felt. Said one Clinton adviser, "This is more an issue of tone than content. The [Gore] tone is off for these times."[11]

Gore's sudden populist stand certainly took many by surprise. At a most basic level, there was a legitimate question about whether the New Gore's message was consistent with the Old Gore's behavior. Gore earlier that year had cast himself as a friend of Wall Street, appearing with former Treasury secretary Robert E. Rubin (then cochair of Citigroup, the nation's largest financial institution) to make the case that he would keep the bull market charging. Whiffs of large campaign donations from Buddhist monks who had taken a vow of poverty still lingered in the air. The Democratic convention was showered with an avalanche of big money, much of it coughed up by the same powerful interests (big oil, Hollywood, polluters, even tobacco) that were attacked by the nominees from the podium.[12] Gore himself was heir to an oil fortune, while running mate Joseph Lieberman, newly passionate champion of the oppressed healthcare consumer, had received more campaign cash from insurance companies (many based in his home state, Connecticut) than any other Senator, and third most from pharmaceutical giants.[13]

Candidate Gore was simultaneously telling voters they'd never had it so good as under eight years of the Democrats *and* that they were getting the shaft from big business. In attempting to triangulate into pockets of swing voters, he was hoping to have it both ways. Thus, no matter what political tack he took Gore could not escape perceptions of pandering, of insincerity, of "saying anything to get elected." But this charge against Gore, while certainly true, was also comical. That's how *all* Winner Take All campaigns are conducted today. *All* campaigns, especially in close races, use the modern technologies—polling, focus groups, dial-meter groups, thirty-second ads—to figure out who the swing voters are, to figure out what campaign messages will motivate them ("crafted talk" and "simulated responsiveness"), and then to regurgitate those messages back at the swing voters.

But the fact that Gore got called on it, was chastised and even ridiculed, much more than his opponent, sent an additional warning that reverberated as subtext throughout the campaign, and to all future candidates: in this new era of staged, even farcical Winner Take All campaigns, the candidate with the greatest advantage will be the one that can project the most sincerity and authenticity *amidst* the fakery. Yet that quality itself—sincerity, authenticity, character—is simply another strategy, another sound bite, determined via polling and focus groups to be electorally advantageous.

Enter George W. Bush. The former Texas governor, much more than Al Gore, is the heir to Clinton. In certain ways, the Bush campaign represents the ultimate triumph of cynicism—the culmination of a downward spiral pattern that began with Reagan, who handed the piloting to George H. W., then to Clinton, and thence to George W., who crash-landed the great ship of state in UnElection 2000.

George W. Bush: the "anti-poll" poll-driven politician

Various commentators and news stories observed how much Bush had "stolen weapons from the Clinton arsenal," as one headline blared.[14] David Broder wrote that in Bush's acceptance speech at the Republican national convention three of the five goals highlighted—expanding and extending Medicare, reforming education, and strengthening Social Security—had "come right out of the Democrats' playbook."[15]

Indeed, looking back at the presidential race and comparing it to Bush's first six months in office, it is remarkable how much the "campaigning Bush" at times sounded like a liberal Democrat. He pledged himself to "tear down the wall" of poverty and prejudice separating too many people from sharing in the American dream. He pledged to "save Social Security and Medicare," programs that Republicans once decried as "creeping socialism." He vowed that his administration would focus on education, a remarkable Republican turnaround for a party that only a few years ago had sworn to abolish the Department of Education. At one Michigan rally "compassion conservative" Bush took a giant step away from Reagan when he declared "we're a nation that says that when somebody can't help themselves, we will as a government."[16] The *New York Times* wrote that "over the course of his campaign, Mr. Bush created a new Republican synthesis; he ran against Bill Clinton's legacy and sounded like him at the same time."[17]

In fact, as the Texas governor made his way from schoolhouse to health clinic photo-op, image after image eerily seemed to *mimic* Clinton's 1996 campaign. In one classroom Bush proclaimed that every child should know how to read by the third grade—flashing back to the 1996 campaign, and Bill Clinton reading along with two tow-headed tykes at a Michigan public library and declaring that "all America's children should be able to read on their own by the third grade." Then, in Pennsylvania, the "environmental" Bush announced a plan to advance the cleanup of contaminated, abandoned industrial sites. Said candidate Bush: "Every environmental issue confronts us with a duty to be good stewards. As we use nature's gifts, we must do so wisely." The setting, the words, the media image recalled foggy memories of Clinton's tour of a contaminated field in New Jersey in March '96, when he called for the cleanup of urban industrial sites and spoke of "the natural blessings God gave this country."[18] Was Bush actually aping Clinton in 1996, some wondered? Was he simply lifting many of Clinton's best lines and images that had been so effective with swing voters and recycling them four years later—but doing it as a *Republican*?

Like the Reagan and Clinton campaigns, the Bush campaign employed an expert army of admen and message masseurs who marinated the public in the chosen images of the candidate: not as the well-bred scion of the closest thing America has to a political dynasty, but as a regular guy, a "good ol' boy" from the heart of Midland, Texas; not as a privileged and spoiled Ivy League frat boy plugged into his father's old-boy network, but as a sunny, Reagan-like figure on his ranch behind the wheel of a beat up Ford Bronco;[19] not as a staunch conservative but as a pragmatic deal-maker who rises above partisanship. Midland, Texas, was terra firma, the place to anchor Bush in the popular imagination, "the place where the sky is as big as your dreams," as one Bush aide gushed.[20]

Similarly with the national convention: the Bush mythmakers went to work, fashioning national images that would resonate with targeted swing voters. Thus, they shunted party ideologues to the wings and staged what some called a slick minstrel show, showcasing black and Latino faces onstage even as the Republican delegates were 97 percent white (whiter even, it turns out, than the Republican convention of *1912*).[21] Bush spoke in coded words that his core constituency and conservative base understood as saying that he was "on their side," even as he avoided ever mentioning the words abortion, school vouchers, and other lightning rods that polls and focus groups had shown would alienate their primary audience of swing voters—that is, moderate suburbanites who had abandoned the party of Reagan in the last two elections to vote for Bill Clinton.[22]

In many ways, candidate Bush remained something of a political Rorschach test, purposefully so, "rounding off the edges of ideology and image enough for voters to see in him what they wanted to see," as the *New York Times* wrote.[23] At times during the campaign, Bush "simply seemed to be selling his infectious optimism to the point that it almost did not seem to matter how much he tortured the English language or what he was really trying to say." Said Marshall Whitman of the ultra-conservative Heritage Foundation, with evident satisfaction, "[Bush] has packaged the traditional conservative positions with completely new covering."[24] As Clinton once outflanked the Republican Congress by a triangulation that embraced many Republican issues, Bush waged a Winner Take All campaign by showcasing issues usually associated with Democrats and giving it a now-famous name—"compassionate conservatism."

Much of this, of course, was what we have come to know as standard canned fare for a modern Winner Take All campaign. The Bush campaign's practitioners slickly employed the usual gaming techniques: polling, focus groups, dial-meter groups, manipulation of images, thirty-second TV spots and more. "Crafted talk" and "simulated responsiveness" were the menu du jour. But what set George W. Bush apart from the likes of Clinton, Reagan, Dole, his dad, or Gore was that, at the same time the Bush campaign was employing all the modern campaign technologies, it publicly *disdained and denigrated* the same technologies as proof of Bush's own titanium character. Indeed, Bush ridiculed Gore whenever he could for using them.

"If you're tired of what's going on in Washington, DC, if you're tired of polls and focus groups, come and join this campaign," Bush shouted at one rally.[25] "We take stands without having to run polls and focus groups to tell us where we stand," he bellowed at another. "I don't need polls to tell me what to think," was a standard part of his campaign stump speech, as he told audiences that he was a "plainspoken man."

Yet when Bush used the term "education recession" thirteen times in a single speech in October just prior to one of the debates, it turned out that phrase had been cooked up by a Republican media strategist and so thoroughly poll-tested and put before focus groups that aides could cite the exact percentage of women who reacted favorably to the phrase in every key battleground state.[26] Bush's vocabulary choice and "crafted talk" were determined by polling and focus groups, as he refused to use the "V word" for school vouchers, opting for "school choice" because the latter tested better. The same with Social Security—in a bout of "simulated responsiveness," rarely did Bush call for "private" retirement accounts, instead the term "personal" accounts was less scary, polls had showed.

When Bush mocked Gore's promise to give tax cuts only to "the right people," it was focus groups that told him such an assault would work. Bush's acceptance speech at the Republican national convention had been thoroughly tested via focus and dial-meter groups; indeed, the entire speech, one phrase after another, one image and hyperbole after another, were ones selected because they had scored high among focus group participants. Similarly, when running mate Dick Cheney gave his acceptance speech, Republican pollster Frank Luntz had assembled a focus group of thirty-six undecided voters—one dozen each of Republicans, Democrats, and independents—and sequestered them in a stuffy hotel room where they held "happy meters" to record their reactions to specific words and phrases as Cheney spoke.[27]

According to conservative columnist William Safire, during the Republican primaries the Bush campaign lined up focus groups in Iowa, New Hampshire, and South Carolina to test TV spots extolling Bush's virtues and responding to anticipated negative attacks coming from fellow Republican candidates.[28] In another Bush campaign focus group, they concluded that Gore's biggest liability with voters was his personality, particularly when he was in attack mode. The information collected there as well as other polling data persuaded the campaign to make a crucial change in its strategy—instead of using direct and frequent attacks on Gore, which the Bush camp had indicated in March would form the core of its campaign, the campaign decided to take the high road.[29] Even Bush's mantra about setting a "positive and constructive tone" and being the candidate that could "heal the bitterness and division that too often characterizes Washington, DC" and bring "civility and bipartisanship," it turns out, exactly matched the strategy dictated by focus groups conducted by Luntz.[30]

Bush used at least three different campaign slogans throughout the campaign season, starting with "Compassionate Conservatism," morphing when convenient to a "Reformer with Results," and ending the campaign with some version of "Real Plans for Real People."[31] Displaying a capacity to pander that rivaled Gore's, Bush responded to a question about the Confederate flag flying over the South Carolina capitol by saying, "I trust the people of South Carolina," and when asked if he had a personal reaction to the Confederate flag, he replied, "Not in South Carolina."[32] When one alert reporter asked "Reformer with Results" Bush what had happened to his old campaign slogan of "Compassionate Conservatism," Bush replied, in his own inimitable, malapropian style, "A 'reformer with results' is a conservative who's had compassionate results in the state of Texas."[33]

So, while Gore was accused of reinventing himself, of "saying anything to get elected," in effect of being willing to "change his clothes," metaphorically as well as actually, the Bush campaign repackaged and canned itself just as readily—they were just better at it. Better, that is, at convincing their audience of their candidate's sincerity among the humbuggery. They were masters at Jacobs and Shapiro's "crafted talk" designed to "simulate responsiveness," to find words and phrases to manipulate and mislead voters—they were the ultimate gamesters.

In a continual search for fresh gimmickry that might give them the winning edge, both the Bush and Gore camps began to feature "real people" at their campaign stops in key battleground states. The idea of the "real people" was that they were citizens specifically chosen to model for the television cameras how the campaign's policy-of-the-day on Medicare, tax cuts, or Social Security would positively affect the family in question and how their opponent's plans would negatively affect them. These campaign events were thoroughly scripted by the media consultants, political strategists, and advance teams to project the desired message to targeted audiences. The "real people," intended to be authentic slices of Americana, were used more like props in the candidates' choreographed dramas, creating for the media reels of prepackaged programming.

So Gore and Bush matched each other, real person for real person. The Whites of Kansas City, the McKinneys of Milwaukee, Wisconsin, the Saavedras of Land O'Lakes, Florida, the Strunks of Allentown, Pennsylvania. To find such people, the Bush advance team sometimes put in eighteen-hour days, screening ten to fifteen families a day in an effort to vet the "real people" and avoid potential embarrassments. Nevertheless, the mother of one Bush campaign "real family" in Wilkes-Barre, Pennsylvania, it turned out afterward, was less than certain about her support for Bush. "Actually, you really don't know who to believe," she said after the event. "You take your chances when you vote."[34] Those words were perhaps the truest spoken of the entire campaign, on *either* side of the political aisle.

Following the Gore campaign's bump in the polls after the Democratic convention, which vaulted Gore into a ten-point lead, the "candidate of character," the candidate of "sincerity" who "knew his own mind" and who previously had decried "the negative tone of Washington, DC" panicked—and promptly went negative on Gore (just as Bush previously had done in the Republican primary against John McCain).[35] Using the preferred weapon of character assassination—the thirty-second TV spot—attacks on Gore escalated throughout the remainder of the campaign (as did Gore's attacks of Bush). In a preview of a governing style that would mark the first eight months of his presidency—namely, saying one thing but doing another—Bush continued his call for an end to the "politics of division" even as he savaged Gore's credibility and Republican Party ads accused Gore of lying. The Democratic Party was waging its own version of two-faced campaigning, but Bush, still trying to lay claim to the poll- and focus-tested turf of running a positive campaign, maintained with a straight face that his ads were not negative and personal. Yet as *Newsweek*'s Jonathan Alter commented, "If suggesting your opponent is a liar and hypocrite" isn't negative and personal, then what is?[36]

The media was slow to pick up on the specter of this "candidate of character" who "speaks his own mind" and who "doesn't listen to polls and focus groups"—yet was thoroughly informed by polls and focus groups about what campaign slogans to use, which themes to emphasize, even which strategies to pursue. Indeed, so cynical and hypocritical was the Bush campaign's use of the modern campaign technologies that it seemed that the very theme of not paying attention to polls and focus groups was itself derived from polls and focus groups. This caused two veteran reporters to speculate that "the next time Bush says, 'I don't need polls to tell me what to think,' voters might fairly wonder, Did a pollster tell him to say that?"37

Truth or Consequences

While George W. Bush bellowed over and over in his campaign that "he trusted the American people," his packaging and reliance on new campaign and gaming technologies told us just the opposite. In another preview of his first half-year governing style, he bet the farm that he could hide his hard-right conservative agenda behind a Reaganesque sunny smile, contrived images, sound bites like "Compassionate Conservative," and targeted messages derived from focus groups and polling. In short, his campaign had been a slick con job, no more or less than Al Gore's or Bill Clinton's. His campaign at times had looked a whole lot like Bill Clinton's in 1996, right down to the images, backdrops, settings, and sound bites, playing the familiar hit tunes of education, the environment, Social Security, and Medicare.

The copycat nature of the Bush strategy raises the uncomfortable specter of the "canned campaign"—might a cookie-cutter formula, one wonders, become the *Groundhogs Day* campaign, endlessly replicated again and again every four years for national electoral consumption? Might we see in 2004 the candidates trekking to the same classrooms and the same toxic waste sites, uttering slightly different versions of the same sound bites from the Clinton 1996 and the Bush 2000 campaigns? If so, does that mean the essential factor that candidates will use to distinguish themselves will have little to do with policy or national vision, but instead will rely on projected character traits like sincerity, authenticity, and congeniality, in short: which candidate seems to be most sincere and likable, or alternatively exciting and fresh, amidst all the humbuggery?

New York Times columnist Frank Rich has called this new-fangled presidential selection process the "Survival of the Fakest."38 In an era of a dwindling number of battleground states, and of declining citizen participation not only in the voting booth but in the numbers of people paying attention *between* elections, the presidential campaigns of the future seem slotted to assume an ominous character: it may not matter much what the current administration has done or not done the previous three years, as long as it can use the modern campaign technologies to hoodwink the muddle-headed swing voters in the handful of swing states, three weeks before the election. Political consultants will intensify their use of the modern campaign technologies to use centrist rhetoric and sunny Reaganesque images in an attempt to mold the impression of their candidate in the eyes of this critical wedge of swing voters, to make these voters "feel good" about their candidate regardless of all evidence as to their actual abilities for the office or their political beliefs or policies. In other words, in a reworking of the famous carnival impresario P. T. Barnum's maxim, the successful candidate doesn't have to fool "all the people all the time," he or she just has to fool a handful of swing voters in swing states a few weeks before Election Day.

If this is the direction of our two-choice, Winner Take All politics—and there is every indication that such is the case—then actors and other types of pretenders will make the ideal candidates. Arthur Miller, who as a playwright has dealt with his share of actors and staged drama, has pithily observed that political leaders have become actors who now understand "that to govern they must learn how to act;"[39] and the audience—the dwindling number of voters who still attend the show—have come to accept artifice for politics. Thus, it made complete sense, and perhaps signaled the future of "feel-good" presidential campaigning, when during the campaign George W. Bush shared an early morning talk show with a man who broke thirty-one boards on his head in thirty seconds and a truck-driving member of the hit TV show *Survivor*. Candidates of the future will prefer the Oprah-Letterman-Leno-Regis circuit to answering more substantive questions from the traveling press corps or fellow citizens. But, as the *Washington Post*'s Howard Kurtz commented, "When Oprah Winfrey tosses such toughies as 'What's your favorite cereal?' it's not exactly a high-fiber diet for the voters."[40]

The Triumph of Cynicism

Campaigns, ideally, should be a time for the entire nation to contemplate ideas, policy, and principle. Campaigns should be times when voters become more informed and most acute about policy differences between the candidates and parties, and make a deliberative decision that, in its aggregate, decides the direction of the nation. Campaigns ought to be a high civic moment when the nation's best and brightest debate and make a bid for our democratic allegiance and our vote.

Yet this is hardly what happens on Election Day. Unfortunately, Winner Take All politics in the United States, led by the nose by campaigning and targeting technologies masterminded by mad scientist consultants and pollster-geists, is running headlong in the *wrong* direction. Between the precise targeting of swing voters, swing districts, and swing states, most voters are sliced and diced right out of the election. As the nation becomes more polarized—regionally, racially, culturally, and by partisan identification—more and more people are ignored because they are either in "locked-up" states and districts, because they are in the wrong demographic, or because they aren't "likely" enough to vote.

To understand how far we've fallen, it is instructive to recall previous historic watersheds in our nation's political history, such as the Lincoln–Douglas debates. In 1858, U.S. Senatorial candidates Stephen Douglas and Abraham Lincoln from Illinois engaged in seven debates, each lasting approximately *three* hours, debating hot button issues of the day like slavery, states' rights, economic protectionism, westward expansion, and the *Dred Scott* decision. By all accounts the debates were electrifying and artful, attended by large crowds who witnessed two master orators at the peak of their abilities. The toughest issues of the day were debated head-on without waffling or evasive rhetoric. In 1860 the transcript of these debates was published and used as an important campaign document in the presidential election that launched Lincoln to his date with destiny. The Lincoln–Douglas debates are now a revered part of American political folklore.

Similarly, during Franklin Roosevelt's thirteen years as president, he delivered some thirty fireside chats by radio, averaging two or three a year—and only one during a presidential campaign. Yet, as historian Doris Kearns Goodwin has written, each fireside chat commanded a huge audience—more than 70 percent of the home audience. To understand the magnitude of that figure, says Goodwin, one need only realize that America's top-ranking radio comedy shows—Jack Benny, Bob Hope, *Fibber McGee and Molly*, *Amos 'n' Andy*—were then garnering what were considered fabulous ratings of 30 to 35 percent. Novelist Saul Bellow recalls walking down the street while Roosevelt was speaking. Through lit windows families could be seen sitting at their kitchen tables or gathered in their parlors, listening to the radio. Drivers had pulled over and turned on their radios to listen. "Everywhere the same voice. You could follow without missing a single word as you strolled by."[41]

But it's hard to even *imagine* listening to today's candidates debate for three hours at a stretch, with their sound bites, sneers, and scripted slogans substituting for substance. And absent a frightful war or foreign attack like that on the World Trade Center, it is extremely difficult to envision either of the two major parties' candidates addressing the nation with such dignity, gravitas, and a sense of national purpose that the nation is *compelled* to tune in. The debates between George W. Bush and Al Gore were considered snoozers by everyone except the professional pundits, with TV ratings dropping with each debate.[42] The national conventions for both parties, pale infomercials for the already-anointed, were similarly bereft.

In fact, few voters actually voted *for* either Gore or Bush as much as voted *against* the other side. They voted their fears instead of their hopes—to keep someone *out* of office rather than get someone in. Indeed, playwright Arthur Miller has written that by the end of the presidential campaign "it seemed like an unpopularity contest, a competition for who was less disliked by more people than the other, a demonstration of negative consent."[43] More and more, that kind of adversarial temperament and negative consent defines our Winner Take All politics, from top to bottom, from the parties and their candidates right down to most voters. Most voters in Bushlandia and New Goreia are locked-up; no matter how bad their candidate, they are united in how much they detest the other side's candidate. Our politics has been reduced to a hollowed-out, rotten vessel of negative consent and fakery.

Fifty years ago George Orwell anticipated the caliber of candidates and campaigns that plague the United States today. "When one watches some tired hack on the platform," said Orwell, "mechanically repeating the familiar phrases . . . one often has a curious feeling that one is not watching a live human being but some kind of dummy." Indeed, in the toxic soil of Winner Take All, the quality of political leadership has declined and the idea of serving one's nation or community via politics has become a dubious career track. Large numbers of intelligent and gifted people eschew politics altogether, particularly rejecting any type of career in formal politics. Ideas and policy have become anathema to politics, and elections now are more akin to a con job. Unsurprisingly, increasing numbers of voters have come to actively detest the whole business as a meaningless and undignified charade that requires political leaders to compromise and debase their integrity.

Moreover, because of the way they now conduct Winner Take All campaigns, the two major parties have lost the ability to articulate real conflicts of interest in society. The packaging of politics and the gaming incentives of Winner Take All have led candidates to target such a narrow, nonideological swath of voters that even strong policy disagreements often aren't discernable in rhetoric. "Compassionate Conservatism," "New Democrat," these are terms meant to blur partisan differences as a means of attracting targeted swing voters. Consequently, campaigns are no longer a vehicle for defining or articulating thorny national problems or issues, nor are they a step toward national resolution, particularly when following the election the presidential winner abandons the center and lurches back toward his party base.

Nor are campaigns any longer a time for the ascension of dynamic national leadership. Indeed, it has been said that neither Franklin Roosevelt, Abraham Lincoln, Thomas Jefferson, nor Teddy Roosevelt—three of them revered faces on Mount Rushmore—could ever make it to the White House today because they were too much orators for today's sound-bite campaigns. On the contrary, Winner Take All is producing McCampaigns of "crafted talk," contrived images, and "simulated responsiveness," repeated like mindless advertising jingles as a substitute for real debate. Lincoln and Douglas would be lost in the world of politics today, and politics is lost without the Lincolns, the Douglases, and the Roosevelts.

But it is important to recognize that this contour of the political landscape is not the result of politicians or the political parties being evil or base personalities, unwilling to rise above self-interest or partisanship. Rather, it flows from the Winner Take All, two-choice dynamic which provides peculiar incentives and ultimately rewards those who wage the zero-sum game best.[44] At a basic level, a battle is occurring between voters' belief in the legitimacy of our political system, on the one hand, and modern campaign methods of gaming and targeting, on the other. Will image permanently triumph over ideas? Will campaign technology trump face-to-face political engagement? Will cynicism permanently move into the house of American democracy, like termites gnawing away its foundation? Only time will tell, but the prognosis under Winner Take All is not encouraging.

CHAPTER TEN

The Winner Take All Media
The Fourth Estate Sells Out

And a people who mean to be their own governors, must arm
themselves with the power that knowledge brings.
—JAMES MADISON

L
ike the politicians and their campaigns, the media also follow the straitjacket dictates of Winner Take All. Indeed, the media has systematically
shut out political candidates that are judged by editorial boards and TV
producers to be nonviable, even if those candidates have sound ideas
and legitimate credentials. In the process, voters are robbed of opportunities to
hear stimulating political debate, since they only hear from the media's anointed candidates.

When Carol Miller decided to run for Congress in 1998 from the third congressional district in New Mexico, she felt she was fulfilling a public service.
Miller had spent much of her adult life as an advocate for health issues, particularly for the inhabitants who lived in the sparse rural areas of northern New
Mexico where she lived. Miller had seen the issue from many angles. She had
been a Commissioned Officer in the U.S. Public Health Service, appointed in
the Reagan Administration, and an appointee to the White House to serve full
time on Hillary Clinton's Health Care Task Force. She had been a lobbyist
inside the "hall of mirrors" of Washington, DC, dedicated to keeping under-
funded local health clinics open in the poorest, smallest communities. Running
for Congress seemed like a logical step as part of her advocacy work for healthcare on behalf of the rural poor.

But instead of running as a Democrat, which had been her political affiliation
since the mid-1980s, in a congressional district that had elected Democrats like
Bill Richardson for the past twenty years, Miller decided to run as a Green Party
candidate. Frustrated with what she had seen from the Democratic Party as a
lobbyist and as a healthcare advocate—under Clintonism "health care for all"
had gone from being a central part of the Democratic Party platform since Truman to barely a footnote—Miller forsook her Democratic roots and ran on the
firmer principles of the Green Party.

"The Democratic Party had sold out," she says. "I watched them sell out,
throughout the '90s. It turned my stomach."

Miller met enthusiastic supporters wherever she went in her district. "People
seemed overjoyed to have another choice, for a change," she says. "The Democ-

rats had taken so many people for granted for so long." The one place where she did not always find a warm welcome was from the media. After winning a remarkable 17 percent of the vote as a Green Party candidate in a 1997 special election to fill a congressional vacancy in her district, many claimed that Miller's votes had caused the Democratic candidate to lose a close race.[1] So when she ran again in November 1998, the broadcast and print media of New Mexico closed ranks around the Carol Miller for Congress campaign. In fact, they tried as hard as they could to pretend the campaign wasn't happening.

Why was that, one might wonder? Here was an accomplished, articulate, respected, and experienced public servant, spending her own time and money and that of her supporters in an effort to emphasize issues of healthcare, the rural poor, grazing rights that were hurting agriculture, native treaty rights, and other issues important to her northern New Mexico district. Already she had demonstrated a degree of electoral viability by pulling 17 percent of the vote in a special election. And the media was acting like she was some sort of pariah.

"So I called up a somewhat friendly editor of the local daily newspaper, the *New Mexican*," says Miller. "And I asked him: why aren't you guys covering my campaign? I almost wish he hadn't told me."

What the editor said was the following: Miller's campaign was not being covered because "he wanted me to drop out of the race," since he was supporting her Democratic opponent. He also told her that the only coverage she would be "allowed" was one op-ed. But when Miller wrote the op-ed, the editor then informed her that he had received it a couple of hours too late for the deadline and refused to print it. Yet this was a *daily* newspaper with deadlines every day.

"My teeth nearly dropped out of my jaw when he told me that," says Miller. "It shattered what little faith I had left in the free press, so-called." Editorial boards of the state's two largest newspapers, the *Albuquerque Journal* and *Albuquerque Tribune,* refused to meet with Miller for an endorsement hearing, saying they hadn't been asked on time. But Miller's staff records show phone calls made early and often, requesting the meetings. What was particularly odd was that both of these newspapers previously had *endorsed* Miller in 1997 for the special election. But after her 17 percent showing apparently had spoiled the electoral outcome for these newspapers—and for the Democratic Party—they came home, so to speak. They refused even to grant her the courtesy of an endorsement interview.

Miller's experience as a third-party candidate is not uncommon. Every election cycle, hundreds and sometimes thousands of independent candidates as well as third-party candidates from the Libertarian, Reform, Green, Working Families, and Natural Law parties run in races all across the country, fighting an uphill battle with a lack of resources. But what's even more damaging to their efforts is the lack of media coverage. In 2000, the Libertarian Party ran more than 1,430 candidates nationwide. They fielded candidates in 255 of the 435

House races, as well as twenty-five of the thirty-three U.S. Senate seats up for election, the first time in eighty years that a third party has contested a majority of the seats in Congress.[2]

Yet an informal e-mail survey of their candidates revealed an appalling pattern of exclusionary treatment at the hands of the media, particularly television broadcasters and daily newspapers. Libertarian Party candidates were routinely excluded from media campaign coverage, televised debates, and editorial board interviews, with reasons that ran the gamut from "sorry, we don't cover third parties, it's just our standard policy" to a cavalier "maybe next time." For instance, in Colorado's sixth congressional district race the daily newspapers printed dozens of daily reports about the Democratic and Republican candidates, day after day, but could not find a single column inch for any third-party alternatives. In New Hampshire, the state's largest newspaper not only gave zero campaign coverage to the Libertarian Party's candidate for U.S. Senate, but also the editorial page editor kept postponing publication of an op-ed from the candidate (a tactic similar to that foisted on Carol Miller by the *New Mexican* editor). In Seattle, KING 5 TV and KIRO Radio 710, two of Washington state's largest media outlets, excluded from broadcasted debates the Libertarian Party's candidate for U.S. Senate, Jeff Jared, even though Jared arguably was the kingmaker in the race and his vote totals ultimately spoiled the tight race for the Republican incumbent, Sen. Slade Gorton.[3]

In Ohio, the *Dayton Daily News* listed all candidates running in various elections, but refused even to *mention* any third-party candidate. When the Libertarian Party candidate called and asked for an explanation, he was informed, "We are only including Republicans and Democrats, because they are the only ones with a fighting chance of winning." In Pennsylvania, the Knight-Ridder owned *Centre Daily Times* refused even to accept *paid advertisement* from the Libertarian Party candidates, specifically $4,600 for about a dozen political advertisements that touted Libertarian candidates as well as prison reform and medical marijuana. In New Hampshire, the Libertarian Party's candidate for governor in 2000 was excluded from all debates, both televised and in public, and during one event when he tried to protest his exclusion he was escorted out by the state police. The specter of law enforcement officials silencing political candidates should make one balk, no matter how nonviable the candidates or what one may think of their opinions.

The smaller, alternative weekly press tends to be somewhat better than the dailies and the TV broadcasters. But the public broadcasting stations, both television and radio, despite their broader mandate to be a public resource, can be just as rigid as the for-profit media. They routinely snubbed third-party candidates and excluded them from debates. In Iowa, the public broadcast station chose to bar a Natural Law Party congressional candidate from its televised debates because he was not considered "newsworthy."[4] A PBS station in Illinois, WILL-TV, barred a Libertarian Party candidate because, he was told, "it would be too confusing for the voters" to have more than two choices. NETV public television in Omaha, Nebraska, hosted a congressional debate for Nebraska's second district—a strongly Republican district that the Democratic candidate could not possibly hope to win—and barred the Libertarian Party candidate. In recent years, the U.S. Supreme Court ruled in *Arkansas Educational TV v. Forbes* that a public broadcast station can legally bar certain candidates from participating in a debate, prompting many First Amendment supporters to ask, "What happened to the 'public' in the Public Broadcasting System?"

The media's ostensible reasons for these exclusions vary, but most often the reason cited is that these candidates are not viable—they can't win. But as we have seen, *most* legislative races across the country are safe seats for one major party or the other, and not competitive for either a Democratic or Republican candidate in those races *either*. If that truly were the criteria for coverage, the media only would cover the obvious winner in each race. But they don't do that. Instead, in every district across the country both Republicans and Democrats receive most of the media coverage, however locked-up the seat and whether or not the challenging Republican or Democrat has a chance of winning. Only the independent candidates and minor party candidates are excluded.

What can we conclude from such a persistent pattern? It would seem that most TV producers, editors, and reporters are in the thralls of a sometimes unconscious and other times appallingly conscious loyalty to the two-party system. Yet because they also see themselves as having a warm fuzzy affinity for a kind of Jeffersonian vision of the free press, and perhaps some journalistic standards of objectivity, they cannot come right out and crassly *say* they are card-carrying members of the duopoly. Thus, they concoct their transparent ruse: "We don't cover *these* candidates because they can't win."

The media's dissembling can reach absurd levels. In 2000, Medea Benjamin, a Green Party candidate for the U.S. Senate in California, in typical fashion was being shut out by the California media. Like Carol Miller, Benjamin was an articulate and accomplished public servant, executive director of a $4.5 million nonprofit organization called Global Exchange with over forty employees that was respected around the world and in the halls of governments for its education and advocacy work regarding the impact of globalization on the Third World. Her organization had spearheaded the high-profile, anti-sweatshop campaign against Nike and other corporations, and prior to her Senate campaign Benjamin had appeared regularly on major national media, including the Lehrer NewsHour, ABC, NBC, CBS, and CNN news shows. She also was frequently quoted by California media like the *Los Angeles Times, San Francisco Chronicle,* and various National Public Radio affiliates. In other words, Benjamin was a public personality, a visible leader, and a credible candidate. Her campaign raised several hundred thousand dollars, she knew the issues, excited audiences wherever she went, and already was familiar to major media outlets and numerous reporters. But she was unprepared for the media blackout that she was about to experience.

"We tried everything," she says. "When some reporters told us to do a bus tour like all the major candidates do today, we did that, traveling up and down the state. But still they didn't cover us. We jumped through lots of hoops for very little."

Benjamin was told by one *San Francisco Chronicle* political reporter that his newspaper wasn't covering her campaign because "you haven't bought any TV ads"—their sole measure of viability. Benjamin asked—and then demanded, even to the point of committing civil disobedience in the lobby of the television station—to be included in the televised debates sponsored by KRON-TV between her two opponents, incumbent Senator Dianne Feinstein, a Democrat, and Republican Congressman Tom Campbell. All the polls showed Feinstein with a huge lead over Campbell, at least 60–40, so Campbell's campaign was not viable either; he had no more a chance of winning than Benjamin did. But he was included in the televised debates—Feinstein couldn't very well debate herself. When Benjamin's campaign asked why she was being excluded, KRON-TV officials had a different line than the *Chronicle*'s citing of a failure to buy TV ads. They told her that the Senate debates were applying a similar standard as that used by the commission running the presidential debates, which invite only candidates polling above a certain percentage in public opinion polls. That might have seemed somewhat credible, except for one hook: the Field Poll, the state's most prominent voter survey, as well as other California pollsters, had not even *included* Benjamin in their opinion polls. It was a classic Catch-22.[5]

"They kept moving the goal posts," says Benjamin. "First—not viable. Then—no bus tour. Finally—no TV ads. It became obvious that no matter what we did, they would find more excuses. It was very discouraging."

Unlike Benjamin, the Libertarian Party candidate for U.S. Senate in Massachusetts actually *did* buy television ads. The "Carla Howell for Senate" campaign spent hundreds of thousands of dollars for approximately eighty television ads on CBS, NBC, and ABC affiliates. They spent another $100,000 on radio ads all over the state, including major stations like WBZ, and $25,000 more on movie screen ads that previewed before major motion pictures on twenty-nine screens for four weeks. According to the campaign, they posted over 10,000 yard signs, had 721 volunteers, and raised and spent $820,000. They used a pollster, a slick Web site, a paid staff, and many other hallmarks of a modern-day professional campaign.

The Republican Party candidate, meanwhile, had few volunteers, no yard signs, and raised only $100,000, too little to prevent his campaign staff from eventually quitting. The Republican campaign was nearly invisible, with little support from the national or state Republican Party organizations because they knew they had an impossible job—unseating Ted Kennedy from his seeming birthright as Massachusetts' Senator. Nevertheless, a Lexus-Nexis search reveals that the Republican Party candidate received *five to six times* the coverage from daily newspapers and television broadcasters as the Libertarian Party candidate.

Apparently, even when a third-party candidate outspends and outorganizes a major party candidate, and is no more or less viable, still the Winner Take All media marginalizes the third-party effort. It is as reflexive as breathing for the media loyalists of the duopoly. Despite the obstacles, Carla Howell finished within 1 percentage point of the Republican Party candidate.

The railroading of articulate and highly qualified candidates like Benjamin, Miller, and Howell is a typical result of the Winner Take All media's knee-jerk allegiance to the duopoly. Editors and TV producers, and to a lesser extent reporters, look at third-party and independent efforts through what only can be labeled "Winner Take All eyes"—that is, through the biases and assumptions of an internalized paradigm, an indoctrinated set of values. The idea that there may be another democratic value worth fulfilling—such as fostering public debate of important policy issues, and engaging the public in considering such issues—rarely seems to implant itself among the ecclesiasts of the Winner Take All media.

This is a great loss for our democracy, as well as a great loss for voters. Lacking news coverage of a range of political viewpoints, voters do not have the opportunity to hear from candidates who may excite them or bring fresh new ideas into the political arena. Is it any wonder that voters are so turned off to politics, with the media's ignoring of fresh political alternatives, the proliferation of poll-tested blandness substituting for campaigns, and the resulting dearth of stimulating political debate?

In fact, the Winner Take All media's refusal to cover political alternatives should be reasonably viewed as an in-kind *donation,* an independent expenditure, to the Democrats' and Republicans' campaigns, subject to federal and state campaign finance disclosure laws. It raises disturbing questions about the tight relationship between the Winner Take All media and the Democrats and Republicans, crushing all political dissent and opposition in a way that is not altogether different from the relationship between the Soviet Politburo and its communist propaganda machines. In fact, a highly respected British think tank, the Electoral Reform Society, observing American elections in 1998, noted this cozy relationship between the duopoly and the American media's duopoly devotees. Their report, called "State of American Democracy," stated that "the media pays little if any attention to third party or independent candidates. . . . On all counts, the voter is restricted in the number and diversity of ideas expressed to him or her, thus negatively impacting the quality of representation a voter receives. . . . A vicious cycle is created, alternative parties cannot get their message to the voters, and the voters cannot expand their limited options."[6]

Clearly, the American voter and political system are badly in need of some kind of *perestroika*—an "opening up"—of the Winner Take All media. But where is the American Gorbachev who will cast off his "Winner Take All eyes" and pave the way?

The Great Free Press—or the Media Monopoly?

Ross Perot in 1992 figured out a way around this media blackout of independent and third-party candidacies—he used his own considerable wealth to *buy* thirty-minute blocks on prime time television. He created his own political infomercials, complete with charts and visual aids to explain his political program, philosophy, and policy proposals. Based exclusively on his wealth and a patented folksy talent for simplifying issues and rallying a populist outpouring, Perot suddenly was viable. And in a perverse twist of logic, that meant he was "news," and so the free media coverage ensued. It was the first time since John Anderson's independent candidacy for president in 1980, and before that George Wallace's third-party candidacy for president in 1968, that the Winner Take All media had deigned to cover an independent or third-party candidate for president. But when a personal fortune is necessary to garner media attention to a political campaign, essential democratic values suffer, public perception becomes jaundiced. And obviously that severely limits political debate, as well as voters' choice in the voting booth.

Jesse Ventura's remarkable bid for Minnesota's gubernatorial seat in 1998, on the other hand, nearly suffered the same fate as those of most third-party or independent candidates. Without Perot's deep pockets, Ventura's fortunes looked like the typical David going against Goliath. Fortunately for his fledgling campaign, Minnesota had some public financing for candidates. This allowed him to mount a credible campaign that was aided by his inclusion in the televised gubernatorial debates. Ironically, Ventura was included in the televised debates not out of any sense of fairness or the need to provide voters with information, spirited debate and choices, but because each of the major party candidates thought that Ventura's inclusion would hurt their main opponent. Their blatantly self-interested subterfuge backfired, and the two-party system in Minnesota received a staggering jolt when Ventura captured the crown in an astounding victory (albeit with a low plurality of only 37 percent of the vote).

In January 2000, in anticipation of televised debates for the upcoming presidential campaign, a body with an official-sounding name, the Commission on Presidential Debates (CPD), established criteria for who would be permitted to participate in the September–October debates. After backroom deliberation for which no public input was solicited, the CPD decided that candidates must have at least 15 percent of the vote in five national polls a week before a debate. The criteria established were so severe that the only minor party or independent presidential candidate who would have qualified in the last sixty years was George Wallace in 1968. Ross Perot would not have qualified in 1992, despite ultimately winning 19 percent of the popular vote after he was included in the televised debates. Neither would John Anderson, independent presidential candidate in 1980. Using the CPD's criteria, Gov. Jesse Ventura of Minnesota would have been barred from participating in his state's televised gubernatorial debates.

The CPD, it turns out, was nothing more than a *front group* for the Democrats and Republicans. It was a commission of, by, and for the duopoly, funded primarily by a beer company and other corporations, posing as a national arbiter. The CPD would have us believe that the debates were only about choosing between the two candidates who could win, and not about serious discussion regarding our country's future by credible and articulate candidates. Yet this standard is a canard—Jesse Ventura's poll numbers did not rise until *after* he appeared in Minnesota's televised debates, and voters could contrast him with his competition by watching him go toe-to-toe.

Using criteria established by the two major parties to exclude all other participants, the televised debates went forward. And the loyal two-party media dutifully televised them (although NBC bowed out of one debate to televise the baseball playoffs and Fox relegated the debates to its for-pay cable channel).[7] But without a Jesse Ventura, Ross Perot, or Ralph Nader to jazz things up, the debates were predictable snoozers of sound bites, poll-tested blandness, and wooden affect. Both Gore and Bush recited their pat responses against the other's pat responses, and then played the "I Love America" hit jukebox tune a few times so viewers could follow along. The media went along with this ruse, declining to include other candidates guaranteed to increase ratings and give viewers a bang for their buck, if that was their criteria. Televised debates with a fiery Pat Buchanan and erudite Ralph Nader flanking the stiff Gore and bumbling Bush could have provided American viewers the best "reality TV" of all. Certainly it would have been more interesting and entertaining than what the duopoly and its puppet commission served up. But that was not in the cards for the Winner Take All media.

These sorts of incidents, and numerous others like them, raise disturbing questions about the conduct of the so-called Great Free Press, and their relationship to the two-party duopoly. The national and local media have colluded in—indeed fostered—the dumbing down and flattening of political debate that is familiar to us as Winner Take All campaigns. The Winner Take All media has systematically shut out political candidates who are independent of the two major parties, even if those candidates have sound ideas and legitimate credentials, even if they have raised hundreds of thousands of dollars and have armies of volunteers or a campaign bus, even if they have bought television ads, under the bogus pretense that they can't win. But the exclusion of such candidates from mainstream media has denied these candidates the ability to get their message out to voters, thereby *creating* the self-fulfilling prophecy that these candidates are not viable.

At the same time the exclusion has robbed voters of a chance to hear a range of ideas and analysis, indeed, a stirring political debate of important issues and themes. Yet, as the examples of Ross Perot and Jesse Ventura illustrated—and Carol Miller, too, who received 17 percent of the vote for New Mexico's 3rd congressional district, spoiling the Democrat—when a means is provided to get information from alternative candidates into voters' hands, voters respond with a ravenous appetite that is itself a comment on the paucity of the standard fare. Politics receives a healthy injection of enthusiasm and vigor from alternative candidates to the two parties—yet in most cases the TV news producers and editors of the Winner Take All media decide if and when these candidates will be heard. The media's rationalizations about viability merely conceal their own two-party loyalties and their "Winner Take All eyes."

There is something troubling about a free press that decides what ideas and candidates the public may hear. Apparently "free" means free to print or broadcast anything you want, and *only* what you want, without responsibility to the richness of the public debate. But once our analysis stretches beyond platitudes to the "freedom of the press," we see some disturbing qualities to the exclusionary practices of the Winner Take All media.

For the media's behavior goes beyond merely a strong allegiance on the part of powerful editors and TV producers to the two-party system, although as we have seen there is plentiful evidence of that. Even more disturbing, in an age when the Great Free Press is wholly owned by mega-merged corporations, the two-party system functions as a cash effluent that is extremely profitable for these corporations' bottom line. While the Winner Take All media is quick to hide behind First Amendment protections whenever their dominion is challenged, in fact there is little corporate concern for the "robustness of public debate" like the kind championed by First Amendment hero Justice William Brennan, or even for the "public interest," as broadcasters have legally pledged to uphold in exchange for receiving license to the public's airwaves.

The death of political discourse

> My people and I have come to an agreement which satisfies us both. They are to say what they please, and I am to do what I please.
>
> **—FREDERICK THE GREAT, KING OF PRUSSIA**

Sometime in the 1990s, the Winner Take All media, particularly television broadcasters, discovered an extremely lucrative mother lode of revenue that augurs poorly for the future of political discourse. As political campaigns and the candidates themselves have become mere vapid displays of poll-tested sound bites, and as citizens have become alienated from most things "political," television broadcasters in perennial search of higher ratings have slowly reduced their political coverage. This has produced at least one unfortunate side effect: increasingly, politicians in a campaign season have no choice but to buy more television ads. *Lots* of television ads, bringing in an estimated *$1 billion* in revenue to broadcasters. Some media analysts have theorized that this has been a brazenly conscious move on the part of television broadcasters to increase advertising revenue—decrease political coverage, forcing candidates to buy more TV time. Others dispute this, claiming that broadcasters are merely chasing viewers who are turned off to politics. Either way, the move has been a veritable gold mine that has dramatically enhanced TV broadcasters' bottom line and has pushed our nation another notch along its political race to the bottom.

According to Wall Street analysts, an estimated $1 billion of the more than $3 billion raised and spent on political campaigns in 2000 went to pay for ads on broadcast television. That's a fivefold increase over what the television industry raked in during the 1980 campaign, even after adjusting for inflation.[8] This cascade of cash has been gathering steam throughout the 1990s; revenue in 2000 from political spots was up 40 percent from 1996. Political commercials, which only appear for a few months out of the year, nevertheless were the third-largest source of TV advertising revenue for broadcasters, trailing only automotive and retail ads, according to an analysis by investment company Bear Stearns.[9] The prospect of such a cash cow caused *Broadcast & Cable Magazine* to gush a euphoric headline at the time of the 2000 primaries: "Happy Days Are Here Again." Said one campaign consultant, "The stations are salivating."[10] Without question, the broadcast industry has become the biggest beneficiary of the "business of politics." Whatever the initial motivations of the broadcasters, now that they have discovered this lucrative new revenue stream, there is little incentive to decrease it by increasing political news coverage.

Not surprisingly then, over the same time period that political ad revenue has been surging, the amount of campaign coverage by the broadcasters has been decreasing. Robert Lichter of the Center for Media and Public Affairs said, following a study his organization conducted of the 2000 election, "Coverage is way down from eight years ago. That means, if you work out the numbers, two elections ago the three networks together gave you about 25 minutes a night of election news, or about eight minutes apiece. This election they gave you about 12 minutes, or four minutes apiece per night."[11] Of that reduced amount of election news, a study by the Annenberg Public Policy Center found that only an average of sixty-four seconds per night was quality "candidate-centered" time during which the candidates themselves had an opportunity to discuss issues or their views. The rest was heavily filtered reporting about the suspense of who might win the horse race—in other words, entertainment.[12] In 1968, the average presidential campaign sound bite on network news was forty-three seconds. In the 1996 election, it dropped to 8.2 seconds. As Gary Ruskin, director of Commercial Alert, commented, "Third graders communicate in longer segments than that."[13]

So not only has the raw amount of election news decreased dramatically, but the quality of the coverage also has taken a nosedive. Thomas Patterson, professor at Harvard's Kennedy School and director of the Vanishing Voter Project, which studied the 2000 presidential election, wrote that the "news coverage that is provided too often serves to discourage or misdirect the public. Both Bush and Gore had more bad press than good press, in both television and newspapers, in the closing weeks of the campaign, and the stories told often were trivial."[14] The Annenberg study found that only one in four campaign stories aired in the month before the election were issue-oriented; the rest focused on the bumps and dips of polls and campaign strategy. Lichter, assessing the quality of the coverage, commented, "If you actually add up the airtime, journalists talking *about* the election accounted for 74 percent of the airtime. Candidates actually shown *speaking* accounted for 11 percent of the airtime. So the news is highly mediated, and I think that's what's driving candidates into talk shows. To give them time just to present themselves more as full human beings to the public." Indeed, rather astoundingly, Lichter's study discovered that when Bush went on the David Letterman show he got more airtime *in a single block* than he got the entire month of October on all three network newscasts combined.[15]

A study by the Alliance for Better Campaigns found that the decline in network news coverage also extended to primary debates, party conventions, campaign speeches, and presidential debates, prompting veteran ABC newsman Sam Donaldson to remark that his network's election coverage had "forfeited the field" to cable TV. The imminent death of political coverage has drawn attention even from the likes of U.S. Senator Robert Torricelli, one of the Democratic Party's soft money kings. During a September 6, 2000, floor speech Torricelli railed against broadcasters, saying, "During the final two weeks of the New Jersey Senate primary, viewers in Philadelphia and New York markets were 10 times more likely to receive a communication from a candidate through a paid advertisement than they were through an actual news story. . . . This collapse of news coverage is leading candidates to raise more money and buy more advertisements."[16]

It's not just that the broadcasters reaped the benefits of too many well-funded political players and their ads chasing too few TV spots—in other words, too much demand chasing too little supply, creating a "crowding out" effect, as some have rationalized. The broadcasters are actively *gouging* campaigns during the political season. As Election Day approaches, prices for TV spots typically double and triple. Some media consultants found the rates rising within hours. One consultant from a firm handling congressional races across the nation reported how a Philadelphia station quoted a $900 price for a particular TV slot. "When my time buyer called a few hours later to place the ad, she was told, sorry, the price is now up to $1150." In Portland, Oregon, the Sierra Club found that the price of a thirty-second spot more then tripled in less than one month.

A Brigham Young University study of broadcast television political ad spending in seventeen hotly contested U.S. Senate and congressional races in 2000 found that the average cost for all political spots rose from less than $500 in mid-August to more than $1,200 in the final week of the campaign.[17] A thirty-second prime time ad in New York City was, in effect, being auctioned to the highest bidders and going for $50,000; in Chicago, $20,000. Said Neal Oxman of the Campaign Group Inc., a Philadelphia media consulting firm, "[Local TV stations] are getting away with flat-out stealing compared to what they're delivering."[18]

Oddly enough, in 1971 Congress enacted a campaign system to insulate candidates from such price-gouging practices. This system, called the "Lowest Unit Charge" (LUC) system, bound television broadcasters as a condition of receiving their license of the public airwaves to charge their lowest rates to political candidates. But the system included a gaping loophole that has rendered it an utter failure. That's because the lowest LUC rates come with a catch: ads sold at the LUC rate can be preempted by the station, often without any notice, if another advertiser wants that particular time slot and is willing to pay more for it. When this happens, candidates are entitled to a refund or to have their ad run at a later date, but that's small consolation. Unlike many product advertisers whose chief objective is to build brand loyalty over the long haul and who can therefore afford to be flexible about when their ads run, candidates need assurance their ads will run exactly when and where they place them. In the heat of the political campaign, if an opponent's attack ad is running on the evening news, the candidate needs to know that a counterattack ad will run at the right time to the right audience.[19]

Local broadcasting stations understand these dynamics—and too many exploit them. In effect, they too game the system, not necessarily to win political campaigns but to profit from the business of politics. "It's become common practice for station ad salesmen to pressure you out of buying LUC into buying non-preemptible by telling you it's the only way they can be sure the ads will run when you want," says Cathie Herrick, a media consultant with a political time-buying firm. Some have compared it to extortion. "It's the ultimate squeeze play," says Peter Fenn, a longtime media consultant. "The stations know it's their way or the highway. That's why you end up paying top dollar. They've done this kind of gouging in the past, but in 2000, they broke through some kind of ceiling. They've just become vacuum cleaners for political money."[20]

A study by the Alliance for Better Campaigns of ten stations in major media markets showed that, in the final months of the 2000 elections, candidates paid ad rates for over 16,000 ads that were 65 percent above the candidate LUC rate.[21] Political parties and issue group advertisers, which are not entitled to LUC protection, saw their rates rise even more, doubling and sometimes tripling in busy markets between Labor Day and Election Day. Obviously the thirty-year-old LUC law, designed to protect candidates from gouging, has collapsed into its own loopholes. The biggest beneficiaries have been ABC/Disney, CBS, and NBC/General Electric, which between them own fifty-eight local TV stations, most of them in the nation's largest cities, that took in tens of millions of dollars in political ad money. Once a minor blip on these corporations' balance sheets, cash from candidates, interest groups, and political parties now adds up to serious dollars that, according to the *Washington Post,* can affect their bottom lines and even their stock prices.[22]

Tellingly, at the time that NBC and Fox refused to broadcast one (NBC) or all (Fox) of the presidential debates, they already had profited handsomely from the political season, with the thirteen stations owned by NBC/General Electric running 15,819 political ads that raked in $23.5 million, and Fox stations running 14,532 ads, earning $9.2 million.[23] Former Senator and presidential candidate Bill Bradley has commented wryly, "Today's political campaigns function as collection agencies for broadcasters. You simply transfer money from contributors to television stations."

Not surprisingly, the broadcasters have fought any legislative or public interest attempts to curtail their billion-dollar cash cow. Following the passage of the deeply flawed Telecommunications Act of 1996, which further deregulated the media market to allow for even larger mega-mergers, the Clinton Administration doubled the amount of spectrum space it licensed to television broadcasters in order to facilitate the industry's transition to digital technology. Estimates of the value of this additional spectrum space ranged up to $70 billion, and once again it was given to the broadcasters for free, provoking cries of "corporate welfare." As a sop to critics, Clinton appointed an advisory panel to "assess and update" the long-abused "public interest obligations" of television broadcasters in the wake of this valuable gift of the public's assets. The panel, composed of scholars, public interest advocates, and broadcasters (including the president of CBS), recommended among other things that all television broadcasters voluntarily dedicate a minimum of five minutes a night in the thirty days before the presidential election to what was called "candidate-centered discourse"—news coverage where the candidates are discussing their views and issues, either via interviews, mini-debates, or other formats—as opposed to election news about the Winner Take All horse race or the latest dips in the polls.

But still the broadcasters balked. In Election 2000, over a million political ads ran on 484 local stations, the equivalent of 595,468 minutes of ads, 9,924 hours or 413 solid days of advertising—and yet nearly all broadcasters were unwilling to dedicate even a minuscule amount of air time to such "candidate-centered discourse." In fact, the networks mobilized to undermine the White House commission's proposal. But aware of the public sentiment (and legal reality) that in fact the airwaves are owned by the public, and that they had taken a pledge "to serve the public interest," the broadcasters worked behind the scenes to kill the plan. They even employed newspapers *owned* by them to do their dirty work.

A study of forty-one newspaper editorials from thirty-three newspapers weighing in on the "five minutes per night" proposal found that seven of ten newspapers owned by media conglomerates with television broadcast holdings editorialized against it. The same ratio, seven out of ten newspapers, owned by media companies *without* TV broadcast properties favored it. The study found that economic self-interest was more closely linked to a paper's stance than its political leaning: papers that endorsed Clinton in 1996 were no more likely to support the White House plan than papers that did not endorse him. But even more troubling, as the study's author pointed out, "in no cases did the [opposing] newspapers divulge their ownership interests in their editorials."[24] Instead, the broadcasters stealthily hid their conflict of interest behind their newspaper mouthpieces.

Given that hostile posture, not surprisingly only a handful of TV stations committed to "candidate-centered" time.[25] The Annenberg study found that ABC, NBC, and CBS "failed to meet the recommended public interest standard that they air five minutes—300 seconds—of nightly candidate issue discussion in the final month of the campaign." Instead, on average, there was just sixty-four seconds of candidate-centered discourse per night per network, the study found. Sixty-four seconds. Barely a minute. That's one minute per night for democracy and political debate, in exchange for the $70 *billion* in additional spectrum space given for free by the Clinton administration to the corporate media, which is in addition to the $367 billion giveaway they already had received.

The surging greed of Winner Take All media corporations in a deregulated media market has created a commercial bazaar in which TV stations sell to the highest political bidder what the government has given them for free. The $367 billion plus $70 billion corporate welfare giveaway from the public to huge media conglomerates in exchange for a commitment to the public interest is being grossly abused. Paul Taylor, director of the Alliance for Better Campaigns, has said, "When it comes to serving as public trustee, the industry doesn't see beyond its own bottom line."[26] Said Fred Wertheimer, president of Democracy 21, a nonprofit organization working for campaign finance reform,

"The industry has a sweetheart deal, and is not interested in making any moves to open the door to make it work better."[27]

Most of the corporate media, of course, cry foul over this negative assessment of their industry. They point out that they are the ones assuming the risk of research for developing digital television, cable, and other broadcast technologies. But having crisper, sharper TV images, or sense-around sound, or interactive television, or five hundred channels "with nothing on," or any of the other digital and cable TV marvels promised by the industry to consumers is hardly a worthwhile trade-off for a dumbing-down of politics and the withering of political discourse.

Media defenders also cite, as proof of their adequate political coverage, the wall-to-wall airwaves saturation of the post-election debacle that unfolded in Florida. It's true that when the presidential election produced a photo finish, suddenly the media coverage that had been MIA during the rest of the campaign lurched into high gear. But that was because it was O. J., Monica, and Elian all over again (except, as one commentator noted referring to O. J. and Monica, "without the guilt"). The media conglomerates know how to cover a train wreck, and this was a political train wreck of historic proportions. It was drama, it was entertainment, it was a riveting event, without issues or discourse or, for that matter, oddly, politics even. It was *the* horse race, the photo finish of the century; in short, it was *news*, as that has come to be defined at the outset of the twenty-first century.

The Perils of "Bottom Line" Journalism

In a mass democratic society in which millions of people ostensibly take part in voting, representation, and, by extension, governance, information is a lifeblood. Without clear, accurate, and reliable information, collective decision making can't help but become disjointed. By extension then, the entities responsible for delivering that information play a crucial, even progenerative, role. They are one of the Archimedean fulcrums on which the health of the system pivots, akin to a feedback loop of an organism's immune system. If the feedback loop is awry, if the information received is tainted, flawed, or incomplete, then the organism misdiagnoses or reacts inappropriately, perhaps even dangerously.

For a century now, dating back to the wildcat days of autocrat media tycoons William Randolph Hearst and Henry Luce, the Great Free Press has hid behind the First Amendment and an ironic kind of Jeffersonian nostalgia to veil the fact that the broadcast and print media have become synonymous with big business.[28] Today, the Great Free Press is dominated by huge mega-merged corporations that have become more like media monopolists, not so much committed to a robust public debate, an informed citizenry, or the public interest as much as to own bottom-line commercial interests. The collective functioning of our representative democracy depends to a troubling degree upon these profit-mongering media monopolists, the Winner Take All media.

That's a scary thought. Besides the omnipresent bottom line, what are the ethics and values of the Winner Take All media? First, they are about political scandal and conflict. Why? Because scandal and conflict, drama and sensation, sell—the familiar Hearst and Luce combination of sensationalism and entertainment packaged as news. Ever since the *Miami Herald* put a tail on presidential candidate Gary Hart in 1987 and found him spending the night with a young woman, political sex scandals have become a staple of modern political reporting. When Hart bowed out of the race he complained that the whole system "reduces the press of this nation to hunters and presidential candidates to the hunted." A number of journalists agreed. *New York Times* columnist Anthony Lewis wrote at the time, "When I read about the *Miami Herald* story on Gary Hart, I felt degraded in my profession. Is that what journalism is about, hiding in a van outside the politician's home?"[29]

Bill Clinton, obviously, was an extremely lucrative cash cow for the Winner Take All media. With the partisan GOP pit bulls in the House and their wealthy conservative backers sniffing for blood, and with Clinton's considerable gaps in personal integrity and behavior, scandal followed the president like a trail of ants to a carcass. His personal peccadilloes sold newspapers and salaciously engaged and disgusted TV viewers. It was riveting political theater. But the global publishing of the Starr Commission's report over the World Wide Web, with its graphic details about spicy events and sexual props like cigars used in the Oval Office with intern Monica Lewinsky, was another "first" in modern politics that the nation would just as soon have done without. Once again, other nations and peoples around the world were laughing and shaking their heads at the utter madness of American politics, wrapped by the media as sensationalist and titillating entertainment, and the excesses to which it periodically leads.

"Bottom-line" journalism has become synonymous with a kind of "pack journalism" that can snowball into what political scientist Larry Sabato has called a "feeding frenzy," where "the news media, print and broadcast, go after a wounded politician like sharks in a feeding frenzy." Sabato has described this as "a spectacle without equal in modern politics." Certainly the Internet, the World Wide Web, and twenty-four-hour cable TV have an unparalleled ability to make whispered rumor and innuendo a defining feature of what is now considered "news." The lives of politicians have transmogrified into a kind of *Truman Show* fish bowl, where it is harder and harder to find the "off" switch to vicious cycles of scandal.[30] Unquestionably this kind of sensationalism and scandal sheet journalism have been good for the Winner Take All media's bottom line. Could that be why the media today engages in so much of it, rather than in real political and investigative journalism?

Even the more respected outlets like the *New York Times* and the Lehrer NewsHour play into this penchant for conflict, scandal, and mudslinging. One study found that these outlets actually *encourage* such conflict by featuring more frequently those politicians from the ideological extremes of their parties and underrepresenting the moderates. The media, the study concluded, "highlights the public's most abhorrent characteristics of politics: conflict, bickering, and games playing. . . . In short, ideological position affects press coverage," even more than other factors that should lead to more coverage such as powerful committee or party leadership positions.[31]

Meanwhile, the Winner Take All media has fought even the smallest encroachment on its monopoly. An unlikely coalition composed of the industry corporate lobby National Association of Broadcasters (NAB) and the nonprofit National Public Radio fought a Federal Communications Commission (FCC) decision in 1999 to democratize America's airwaves by issuing hundreds of noncommercial, low-power FM radio licenses. So-called "micro-radio" stations would have the capacity to broadcast anywhere from 1 to 3.5 miles, an infinitesimally small range compared to the powerful transmitters of commercial stations. FCC engineers determined that there were no technical issues, as opponents claimed, regarding spectrum integrity or interference with the signal of established stations. The micro-radio stations were going to be low-tech *community* stations, both rural and urban, providing provincial programming about local events and themes that the mega-commercial stations seeking a larger audience consistently overlooked. It seemed to many to be an appropriate marriage of Big and Little, enriching the milieu of all.

But the rich broadcasters and NPR saw it differently; they saw their profits and/or their hegemony being potentially challenged, so they fought vociferously to stop micro-radio.[32] NAB has been described by Sen. John McCain as one of the most powerful lobbies in Washington, and its president, Edward O. Fritts, was a friend and college classmate of then–Senate Majority Leader Trent Lott.[33] NAB spent millions lobbying Congress against low-power radio stations and other issues. With political cover provided by the increasingly corporate-sponsored NPR (once again, "what happened to the 'public' in National Public Radio?" as one critic bemoaned), the FCC decision was effectively bottled up.

Like a fuzzy television screen that is slowly coming into focus, a pattern is emerging here. The Great Free Press *cum* Winner Take All media monopoly, like any business, is motivated substantially by profit. It takes positions based on the Bottom Line: what will increase profits?—like political sex scandal, reducing political coverage and forcing more ad-buys, or marketing violent material to children[34]—or what will impede them?—like the infinitesimal signal of a micro-radio station or airing presidential conventions, debates, and other political coverage. That is the mentality, that is the ethics, of the Winner Take All media. It is *not* motivated by the public interest.

Yet when the Communications Act of 1934 granted broadcasters free and exclusive licenses to the public airwaves, it did so on the condition that they agreed to serve "the public interest." The value of the public airwaves has been estimated by a leading media analyst to be worth currently $367 *billion*—that is a $367 billion giveaway, corporate welfare, from the public to huge media conglomerates in exchange for a commitment to the public interest.[35] But obviously the latter part of the equation has been entirely lost in the ensuing sixty-plus years.

The Telecommunications Act of 1996 deregulated the telecommunications industry and made takeovers and mergers even easier. Many experts predicted the Telecommunications Act would inevitably result in increasing media centralization, and since its passage corporate media takeovers have proceeded apace. Disney's subsequent takeover of ABC created the world's largest media company at the time, until the $100 billion AOL–Time Warner merger came along. And the Australian magnate Rupert Murdoch, probably the closest we know to a modern-day William Hearst, has been slowly adding to his media empire.

For the corporate Winner Take All media, the Telecommunications Act has been a kind of "free trade" agreement to increase profits. Like our politics, where the winner takes all, our Winner Take All economy similarly rewards the biggest winners in a disproportionately lucrative fashion, as outlined in economists Robert Frank and Phillip Cook's superb *The Winner Take All Society*.[36] In the specter of the modern media cartel we see a monopolistic convergence of Winner Take All politics and Winner Take All economics, using First Amendment arguments to attack any barriers to its present lucrative existence or future growth. In an era when *effective* speech is equivalent to how many TV stations or radio stations you own, the First Amendment itself has become like a free trade agreement for media corporations. It keeps the government at bay, creating a deregulated media market no less than NAFTA or GATT. Within this "free trade–free speech" zone, corporate speech can gobble up competitors and, ironically, decide who will speak and, more importantly, who will be *heard* in our Winner Take All political system.

As legal and media experts like Yale law professor Owen Fiss, Robert McChesney, and others have pointed out, the First Amendment paradigm of the political dissident standing on their street corner soap box, inveighing against politicians and society's ills until hauled off by the cops, is mostly an anachronism.[37] The terrain of the First Amendment today is dominated by huge media conglomerates who have a lot more and a lot louder speech than everyone else. It's as if they have turned up *their* volume and drowned everyone else out. It's not that others cannot speak, it's just that we cannot hear them, their speech is not effective, compared to the booming speech of the Winner Take All media. And traditional, civil libertarian–type First Amendment defenses protect this status quo. The paradigm has dramatically shifted, but civil libertarians and First Amendment fundamentalists are still stuck in the old "individual autonomy" paradigm, refusing to recognize the new reality.

All of this, of course, has huge ramifications for politics and political discourse. In its customary, dissembling fashion, the Winner Take All media pick and choose what to air, and the evidence is overwhelming that their criteria for choosing America's information fare has little to do with the public interest or stimulating political discourse. With a Winner Take All media saturated by the values of sensationalism, entertainment, and profiteering, there is little room on the dial for the values of "robust public debate," discussion of ideas and policies, or political pluralism. Their motto is, "If you can't pay, you can't play," and only a shrinking number of players can afford the price of admission. With a hundred channels of laugh tracks, home shopping infomercials, and pay-for-view, the information necessities of democracy and a free-thinking society are swallowed up in the unregulated, free-for-all regime dominated by the corporatized Winner Take All media.

The future of the Winner Take All media

John Peter Zenger must be rolling over in his grave. Arrested for libel on November 17, 1734, for publishing a newspaper criticizing the British colonial governor of New York, Zenger was imprisoned for nearly ten months. When finally brought to trial he was represented by the young Alexander Hamilton, and to the acclaim of the public the colonial jury acquitted Zenger on the grounds that his charges had been based on fact—a key consideration in libel cases since that time. Zenger became a champion, setting a standard for the gallant free press standing up to autocracy. The Zenger case struck a tremendous blow for freedom of the press and a classically liberal tradition that eventually led to the First Amendment.

How far we have traveled in 260-plus years. Today, the Great Free Press, the corporate Winner Take All media monopoly, *is* the embodiment of autocracy. Soaking off the fat of a public dole for their own enrichment, in a very real sense the corporate media has become a *threat* to free speech, certainly to political speech and to political campaigns. Broadcasters, in essence, are guardians of something precious—the modern-day equivalent of the public square. Except *they* decide who will address the "assembled" audience. The specter of the media, particularly the *corporate* media and its values, deciding the viability of political candidates—and, by extension, which issues and policies voters will hear about during campaigns—should be utterly offensive to a democratic society. A congressional district now contains over 600,000 people, making grassroots campaigns impractical in most cases, so television and radio campaigning have become near-essential in most congressional elections, and even in state elections, particularly the most high-profile, and close races.

The corporate media has its own agenda, which is not unexpected, but every candidate should not have to squeeze her or himself through the pinhole of corporate media preconditions.

Moreover, as we have seen, broadcasters, having been the recipient of ridiculously generous corporate welfare, have managed to wrest control of the people's airwaves from the people and their representatives, and now have huge financial incentives to keep political coverage of campaigns and candidates to a minimum. That allows them to *sell back* to candidates the airwaves that they have been given for free. The Winner Take All media conglomerates were not elected or even appointed to act as the arbiter or the mediator of our democratic process or our national politics, yet the crucial telecommunications technology they control has allowed them to assume this position, uninvited. Now in custody of this crucial infrastructure of our representative democracy, the Winner Take All media has become a powerful special interest that uses the public's airwaves to perpetuate its domination, a kind of self-fulfilling cycle. It seems a sort of collective stupidity, an implacable insanity, that no one knows how to stop.

The evolution of the Winner Take All media has reached a fork in the road. Voters are being robbed of the fullness of a debate of ideas and policies, and the challenging viewpoints that a Perot, a Ventura, a Benjamin, a Miller, or a Howell brings to a campaign. The fork in the road can go only one of two ways—either toward reform or toward further deform. It has already cut political coverage down to the bone—only sixty-four seconds per night—and raised advertising rates to exorbitant levels. There's not much more profit to be wrung out of the system. So the logic of reform makes more and more sense, even to those who profit from the system. Many broadcasters say privately that they are appalled by the soaring amounts of money spent by candidates on TV ads. CBS President Leslie Moonves cochaired the White House panel that recommended five minutes per night of candidate-centered time. A sales manager for KTNV-TV in Las Vegas said, "Speaking as a citizen, the system screams for reform."[38]

But lacking serious and profound reform, the current trajectory of the Winner Take All media does not augur well for the American future. Indeed, it is one of the most disturbing trends contributing to our downward spiral into a voterless and internecine post-democracy. An ominous dark cloud moved over an already-gloomy horizon in September 2001 when the largest media conglomerates, including Fox, NBC, CBS, and AOL–Time Warner Inc., filed suit in federal court to overturn FCC rules that bar a company from owning television stations that collectively reach more than 35 percent of viewing households or that prevent one company from owning television stations and cable systems in the same market.[39] The court challenges, if successful, will allow big media companies to become even larger through mergers and acquisitions—and to further garrotte the free flow of information. Ironically, the corporate plaintiffs are employing civil libertarian–type First Amendment/free speech arguments, claiming that "every day the rule is in effect, we are being deprived of our ability to speak to 65 percent of the nation's households"—the First Amendment as "free trade" agreement for the Winner Take All media.[40]

If the media corporations prevail in this audacious gambit, that may initiate the first steps toward what might be called the "Berlusconization" of the American media. Silvio Berlusconi is the Italian media magnate who managed to gobble up nearly all private media in Italy, and then used that resource as a personal steppingstone to a political career. The exquisitely dressed Berlusconi's campaigning method consists of sailing up and down the Italian coast in his private yacht, and pulling into ports where his TV stations cover his press conferences, beaming his perennially tanned face to Italians all over the country. Berlusconi's intertwined political and media careers culminated diabolically in 2001 with his winning the prime ministership of Italy, a kind of Italian version of a William Randolph Hearst.

If the U.S. corporate media plaintiffs succeed via the courts in overturning the rules preventing even greater media mergers, or if the FCC waives these rules, it moves us a giant step closer to a Berlusconi-type figure lurking on America's horizon—a demagogue like Hearst with political aspirations, who personally controls huge portions of the electronic media infrastructure and programming, all on the public dole—a person who is part Rupert Murdoch and part Newt Gingrich. Given the current trajectory of the Winner Take All media—of the corporate media monopoly immersed in the Winner Take All political system—such an American future is not outside the pale of possibility.

CHAPTER ELEVEN

Caught between a Poll and a Hard Focus Group
The Loss of Political Ideas

I find myself speculating whether the relentless daily diet of crafted, acted emotions and canned ideas is not subtly pressing our
brains to not only mistake fantasy for what is real but to absorb
this process into our personal sensory process. This last election
is an example.

—ARTHUR MILLER, PLAYWRIGHT,
30TH JEFFERSON LECTURE IN THE HUMANITIES,
MARCH 26, 2001[1]

Under the mind-numbing influence of the new campaign technologies and the Winner Take All media, electoral politics in the United States has become like cotton candy for the political faculties. As we have seen, Winner Take All provides incentives for candidates in close races to use "crafted talk" and "simulated responsiveness" in a bid to stay as close to the political center as possible (at least in rhetoric, if not in policy), to push personality and scandal above ideas or policy, to ignore whole swathes of voters who aren't among the lucky few targeted as swing voters, and for the media to ignore independent and third-party candidates. An unwritten, cozy convergence has occurred between all the major players involved—the party leaders, candidates, political consultants, the media bosses and reporters—per-petuating this Winner Take All reality.

Consequently, what we are witnessing is a wholesale and widespread under-development of the American voter. Campaigns and candidates under the sway of mad scientist political consultants and garbage pail snoopers and their bags of tricks are contributing to the atrophy of the national political consciousness. Voters are not challenged or stimulated to think about the great issues of our times because these issues are mostly left on the political sidelines by both the Winner Take All campaigns and the media. And the issues that *are* discussed are done in such a simplistic sound-bite fashion that they contribute little to the understanding of complex matters. Fostering understanding and debate of issues is simply not the way you win elections today under Winner Take All's two-choice duopoly. Tragically, at the *exact* historical moment of rapid techno-logical, ecological, foreign policy, and global change, when fresh, creative solutions for dealing with looming challenges are at a premium, our nation is in the throes of an alarming loss of political ideas.

The fizzled flatness of the presidential debates in October 2000 perfectly illustrated this zombielike state of our national political discourse. During the second debate, Gore agreed with Bush so many times that at one point Bush quipped that the debate was beginning to look like a "love fest."[2] "From the debates," wrote *Washington Post* columnist Mary McGrory, "you get the idea that the American electorate has been boiled down to one 65-year-old woman with arthritis."[3] Nader described the debates, quite accurately, as the "drab debating the dreary." Yet that was the best that the American political system — the Winner Take All system—and its mediating institutions could produce.

At this point official political discourse is so arbitrated by the handlers, the consultants, the polling numbers, and the focus groups; by party leaders salivating to win; by the Winner Take All media, and so subjugated to the gaming incentives to win, that it has become utterly devoid of anything resembling a spirited debate of ideas, policies, or vision. Likewise, legislative policy—indeed, our national direction, our national political maturation—has become stunted because it has been robbed of the opportunity to find a consensus via a fully informed debate in the marketplace of ideas. With the advent of the permanent campaign, this "discursive depression" now extends throughout the legislative session. The loss of political ideas is becoming an entrenched feature of our Winner Take All political landscape.

Ideological monocultures:
"It's hard to debate when only one side can be heard"

The loss of fresh policy ideas, even as the world becomes more complex and internationally intertwined, is perhaps the greatest measure of how obsolete and antiquated our eighteenth-century Winner Take All system has become. Due to the way you win elections in a two-choice/two-party system, Winner Take All severely restricts not only which ideas and policies will be discussed, but also *how* they will be discussed. From the issues of labor and trade, food safety, energy policy, and healthcare to globalization and vital issues for low-income people and young voters, debate of ideas and policy options has become severely constrained by the Winner Take All conundrum and the two-choice tango. Here are a few examples that illustrate the anatomy of this dynamic.

Labor and trade policy

In a time of globalization and rapid technological change, policy discussions related to labor and trade policy are conducted along rigidly constricted lines. Both the Republicans and Democrats prioritize "the growth of our economy" and "the rising tide that lifts all boats," avoiding like the plague those policies or discussions targeted at distribution of wealth or per capita inequality. To be sure, both sides profess sympathy for "the working man," but to a slavishly opti-mistic degree both expect that the invisible hand of the free market eventually will iron out any irregularities or inequalities. Any dissent to this fundamentalist position rarely finds expression in the halls of Congress.

The labor stances of even the most pro-labor Democratic leaders pale by comparison, for instance, to the Social Democratic parties of Europe, whose labor and trade policies more conform to human and worker needs rather than the other way around. On a whole slew of indicators, including healthcare, day-care for working parents, equal pay for equal work, length of the workweek, paid vacation and holidays, free and equal education (including free tuition to universities), and more, the European political center is where the U.S. labor movement and many American workers would love to be.

How has Winner Take All contributed to a comparative decline for Ameri-can workers, even during a time of prosperity? As we saw in Chapter 3, the democracy technology of Winner Take All tends to foster a two-party system in which minor parties, like a European-style Labor or Green Party, that might offer voters a different kind of perspective than the doo-wop chorus of the duopoly, flounder. Not surprisingly, in the carnivorous climate of Winner Take All, ideas that put forth labor, trade, and social policies on the order of the social democracies of Europe have gotten chewed up by the corporate and PAC-fund-ed duopoly. In recent years, campaigns for swing voters' allegiances have cen-tered on conservative issues like tax cuts, deficits, the war on drugs and crime, and, most recently, Social Security, a patient's Bill of Rights and education (although, curiously enough, European-style free university education is nowhere on the radar screen), with a political smear or two here and a dollop of race-baiting there crafted to attract conservative white swing voters.

So labor and trade policy does not figure heavily in campaign sound bites, not because these issues are too complex to boil down to a sound bite, but because they are too controversial and unpredictable in how they will play across political lines with swing voters. A candidate needs to amass a lot of votes to win, and this preselects what type of ideas will receive attention from the two major parties during a Winner Take All campaign.

Moreover, Winner Take All's constricted two-choice conundrum does not allow complexities in the electorate to emerge or find political expression. For example, blue-collar, pro-gun workers must choose between labor's traditional support for the Democrats and the pro-NRA Republicans. The racially conser-vative white working class must choose between the pro-labor, pro-affirmative action Democrats and the anti-affirmative action, anti-union GOP. Among many of these same blue-collar workers the death penalty has come to represent "toughness on crime"; it is unlikely that an opponent of the death penalty could run a credible campaign for president or for most legislative offices because Winner Take All elections make nuanced positions difficult. The political monocultures engendered by regional demographics, i.e. Bushlandia and New Goreia, as well as the huge numbers of safe seats located even outside these regions, bury the natural diversity of opinion. As Rob Richie of the Center for Voting and Democracy has pointed out, if the Pope could vote in the United States he would be bedeviled by the Winner Take All conundrum, demanding that he weigh his fervent opposition to abortion against his support for social justice such as a humane welfare policy. Republican or Democrat, either way the Pope loses. While the Pope can't vote, many similarly minded Catholics do have to choose in key battleground states like Ohio, Pennsylvania, and Michigan.

Because of these dynamics unleashed by Winner Take All, with its incentives for hack-attack politics and targeting campaigns at swing voters, new or controversial ideas are very difficult to put before the American people. Instead, the modern technology used for Winner Take All campaigns is ideal for "divide and conquer" strategies in which the two major parties triangulate into each other's political base with contentious "wedge issues" like gun control, gay rights, race, affirmative action, the death penalty, and abortion. Thus, while in theory there ought to be a large constituency of American workers out there demanding better wages and working conditions, in fact that constituency is splintered and fractured along multiple lines. The two-choice Winner Take All system, with its gaming incentives to target key groups of swing voters with powerful sound-bite campaign slogans that resonate and motivate, simply cannot cope with this kind of complexity.

Of course, it would help substantially if American workers *knew* about their relatively low status among the global workforce. Unfortunately, the Winner Take All media and the two major parties don't bother informing them of this. While the Dow and Nasdaq were high-flying in the mid- to late-1990s, we were regaled daily with headlines and statistics about the robustness of the U.S. economy, including the latest IPO success stories and "get rich quick" gazillion-aires. Americans have become so used to thinking that we are the best, "the wealthiest economy," the "most powerful nation," the "lone remaining super-power," that we fail to recognize how few Americans actually shared in our great fortune during the 1990s. Let's briefly summarize the evidence.

Comparing American workers to European workers, French, Swedish, German, Italian, Belgian, and Spanish workers have seen reductions in their work-week to anywhere from thirty-five to thirty-nine hours as their wages stayed even or increased, but in the United States we have an unenforced forty-hour workweek, and the average full-time worker in the late 1990s worked forty-four hours per week—a full day longer *per week* than French workers. Some Americans work even more hours because certain industries pressure employees to work overtime, including grueling twelve-hour shifts as employers move to continuous twenty-four-hour production. Besides working greater hours than their European counterparts, according to the Bureau of Labor Statistics American workers also have less parental leave, less affordable daycare, and the least number of paid holidays and vacation, in many industries and occupations as low as only ten vacation days (two weeks) per year—the European standard is to give all workers five weeks of paid vacation per year. In short, the average American worker now has lower wages per hours worked, less vacation and paid holidays, and a longer work week than their European or even their Japanese counterparts.

According to the Department of Labor, a majority of American workers now make less income in real (inflation-adjusted) dollars than they did twenty years ago, even as they work *160 hours more a year*. One study found that the booming late 1990s appears to have left the middle class in many states no better or even worse off than it was a decade before.[4] According to the Economic Policy Institute, more than one in four American workers earned poverty-level wages in 1999—at the *height* of the prosperity cycle—which translates into $8.19 per hour or less, or approximately $17,000 per year. Lacking sufficient income, American workers have had to go deeper in debt, consumer indebtedness now soaring to over $6.2 trillion—for the first time in history total household debts (including mortgage loans) surpassed total after-tax incomes, a precarious level not even reached pre-1929.[5]

Nationally we have 20 percent child poverty, the highest percentage—by far—in the Western world. Among the major European countries, only Russia, at 23.2 percent, has a higher percentage of children living in poverty than the United States (but within the U.S., two of our most populous states, New York and California, have higher percentages of poverty-stricken children than Russia).[6] By numerous measurements there exists a two-tiered economy where the top 10 percent is doing quite well, the top 1 percent spectacularly. But as Jeff Gates pointed out in his book *Democracy at Risk,* the top 1 percent of the richest people in this country have financial wealth equal to the combined 95 percent of the American people.[7] That's an inverted pyramid of inequality that has troubled even Alan Greenspan.[8]

Why, one must suppose, did we not hear much about *that* reality in the 2000 presidential campaign? The answer has a lot to do with our Winner Take All practices and methods. Without the presence of a multiparty system based on proportional representation that permits the viability of a political party and candidates who are explicitly pro-worker and willing to raise issues regarding the lopsided distribution of wealth, the American labor movement has had little choice but to support the Democrats. This has left the Democratic Party, under the leadership of Bill Clinton, Al Gore, and the centrist Democratic Leadership Council, free to drift as far to the right as they dare. Thus, under the pinch of Winner Take All, uninformed about their low economic status and with nowhere to turn electorally, American workers have been slowly losing ground compared to other established democracies, even during a time of great prosperity. The economic boom of the 1990s was not equally shared, not by a long shot, in part because the strictures of the Winner Take All system and the prejudices of the corporate-owned Winner Take All media did not permit a widespread transmission of varied information sources or a substantive debate of important policy issues related to distribution of wealth and income.

Caught between the pincers of swing voters and the latest polling numbers, Al Gore's flirtation with populist rhetoric was extremely short-lived. Yet when he abandoned that campaign ploy there was little that labor and its supporters felt they could do but tag along. Ralph Nader tried to do the heavy lifting of raising these issues in the 2000 presidential campaign, but he was mostly ignored by the corporate media and excluded from the televised presidential debates by the duopoly's puppet Commission on Presidential Debates. The incentives of the two-choice, Winner Take All system combined with the biases of the Winner Take All media simply do not permit the ascension of a political party or candidates that can articulate an unabashed worker-oriented and wealth redistribution program and mobilize that natural constituency in the electoral arena. Thus, under the vice grip of Winner Take All, American workers are being slowly and inexorably squeezed.

Food safety

Another example of how the two-choice tango of Winner Take All restricts the parameters of the debate and leads to an ideological monoculture is the issue of food safety. The past decade has seen astonishing, even frightening, advances in biotechnology. Genetically modified (GM) Franken-foods and biologically redesigned "pharm animals" and "super-fish" have made Hollywood science fiction a present-day fact. On the European side of the Atlantic, genetically modified foods have been the subject of fierce public debate and parliamentary deliberation. Elected representatives to national governments as well as the European Union's parliament, led by representatives from the various Green Parties, have introduced and passed laws restricting manufacture and import of GM foods.

But on the other side of the Atlantic, in good ol' Winner Take All USA, corporate and Clinton Administration boosters of GM foods launched this technology forward with nary a public or congressional debate. European skepticism over GM foods was blamed on "old-world conservatism," on their being "culturally risk-averse to trying new things," and on "agricultural protectionism." Meanwhile, Americans have been portrayed as more sophisticated consumers who are more accepting of technology "based on science and not on anxiety." A *New York Times* article suggested that U.S. consumers "seem hardly to care" about genetic alterations of what they eat.[9]

But in fact numerous consumer surveys have shown huge majorities of Americans support mandatory labeling of genetically modified foods, and would avoid buying them if they were clearly labeled. Consumers Union, the oldest and largest association of American consumers with 4.7 million member households, has repeatedly and persistently opposed government failures to adequately handle this new technology. In 1997, even biotech giant Novartis found 93 percent of Americans in favor of labeling; a poll conducted by the U.S. Department of Agriculture in 1995 found 84 percent in favor, and a *Time* magazine survey in 1999 put the percentage at 81. Among those calling for food safety testing and labeling were the Attorneys General of eight states and the several-million-strong American Association of Retired Persons. In June 1999 a petition carrying 500,000 signatures in support of labeling was presented to the White House, Congress, and governmental agencies. As University of Washington professor Phil Bereano has pointed out, "this is hardly the mark of apathy."[10]

Yet this kind of public opposition found little expression in the halls of Congress. The reason why is closely related to our use of Winner Take All. In Europe, the electoral system is based on proportional representation systems; like-minded groups such as the environmentalists and social justice activists who formed the Green Parties are represented in the legislative bodies as long as they attract a sufficient number of votes to cross a certain threshold of support (typically a minimum of 5 percent of the popular vote). From this vantage point, the Greens and their Social Democratic supporters have been able to insert genetic engineering concerns into public and legislative discourse. As the number of food scares have increased in Europe, as well as the concomitant concern over food safety, so has the success of the Green Parties, to the point where they have become junior coalition partners in five European countries, including the two largest. The proportional voting systems, in other words, have allowed an upwelling of popular response to register in the electoral arena and in the legislatures.

But in the United States, due to the peculiar Winner Take All incentives, significant political minorities—along with their ideas and issues—have been ignored by legislative representatives. Practically never does the Green Party or any other political party with a strong position questioning GM foods get elected to our national or state legislatures (although there have been some modest successes for the Green Party at the local level).[11] Consequently, the issue of food safety, like many other new and innovative ideas that begin with significant public support though not yet majority support, has been left on the cutting room floor of legislative debates and political campaigns. Not able to penetrate the corridors of the duopoly's legislature, mass popular opinion regarding GM foods and the broader theme of globalization's impacts has had to forcefully assert itself via protest and civil disobedience amid tear gas and police reaction, first in Seattle and then elsewhere. That, combined with Europe's refusal to import American farmers' GM crops, have stalled so far the GM industry juggernaut in the United States.

Energy policy

The energy crisis in 2001, both in California and nationwide, similarly was affected by the lack of any political opposition or a political party that could bring new ideas to the table. As gasoline prices doubled and electricity and natural gas prices tripled and quadrupled, with no end in sight, the crisis initiated a predictable round of political brinkmanship between the Bush White House and congressional Democrats.

The United States, with only 4 percent of the world's population, consumes one-quarter of the world's energy, and reliance on foreign energy over the last two decades has become greater than it had been before the 1970s Arab oil embargoes. But recalling the political damage suffered by the Carter Administration during the oil spike of the late 1970s, both parties ducked for political cover. First, White House spokesman Ari Fleisher, when asked whether Americans would need to curb their voracious appetites for energy, tried a version of "the patriotic pander:" "That's a big no," he said. "The president believes that it's an American way of life, and that it should be the goal of policymakers to protect the American way of life. The American way of life is a blessed one."[12]

But the Democrats were hardly any better. House Democratic leader Dick Gephardt said, "We have a society, like it or not, where gas and electricity is like air or water." Democrats tried to offer a "kinder, gentler" version of Republican pander by genuflecting briefly toward the environment, with Gephardt saying, "We think there are effective, intelligent ways to work through these problems so that we don't suffer in terms of price, we don't suffer in terms of supply, and we don't suffer in terms of the environment." Yet when the House voted on President Bush's energy package in August 2001, Democratic House leaders like Gephardt, minority whip David Bonior, House caucus chair Martin Frost, and others broke ranks to oppose big increases in automobile fuel efficiency. Three dozen Democrats, including at least five members of the Congressional Black Caucus, supported drilling in the Arctic National Wildlife Refuge (ANWR) on the flimsy and unsubstantiated grounds that it would create thousands of jobs. On both issues, Democratic Party votes provided the margin of victory.[13]

In truth, Democrats were recalling with a shiver President Jimmy Carter donning a cardigan sweater and urging Americans to curb their energy appetites. Clintonian Democrats know their party's history: they knew that Carter had been a one-term president.[14] So between the increasingly closed political spaces separating Democrats and Republicans, on the energy issue there was little political opposition demanding, for instance, not only conservation, anti-ANWR drilling, and higher fuel efficiency standards, but also alternative energy fuel sources or, heaven forbid, public power. Yet throughout the California energy crisis, the cities of Los Angeles and Sacramento had been islands of calm in a sea of deregulatory chaos. The reason? Both had their own municipally owned utilities that kept costs down and energy flow stable for millions of households and businesses. In fact, the publicly-owned Los Angeles municipal power stations were *selling* excess power to the rest of the state.

But without legislators elected to our state or federal legislatures willing to champion these issues, values, and solutions, the parameters of the debate were exceedingly narrow. The only opposition came from protesters on the Capitol steps in Sacramento and those attending meetings of the Public Utilities Commission, wearing tombstone props around their necks reading "RIP California Dream." Thus, like an addict needing a bigger fix, the oilmen who occupied the White House and their Democratic Party accessories prepared to drill in the last remaining unspoiled wilderness areas in the fifty states for more of the precious liquid to fill their industrial veins.

Healthcare

In October 1999, the *Washington Post* reported that "the number of Americans who lack health insurance continued to increase, climbing to 44.3 million in spite of a prosperous economy."[15] Yet you would hardly notice this national privation by listening to the rhetoric of the campaigns for president and control of the Congress in 2000. That's because those people without insurance also are disproportionately poor people who lack political power, and that's not who politicians appeal to for votes and campaign donations. Elections are won and lost in the suburbs and in swing districts with swing voters, and politicians know this in every fiber of their political beings.

Thus, the health care debate dwelled, not on figuring out a way to insure the uninsured, but on a patient's Bill of Rights, prescription drugs for Medicare beneficiaries, and HMOs. In other words, the debate was over how to treat people who already *have* insurance. Winner Take All elections are a zero-sum game, and along the way the poor and the uninsured got abandoned on the political sidelines. The rightward-drifting Democratic Party, which once had featured universal healthcare as a major component of its party platform, has relegated it to a minor plank.

To be sure, during the Democratic presidential primary season, both candidates Bill Bradley and Al Gore talked about the plight of the uninsured. "We must redouble our commitment, as an American community, to bring the uninsured into our community of care," Vice President Gore had said in releasing his health plan. "It is not right that uninsured Americans face illness alone," former New Jersey senator Bill Bradley said as he set forth his own, somewhat more ambitious plan. But once the primaries were over and Al Gore had locked up the nomination, Candidate Gore, keeping true to the old political saw about "running to your base in the primaries and to the center in the general election," dropped the uninsured from his campaign rap in favor of better health care for seniors and a patient's Bill of Rights.[16] Gore was yielding to the incentives under Winner Take All to chase fiscally conservative swing voters who are passionate in their opposition to "big government." Thus, without a political party committed to the idea of "healthcare for all" as more than a temporary campaign, that policy option mostly has fallen by the wayside. Consequently, nearly one-sixth of our population, most of them children, continue to lack basic healthcare despite our nation's great wealth, and despite per capita spending on healthcare that is the highest in the world.

Demographic Dropouts: low income and young voters

In Election 2000, low-income, working-age Americans of all races, among the least likely voters in a country with the lowest voter turnout among established democracies, appeared to be doubly alienated. Not only had they watched the nation's longest economic boom lift seemingly every boat but theirs, but then the major presidential nominees talked conspicuously past them about tax relief for the middle class and prescription drugs for the elderly.

Even in heavily targeted states like Pennsylvania, low-income working-class voters were left out of presidential calculations. Even in a swing state, it turns out, you did not count for much if you were in the wrong demographic. Millions of "demographic dropouts" littered the American political landscape in Election 2000.

"None of what they're saying is about us," said Mary Eakle, twenty-five, a $7-an-hour assistant deli manager and mother in Carbondale, Pennsylvania, to a *Washington Post* reporter when asked about the bombardment of ads featuring suburbanites and elderly people.[17] In the past, Democrats were the party of working people and Republicans the party of business. It was a lot easier for families like the Eakles to figure out who to vote for. But now, with both parties rhetorically targeting the same voters, the differences have blurred. So Mary Eakle didn't even bother to vote.

"I'm so busy working and running after kids," she explained, "I'd never figure out who to vote for."

Sally Kurtz, fifty-six, a cleaning woman in Scranton's Steamtown Mall restocking toilet paper and scouring washbasins, echoed Mary Eakle's plaintive words of woe. Ms. Kurtz at the time lived with her daughter, a presser in a pants factory, and her young grandson, on a household income of about $25,000. She said she wasn't planning on voting because "I wouldn't know what to do when I went behind the curtain." Asked what a candidate could say to make her want to participate, she thought hard: "I'd like to be able to have a house."[18]

With the presidential race one of the tightest ever, the campaigns had zeroed in on undecided swing voters in key battleground states, whom polls found concentrated among middle-income families, suburbanites, and the elderly—not low-income, working-class voters. Bush touted his plan to cut taxes by $1.3 trillion over nine years by saying a typical family of four would save $2,000 annually. But the family in his sample made $50,000 a year. The Eakles make less than half that amount—too little to owe income taxes for Bush to cut. For Mary Eakle and Sally Kurtz, the campaign was like one coming from Mars.

Young voters are particularly turned off by the swing dancing of the two-choice tango. When they are asked why they do not vote—which is not often—many young people are very clear and articulate: uninspiring candidates and uninspiring issues that do not address their needs or interests.

The Center for Voting and Democracy sponsored a contest in 2000 for youth ages sixteen to twenty-four that gave $1,000 to the best answer to the question: "What changes in our electoral system would increase political participation by young people?" Nearly 9000 entries from all fifty states weighed in on the subject. Scattered among the thousands of essays were recurring sentiments like, "The issues, however important, do not relate directly to young people today"; "Often the ideas of youth are brushed aside and rarely offered the protection of representation"; "It would be nice if everyday citizens had a better chance to run for office, not just the extremely wealthy businessmen, lawyers, and military leaders."

Some of the young essayists wrote bluntly—and often brilliantly—about the narrow menu of issues offered as standard political fare during political campaigns. "The traditional issues are not necessarily at the forefront of young minds, and will not stir them to voice their opinions. Yes, the budget deficit is decreasing, and that is a good thing, but why has Tibet not gained more freedom? Why are alternative fuels, or even alternative lifestyles brushed aside by political tycoons?" "Most youth feel that local, state, and national politicians do not speak to them, and they have good reason to feel that way. . . . Great and monumental decisions that will dramatically affect our future are being made without us"; "The United States political scene is becoming increasingly stagnant as incrementalist politicians pursue visions of mediocrity and the mere absence of popular disapproval; the concerns of many facets of society, including young adults, are thereby often neglected"; "Politicians and campaign managers work nearly exclusively within the tried and true aspects of politics, addressing the same issues time and again."

Other young essayists eloquently conveyed the sense of alienation they feel from politics and politicians. "X generation sees both Republicans and Democrats as devoid of leadership that actually stands and delivers on promises"; "We feel as though our candidate has no chance of winning, so why vote?"; "We have been told that democracy is the way that the people rule and control our own nation, but we have seen repeatedly that 'the people' are merely the rich, the privileged, the elite"; "The lack of competition and excitement lose the attention of the people. Let's face it, does one vote really matter in a landslide political campaign?"; "Give us something worthwhile to vote for and we might start showing up at the polls"; "All I ask is that if you expect us to take part in your games, that you at least give us a fair voice"; "As a member of this so-called 'younger generation' I have gotten quite detached from the political system. To me the government is simply a channel on television (C-SPAN), which I hastily flip by on my way to MTV or Animal Planet"; "We turn on the TV and we see our elected officials screwing interns and building missiles and slaughtering thousands of innocent lives"; "You ask why we do not vote or participate actively in politics. I ask why should we choose between two evils, two wrongs?"[19]

Various essays cited Jesse Ventura and John McCain as two admirable candidates, specifically because they had reached out to youth. One essayist stated, "As a registered voter of Minnesota I have seen first hand what it takes to get the younger generation to vote. . . . How did a Pro-Wrestler get elected to office? Simple, he spoke to everybody. . . . As a result of this Jesse produced the greatest turn out of 18-24 year-old voters in Minnesota history." Another essayist was so moved by meeting John McCain and McCain's "asking our opinions and giving us his, telling us that we need to get involved," that he took a job chairing the national teen effort for McCain's campaign.

In contrast, Gore and Bush paid little attention to young people, the working poor, or their issues. Neither the "New Populist" Gore nor the "Compassionate Conservative" Bush could find these demographic dropouts on their radar screens. In three presidential debates, Gore and Bush kept to their prepared scripts and barely mentioned what their "leadership" would mean for young people, nor for that matter the poor, city-dwellers, racial minorities—constituencies important to the future, but solidly in one camp or the other, unlikely to vote, or both. So Al Gore could put Social Security in a lockbox and George Bush could talk about compassionate conservatism, yet neither addressed at all the lock on the future of millions of children in poverty or the missing compassion for 30 million children without healthcare. Those children don't vote, and most likely neither do their parents. They are expendable in a Winner Take All system, electoral *desaparacidos*—"the disappeared ones"— without a future or a voice. There are no faces on "political milk cartons" for these unfortunate ones.

Mario Velasquez, president of Rock the Vote, which registers young people to vote, commented on this kind of electoral gaming. "Candidates are controlled by demographics. Demography, I like to say, is the death of democracy. If you have precision demographics, you are only talking to people who vote, not to the entire country."[20]

Nationally, voter turnout is much lower among youth and poor Americans than among other demographic groups. Only 12 percent of eighteen- to twenty-four-year-olds and 8.5 percent of eighteen- to nineteen-year-olds voted in the 1998 elections.[21] Among income categories, turnout was highest among people making $50,000 or more, with 65.7 percent of eligible voters voting in the 1996 presidential election, but turnout declined steeply and consistently as income dropped. Just 48 percent of people making $25,000 to $35,000 voted, 42 percent of people making $15,000 to $25,000, and just 28.6 percent of people making less than $10,000 a year voted in the 1996 presidential election.[22]

Thus, Winner Take All campaigning further fragments the electorate. Whole swaths of people—potential voters—are dropped from the guest list of this "invitation-only" election. It raises a mischievously *noir* suggestion about a way to save much of the cost and inconvenience of periodic elections: perhaps in the uncontested and safe-seat areas—most of the country—we should simply cancel elections and declare presumed winners, as indicated by pollsters; and in the remaining slices of the country we should officially de-register and forget about unlikely voters—about half of all voters—which is merely recognizing what unofficially occurs right now. That such a course is both Orwellian *and* logical within the trajectory of Winner Take All should be a cause for great alarm.

Third parties: the laboratory for new ideas

Our economy has become an *information* economy, and consumer choice is one of the mantras of the times. Yet our politics is running headlong in the opposite direction—toward less choice, less quality information, and less innovation. Winner Take All is producing lackluster, undistinguished, even lifeless politics that fails to inform or inspire. At a time when the need for reliable and well-presented information is at a premium, new political ideas and innovation are having more and more difficulty percolating to the surface.

John McCain, for a few brief shining moments in 2001, overturned the usual stale campaign formula. Facing an opponent with the full support of the Republican Party establishment, McCain tried to win the Republican presidential nomination by appealing to—non-Republicans. In several major primaries, McCain actually pulled over half of his support from voters who described themselves as independents, Democrats, or moderates. It almost seemed that McCain was running for the nomination of a party that was not quite the Republican Party—let's call it the Republican-Independent Party. And lo and behold, swarms of voters, tired of the traditional two-party tango, responded. The boost in turnout in the 2001 presidential primaries was mostly because of McCain. Where he didn't contest races, such as Iowa and Delaware, turnout dropped despite George W. Bush's big spending.

Like Perot's insurgent presidential bid in 1992, McCain's audacious move to capture the Republican flag by appealing to independents and reform-minded moderates revealed a gaping hole in the American political spectrum. Yet the hole was not so much ideological as it was "methodological"—the innovation McCain brought to the tedious template and poll-tested blandness of a politician was a bit of spontaneity, a bit of self-effacing humor, and the mild mantle of a reformer. Even though McCain was a career politician, had been snared in the Keating Five savings and loan scandal, and held viewpoints on most issues similar to that of the GOP establishment, amazingly enough he managed to run as an "outsider." That in itself was a comment on the paucity of the standard fare, and how hungry the public was for something or someone to break up the political dreariness. After McCain dropped out of the race, Bush and Gore attempted to reel in those McCain voters with a dance to the center, but watching the two leopards trying to change their spots just reinforced the perception that, compared to someone like McCain, most politicians will say anything to get elected. To the extent that Gore and Bush succeeded in attracting McCain voters, it was because many American citizens felt duty-bound to hold their noses and vote anyway, often for the "lesser of two evils" to keep someone out of office. But that sort of "negative consent" hardly filled the political void.

McCain's ebullient candidacy, like Ventura's and Perot's, and even Nader's mass super-rallies, revealed that never in recent memory has there been a better time for the emergence of new faces and new perspectives on the political scene. One of the significant antidotes to a lack of fresh ideas and innovations is simple enough—independent candidates and third parties. These, in essence, are the laboratory for new ideas. Without independent candidates and third parties, fresh perspectives, policies, and analyses about a fair economy, healthcare, food safety, youth or low-income issues, and more get strangled in the crib by Winner Take All's two-party duopoly and the duopoly's identi-kit politics. New ideas that do not start out with majority support, or that do not appeal to swing voters, die a quick death, never having a chance to find support and take root in the toxic Winner Take All soil.

Third parties have long played an important role in American politics, despite draconian rules restricting them and efforts by major party politicians, academics, and the Winner Take All media to dismiss them at every turn. Repeatedly, major American ideas—both good and bad—have become part of our culture because of precisely the sort of politics Nader, Ventura, Perot, and Buchanan have practiced in recent years. Author Sam Smith, who has researched the influence of third parties, says that the list of significant ideas that were first brought forth by third parties include the abolition of slavery (Free Soil Party), prohibition (Prohibition Party), the income tax (Populist Party), social welfare programs (Socialist Party), the New Deal coalition (Progressive Party), and balanced budgets (Reform Party).[23] Other ideas advanced or helped along by third-party efforts include women's suffrage, the forty-hour workweek, ending child labor, Social Security, food and drug safety laws, workers' compensation, unemployment insurance, public education, public libraries, direct election of U.S. Senators, and government regulation of monopolies.

Above all, third parties have repeatedly revived conventional notions of "good government," and the idea that our government should serve the people instead of special interests—a quintessential McCain or Ventura theme. Writing in the *Journal of American History*, Mark Voss-Hubbard stated, "Third partisans, of whatever time and place, expressed a common ideal when they imagined how politics and government ought to work. Governance should be guided by a larger moral vision than simply electoral victories and party control over public affairs. It should serve the public interest, not narrow partisan agendas."[24]

The importance of third parties and independent candidacies is that they introduce not only new types of ideas and issues, but also a new type of *candidate*, candidates that speak directly to various constituencies and mobilize them with a personal touch that only an "authentic" candidate can provide. For instance, it is hard to imagine how the standard political menu—usually some smiling white guy in a necktie—could ever inspire inner-city youth to participate in the electoral process. Conversely, it is not hard to imagine why inner-city youth might think that if a candidate doesn't talk their talk and walk their walk, then why should they talk and walk his? But if a young, black, socially conscious rapper were to enter politics, *and* we used some sort of proportional representation system that allowed such a candidate to actually win, suddenly the Winner Take All straitjacket would be transformed.

For example, in New Zealand, where they use proportional representation elections, one Green Party candidate elected to Parliament is a young, half-African, dread-locked Rastafarian who is an articulate spokesperson on issues of ecology and genetically modified foods and has particular appeal with younger voters. He has a constituency, and that constituency has an elected representative that can speak both to and for them. But in Winner Take All USA, such a candidate could never be viable, and the typical response is to write off the potentiality of voters attracted to such a candidate. Thus, we miss out on an opportunity to incorporate and integrate electoral dropouts like young people and poor people and their views and instincts, indeed their unique brilliance, into the fabric of American politics and society.[25]

A December 1999 poll by Harvard's Vanishing Voter Project found that a mere 23 percent of Americans agreed that "the two-party system works fairly well." About half wanted to consider a third-party candidate no matter who won the major party nominations. A January 2000 poll by Rasmussen Research found that if a third-party candidate had a legitimate chance of winning a congressional race, 30 percent of likely voters would vote Democrat, 25 percent Republican, and 26 percent for the generic third party. In observing the Winner Take All two-party duopoly in the United States, former U.S. Senator and governor from Connecticut, Lowell Weicker, has commented, "The only way you're going to shape up American politics is by a third force, nationally. Politics—the intellectual business—is no different than the economic business. When you have an economic monopoly, you get high prices and bad products. You've got an intellectual monopoly in this country, and you've got bad ideas and bad candidates."[26]

The Prospects of Multiparty Democracy under Winner Take All

Unfortunately, within the confines of the established Winner Take All rules, it is extremely difficult for a third political force to gain a foothold and grow. Nearly half a century ago, Duverger's Law showed that Winner Take All voting systems tend to result in a two-choice/two-party political system.[27] It is not a matter of which political parties have more money or better candidates or more activists—it is a matter of the mechanics of Winner Take All, and how the prevailing demographics and distribution of voters express themselves through that political system. Or, as politicians like to say, it comes down to votes, and third parties or independent candidates by definition usually don't have as many voters as either of the two major parties. In a Winner Take All system where the "highest vote-getter wins," rarely will the candidate from a third party be the highest vote-getter, and that poses a huge barrier to "third force" politics.

But in addition to the limitations of Winner Take All, the two major political parties and the media have erected a byzantine array of legal mazes, snafus, and Catch-22's designed to keep third parties down. In fact, as one observer has put it, the duopoly has erected various rules "that are as efficient at wiping out minor parties as any state police has ever been."

For instance, the ballot access laws in most states make a mockery of democracy. Acting like the Microsoft of politics, the duopoly has rigged a legal hodgepodge from state to state *designed* to keep competitors off the ballot. In North Carolina, for example, a third party needs to gather 58,000 signatures on a petition to qualify for the ballot. This high threshold kept Ralph Nader off the 2000 ballot in North Carolina, yet it was upheld by the courts. In the entire history of the state, Ross Perot in 1992 has been the only independent candidate to qualify for the ballot. In Georgia, the ballot access requirements, including the unusual requirement of separate petitions for each *individual* candidate for partisan office rather than one statewide petition for the whole party, are so onerous that there hasn't been a third party candidate for a U.S. House seat since 1964. Florida charges its candidates for the U.S. House an exorbitant filing fee of approximately $8,500 simply for the "privilege" of running, high enough to discourage most third-party candidates.

In Alabama, a third party must win 20 percent of the vote for any statewide office in order to stay on the ballot—more votes than Ross Perot won for president in 1992. Until 1997, North Dakota's ballot access law *automatically* granted ballot status to Democratic and Republican Parties, but required third parties to jump through various electoral hoops to stay on the ballot (that blatantly discriminatory policy was abolished recently). Probably the most ridiculous requirement is that of West Virginia: the duopoly has made it a *crime* if the signature-gatherer does not inform the person signing that "if you sign this [third-party] petition, you cannot participate in the upcoming primaries" of the

Democrats or Republicans. In 1992 the Secretary of State actually hired and deputized a private investigator who arrested and hauled off to jail a Libertarian Party petitioner who forgot to inform a signer about this unreasonable and preposterous requirement.[28]

As a contrast, Great Britain uses uniform ballot access procedures that are identical for all candidates in all regions of the country: a slight petition (approximately ten signatures) and payment of a small fee (about $700), which is returned if the candidate polls 5 percent. The filing deadline is only sixteen days before the election, giving candidates and third parties maximum time for qualifying.[29] There are no good reasons why ballot access laws in the United States cannot be just as welcoming, except for the fact that the Democrats and Republicans stomp around like the Microsoft of politics. Consequently, third parties and independent candidates are routinely shut out of the process by legal tricks, and voters are robbed of the opportunity to hear their political perspective and to be informed by the stimulation of political debate and policy options.

It is instructive to recall, as we saw in Chapter 3, that out of the more than 7,000 state Senate and House seats scattered across the United States, five currently are held by third parties, all in Vermont (a fairly constant number, year after year, election after election). Out of 535 Congressional and U.S. Senate seats, only two are held by an independent representative (one each from Vermont and Virginia), and none by third parties. It has always been that way in the United States (and, to some degree, in other Winner Take All democracies as well). Out of the approximately 21,000 U.S. House races in the twentieth century, minor party and independent candidates won a mere one hundred times, plus another seven special elections, a total of 107 victories—or about 0.5 percent of the time, statistically (and politically) insignificant.[30] Political scientist David Gillespie, commenting on the vast gap between Americans' *desires* for third-party candidates and the bleak prospects under Winner Take All, said, "Americans increasingly have shown they yearn for third-party alternatives. . . . Unfortunately, the cards are stacked against it."[31]

The quest for a fair economy, or better healthcare, or safe food, or sane energy policy, or adequate housing, can be put in its proper perspective by answering a simple question: who is to benefit? But the Winner Take All system does not permit such carefully nuanced discussions to take place in the political arena, particularly with the new campaign technologies that are so sinisterly suited to gaming and carving up the electorate and targeting campaign spin in a bid to win elections in our two-choice system. Such discussions now are plagued by the relentless unholy trinity of crafted talk, canned ideas, and simulated responsiveness. Instead of informed and consensus-building national dialogue, Winner Take All is producing a kind of collective electoral anesthesia that has gulled the public into mistaking political fiction for reality, artifice for substance. It has produced a political duopoly and media monopoly that have intensified their own predatory practices, stomping around like the Microsoft of politics and political discourse. And it is producing regional sub-nations like Bushlandia and New Goreia, ideological monocultures where new political ideas and innovation are having more and more difficulty percolating to the surface.

But the story in Europe is quite different. There, instead of Winner Take All, they use forms of proportional representation voting systems that allow various points of view and political parties from across the political spectrum to compete for voters' sympathies and to win actual representation instead of phantom representation. In Europe, there appears to be a greater commitment to political pluralism, to a flowering of opinion and thought that finds expression in campaigns and in the legislatures, even in more politically diverse media outlets, including more robust public television and radio networks and numerous daily newspapers (many taxpayer subsidized), with editorial slants from the right to the left to the center. Ironically, compared to the United States, Europe today displays much more of a Tocqueville–like climate, as the political activity and rousing "tumult" Tocqueville once observed on the American continent has waned, while in Europe such pluralism has been encouraged by its political and media institutions. It appears the torch has passed.[32]

Some of these European democracies have constructed the electoral rules to allow a multiplicity of political parties (some say too many parties); others use electoral rules that have the effect of limiting their multiparty democracy to perhaps four or five political parties that win seats in the legislature.[33] In any case, the European political system has flourished under a multiparty/multichoice environment that has fostered political parties across the spectrum; and this in turn has fostered spirited debate of globalization and related issues like GM foods and food safety, labor rights, trade, the social compact, and the secrecy of the World Trade Organization, to a degree that has been far more substantive and inclusive than in the United States under Winner Take All's two-party tango.

Given all the barriers in place in the United States, the prospects in the near future for a vibrant political pluralism founded on the bedrock of a multiparty democracy are not bright. Certainly it is difficult to imagine those dedicated red cabooses huffing and puffing around the American political landscape, with names like Reform Party, Green Party, New Party, Working Families Party, Libertarian Party, and others, puncturing through to any stirring degree of electoral success. Since third parties and independent candidates are the laboratories for new ideas, that itself is a measure of how distant we are from a fresher, more innovative kind of politics.

Lacking fair ballot access laws, lacking public financing of elections, lacking competitive elections or stimulating campaigns, lacking some form of proportional representation and the new voices and ideas it brings to the table, lacking a pluralistic media dedicated to debate and discourse, the abject state of our politics has produced a post-traumatic public quiescently awaiting the fractious, voterless post-democracy that is beginning to rain down upon our heads. Some still vote, most don't bother. The electoral choices are increasingly unappealing because the typical Winner Take All candidate does not address the larger issues confronting our nation, nor the ones that many people are concerned about in their daily lives. Instead, politicians only address the narrow selection of issues that will help them curry favor with swing voters and win elections. As a consequence the Winner Take All system has created a log-jammed process in which new and good ideas have difficulty percolating to the surface, and that augurs badly for our collective future. Oddly—for a democracy—the public itself is becoming less of a factor in our politics, practically bystanders, with decreasing participation and declining expectations. Winner Take All is utterly failing us; we have arrived at a scary bend in the road, and around the next corner lies post-democracy.

Not surprisingly then, the American sensibility and *appreciation* for representative government is atrophying, like shriveled grapes on the vine. Government today certainly has acquired a bad reputation, despite the many good things it has done over the years in numerous and important areas of life, safety, business, transportation, communication, and health. But for lack of fresh ideas, of effective policy informed by spirited debate, and of a diverse menu of compelling candidates who can appeal to various constituencies and voters, our political respiration is becoming a flat-line on the oscilloscope. Whole swathes of voters are at this point so alienated and democratically moribund that it will require a miracle on the order of Jesus raising Lazarus from the dead to revive them. One former Vermont state legislator recounts how difficult this sort of electoral CPR has become:

> I have campaigned door-to-door for over two decades in my city council and legislative districts, and have a very clear notion of why at least low-income folks don't register or vote, even when all they have to do is sign the form placed in front of them. Most refrainers consciously *choose* not to vote. They either have disdain for politicians—either a perception of the lack of difference between the major parties, and/or disgust generated by the batch of negative TV ads—or they feel that politics is totally irrelevant to their lives. Campaigns don't seem to deal with the most important concerns of working and low-income folks (their powerlessness at work, fear of their landlord, how they can improve their relationships within their family or take a vacation, etc., etc.). Many U.S. refrainers think of candi-

dates or voter registration volunteers knocking at their door the way I think of Jehovah's Witnesses knocking at mine.[34]

The deep-sixing of millions of voters—100 million, to be exact, who did not participate in the 2000 presidential election, larger than the population of most nations—has left a lasting scar on our representative democracy. It is as if our fractious, voterless post-democracy is being interred, slowly, inexorably, one shovelful at a time.

PART FOUR
Majority Rule? Or Majority Fooled?

CHAPTER TWELVE

Winner Take All Policy
Where the Majority Does Not Always Rule

> A democratic government provides an orderly and peaceful
> process by means of which a majority of citizens can induce the
> government to do what they most want it to do and to avoid doing
> what they most want it not to do.
> —ROBERT A. DAHL, *DEMOCRACY AND ITS CRITICS*

Finally, after analyzing the impact of Winner Take All and its gremlin progeny on campaigns, representation, participation, and national division, we arrive at policy. If it were merely high-minded democratic ideals and destinies like "fair representation," "voter participation," "electoral competition," and "informative campaigns" taking the direct hit, while governance and public policy stayed on track, the reaction to Winner Take All post-democracy might justifiably be a collective national shrug. Americans, now the least exuberant participants in our democracy in the established democratic world, have become used to diminished expectations. As long as national policy is still somewhat on target and the economy is chugging on the tracks, some will think less democracy an acceptable price.

Unfortunately, as a result of Winner Take All progenies like phantom representation, artificial majorities, swing voter serenade, two-choice tango, the redistricting roulette, and the Winner Take All conundrum, neither governance, policy, nor the national interest escape collateral damage. Indeed, Winner Take All shenanigans have compromised national policy on a host of pressing public fronts, including the impeachment and subsequent trial of the president, military appropriations, Social Security, gun control, our decaying cities, anti-crime policy, the minimum wage, the enormous 2001 tax cut, agricultural policy, and more.

There actually has been a fair amount of debate over the years among pundits, political scientists, and theorists about the impact that Winner Take All has on policy. Defenders of Winner Take All—and there are many—like to point out that Winner Take All, for all its faults, is still superior to other alternatives because it provides centrist, majoritarian policy and decisive government, and that's all that matters. For the torch-bearers of Winner Take All, effective and decisive policy is where the rubber hits the road, the sine qua non of political desirability. But as the next two chapters will demonstrate, policy enacted under Winner Take All does not stay on track, nor is it necessarily centrist or majoritarian. In fact, under Winner Take All, the majority does *not* necessarily rule.

Arrow, Downs, Hotelling, and vendors on the beach

Kenneth Arrow was awarded a Nobel Prize in 1972 for using logic and mathematical models to show via his appropriately nicknamed "impossibility theorem" that no election system is perfect. Like three legs on a stool, between the choices of equality, collective rationality, and decisiveness/effectiveness, when you try to greatly maximize any one of the three ultimately you shorten the other two legs and destabilize the whole stool.[1] In other words, every voting scheme will, at times, exhibit shortcomings. To a certain extent it is a natural zero-sum game, and a balance is to be struck. But for defenders of Winner Take All that balance must tilt inexorably toward decisive, centrist and effective policy.

Studying the impacts of voting systems on policy is a tricky business, often shedding more heat than light. Rational choice theory seems to demonstrate that because there is no single preference that a majority prefers to all other preferences the seemingly infinite array of citizens' preferences are almost always collectively uninterpretable. A process of sequentially pitting one preference against all others almost always can lead to any outcome. Moreover, as Stanford law professor Pam Karlan has pointed out, there's a paradox at the core of democratic politics: "We use elections to tally up our preferences and to determine the future direction and structure of our government, but the current structure of our government powerfully influences our preferences and dramatically limits the choices available to us. The kind of democracy we have, and can imagine, is thus quite path dependent. Think about the famous M. C. Escher print of a hand drawing itself drawing a hand."[2]

Nevertheless, within the confines of Arrow's parameters and these other paradoxes, certain conclusions are possible. When studying the impact of voting systems on policy, the key terminology in the political science literature is what political scientists call "congruence." Congruence is an ivory tower way of saying, as noted political scientist Robert Dahl has sensibly written (quoted at the beginning of this chapter), "does the government do what a majority of citizens most want it to do, and avoid doing what they most want it not to do?" Without congruence, there is no legitimacy. There is little point to representative government if the majority does not rule or, conversely, if a minority of citizens still rule over the majority.

The seminal works on congruence, the patriarchs of the fold from which the offspring then propagated, are Harold Hotelling's 1929 paper "Stability in Competition" and Anthony Downs' famous 1957 work *Economic Theory of Democracy*. Hotelling and Downs were both economists who used game theory and spatial equilibrium models to say some interesting things about competition in a duopoly, i.e. a two-choice, situation. Hotelling, Downs' intellectual forebear, devised a clever model that analyzed two merchants selling their wares and how sales would be affected by their physical location. He then applied his model to other real-world applications, like politics.

Paraphrasing Hotelling, imagine his merchants as two ice cream vendors, selling ice cream cones to bathers scattered along a crowded beach. The bathers are assumed to be scattered uniformly along the beach; it is also assumed that the vendors charge exactly the same price for their ice cream cones and that the bathers will consume the same number of cones no matter the distance they must walk to buy them. Where will each of the vendors set up their ice cream stands in order to make the most sales?

If one vendor sets up about at the center of the left side of the beach, and the other about at the center of the right side, they'll split the customers evenly in half, and no one will have to walk farther than a quarter of the beach to buy an ice cream cone. This would seem like an ideal situation. But one of the clever vendors quickly realizes the obvious: if she moves to the center of the beach, she will be closer than her competitor to a larger portion of bathers and will be able to steal customers from the other vendor. In fact, if she sets down *just to the outside* of the other vendor, she will capture nearly all the market, since her ice cream stand will now be closer than her competition to three-fourths of the customers.

So the other vendor, seeing his competition moving closer to him, begins to do the same. They both move closer and closer to the center, until finally they are right next to each other, exactly in the middle of the beach. Any other location by either of the vendors would give their competition a larger share of the customers.

Hotelling briefly applied this microeconomic model to more general circumstances, like the distribution of churches and political parties. For the latter, he assumed that voters were evenly spaced along the "political beach." He reasoned that competition in a two-party system would cause each party to converge, that is, to move toward the ideological center, as a way of maximizing the numbers of voters they can reach, and cited anecdotal information to buttress his claim.[3]

Thirty years later, Anthony Downs renewed the Hotelling microeconomic model's application to competition between two political parties, but he tossed out the unrealistic assumption that voters were evenly spaced along the political spectrum. According to Downs' adaptation of Hotelling's model, a two-choice/two-party system—a relative proxy for Winner Take All—will cause the two parties to move toward those two ideological points where the most numbers of voters are amassed. But for Downs, these two ideological points could vary. Thus, Downs modeled different distributions of voters and predicted what the reactions of the vote-maximizing parties would be to those distributions.

Of particular interest were two specific distributions: (1) when most voters are amassed at the ideological center, that is, the median-middle (illustrated by a one-humped curve) and (2) when voters are polarized into two ideological camps to the right and left of the center (a two-humped curve). In the first instance, Downs basically agreed with Hotelling: given a voter distribution where most voters are amassed at the middle of any particular political spectrum, the two political parties will tend to converge—that is, they will locate like Hotelling's vendors at the middle of the electoral beach, where most of the electorate is concentrated. Both parties will tend to adopt the views of what is called the "median" voter—the voter closest to the middle of the political spectrum. That's because the strategic incentives for the two parties, and the rational choices for voters picking the best of what's available in a limited two-choice field, act together to provide victories for the party that is closest to the median.[4] A party that fails to converge to the median can always be defeated by a party that does (with one important addendum, known as Smithie's refinement, that fear of losing their own extremist voters would keep the two parties from drifting completely to the median-center, "becoming identical").[5]

Thus, according to this Hotelling–Downs model, what has been called the "tweedle dee" or "tweedle dum" choice of near-identical Democrats or Republicans actually is rational behavior by politicians trying to win elections in a two-choice field. Given a "one-humped" distribution of voters amassed in the middle of the political spectrum, if either of the two political parties locate too far toward the margins, they will yield more of the political turf to their opponent. So both parties stride toward the middle. This reality has given rise to a classic political strategy that says "in the primaries run to your base, but in the general election run to the middle"—different elections with different median voters, with primaries determined by median voters considerably more partisan than in a general election. Certainly George W. Bush and Bill Clinton masterfully utilized such a strategy, and the Hotelling–Downs spatial equilibrium model purports to tell us why.

But Downs proposed an important "two-humped" exception to this application of Hotelling to politics: what if, he asked, the distribution of voters is not humped in the middle of the ideological-political market? What if instead the electorate is polarized? In that case, Downs showed, the two parties will "diverge toward the extremes rather than converge on the center. Each gains more votes by moving toward a radical position than it loses in the center."[6] When the electorate is polarized, Downs' model portrayed the distribution of voters as two-humped, equal in size, like a Bactrian camel's back. In such a situation, Downs goes on to predict that "regardless of which party is in office, half the electorate always feels that the other half is imposing policies upon it that are strongly repugnant to it. In this situation, if one party keeps getting reelected, the disgruntled supporters of the other party will probably revolt; whereas if the two parties alternate in office, social chaos occurs, because government policy keeps changing from one extreme to the other."[7] Thus, Downs concluded, the two-party system "does not lead to effective, stable government when the electorate is polarized."

The strip-mining of Downs

Downs' work was enormously influential over the ensuing decades. His rational choice formulation of politics permeated throughout the academy, even the culture at-large. Here, finally, the incessantly irascible pandemonium known as politics had been modeled and reduced to "natural law," just like economics or physics, in a way that seemed to make sense out of the chaos. Testifying to its enduring clout, a search of Downs' *Economic Theory of Democracy* in the Social Science Citation Index turns up over one thousand entries in the 1990s alone.[8]

But in the ensuing four decades following Downs' seminal work, various neo-Downsians in the media, editors, pundits and politicos, and even researchers in the academy, selectively strip-mined Downs for their own purposes. Their interpretations of the Downs model ignored what apparently did not fit in with their preferred vision of America as a nicely organized, single-humped electorate. Thus, Downs' formulation of what happens to a democracy when the electorate is polarized into two voter distribution humps somehow was left on the cutting-room floor.

What remained was Downs' reworking of Hotelling's "vendor on the beach" model, and the two-party system was transmogrified in many minds into a proxy for moderate, majoritarian, centrist government. Down's *median* voter acquired a reputation as a political *moderate,* and even more as an *undecided,* i.e. a *swing,* voter. And the policy passed by that government was presumed to be preferred by the majority of voters. Congruence had been more or less achieved, at least theoretically according to the neo-Downsians, and unsurprisingly it looked quite a lot like two-party government in the United States.

But this was certainly a misreading of Downs. Downs himself had postulated an important exception: *except* when a polarized electorate leads to a more difficult brand of democracy. For Downs, the behavior of both vote-maximizing parties was determined by the *distribution of voters,* not vice versa. One of the strengths of Downs' model was that it was flexible, and it examined the reaction of political parties pursuing votes from *different voter distributions.* Yet an unsubstantiated assumption had crept into the neo-Downsians' revisions of the model, from the perspective of policy determination: like a kind of political conveyor belt, the two-choice dynamic, in aggregate, was presumed to drag both parties inevitably to centrist positions of moderation, leading to a *politically* centrist, moderate, majoritarian government—regardless of the distribution of voters.

The "polarized electorate" exception had been dropped inexplicably from the neo-Downsian canon. But politics in the real world is not always very cooperative or kind to those who try to bend theory to their will. The outstanding question was: which distribution of voters was applicable to American politics? The "one-humped" majority of voters amassed around the ideological median-middle? Or a "two-humped" polarized distribution of voters? Or perhaps a distribution somewhere in between the two extremes, or one that fluctuated between the two extremes over time? There was a one-hump versus two-hump uncertainty to figure out—only after answering that question could anyone begin to speculate whether the politics of policy making would lead to moderation and centrism, or to polarization and paralysis.

Now recall the post-presidential election map published in *USA Today* discussed in Chapter 1. Recall the flaming fields of red Bush counties and the high-population island outposts of blue Gore counties—Bushlandia versus New Goreia. For many political observers—particularly those more soberly contemplating the Downsian model—that map of the national vote caused the hair on their necks to raise, precisely because of what it conveyed: a national two-hump distribution of polarized voters, cleaved along starkly regional lines. It was like some sort of two-humped Godzilla, rising up out of the sea.

The same two-humped Godzilla also appears, it turns out, when analyzing congressional elections. Political scientist Elizabeth DeSouza reevaluated the Hotelling–Downs game and some of its most basic assumptions for U.S. House races. In particular, she reevaluated the neo-Downsian notion of the distribution of voters, challenging the depiction of the median voter as a neutral, undecided, or swing voter in congressional elections.

DeSouza's model included the more real-world condition that most congressional districts actually were noncompetitive *safe seats,* favoring one party or the other by landslide margins. In examining House races from 1974 to 1996, DeSouza found a strong link between vote shares and partisan legislative behavior: the safer the seat, the more partisan the legislator. All other things being equal, a legislator in a safe district was more likely to vote positions corresponding to the party's *wings,* not the center, compared to a legislator from a competitive district. It is only as vote shares decreased, that is, as races became more competitive—fewer and fewer such contests every year—that representatives' positions gravitated toward the political center.

In the modern era, where, as we have seen, 70 to 80 percent of U.S. House seats are won by overwhelming landslide margins and 90 percent are won by at least ten-point victory margins due to natural partisan demographics and partisan gerrymandering that create safe seats for one party or the other,[9] "very few [House] members will have *any* incentive to moderate their positions," and "the logic of party convergence collides with the unmistakable party wars," DeSouza concluded. The overwhelming numbers of safe seats, as DeSouza pointed out, gave political parties and their candidates "the political equivalent of academic tenure without the tenure process," and produced a lack of accountability that in turn produced "the rise of the ideologue."[10]

Yet neo-Downsian rational choice models based exclusively on a single-hump voter distribution had predicted the *opposite* pattern. According to the neo-Downsians, the "drive to the center," toward median voters—toward *mod-*

erate voters—was a proxy for a two-choice, Winner Take All system that on the whole produced centrist political winners and majoritarian governments of moderation. But, as DeSouza observed, in the vast majority of House races (and most state legislative races as well), a voter whose party identification favors one of the major parties casts the decisive vote. In other words, *partisan* voters, not centrist or moderate voters, are the *decisive* voters in most legislative elections today.

One conclusion was glaring: for the past two and a half decades, since the mid-1970s at least, Downs' two-humped model had been the more accurate descriptor for most U.S. House races, with one partisan hump larger than the other, usually drastically so, depending on the district (i.e., in landslide, safe-seat districts, which typify three-quarters of U.S. House races). "This finding contradicts the theoretical premise that political victories are called by neutral voters. . . . The median voter is not necessarily a neutral voter. More often than not, the median voter is a member of the victor's political party."[11] DeSouza concluded that "rather than having strong incentives for centrist politics, we have a system that favors partisan politics: politicians are rewarded for staking out extreme positions because most owe their seats to ideologically skewed electorates."

Thus, just as with the national vote revealed by the red vs. blue *USA Today* map of the presidential election, Downs' two-humped model had been the operative voter distribution pattern for most congressional races as well. More-over, as more House districts have become lopsidedly partisan throughout the 1990s, fewer moderates have been elected to the House. Because of the dynamics of Winner Take All districts, the U.S. House has split into two polarized camps, a more solidly liberal Democratic Party and a more solidly conservative Republican Party, like two tectonic plates drifting in opposite directions, with a dwindling number of moderates between them trying to bridge the gap.

Downs' original model that included one-humped *and* two-humped voter distributions, it turns out, had been exactly right. But those who strip-mined the fullness of Downs' theory tried to bend it to suit their "Winner Take All eyes." Not only that, but these neo-Downsians had thrown their weight around for decades. Over time, their half-baked version of Downs's reworking of Hotelling acquired a vast degree of influence. Neo-Downsianism rose to the level of political dogma; indeed, it became a kind of priestly orthodoxy: two-party, Winner Take All political systems produce centrist, moderate, majoritari-an government. The dogma trickled down to popular culture; it was insinuated ad nauseum in the mainstream press, taught in the universities and civics classes with a kind of nationalist pride, with the *Wall Street Journal* and *New York Times* acting as high priests of the canon.[12]

Typical of this viewpoint were those who claimed, as did one political scien-tist, that our "exceedingly fluid two-party system" is built upon "tenuous compromises" between ideological factions and special interests "which are forced at every turn to moderate their claims."[13] Even Supreme Court justices like Scalia and O'Connor, straining in some of their opinions to sound erudite, fell back on unsubstantiated neo-Downsian characterizations.[14] In the end, Downs' clever and provocative model had transmogrified into a stultifying stereotype: everyone knew, it seemed, that the kind of government and Winner Take All political system used by the United States was the best in the world because it led to effective, centrist, stable, majoritarian government.

Other recent studies and analyses have added further empirical evidence to DeSouza's and others' controverting of neo-Downsian dogma. A *New York Times* story reported that some scholars and analysts had concluded that the "lack of competition has consequences for how Congress operates—such as the creation of an ever more polarized House, with incumbents increasingly insulated from challenges from the other party that would push them to the center. It may also help explain such political puzzles as the impeachment of a president in defiance of the public opinion polls."[15]

Evidence of partisan polarization and its impact on policy continued to pile up in the late 1990s. Researchers Alan Abramowitz and Kyle Saunders found that the U.S. electorate underwent a slight ideological realignment during the 1980s and 1990s (as we saw in Chapter 6, some analyses estimate a national swing from Democrats to Republicans of approximately 5 percent nationally, a small but significant shift, to a point where the two parties now are essentially dead-even in terms of voters' sympathies). Increased ideological fervor of the Republican Party during the Reagan–Gingrich era led to a growing awareness of party differences among the electorate, allowing more citizens to choose a party identification based on their own policy preferences.

Following this realignment, conservatives in general, and conservative Republicans in particular, comprised a much larger portion of the GOP base.[16] Republican incumbents, especially in the House, are now much less dependent on votes from moderates, independents, and Democrats. A Republican legislator is now more likely to vote in agreement with a majority of the Republican Congress than at any time in the last five decades. Likewise, Democratic legislators are setting modern records for party unity. In other words, within the U.S. Congress the parties have become both more polarized and more internally cohesive.[17] Elected moderate representatives of both parties have declined greatly in numbers (one estimate charted the decline from 25 percent of the House membership in 1980 to 10 percent moderates in 1996).[18]

This was further empirical evidence of what DeSouza and others had discovered, about the extreme partisanship of safe-seat politicians instead of their alleged centrism or moderation. Like the researchers cited by the *New York Times*, Abramowitz and Saunders also speculated that "this may help to explain the strong support by House Republicans for impeachment and other conservative causes in recent years—causes that were highly popular with the GOP base if not with the rest of the country."[19]

Compiling the conclusions of DeSouza, Abramowitz, Saunders, et al., it would seem that because the neo-Downsian spatial model had selectively ignored Downs' two-humped distribution, it now had limited relevance since it only applied in a handful of the closest races—that is, in the infamous swing districts and in swing states for presidential or statewide elections, important constituencies that may decide legislative majorities and presidential contests. Only in those races was there a greater chance that a neutral, independent, or undecided voter also would be the decisive voter. But for the vast majority of legislative races, the neo-Downsian revisionism simply did not apply. And neither did its supposed implications about the two-party system producing majoritarian governments of moderation where the two parties converge at the ideological center. Those who swear by Winner Take All's alleged centrism would have us believe that today we can have a U.S. House of Representatives that is populated by more unabashed liberals and conservatives and fewer and fewer moderates, and yet somehow this two-humped Godzilla monster will find its way to enact centrist, moderate policy. It would be a miracle if such were the case.

But presumably Downs himself, with his important caveat "democracy does not lead to effective, stable government when the electorate is polarized," would find nothing troubling or unexpected about this conclusion. As our politics have fragmented and polarized, the *fuller* version of Downs' model, including the two-humped "polarized electorate" exception, would have predicted such fragmentation and the distorted policy that results. But because the neo-Downsians in the media and the academy had selectively strip-mined Downs, we ended up with a stereotype instead of a flexible and cohesive predictive model full of utility.

With the recent research of DeSouza, Abramowitz, Saunders, and others, as well as the past theoretical work of people like Donald Stokes,[20] the neo-Downsian revisionism was in trouble. Centrist, moderate, majoritarian government, it turned out, was not guaranteed at all by a two-party system. In fact, under Winner Take All's two-choice/two-party paradigm, it was somewhat of a crapshoot.

The incongruous Congress

Another of the Downsian model's assumptions that has been challenged by recent congressional events was that "government policies at root follow whatever a majority strongly desires."[21] Implicit in this assumption is that, theoretically at least, we can take an opinion poll and find out what a majority of the public desires on any particular issue, and the majoritarian government they elected naturally will enact this desire.

But political scientists Lawrence Jacobs and Robert Shapiro found just the opposite: their research going back two decades tracked Americans' views on a range of political issues and compared them with the relevant legislation that Congress eventually approved. Their empirical data found increasing policy dissonance between policies enacted and the views of the majority of the voting public. Twenty years ago, according to the researchers, lawmakers did what a majority of Americans wanted about two-thirds of the time. Today, Congress is on the same page with the public only about 40 percent of the time. They also noted that the split between politicians and the people accelerated in the 1990s, as Congress became increasingly polarized and partisan.[22]

In their book *Politicians Don't Pander,* Jacobs and Shapiro added a further challenge to the neo-Downsian notion that "competition for the median voter" would motivate parties and politicians to respond to public opinion. Jacobs and Shapiro were trying to figure out how Americans could hold simultaneously two contradictory beliefs: that, on the one hand, there is a public perception that the growing influence of opinion polls has increased pandering by politicians, and so in one sense increased politicians' *responsiveness* to the public; but, on the other hand, there is a perception that the pernicious combination of money in elections and partisanship causes officeholders to ignore the wishes of the public in favor of pursuing the agendas of various special interests. How can both be true, the researchers wanted to know?

As we saw in Chapter 8, Jacobs and Shapiro discovered the answer in their conception of "crafted talk" and "simulated responsiveness." That is, indeed, politicians rely heavily on opinion polls, focus groups, dial meter groups and the like; but more importantly, the authors showed that politicians use those electoral tools not so much to pander but instead to find words and phrases to manipulate and mislead voters, using "crafted talk" designed to "simulate responsiveness." Moreover, with fuzzy-headed swing voters—those most gullible and swayed by crafted talk—determining who wins close races and, ironically enough, control of a closely balanced Legislature or a close presidential race, policy dissonance can easily result. Using the modern campaign technologies to rhetorically trick their audience about their alleged centrism, politicians are able to prevail today by masking the extent to which they diverge from the more pragmatic, less ideological sentiments of the voting public. Consequently, the views of a partisan few—party leaders, party activists who hold the most extreme ideological views, and their donors—are the real purveyors of actual policy, and successful politicians use centrist rhetoric to cover up their noncentrist policy.

Not surprisingly, said Jacobs and Shapiro, "We have found a dramatic decline of political responsiveness to the wishes and preferences of the public on major policy decisions." Like other researchers, Jacobs and Shapiro also reached a conclusion about the impeachment spectacle, namely, that it revealed "one of the most important developments in contemporary American politics—the widening gulf between politicians' policy decisions and the preferences of the American people toward specific issues."[23]

This finding critically undermines Downs' model. If there was one thing fundamental to the entire model, it was that the behavior of parties and the policies they gravitated toward were completely *dependent on the distribution of voters*—whether one-humped or two- or three-, and so on. But with the use of "crafted talk," "simulated responsiveness," and modern campaign techniques to game and fool voters into thinking that the party and its candidates are more centrist and more responsive than they actually are, the link between Downs' distribution of voters and actual policies pursued by the parties has become increasingly strained. The Downsian connection still exists between median voters and campaign promises, but under the influence of the modern campaign technologies, promises and rhetoric have become divorced to an unsettling degree from policy. A widening schism has developed between Down's median voter, between what politicians *say* they will do to attract that voter, and what they *actually* do once in office.

A great deal of empirical evidence and real-world behavior, then, contradict any spatial voter distribution models that predict a two-party Winner Take All system will produce moderate, centrist, or majoritarian policy. As political scientist David King has written, "Political scientists may instinctively suspect that polarization is an irrational strategy for party elites running the parties. The party locating its policy positions closest to the preferences of the median voter is supposed to get the most votes, or so we have been taught [by neo-Downsian theory]. With that model in mind, it makes little sense to allow one's own party to become extreme, but that is precisely what has been happening."[24]

Here we arrive at the crux of the dilemma that is utterly undermining any neo-Downsian incentives toward centrism. It is as if the two political parties have slickly substituted centrist *rhetoric* for centrist *policy*. The Democratic and Republican parties today, their leaders, candidates, and their mad scientist consultants, use modern campaign techniques like polling, focus groups and dial meter groups to figure out what to say to the all-important swing voters that determine close elections and control of legislatures. The sound bites, the contrived images, the permanent campaign, all of these are designed to produce Jacobs and Shapiro's "crafted talk" in order to dupe certain crucial slices of voters. Hence, the distribution of voters today—the very foundation of Downs' model—is stuck like fly paper to campaign rhetoric but not necessarily to policy. If there are any Downsian incentives toward centrist policy, increasingly they are "simulated" ones.

There was no better evidence of this than George W. Bush, who campaigned as a "Compassionate Conservative," waltzing toward the rhetorical center—classic Downsian theory—and once elected lurched hard to the right policy-wise and worked for straight party-line votes to enact his programs.[25] Interestingly, both the first year of the Clinton presidency in 1993 and the early months after Republicans took control of Congress in 1995 also were marked by party-line votes, and the battles set an uncompromising tone of confrontation that remained throughout the legislative sessions. Then, parties drifted back toward the center, at least rhetorically, as the next election approached, a kind of roller-coaster pattern that has become familiar. Accordingly, as the 2002 midterm elections approach, we can expect that the Bush administration once again will go before the TV cameras to propose centrist policy initiatives ("simulated responsiveness"), whether those initiatives pass or not, and fold the photo-ops into campaign rhetoric ("crafted talk") in an effort to win congressional elections. And so it goes on the tumultuous roller-coaster ride of Winner Take All policy.

Comparative clues from other democracies

Political scientists John Huber and G. Bingham Powell drove perhaps the final nail in the coffin of the absolutism of the neo-Downsian model. As if they were explaining what Jacobs and Shapiro had discovered—chronic policy dissonance between voters and the dominant majoritarian party—their comparative research of several Western democracies clarified that policy resulting from a Winner Take All, two-choice system in fact was *not* particularly close to the median voter.

Huber and Powell in 1994 assessed what they called "congruence between citizens and policymakers" under different electoral systems. They divided thirteen democratic nations into three system types: Majority Control vision, Proportionate Influence vision, and a mixture of the two. The Majority Control vision was, to a large degree, a proxy for a Winner Take All voting system, since the three countries lumped into this category all used the purest forms of Winner Take All and single-seat districts.[26] The Proportionate Influence vision was a proxy for a multiparty system elected by some variant of a proportional representation voting method.

Central to Huber and Powell's study of congruence was the relationship between the positions of policy makers and the position of Hotelling–Downs' median voter. Imagine, the authors wrote, that the voters did not elect representatives but rather voted directly on policy. "We should expect these voters to adopt (eventually) a policy position that corresponds to the policy decision of the median voter because the median voter's position is the only one that cannot be defeated by a majority. If some position other than the median is adopted, a minority has prevailed over a majority." To measure the degree of convergence, Huber and Powell used a regression analysis to compare separate surveys in which citizens in these respective countries placed themselves on a left-right ideological continuum to other surveys where experts, academics, and journalists estimated the positions of governments and policy makers on a left-right scale. Was there convergence between the two? If so, how much? And by which system—Winner Take All? Or proportional representation?

Huber and Powell concluded that "despite the plausibility of Downsian theory and some of the other formulations of majoritarian democracy that predict congruence . . . on average the failures of electoral competition in the Majority Control (and Mixed) systems seem more serious for congruence than does the failure of government formation in the Proportionate Influence systems. . . . The winning parties in the Majority Control systems are often not very close to the median." In addition, the authors concluded that "Proportionate Influence systems are on average significantly closer to the median voter than are governments in the Majority Control and Mixed systems." Moreover, Huber and Powell found, contrary to the established dogma that one-party majorities in strong, Winner Take All governments will produce the most majoritarian policy, that "giving some (but not too much) policymaking weight to the opposition will typically increase congruence." That's because "many of the [Majority Control] governments are quite far away [from the median] and have, on average, a good deal to gain in congruence from forces pulling them toward the center."

But, again, this is precisely the *opposite* of what the neo-Downsians had predicted. Yet it was a more accurate descriptor of what actually occurs in a two-party system, particularly when the two parties are severely polarized—like they are now. Indeed, as Downs himself had predicted, the parties may pull inexorably apart like tectonic plates when the distribution of voters is polarized, leaving a rift between them. And in that rift is where the median voter—and majoritarian, centrist, moderate policy—wallows, in abandoned isolation, until some third force (like a Ross Perot or Jesse Ventura) steps into the void.

Powell updated and expanded this research and thesis in a book published in 2000, in which he examined over 150 elections in twenty democracies over the past quarter century. Once again, Powell laid out how the two models of democracy—majoritarian vision and proportional vision—dealt with voters' intent and desires. While both political systems have their merits, Powell concluded, the proportional vision produces greater policy congruence between what the public wants and actual government policy. Proportional vision systems have outperformed the majoritarian ones by better reflecting the populace's needs and better representing the voter's wishes.[27]

Thus, contrary to popular and even political science stereotypes, Winner Take All does not necessarily lead to moderate, centrist, stable, or majoritarian government or policy. Recall the criteria of Robert Dahl at the beginning of this chapter: "A democratic government provides an orderly and peaceful process by means of which a majority of citizens can induce the government to do what they most want it to do and to avoid doing what they most want it not to do." With Winner Take All, driven by its disruptive progenies and gremlins, what the majority wants or doesn't want does not necessarily translate into policy. The theorized neo-Downsian policy congruence has been undermined by "crafted talk" and "simulated responsiveness," modern techniques of campaigning that extend the "permanent campaign" into the legislative cycle, a fundamental lack of competition in most lopsided legislative districts, partisan rather than neutral voters comprising the decisive voters in most elections, distorted electoral results that produce artificial and exaggerated majorities and political monocultures, political gaming that manipulates policy initiatives, and the increasing polarization of the two major parties' candidates and activists.

Introducing: the Winner Take All policy goblins

Despite the neo-Downsian model having encountered so much downstream debris, the mainstream of political thought is still catching up. The fact of the matter is, once a city, state, or nation elects to use the Winner Take All voting system, with all its disruptive gremlins (the redistricting roulette, phantom representation, artificial majorities, the Winner Take All conundrum, the swing voter serenade, and the two-choice tango), a host of other disruptive dynamics kicks in. For instance, in previous chapters we saw how artificial or exaggerated legislative majorities have prevailed in various state legislatures and in the U.S. House and U.S. Senate, due to the distortions of our Winner Take All system. Sometimes an undeserved majority was won by a political party with a minority of votes (like the current GOP majority in the U.S. House, or like Texas Democrats in 1994, where they won only 42 percent of the popular votes—fewer votes than the Republicans—yet ended up with a Tony Blair–like 63 percent of the state's U.S. House seats); other times an overrepresented party won a veto-proof majority capable of ramming through radical policies without a popular mandate. Such representation distortions in our legislatures contribute to policy distortions on a regular basis.

Beyond such representational distortions and other Winner Take All gremlins present in the legislature, any polity that uses Winner Take All will see their policy making haunted by an additional circus of mischievous goblins. These goblins produce a hair-raising roller-coaster ride that disfigures many a proposed legislative bill. Some of these goblins have been suggested in previous chapters, but it will be helpful now to spell them out more explicitly. Here are the typical Winner Take All policy goblins.

- *Pit bulls on the prowl.* Politicians gerrymandered into safe seats often lead the charge for their party on certain unpopular issues. The pit bulls can push an issue or policy before it is popular, or even long after the policy should have died, because they are not bound by the Winner Take All conundrum—they lord over a safe district where they cannot lose. No matter how obnoxious or obstreperous their behavior, the pit bulls can sink their teeth in and clamp down hard in dedication to their righteous cause, ignoring the public outcry. A recent, poignant example is the way a few Republicans were able to spearhead the impeachment of a popular president in 1999, despite a lack of nationwide support, because support was high in their districts.

- **Bumper-sticker policies for political positioning.** In a two-choice field, neither political party has to watch its back much, since the voters don't have any other electoral place to go. You can more easily strip-mine your opponent's record, highlighting certain positions and ignoring others, without any third candidate intervening with conflicting messages. The ideological space is relatively wide open and undefined, leaving the two parties more free to blur the policy and ideological lines using crafted talk, symbolic overtures, and bumper-sticker politics that reduce complex policy proposals into slogans. This strategy extends into policy making, as the two parties play off each other to craft policy initiatives targeted at ever smaller slices of swing voters.

- **Simulated responsiveness.** A subset of political positioning, simulated responsiveness is a gaming tactic whereby specific legislative bills are introduced by a representative or political party designed to bolster their ongoing political prospects. Everyone knows the particular bill has no chance of passing, but by introducing it, individual representatives or party leaders can then say to their constituents or to the public, "I voted to cut your taxes" or "I voted to support the minimum wage." Such "simulated responsiveness" is legislative jujitsu designed to provide the illusion that individual representatives or a political party is responsive to the public or to particular issues that the public supports. Often the positioning is timed to influence swing voters at election time. Some policies will be rushed forward and others will be slowed to a standstill as the pollsters and consultants forecast to the party leaders "what plays in Peoria." This can dramatically affect the types of policies pursued in a legislative session.

- **Pork barrel politics.** The legendary episodes of pork-laden politics that have plagued every legislature are part and parcel of Winner Take All, which at its core is about the politics of geography. Once you carve up the political map into geographic districts, every pig of a politician has tremendous incentive to bring home the bacon, with severe impacts on policy making. The larding of pork is based not on merit or on where federal appropriations are most needed, but on strategic considerations like political geography, strong-arm might of party leaders, and the wooing of swing voters. In the Senate, low-population rural states, which have disproportionate representation, are awarded disproportionate shares of federal subsidies.

- **Geographic polarization.** The political differences associated with geographic regions are exaggerated and polarized by Winner Take All. As the red and blue *USA Today* map illustrates so dramatically, geography largely has become a proxy for partisanship, culture, and race—racial minorities, liberals, and progressives living in the urban areas of New Goreia, whites and conservatives in the vast rural areas of Bushlandia, with the suburbs still majority-white but a salad mix of partisan sympathies. Yet due to its exclusive reliance on geographic representation, Winner Take All produces distorted regional representation and political monocultures with polarizing effects on policy.

- **_Intensity versus preference._** Paraphrasing what Grover Norquist of the NRA has said regarding the issue of gun control: the question is intensity versus preference. You can always get a certain percentage to say they are in favor of a particular issue. But are they going to vote on that issue? In other words, how *passionate* are voters opposed to or in support of a particular issue or policy? Passionate voters are mobilized voters, and a small number of mobilized voters can overcome a larger number of opinionated but unmotivated voters. These dynamics become particularly important in close races (i.e., in swing districts and swing states), where knee-jerk wedge issues like gun control, crime, or tax cuts can mobilize a party's base or act as a key wedge of swing voters. Politicians and political consultants understand this, and they gauge their policy making and position taking accordingly.

- **_End-of-the-decade partisan muggings._** At the end of every decade, with the Holy Grail of redistricting looming closer, both parties have intensified pressure to win control of state legislatures, which for the most part control legislative line-drawing for state and federal districts. Policies and positioning often will be weighed by how they will affect the last two election cycles of the decade, which determine who will win the divine right to redistrict.

We can boil these seven goblins policy down further by noticing that all of them are by-products of either a *two-choice* system, a *geographic/district-based* system, or both. Pit bulls: resulting from safe districts in a two-choice system; bumper-sticker politics: resulting from the two-choice system where swing voters and swing districts and states determine who wins and loses; simulated responsiveness: political positioning vis-à-vis your lone opponent, using "crafted talk" to attract a targeted group of swing voters; pork barrel politics: resulting from incentives of geographic-based districts to "bring home the bacon;" regional polarization: resulting from the two-choice system and partisan demographics, where one side dominates entire geographic regions while the other side gets ripped off; intensity versus preference: politicians in a two-choice system gauging the strength of conviction among swing voters in close races; and end-of-the-decade ambush: resulting from redistricting of single-seat districts. And oftentimes these seven goblins will work in tandem, double- and triple-teaming to upend policy making.

Thus, underlying much of what plagues policy formation in our representative democracy are the most fundamental aspects of Winner Take All, indeed, the very essence of it: geographic, district-based representation with only two uninspiring electoral choices. The gremlins and goblins of Winner Take All flow from those defining characteristics, combining to thwart sound national policy at frequent turns.

In fact, as we will see in the next chapter, on a host of policy fronts during recent years, Congress has been badly out of touch with the majority of Americans. Defenders of the status quo would have us believe that you can have a political system that depresses participation, that underrepresents certain constituencies (indeed entire regions and states) and overrepresents others, that manufactures artificial and exaggerated majorities, that provides incentives for shallow, sound-bite campaigns, crafted talk, and simulated responsiveness, that produces excessive legislative posturing and two-party tango, and that exacerbates political and racial division and polarization, and yet somehow it will produce moderate, centrist, majoritarian government. It would be a miracle if such were the case. Unfortunately, it is not the case.

Instead, during the tenure of the 106th and 107th Congresses we saw agonizing evidence of a rogue legislative body unrestrained by majoritarianism instinct or the will of the people. In the next chapter we will analyze examples of recent specific policy debates and legislation in the Congress that illustrate the Winner Take All policy goblins at work. The resulting policy distortions can be laid at the feet of our two-choice, geographic-based political system. Under Winner Take All, the majority does *not* necessarily rule.

CHAPTER THIRTEEN

The Roller-Coaster Policy Ride of Winner Take All

A s we saw in the previous chapter, research by political scientists Lawrence Jacobs and Robert Shapiro estimates that the United States Congress is now on the same page as the American people a mere 40 percent of the time. Policy dissonance rules. Yet this hardly should be surprising. Even casual observation of the Congress in recent years should have given more than a hint to unbiased eyes that Winner Take All does not necessarily fulfill Dahl's criteria for majoritarian government—government does not always do what the majority wants it to do. The following are examples of recent specific policy debates and legislation in the Congress that illustrate the Winner Take All policy goblins at work.

Pit bulls on the prowl, end-of-the-decade calculations: impact on impeachment—"if you lose, I win"

It was surprising how little discussion there was about how Winner Take All dynamics substantially drove the Clinton impeachment debacle. Often the goblins unleashed by Winner Take All will operate in tandem; in the case of impeachment, partisan pit bulls nosing around for end-of-the-decade redistricting advantage hit huge pay dirt.

Firstly, the bay hounds who pursued the hunt were mostly safe-seat Republicans, courtesy of the 1991–1992 redistricting, who lived in heavily partisan districts with no chance of losing reelection.[1] Displaying a dash of tribalism that was as impressive as it was mortifying, they were free to don their righteous armor and wage their quixotic war without worrying about career repercussions.[2] The visibility and voraciousness of congressional pit bulls in recent years has been aided, as *Chicago Tribune* writer Charles Madigan has pointed out, by declining voter turnout.[3] Party primaries in particular have become notorious for extremely low voter turnout, sometimes lower than 10 percent of eligible voters and rarely higher than 40 percent. Writes Madigan, "the smaller the number of people who vote, the more power the general population yields to special interests who are motivated enough to cast ballots."

Because most states do not require any sort of runoff in primaries for congressional elections, this can tilt these contests toward extremely partisan candidates with a highly mobilized but relatively narrow base of support who win their party primary with a very low percentage of the vote.[4] Enough of these highly partisan candidates are successful in the general election to result in a number of winners who are more partisan, more extreme, than most of the constituents they represent, even from their own party. For this reason, an editorial by the *St. Petersburg Times* opposing a proposal in Florida to get rid of runoff elections for party primaries said: "Without runoffs, the two major parties would be vulnerable to coups by their most extreme factions, presenting the voters with poorer choices in November."[5]

These districts have been some of the "breeding ground districts" for partisan pit bulls, particularly for Republicans of that breed. Safe-seat Republican House members like Tom Delay, Newt Gingrich, Dick Armey, Dan Burton, and Henry Hyde not only led the crusade for impeachment and other GOP causes, they also rose to heights of Republican House leadership. Yet they were answerable only to their party's primary voters in their district, particularly the most motivated, right-wing activists.

Also, let us not forget that the last two legislative elections of every decade determine which political party will oversee the redistricting process in all fifty states. So from the Republican point of view, Clinton's troubles, and by extension those of his party, couldn't have come at a better time for energizing their electoral base. The GOP sharks in the water smelled blood, and they lunged for the jugular; the Democratic faithful, unsurprisingly, circled the lifeboats. The fact that the GOP strategy is widely believed to have backfired in the 1998 congressional elections (the Republicans lost seats) doesn't change the fact that the Winner Take All calculation at the end of every decade is to leverage any situation extant for partisan advantage in the impending redistricting process. In these sorts of partisan gambits there is always more than one prize. The 2000 presidential outcome was probably affected by the Republican impeachment stratagem: nearly half of all voters across the country said the impeachment scandal was very or somewhat important in determining their vote, and three-quarters of them voted for Bush.[6]

Thus we arrive at one of the most maddening aspects of the recent impeachment fiasco—that a rump of safe-seat House Republican pit bulls was able to whip-saw the overall Republican hulk to impeach, oddly enough, one of the most *conservative* Democratic presidents in recent memory. Clinton, arguably, helped the GOP implement more of their conservative agenda than any previous Republican president, on a whole range of issues including welfare, crime, free trade, foreign policy, civil liberties, law enforcement, affirmative action, and more. If it took Nixon to go to China, it took Clinton to sneak significant chunks of a conservative agenda past liberal guardians. But that wasn't enough for certain Republicans. For the logic of Winner Take All dictates a singular ambition: that you beat the other side. It's instinctual to the Winner Take All mentality, like a pit bull trained as an attack dog, salivating to go on the offensive.

Most Americans, while uncomfortable with Clinton's prurient behavior, were able to recognize that the impeachment episode was a farce, a national catastrophe that was not about policy or issues or even presidential lying but about destructive partisan attacks driven by the gaming calculations of Winner Take All.[7] Certainly opinion polls showing upward of 65 percent of respondents rallying around their beleaguered president suggests that conclusion.[8] Most Americans aren't used to such bitter partisanship; we usually think of it as something that happens in other nations, either between Irish Catholics and Protestants or Arabs and Israelis. But the potboiler had been building for at least a decade, during which time the political parties became more extremely partisan than the electorate.

Welcome to the wacky world of Winner Take All and its two-choice tango, where it doesn't matter what the nation wants, for the partisan calculations are this: whichever side is left standing at the end of the *mano a mano* wins. And in that battle, pit bull attack dogs from safe districts play a crucial role, especially at the end of the decade when redistricting is at stake. Oddly, even in post-impeachment analysis by the Washington Post and others, rarely were these Winner Take All factors even considered.[9]

We can estimate the impact of these dynamics by imagining what would happen if we did not use single-seat districts: there would be no safe seats per se, nor any safe partisan pit bulls, and there would be nothing to redistrict. Hence, partisan pit bull attacks would be reduced, and the level and intensity of partisan warfare would diminish. If we used a proportional representation system instead of Winner Take All, as the work of political scientists like Huber and Powell has shown, legislative majorities would align more closely with majority popular opinion.

Pork barrel politics, pigs at the trough:
Impact on Budget Appropriations

The Winner Take All incentives for wasteful pork barrel spending are so powerful that even supposedly fiscal-conservative Republicans, once they assumed the congressional reins in 1994, failed to lasso government spending as they had promised in their "Contract with America." Pork-barrel appropriations, of course, are infamous within and outside the Beltway. They are part and parcel of Winner Take All's reliance on single-seat districts where the representative is subject to electoral pressure to "bring home the bacon." Headlines about military budgets with $200 hammers, $600 toilet seats, and the like have passed into popular folklore as notorious examples of the wastefulness of government bureaucracies. But pork is not just doled out in military budgets—in recent years it also has fed the trough of highway appropriations, airport money, subsidies for agribusiness giants in low-population states, and numerous other pet projects loaded with goodies for favored congressional districts, many of them electing formerly fiscal conservative Republicans.

For instance, in the face of post–Cold War budget reductions, a $96 billion NASA space station left over from the Reagan Administration that no one seemed to want or think the nation needed was kept on life support throughout the 1990s, almost exclusively resulting from pork. Republican districts and even some Democratic districts plugged into the life support, slurping up federal subsidies. For eight years, NASA spent a staggering $10 billion drawing and discarding blueprints without a single piece of metal ever getting cut before the Clinton Administration finally embraced the idea of building it.[10]

But the antics of Rep. Bud Shuster of Pennsylvania, powerful chairman of the House Transportation and Infrastructure Committee, probably best typify how this Winner Take All game is played. Shuster was not nicknamed the King of Pork for nothing. Using threats and strong-arm tactics, Shuster was able to ram through in June 1999 a $56 billion airport bill that made a mockery of his party's 1997 balanced-budget agreement and imperiled the Republican income tax reduction, at the time their central campaign theme. Shuster, a conservative Republican, was the quintessential "safe-seat politician"—he ran unopposed for reelection in 1998, the eighth time in fifteen terms he received 100 percent of the vote in his district. He could threaten and bluster and there was relatively little anyone could do to touch him, including the Republican leadership. But how, conservative pundit Robert Novak asked incredulously in a *Washington Post* column, was Shuster able to get half the Republican House members, including the Republican leadership, to support a bill that Ways and Means Committee Chairman Bill Archer, the GOP's leading tax writer, claimed "could eliminate entirely any net tax relief for the year 2001 and force us to renege on our promise for early tax reduction"?[11]

"They porked out," answered blunt-spoken Republican Rep. Tom Colburn of Oklahoma. Shuster had masterfully used the Winner Take All carrot and stick, sweetening the bill with goodies for individual lawmakers' districts who supported him and icing out those who opposed. Finally he threatened the entire House, warning that he would pull the bill entirely if they insisted on cutting the airport appropriations to keep within the budget agreement—which would have meant no airport money for anyone's home district, a loss of millions of dollars per district. Shuster had performed a similar hijacking a year earlier with a highway bill, giving him an impressive record, Novak noted, of two big pork-laden bills in two years at a time when little else was accomplished by the Congress. Being a safe-seat politician and powerful committee chair, Shuster was able to work the Winner Take All turf with impunity. He sprinkled money around, district by district, and in the process acquired a multibillion-dollar sway over the nation's transportation infrastructure.

While Shuster's tactics gave new meaning to the phrase "it's my way or the highway," he wasn't the only Republican who, once they took over the Congress, was driven by Winner Take All calculations to renege on their fiscal conservatism. The GOP fire-breathers who once wore "Cut Spending First" pins and fought to abolish Cabinet agencies were not willing to revamp Washington's spending culture. This caused another conservative writer, Cal Thomas, to write incredulously in his syndicated column in December 2000 about "those spendthrift Republicans." Republicans, Thomas wrote, had made a lot of political hay in recent years by accusing Democrats of being the tax-and-spend party. Yet, he sputtered, "the last Republican-dominated Congress behaved more like the party of FDR than the party of Ronald Reagan." Specifically what stuck in Thomas' craw was that the Department of Education, which Reagan had pledged to eliminate, had its budget increased 17 percent by a Republican Congress, which added $2 billion *more* than what President Clinton had requested.

Other programs conservatives love to hate enjoyed budget increases as well, including the National Endowment for the Arts, the Legal Services Corporation, corporate welfare, and bilingual education. "You name a worthless liberal social program and chances are its budget went up," said an exasperated Stephen Moore of the Cato Institute. "The 106th Republican Congress spent more money on social programs than any Congress since the late 1970s. . . . Many of the more than 200 programs that Republicans promised to eliminate in the 1995 'Contract With America' now have larger budgets than before Republicans took control of Congress."[12]

The reason for this fiscal conservative hypocrisy was simple: when you are in control of the cookie jar, dispensing the cookies district by district becomes an enormously enticing way to retain that control. Election-year strategies in close races lend themselves to giving away the store, at least temporarily. The conservative *Wall Street Journal* commented that the November 1999 budget deal showed "the Republicans' increased penchant for pork barrel politics" and that "page after page [of the budget bill] is filled with earmarks for home-state projects."[13] Winner Take All calculations are too seductive to ignore, and even supposedly fiscal-conservative Republicans behave like "drunken sailors spending someone else's money."[14]

As a point of comparison, if we used a plurality at-large voting system instead of single-seat districts to elect the U.S. House, or if we used a proportional representation voting system (which usually does not rely on single-seat districts to elect representatives), pork-barrel incentives would be greatly diminished. But because we rely on Winner Take All fiefdoms as the basis of our representative democracy, where there is so much to lose or gain in a contest for a district seat, there is tremendous incentive to bring home the bacon. Even supposedly fiscal-conservative Republicans can't resist the temptations of Winner Take All pork.

More pigs at the trough: Impact on Military Appropriations

The story of the October 1999 military budget illustrates some of the worst impacts on policy resulting from a Winner Take All system. The horrific events of September 11, 2001, in which targeted attacks destroyed the World Trade Center and part of the Pentagon and took thousands of lives, confirmed what most military analysts had been saying since the early 1990s, namely, that today the main "military" threats to U.S. interests are isolated acts of terrorism, biological and chemical warfare, and the escalation of ethnic conflicts and diseases like AIDS—scourges for which high-priced, gold-plated weapons systems like new fighter planes, attack submarines, and Star Wars missile defenses are relatively useless. But you would never know this by looking at the presidential and congressional debate that occurred in 1999 over the military budget.

That's because these debates were driven by the most perverse kind of Winner Take All calculations: the usual twin pillars of pork-barrel politics and political positioning. But in addition, the appropriations from this sorry episode reached unusually ridiculous heights because of the dynamics unleashed when the President became weakened by the impeachment entanglement. As the pit bulls sank their teeth in deeper, a damaged President sought cover by placating a powerful political constituency—the military. The anecdote in this section qualifies as one of the "Top-10 Worst Winner Take All Stories" because of its astonishing combination of shakedown, partisan brinkmanship, pork, positioning, and prowling pit bulls, all working together to mangle any semblance of sane policy.

In the spring of 1998, the conventional wisdom in Washington was that the military budget would remain steady at about $270 billion per year through 2002, as called for in the 1997 balanced budget agreement between the White House and the Republican congressional leadership. But that assumption of a constrained defense budget changed dramatically in the fall of 1998, when key Republicans in Congress and the Joint Chiefs of Staff decided that a president facing impeachment charges was ripe to be shaken down for more military spending.

The Joint Chiefs fired the opening salvo in mid-September when they invited Clinton to Fort McNair for a "closed-door" briefing. No one has revealed what words actually were exchanged, but a leak to the press by a "senior defense official" contained an anti-Clinton spin that was summarized by the *New York Times* as follows: "It has not escaped notice in the Pentagon that the accusations against Mr. Clinton—having a sexual relationship with a subordinate and lying about it—would end the career of any officer." A week later, the President sent Secretary of Defense William Cohen a letter signaling his desire to seek a military spending increase. Clinton movingly pledged—biting his famously quivering lower lip, no doubt—that "the men and women of our Armed Forces will have the resources they need to do their jobs."[15]

There was one small problem with the President's pledge: it broke the spending cap of the balanced-budget accord. So Clinton funded it through budgetary smoke-and-mirrors in the form of a $1.1 billion "emergency" increase for military readiness. But in the inevitable horse-trading needed to close the deal, Congress transformed Clinton's modest readiness increase into a $9 billion grab bag of pet pork projects, what GOP Sen. John McCain described as "the worst pork in recent memory." The additional $8 billion included an extra $1 billion for Star Wars, over $400 million for C-130 transport planes to be built just outside of still-Speaker Newt Gingrich's Georgia district, a $1.5 billion helicopter carrier to be built in Senator Majority Leader Trent Lott's hometown, and $275 million for five F-15 fighters to be built in the St. Louis area represented by House Minority Leader Dick Gephardt. Yes, Republicans and Democrats alike pushed the military pork, this bread was buttered on both sides to ensure its palatability.[16]

But the antics of October 1998 offered only a preview of the main event the following January. At that time, Clinton upped the ante by announcing a six-year, $112 billion increase in Pentagon spending. Conservatives, like those from the editorial page of the *Washington Times*, were incensed, complaining that "Mr. Clinton has appropriated yet another set of Republican issues." Not to be outdone, Senate Republicans promptly upped the ante even further. They added billions of dollars more to the Pentagon budget, beyond what the Pentagon even had requested, for items that were being purchased almost solely to maintain jobs in and around the districts of key members. Successive rounds of one-upmanship pushed the bureaucratic bloat higher and higher until it reached stratospheric heights.[17]

Let's track where this started and add up the score: first came the impeachment attack—driven by safe-seat Republican pit bulls. The attack occurred at the end of the decade when state legislative elections would determine redistricting—and by extension, representation—in all fifty states for the next decade, providing further Winner Take All incentive. The partisan attack on the President created an opening for the military and congressional hawks to shakedown the President. Once the pigskin was put into play, successive rounds of partisan brinkmanship upped the ante—and the price tag—with politicians grabbing for pork for their districts. It became a feeding frenzy, driven by a Winner Take All hunger of individual Members salivating to pull home hunks of pork for their districts and of party leaders trying to position their party for elections.

The package also had one obvious political side benefit for Democrats, including presidential contender Al Gore: as a presidential and congressional election year approached, it inoculated them against the perennial Republican charges that they are "soft on defense," allowing the Democrats to focus the electoral debate on issues where they felt they were stronger, like education, Social Security, and healthcare.[18] To counter expected liberal criticism of more military spending, Clinton included a fund to stimulate the hiring of 100,000 new teachers nationwide. Thus, liberals wanting a greater "peace dividend," along with fiscal conservatives and critics of pork and excessive military spending, had been completely outflanked. The nimble Clinton had turned a political weakness into a slick political victory, but at the price of paving the way for a liberal policy disaster—by now a familiar refrain of his presidency.

The real losers were the American taxpayer and those desiring a peacetime economy. In an era when a supposedly fiscal-conservative Congress has microscopically scrutinized and in some cases severely slashed domestic social spending, when 40 million Americans—most of them children—go without healthcare, and where we have levels of child poverty that approach that of Russia, the Pentagon still runs a bloated and inefficient Cold War bureaucracy. A General Accounting Office report in 1999 stated bluntly that "many of the Department of Defense's programs are still vulnerable to waste, abuse, and mismanagement." Among the report's most jarring findings were that "auditors could not match about $22 billion in signed checks with corresponding obligation."[19] The Pentagon's own Inspector General reported in March 2000 that the military's money managers had to make almost $7 *trillion* in adjustments to their financial ledgers in a rather inept attempt to make them add up.[20] As a result, "the Pentagon doesn't know what it can send troops, can't avoid buying more of something that the military already owns, and can't tell how much its programs actually cost."[21] Yet the military budget passed in October 1999 was the largest increase since the Reagan era, even though the military budget at the time already was more than twice that of the *combined* military budgets of every conceivable U.S. adversary.[22]

Neither Democrats nor Republicans have been willing to muster the political will to stop the waste or even to play much of a watchdog role. As a point of contrast, a third party called the Progressive Party in Vermont holds four seats in the state legislature. One of their legislative roles has been to act as watchdogs exposing bad policies that both Democrats and Republicans support, including a bipartisan corporate welfare tax credit program that was so wasteful that even the *Wall Street Journal* wrote an article criticizing it. Lacking a third-party watchdog at the federal level, and with Winner Take All policy goblins offering powerful incentives for pork-barrel gluttony, political positioning, and partisan pit bull attacks leading to impeachment, the waste and budgetary fraud known as military appropriations has been impossible to stop. Moreover, these appropriations primarily keep alive weapons systems that are not even well-suited to counter today's security threats like those responsible for the September 11 attacks. Amidst the military and patriotic outpouring unleashed by those horrific events, and the subsequent calls for "homeland security," it will be even more difficult to separate out legitimate security and military needs from the pork and other Winner Take All policy goblins that have ensured that the insanity of military spending continues to suck up so much of our nation's human and budgetary resources.

Bumper-sticker politics and electoral positioning: impact on Social Security—"Our party is for old people, theirs isn't"

The congressional debate, and as a result much of the public debate, regarding Social Security has been marred by Winner Take All–type posturing, bumper-sticker politics, mutual distrust, and spin wars between Republicans and Democrats trying to curry favors with swing voters. Partisan muggings, political gaming, and *mano a mano* have become so much a part of the cloth of Congress that the public barely recognizes them anymore. Media pundits shrug their shoulders and assume that's just how politics works, instead of laying the blame where it most belongs—at the feet of Winner Take All.

Polls have shown that solid majorities of the public favor Social Security reforms that will ensure the current level of benefits *and* stabilize the system for the future. And yet the congressional debate in the 106th Congress predictably ground down to a spate of playground name-calling. Here's how the drama played out.

The GOP decided in January 1999 it wouldn't be burned by Clinton on Social Security like it felt it had been burned on other issues. So the Republican majority in the Senate and House set aside S. 1 and H.R. 1—the ceremonial first bills of the new Congress—for Clinton's own legislation for Social Security reform. It was a symbolic move, daring the President to submit a bill that the Republicans could then pounce on. But Clinton didn't take the bait. Knowing that the Republicans were laying for him, he declined to formally draft as a bill his Social Security plan that he had previously announced on national TV. That plan would have had the government dedicate 62 percent of budget surpluses to shore up Social Security's finances and have the government invest some of those surpluses in the stock market.

The Republicans also feared a public backlash if they put out a plan that Clinton attacked. "There are a lot of lawmakers who are skittish . . . and have a big fear of having these issues turned into campaign issues," said Virginia Flynn, spokeswoman for Republicans on the Senate Finance Committee. "We were on the receiving end of a huge disinformation campaign on Medicare in 1996. There's a track record of this administration deciding that . . . they're going to use these programs as political footballs."[23] While it is true that the 1996 Clinton campaign distorted the GOP plan on Medicare,[24] Clinton and the Democrats, having recently survived the Republican impeachment gambit and recalling the Republican scare tactics used to gut health care reform back in 1993, quite rightly scoffed over such whining.

With neither side willing to draw the first fire, the two parties bunkered down in their fox holes. Meanwhile, sound national policy was held hostage. Then, following a period of relative calm—a ceasefire of sorts—in the spring of 1999, both sides cranked up the Cold War–like posturing. Finally, Clinton announced his Social Security plan, and the GOP predictably went on the offensive. Party leaders from both sides began appearing on the ubiquitous talking head TV shows in an effort to take their case to the American people. On one TV show Senate Majority Leader Trent Lott and White House press secretary Joe Lockhart squared off in a typical war of blaming and name-calling. "I don't believe the President will really honestly address Social Security," said Lott; Lockhart countered, "Some in the Congressional leadership have sought to dismiss this debate for political reasons."

The acid tone of the debate and "watch-your-back" atmosphere looked and sounded like sandbox behavior because it was. More to the point, it was Winner Take All behavior, each side using rhetorical ordnance and "crafted talk" in a two-choice field to influence swing voters, particularly among the elderly, the likeliest voting demographic in the nation. With the ideological space so polarized, and with no "third force," that is, no third political party to fill the gap, the two sides remained split from each other as well as from the desires of the American people. Many observers became understandably skeptical of what type of national policy could percolate to the surface in such an inhospitable atmosphere. Nonpartisan watchdog groups shook their heads in frustration and disgust.

"Trust is essential to bipartisan accord," said Harry Zeeve, the Concord Coalition's national field director. "We genuinely hope the importance of the issue can transcend pure partisan games or gamesmanship."

Yet by January 2000 there was still no movement on Social Security reform. The two sides were eyeing each other with weapons at the ready, and elections loomed closer every month—still nearly a year distant, by the public's reckoning, but just around the corner for politicians. Elections are *always* just around the corner for politicians. With the 2000 election deciding control of the presidency, the Congress, and, most importantly, the state legislatures that would redraw the district lines for state and federal elections for the next decade, the Winner Take All prize was too high, and more election-year gridlock resulted.

Finally, Social Security's moment arrived, in a sense, during the 2000 presidential campaign when polling and focus groups in battleground states like Florida propelled Social Security to the front of the "issues pack" (along with prescription drugs, patients' Bill of Rights, tax cuts, and education). But on the roller coaster of a presidential campaign, rational discussion was impossible as each side tried to use the issue to jockey for voters. With the polls so close and the stakes so high, the Hotelling–Downs incentives to "drive to the [rhetorical] middle" were in full force: picture Gore and Bush as Hotelling's ice cream vendors, setting up shop right next to each other in the center of the beach, using sound bites and "crafted talk" to minimize the "political distance" between themselves and as many customers, i.e. voters, as possible. Bumper-sticker politics about "Social Security lockboxes" and "trusting the people, not the government, to invest their own money" prevailed. Once the 2000 elections were over, the slogans morphed but they didn't disappear. With a barely elected President at the helm and an evenly divided Congress, Social Security reform continues to bounce along a bumpy ride, which ought to be of great concern to aging Baby Boomers. Winner Take All policy goblins have produced nothing but stalemate on this issue.

As a point of comparison, Germany recently reformed its own government-run retirement system, and that legislative process was not plagued by the kind of kindergarten behavior and two-choice tango that has infected Social Security debate in the United States. Germany's challenge, if anything, was more difficult, since their retirement pension is far more generous than that in the United States (with 85 percent of retirement benefits coming from the government, as opposed to only 45 percent in the United States) and consequently is considered nearly sacrosanct as part of its welfare safety net for retirees. Unlike the United States, however, Germany does not use a Winner Take All system. Instead, they use a proportional representation voting system where approximately six political parties win seats in the national legislature. Ironically, multiparty democracy, rather than adding to partisan warfare by increasing the number of political parties, actually transforms the partisan blame-game and "if you lose, I win" Winner Take All calculations that plague politics and policy formation in our two-party system. Multiparty democracy mitigates the peculiar positioning and gaming incentives and bumper-sticker politics of the two-choice tango and Winner Take All conundrum. Under proportional representation, triangulation into your opponent's base is more perilous since you may lose the support of other voters, including your own base, who become alienated and now have other political options in a multiparty system. With voters having more electoral choices, a critical mass may abandon whichever political party is perceived as stubbornly uncompromising or excessively vitriolic.

Thus, Germany's multiparty system led by the Social Democratic Party was able to build a consensus among the various stakeholders, including trade unions, retirees, states controlled by the opposition party, and the general public, and to reform their retirement pension system in a way that safeguards it for the future.[25] But back in the USA, it's the same old rerun of Winner Take All gridlock and partisan name-calling.

Simulated responsiveness, intensity versus preference: the 2001 Tax Cut

The enormous $1.4 trillion tax cut of 2001 was a modern watershed, absolutely the defining piece of legislation of a new conservative era of fiscal reprioritization. It amounted to nothing less than a final repudiation of the principles and philosophy of the New Deal and the Democratic Party's four decades of dominance. It was a stunning GOP policy victory. But what was perhaps most remarkable about this episode was how Winner Take All incentives drove the

Democratic Party to embrace tax cuts, and to enter into a game of tax cut brinkmanship from which they emerged, not only as the losers, but as a changed party.

Polls consistently had shown since 1998 that in a time of perceived prosperity, most voters ranked tax cuts behind Social Security, Medicare, debt reduction, healthcare, education, and other priorities as the best use for a huge projected budget surplus. Nevertheless, driven by Winner Take All political calculations in advance of an electoral season, in 1999 a bipartisan consensus arose in both parties that there should be a tax cut. The question was really over how large the tax cut should be, where the middle ground was, and how the Democrats and Republicans in Congress and the White House could get there.[26]

While tax cuts had been a Republican principle for decades, such was not the case for the Democrats and their New Deal lineage. But the Democrats under Clinton were not guided by principle, but by pollsters. Times had changed since the New Deal, the New Frontier, and the Great Society, and the Clinton Democrats abandoned historical policy to sally forth in a quixotic quest to reel in fiscally conservative swing voters like suburbanites who they believed vote passionately on this single issue. The Democratic Party's predicament was captured by U.S. Senator Ernest Hollings, a Democrat from South Carolina and thirty-two-year congressional veteran, when he stated in the heat of the 1999 tax cut debate, "We're fooling the voters. Everybody knows this is not the time for a tax cut, but we [Democrats] have come pell-mell down the road. . . . The only reason the Democrats came in with a tax cut was to offset or neutralize the Republican tax cut." Hollings blamed the politics of pollsters and pandering. "That's pollster pap," he said. "I never knew a pollster who ever spent a day in public office. They don't have any idea of public service. They have the idea of winning— that's all they know how to do. So they know how to neutralize."[27]

Neutralize. In a word, that was the Clinton-led Democratic Party's calculation in this Winner Take All game, that they somehow had to neutralize the GOP advocacy of tax cuts by taking their own steps in that direction—by, in effect, taking the issue off the table as an electoral factor with their own call for tax cuts, triangulating into the fiscally conservative swing voter demographic, and neutralizing the intensity of those voters. It was a typical Clintonesque strategy, but in this case it backfired badly.

So the Democratic leadership in 1999, instead of opposing a tax cut, expressed agreement with a tax cut proposal but took exception to the *size* proposed by the Republicans. Instead of a nearly $1 trillion tax cut proposed by Republicans, the Democrats countered with tax cuts in the neighborhood of $300–$400 billion, a sizeable departure from traditional Democratic Party tax policy. They politically counterpunched by saying that the huge Republican tax cut would miss the country's best chance to shore up Social Security and Medicare and to invest in education, healthcare, and the environment. The

Democrats also claimed the Republican tax cut was disproportionately tilted toward the wealthy—all of which were to become Democratic themes during the 2000 presidential and congressional campaigns. President Clinton, who declared his support for a smaller "fiscally disciplined" tax cut, threatened to veto the near-trillion-dollar measure.

But now that they had started down that path of bipartisan agreement on tax cuts, the Democrats had unleashed a force they could not direct or control. They made at least two fundamental miscalculations, and as a result they were subsequently outmaneuvered in the Winner Take All gambit of partisan brinkmanship.

Their first miscalculation was to think that the GOP would strike a deal to get a tax cut. While a compromise could have been hailed by the Republicans as a victory, it also would have removed the issue of tax cuts from the electoral table—exactly Clinton's strategy. But many of the GOP candidates for Congress and for President preferred to run in 2000 on party-defining issues, unclouded by messy compromises or crossover votes. So while the general public was not much in the mood for tax cuts, the Republicans gambled that trumpeting a tril-lion-dollar tax reduction would ignite their political base by recapturing the conservative fervor of Ronald Reagan's first term as president. Also, they calcu-lated that they could win over fiscally conservative swing voters in key suburban districts who had swung to Clinton in 1996.

Second, the new Speaker of the House, Rep. Dennis Hastert from Illinois, still looking to prove his mettle after being suddenly thrust into the spotlight fol-lowing the resignations in quick succession of Speakers Newt Gingrich and Bob Livingston, made the House passage of the huge Republican tax cuts a test of his leadership. A Speaker's credibility and his party's electoral agenda were on the line. He faced a minor revolt within his own party when moderate Republicans, who leaned toward a compromise plan of smaller tax cuts, threat-ened to bolt.[28] But, in a dress rehearsal of the 2001 tax cut, after twisting a few arms Hastert kept the moderates in line with a meaningless compromise.[29]

Thus, with a crucial end-of-the-decade election approaching, with the U.S. House, the Senate, the presidency, and state legislatures (and their redistricting capacity) all up for grabs, the GOP stuck to their guns and pushed a huge (at the time) near-trillion-dollar tax cut as one of the crown jewels in their electoral strategy for the 2000 elections. Refusing compromise, finally the House Repub-licans with near-unanimity passed a $792 billion tax cut without support from many Democrats (except, of course, those Ds from swing districts). And Clin-ton, as promised, vetoed it.

But as everyone already had figured out, from the GOP perspective passing a compromise tax cut hardly had been the point. One senior Republican con-gressman stated bluntly, "It was a gimmick."[30] The Republicans had the issue they wanted to inspire their conservative supporters in the 2000 elections, even at the cost of not reaching a compromise with the White House and enacting a tax cut. But the "tax cut" ball had been set in motion and had gathered considerable momentum. With Democrats arguing not "if" but "how much," opposition was effectively muted; the game now was being played in the Republican's court, and they were setting the agenda. All that was needed for a truly huge tax cut was a Republican president to sign it.

And, of course, they got that in George W. Bush. Bush immediately upped the ante even further by proposing tax cuts in the spring of 2001 amounting to $2.6 trillion, a staggering figure. The Democratic Party, having started down the path of tax cuts, committing their party as well as individual representatives in a bid to woo a certain slice of fiscally conservative swing voters, found it difficult to backtrack, much less reverse the course. They had been completely outflanked. The Bush Administration ultimately "settled" for a compromise of $1.4 trillion dollars, a tax cut nearly *twice* the size of the one vetoed by Clinton in 1999. In trying to play a Clintonesque game of setting their course by opinion polls and "simulated responsiveness," the Democrats got snared in the nets of the two-choice tango and swing voter serenade, and ultimately were outmaneuvered by the GOP.

As the national economy deteriorated in the summer of 2001 and the budget surplus dried up, threatening Social Security, Democrats blamed the Bush Administration and the GOP for the sudden reversal in our nation's financial health, deservedly so. But the pollster-driven Democrats had entered into the game of tax cut brinkmanship as a vehicle for their own electoral success. By miscalculating, they also bore part of the blame for our nation's sudden financial austerity.

Simulated Responsiveness: election year sop—anti-crime legislation

Most anti-crime bills, as political scientist Anthony King has pointed out, can be best understood as a kind of "symbolic politics," consisting of speechmaking and public position taking in the absence of any real action or any intention of taking action. "Casting the right vote is more important than achieving the right outcome," King has written.[31] Between 1981 and 1994, six of the seven major crime bills were passed in election years, usually late in the year. Crime bills are notorious for their electoral posturing potential, as Democrats and Republicans fall all over each other in an election year to appear "tough on crime." Yet according to King, many of the provisions passed in these crime bills have been of dubious effectiveness.

Usually "tough on crime" legislation is composed of a hodgepodge of adrenaline-rush policy reactions in an effort to woo swing voters. The lineup of crime policy failures, according to King, include mandatory minimum sentences, "three strikes and you're out" provisions, crackdown on crack, so-called police-community ventures like the notorious "Weed and Seed" program, and the extension of the federal death penalty to fifty new crimes. The War on Drugs has been a huge law enforcement and social policy debacle. According to the testimony of numerous judges, law enforcement personnel, and legal scholars, the War on Drugs has been at best useless and at worst pernicious in its effects. It has filled prison cells not with violent criminals but with benign drug users and low-level drug dealers. The big crime bosses and drug kings barely have been affected.[32]

The anti-drug D.A.R.E. (Drug Abuse Resistance Education) program for children and adolescents similarly has been shown to have had little impact, and may even have been counterproductive.[33] The federal death penalty also has been irrelevant; until Timothy McVeigh was executed in June 2001, no federal offender had been executed for more than thirty years, and hardly any offenders were awaiting execution on death row. Thus, the "crackdown" federal statutes, passed amid great drama and anti-crime posturing, were almost entirely for show.

The gaming incentives of the two-choice tango drive this kind of knee-jerk, bumper-sticker politics exhibited by largely ineffective "simulated responsiveness" consisting in this case of tough-sounding anti-crime and anti-drug legislation. Each party tries to gain a leg up in the incessant competition to carve out electoral space and win votes by appearing to respond to an emotional public concern. For close races in swing districts, "tough on crime" sound bites play well to most undecided voters who determine elections. But anti-crime/anti-drug policies and other types of bumper-sticker policies usually are extremely wasteful of tax dollars. That's because they create whole government programs that are superficially designed to achieve one set of objectives but in reality achieve another objective—often, simply the reelection of the politicians and the political party that claims credit.

Simulated responsiveness mows down minimum wage: the poor snagged in the Winner Take All war

Because all 435 U.S. House districts are conducted as individual races, it allows party leadership to introduce and even pass legislative bills designed to help their individual Members in swing districts. Unfortunately, this clandestine form of incumbent largesse can serve to derail badly needed policy. Such has been the case for an increase in minimum wage.

In the late 1990s about 10 million full-time workers were paid the minimum wage, earning about $10,700 a year. Raising their wages to $6.15 an hour would increase their annual earnings by $2,000, enough, supporters say, for a low-income family of four to buy groceries for seven months or pay rent for five months. According to an ABC News poll in October 1999, 83 percent of the public favored such an increase in the minimum wage. That was good news for the poor. Unfortunately, the bad news was that an election year usually is harsh for the poor, as Winner Take All calculations usually drive both parties to scapegoat or ignore anti-poverty policies.

Consequently, in year 2000 minimum wage legislation became a political football. Democrats and Republicans dickered back and forth, both claiming to favor an increase. Finally in March 2000 the Republican-controlled House agreed to raise the federal minimum wage by a dollar to $6.15 an hour. But there was a catch: they cleverly attached the bill to a $123 billion tax-cut package that they knew President Clinton would veto. What the Republican leadership had decided to do was engage in some old-fashioned legislative hijinks to give their Members political cover at home to defuse the politically potent Democratic issue of a minimum wage at the ballot box.

First, they staged separate votes on the two measures, allowing Republicans to vote *for* the minimum wage. Then they merged the minimum wage bill with the tax-cut bill, making the whole package dead-on-arrival at the President's desk. The political effect was that the measures canceled each other out—no minimum wage and no tax cut.[34] But in an election year, what was more important was that certain Republican House members representing swing districts in close races now could go home to their districts and say with all sincerity, "I voted for a minimum wage increase."

But the Republican House members were not the only ones engaging in political positioning via irrelevant votes. Everyone knew that these bills were going nowhere because of the threat of a presidential veto if minimum wage and tax cuts were linked. So forty-one Democratic Party House members representing swing districts with close races were free to join 215 Republicans and one independent in passing the tax-cut measure, 257 to 169. Now *they* could go home to their districts and bluster, "I voted to cut your taxes." In fact, numerous individual representatives, both Democrat and Republican, could legitimately brag to their constituents, "I voted to cut your taxes *and* increase the minimum wage." They could feature this fact on their targeted direct-mail pieces and in their radio and TV ads. All the while, neither the tax cut nor the minimum wage bill passed. It was a gimmick, a free vote.

Members of Congress typically vote on several hundred bills per legislative session. With the approval and advice of their party's leadership, individual members of both parties representing swing districts are always on the lookout for "bargain votes"—those votes where they are free to vote against their party and pick up some future campaign selling points at little or no cost. And the party leadership is always looking for ways to create these bargain votes for their vulnerable Members, even if it means undermining badly needed policy. These kinds of tactics allow representatives to obscure their actual legislative records. What should have been a simple vote to slightly increase the minimum wage— policy supported overwhelmingly by the public and desperately needed by the poor—became derailed by a maximum of political gaming and maneuvering.

In the 2000 election year, this was a strategy that the Republicans used many times: break out important parts of a particular bill and ram it through the House, knowing that the measure's prospects in the Senate were uncertain or that it was doomed at the White House. But in an election year, House Republicans were willing to pocket the bargain votes as campaign fodder for their members in swing districts. During 2000, Winner Take All incentives like this polluted the legislative process, top to bottom, on issue after issue.

Such tactics are much easier to target and mastermind today, with the pinpoint campaigning techniques and demographic data that allow politicians to know the electoral map like the back of their hand. If Members of Congress were not elected from single-seat Winner Take All districts, it would be much more difficult for them to carefully tailor their bargain votes to fit the demographics of swing voters in their districts. Moreover, this would increase the incentives to vote for or against a piece of legislation based on the bill's merits, instead of on the impact of that vote on one's reelection or on one's political party's electoral fortune.

Geographic polarization: Cities versus suburbs

The amount of time presidential candidate Al Gore spent dwelling on suburban sprawl and traffic jams may have seemed excessive to city dwellers, but consider this: fifty years ago fewer than a quarter of Americans lived in the suburbs. Now roughly half do. Every ten years another ten members of Congress represent predominantly suburban districts. Shifting demographics cause shifting politics, and in Winner Take All's geography-based system, "where you live" is of paramount importance.

The focus on the suburbs has dramatically changed how the issues are presented and discussed. As the 2000 battle for the presidency, the Congress, and control of redistricting got under way, population shifts over the previous decade had a more profound effect than ever before on the language and policy proposals of the parties and their candidates. So Al Gore and George W. Bush looked toward suburbs for votes, trolling for ways to appeal to the SUV-driving soccer moms and high-tech workers who populate office complexes along suburban beltways.

Issues like transportation, housing, education, and healthcare are just as pressing in the cities as in the suburbs—perhaps more so—but under the pressures of Winner Take All incentives these issues are framed to appeal to swing voters in the suburbs. So when Al Gore talked in campaign 2000 about reducing traffic, on the advice of his pollster Mark Penn he framed road congestion as a suburban family issue, speaking of parents running to their kids' soccer practice while talking on the car phone to explain to their spouse why they can't get home for dinner. He did not talk about urban dwellers riding a dilapidated public transit system for two hours each way back and forth to work.[35] That's because most urban inhabitants aren't swing voters. Many are poor, black, or brown, some speak English as a second language, and practically all vote Democrat when they vote at all. They are charter residents of New Goreia, and so can be taken for granted by Democrats and ignored by Republicans.

Policies capable of addressing urban decay, homelessness, inner-city youth unemployment, and affordable housing weren't even on the radar screen in Election 2000. National concern raised in the late 1980s about the dramatic rise in destitute, mentally disheveled individuals living on the streets, as well as homeless working families, has been abandoned under the incentives of Winner Take All politics. No mention of these issues appeared on GeorgeWBush.com, the campaign's official Web site, which chronicled two hundred of the Texas governor's top policy positions. Vice President Gore's Web site expounded on everything from "The New Africa Infrastructure Fund" to "Fighting Rural Crime." But neither of the presidential candidates had a cyber-word to say about housing, city youth unemployment, or homelessness. And they didn't talk about it in their stump speeches, either, or in their three debates.[36]

As populations have shifted to the suburbs, and as many state legislatures have tilted more conservative, Winner Take All has resulted in cities being neglected. Republicans have given up trying to win votes in most cities, which are usually Democratic strongholds. Since they don't win elections there, a Republican Congress or state legislature has little to gain politically by supporting cities with badly needed funding. And lacking other viable choices, urban voters have been taken for granted by the Democratic Party. Consequently, we don't hear very much about the issues of crumbling cities in political campaigns because it's just not a sexy part of the courtship of predominantly white suburban and swing voters.

In a Winner Take All political milieu, policies for cities and suburbs get played against each other as a zero-sum game. Not surprisingly, a number of states are being sued over spending discrepancies in school funding between urban and suburban areas. Chicago, for instance, has been a big loser in equitable funding of public schools.[37] In Minneapolis and St. Paul, Republicans controlling the Minnesota House of Representatives pitted urban school spending against the suburbs and rural areas by trying to yank funding from city schools that received special assistance for educating their disadvantaged student population.[38] With most branches of the federal government currently in the hands of the Republicans, urban areas are staring into the barrel of a policy shotgun. Because Republicans don't win often in cities, they have every incentive to run urban policy off the White House, Capitol, and Supreme Court lawns and hang a "Do Not Trespass" sign.

Welcome to the wacky world of Winner Take All, where not only is representation a zero-sum game, but so are the issues and policies that are raised and debated. The geographic basis of Winner Take All legislatures exacerbates regional tensions between urban, suburban, and rural areas and contributes toward neglect of cities.

As a point of contrast, when Illinois used three-seat districts and a "fuller representation" election method like cumulative voting to elect its lower house, we saw a different story. As related briefly in Chapter 2, nearly every Illinois three-seat district had two-party representation, with Democratic strongholds like Chicago electing some Republicans and Republican strongholds like downstate DuPage County electing some Democrats. Numerous commentators noted the cross-fertilization of policy ideas that occurred, resulting in bipartisan policy. But now in Illinois, partisan polarization exacerbated by Winner Take All single-seat districts and the two-choice tango pits cities versus suburbs versus downstate, and plagues most legislative endeavors. Moderate, centrist legislators are nearly a thing of the past in Illinois, as are the policies they promoted. Largely for this reason, a blue ribbon commission in 2001 headed by former GOP governor Jim Edgar and former Democratic Congressman Abner Mikva, along with other prominent state leaders and both Chicago dailies, recommended a return to cumulative voting with three-seat districts.

Geographic polarization: agricultural policy— "Even the pigs have lobbyists"

In contrast to the undeserved neglect faced by cities and their low-income denizens, Winner Take All's geographic-based politics have been a boondoggle for rural areas and low-population states. Overreliance on geographic representation, both in the U.S. House and the U.S. Senate, gives disproportionate influence over policy to certain groups of swing voters in low-population, rural states. Moreover, with entire geographic regions of our nation polarized along partisan lines—think of Bushlandia and New Goreia—policies for federal subsidies follow these polarized trends.

For instance, because of the regional partisanship of Bushlandia and New Goreia, farmers—especially large corporate farmers—are an essential part of the winning Republican electoral coalition in low-population, rural farming states. But this is a new alliance; historically farmers were part of the populist-labor New Deal coalition of Democrats in states like Montana, Iowa, Idaho, and Wisconsin. Having one foot in the past and another in the present gives farmers a disproportionate level of political influence, particularly in the malapportioned U.S. Senate, where each state has two senators, regardless of its population.

Despite the fact that the family farm in the United States has been plowed under by large corporate agribusiness and now is nearly an extinct species with about as much reality as a Norman Rockwell painting, politicians of all political stripes continue to pay homage to the myth of the sturdy, independent American farmer. Thus George W. Bush fixed Tom Brokaw with an icy glare when Brokaw asked at one of the debates, "Why should the family farm . . . be any more protected than the corner drugstore or the little grocery store?" Candidate Bush frostily responded, "If you ask the family farmer in Iowa, *they* don't feel protected."

Yet protection for farmers has not always been bedrock Republican policy. As recently as 1995 the Republican Congress passed the Freedom to Farm Act, a conservative's principled effort to replace the subsidy-based system that guaranteed farm incomes with a market-based system that reintroduced risk. But in 1998 plummeting prices devastated farmers, so the GOP abandoned their principles and agreed to a $6 billion bailout to avoid alienating this small but important constituency. The heartstrings were played for the plight of the family farmer, but in actuality a mere 10 percent of American "farmers" with huge corporate agribusinesses receive over 60 percent of agricultural subsidies.[39] In fact McDonald's is one of the "family farms" that receives subsidies targeted at increasing exports, since McDonalds exports to their own restaurants overseas. So when Congress agreed to extend a helping hand to the little guys, the corporate agribusinesses who own the lobbyists also landed smack in the middle of the generous safety net.

In 1999, crop prices were even worse and for a time the issue became a political football. The Democrats, desperately seeking to assist reelection of their four Democratic senators from South and North Dakota (including Senate Democratic leader Tom Daschle), and also bidding to woo back the farm support they had enjoyed for decades in states like Montana and Idaho (that had elected progressive-populist Senators like Mike Mansfield and Frank Church), tried to outbid the Republicans in a blatant effort to win agriculture votes from these low-population states. The Democrats pushed for a $9.9 billion emergency bailout, and Republicans countered with their own package.[40] Once again the predictable Winner Take All pattern of one-upmanship took over. The policy eventually resulted in a subsidy to each farm of up to $460,000, and the total hit to taxpayers was $22 billion in direct government payments.

In 2001 the agricultural one-upmanship between Democrats and Republicans began anew, with some House Republicans from farm states threatening the Bush Administration that they wanted agriculture taken care of as a condition for their support of huge tax cuts. In the Senate, where seven Democrats from farm states that George W. Bush won with over 60 percent of the vote were facing reelection in 2002, a Democratic proposal with bipartisan support sought to increase spending on agriculture by a whopping $100 billion. In an outright effort to buy the farm vote, the Democratic proposal sought to devote more than one dollar out of eight of the $750 billion allocated for new spending initiatives (including for education, defense, and prescription drug benefits for seniors) to low-population rural areas of the country that comprise a miniscule portion of the national population.

These sorts of electoral dice-rolling prompted *New York Times* columnist

Gail Collins to comment, "My own home, New York City, is . . . crammed with people who work 14 hour days at the family dry-cleaning store or corner bodega. If they founder and lose their life savings, the government may deign to give them a free night-school computer training course." But corporate agribusinesses are subsidized to the tune of billions of dollars, even as the policy is sold as one to "save the family farmer" and the family-farmer way of life, which, Collins wrote sarcastically, "is fundamentally superior to whatever it is the other 99 percent of Americans are living."[41]

Closer to the truth is that the farm vote is an important swing constituency in these low-population rural states that are part of the Republican base in the subnation of Bushlandia. Behind the drive to increase agricultural subsidies are groups such as the Commission on 21st Century Production Agriculture, the American Farm Bureau Federation, and organizations representing huge cotton, wheat, sugar, peanut, and corn producers. The GOP majority in the House does not have much incentive to enact such generous subsidies for multiracial, hardworking citizens living in cities because Republicans *don't win votes or elections there.* But these conservative, low-population, rural states elect two U.S. Senators like any other state and also are beneficiaries of the affirmative action "representation subsidy" in the Electoral College that disproportionately favors low-population states. So Republicans do what they must to keep their base satisfied, even as the Democrats try to swipe that vote back from them.

Thus, once again we see that the geographic foundation of Winner Take All distorts policy. Winner Take All incentives massively favor agricultural policy over urban policy, and low-population states in general, as each are played against the other with consequences over who will receive federal subsidies. Increasingly, this factor is a divisive part of the political landscape as our politics polarize along geographic and regional lines, with racial and cultural overtones. The impacts are nothing less than discriminatory. The geographic-based foundation of Winner Take All is producing more and more of such zero-sum policy, yet it goes mostly unrecognized. Indeed, a *Washington Post* editorial in October 2001, commenting on the breakdown of agricultural policy dependent on huge federal subsidies where "most of the money goes to big farmers," failed to indicate even the remotest understanding of the Winner Take All incentives that drive such bungled and discriminatory policy.[42]

The Winner Take All Congress: bitter partisans in the People's House

Impeachment, pork-barrel military and airport appropriations, Social Security, huge tax cuts, "tough on crime" legislation, gun control, minimum wage, agricultural subsidies, cities versus suburbs versus rural—practically no policy areas are left untouched by the roller-coaster policy ride of Winner Take All. Over and over, in policy after policy and debate after debate, Winner Take All calculations and gaming incentives drove the partisans in Congress to take uncompromising positions, to engage in symbolic and bumper-sticker politics, or to elevate political fortunes over effective national policy—sometimes all of these combined.

Early expectations that prosperity would allow the 106th Congress to seize the moment and restructure Social Security programs to prepare for the coming retirement of the Baby Boom generation evaporated quickly under the Winner Take All calculations of partisan brinkmanship. President Clinton's proposal for a new Medicare prescription drug benefit languished. The horrific shootings at Columbine High School and elsewhere could not propel gun control legislation through Congress, as we saw in Chapter 4. And the Republican Senate's rejection of the Comprehensive Test Ban Treaty—saying "there will be no photo ops for this president"—ended any last pretense of bipartisanship on foreign policy.

While it is certainly true that, to some degree, political positioning and electoral posturing are inevitable results of government itself, it is also true that this dynamic is exacerbated greatly by our *two-choice system* founded primarily on *geographic representation in single-seat districts* and *equal representation in the malapportioned Senate.* All democracies, whether using Winner Take All or proportional representation voting systems, exhibit political positioning on the part of its political parties that affect what policies are pursued. But in the modern era with its new campaign technologies, political positioning in a two-choice/two-party field exhibits significantly different dynamics than a multi-choice/multiparty field. In a multiparty or multichoice field, where most voters have more electoral choices to their left and their right, political parties must always look over both shoulders to make sure they aren't losing support on one front as they gain it on another. There is greater incentive for political parties to define themselves more precisely; to communicate who they are, ideologically and policywise; and to stand on this firmer ground. This acts as a check against campaign fakery, political gaming, and bumper-sticker policy.

But in a two-choice field, neither political party has to watch their back much, since voters behind them are severely constricted by a lack of choice and don't have any other electoral place to go. The ideological space is relatively undefined, leaving the two parties freer to foray into each other's base of support. Each candidate or political party carves out its rhetorical positions vis-à-vis the other candidate or party, playing off the solitary competition with both eyes on the glorified prize—winning elections and control of legislatures.

This strategy extends into a kind of "rhetorical policy making," as the two parties circle each other to craft policy initiatives—simulated responsiveness—targeted at both attracting support from key swing voter constituencies and mobilizing their electoral base. Navigating between the markers of such conflicting constituencies is a delicate Winner Take All dance. With exclusively geographic representation, party leaders eye the electoral map like battlefield generals, maximizing demographic opportunity as they pursue policy designed to win over swing voters, swing districts and swing states. The precision and power of the new campaign technologies like polling, focus groups, dial meter groups, thirty-second TV spots, and more, greatly facilitate this kind of harvesting and rank opportunism. Thus, the policy-making process has become just another part of the permanent campaign, bedeviled by the mischievous goblins and gremlins of Winner Take All.

Partisan gridlock in the 1990s became a familiar refrain, the commentary of numerous editorials, columnists, letters to the editor, even automobile ads and popular songs.[43] By the end of the 1990s both sides were pointing fingers and accusations like bratty children in a sand box. The 106th Congress that began with the traumatic Senate impeachment trial of President Clinton became known as the "do nothing" Congress, with numerous legislative priorities either stuck in post-impeachment gridlock or derailed by pre-election politicking. Various commentators and pundits remarked on this combination of old fights and new battles that produced such gridlock and lackluster legislative accomplishment. James Thurber, director of the Center for Congress and the Presidency at American University, said the 106th Congress hit "a low for production. Republicans have such a thin majority that every issue seems to be a wedge issue."[44]

With our legislatures, indeed our nation, so closely split along partisan, regional, cultural, and racial lines, the hapless 106th Congress may well augur our national future. Certainly the 107th Congress of the Bush Administration, outside the passage of the oversized tax cut, and a much-hyped education bill that amounted to little more than national standardized testing of students K-12 like the kind that has met with mixed results in various states and cities,[45] was similarly lacking in achievement (that is, prior to the September 11 attacks that, in effect, wiped clean the legislative docket).

Moreover, even the temporary partisan truce that prevailed in the aftermath of the September 11 attacks proved to be short-lived. The 2001 session of the 107th Congress finished as it began: in a bitter partisan dispute over taxes and other issues that showed no sign of easing anytime soon. Members of Congress returned to their home districts for the Christmas holiday break with a long list of unfinished business: patients rights, prescription drug assistance for seniors, campaign finance reform, trade and energy legislation, and more. Efforts to pass an economic stimulus bill to lift the nation out of recession collapsed amid acrimony, with proposed GOP tax cuts for corporations and wealthy individuals pitted against Democrats' proposals to extend jobless benefits and health coverage for unemployed workers. The combination of recession, war in Afghanistan, and the previous mammoth Bush tax cut had completely erased the unprecedented budget surplus. In 2002, the Bush Administration was facing budget deficits requiring borrowing through 2005, and the spending of the

Social Security surplus for the rest of the decade. Once again, both parties hurled accusations and pointed the finger of blame, with Vice President Cheney labeling Senate Democratic majority leader Tom Daschle as "obstructionist," and House Democratic leader Richard Gephardt accusing House Republicans of pushing ideologically narrow bills that pleased their conservative base but had no hope of winning in the closely divided Senate. Said Gephardt, "They are trying to get their ideological imprint on things," in anticipation of congressional elections the following November.[46]

While many observers and hopeful members of the public no doubt mourned the loss of their elected leaders' short-lived, patriotic bipartisanship, this is exactly what we should expect from the two-party tango of the Winner Take All system. For, more than "do-nothing" Congresses, the 106th and 107th Congresses were *Winner Take All* Congresses. The peculiarities of Winner Take All, with its geographic-based representation, gaming incentives, and disruptive gremlins and goblins, combined with the new campaign technologies during a time of regional polarization and shifting racial and partisan demographics, are a formula for policy gridlock.

Oh, there *was* one area where the 106th and 107th Congresses managed to craft bipartisan accord—both Congresses gave themselves healthy pay increases.

CHAPTER FOURTEEN

The Gatekeepers of Winner Take All

D espite our society having become a highly technological and complex matrix, our understanding of our *democracy technology*—the infrastructure and rules, the "hardware" and "software" that drive our political institutions and elections—has advanced very little since the time of the Framers. It is another one of these only-in-America paradoxes: we are stalked at every turn by technology, whether we want it or not, and yet our understanding of democracy technology is fairly primitive. Technologists are cramming ever more minute digital chips and memory banks into just about everything—household appliances with computers on board make bread in a shake-and-bake format, warm sourdough at the ready when you arrive home from work; sprinkle lawns at preselected times; and use Global Positioning Satellites to track children for overanxious parents. Ubiquitous PalmPilots have created a new demographic of stylus-wielding neo-Phoenicians, hunched over their sacred life-organizers, scribbling a peculiar hieroglyph. Daily headlines barrage us announcing, often times with trepidation, the latest laboratory miracle or techno-abomination, including in vitro babies, cloned sheep, designer genes, genome mapping, gene-altered pink-glo bunny rabbits, space shuttle flights for tourists, and the latest in military wizardry, including pilotless spy planes and robo-bombers.

And yet we are still using substantially the same primitive, Winner Take All democracy technology invented by the Framers in the eighteenth century. Our wholesale neglect of our national electoral infrastructure, from voting machines to voting systems, is nothing short of a disgrace. In the 2000 presidential election, ballots from as many as 6 million voters nationwide—nearly 6 percent of the total—were never counted, due to either faulty voting machines, poorly designed ballots, polling place failures, or foul-ups with registration or absentee voting.[1] We have paid a steep price for our state of disrepair. Following the Florida meltdown there was much badly needed and long overdue talk of modernizing voting equipment and other aspects of election administration. Fortunately that momentum was not permanently sidetracked by attention to national security in the wake of the September 11 attacks. But if we don't also deal with the daunting problems presented by our antiquated Winner Take All voting *system*, we will continue to watch our politics lurch in and out of one mishap after another.

Voting systems are largely esoteric to most audiences, especially American audiences. Most people in the United States, even most political scientists and constitutional lawyers, don't speak even the most basic lexicon of voting systems—terminology like Winner Take All, First Past The Post, single-seat districts, multiseat districts, proportional representation, plurality at-large, choice voting, single transferable vote, cumulative voting, limited voting, and the like. A glance at any university course catalog in the United States shows that voting systems are not studied or researched in any widespread and systematic manner, either at graduate or undergraduate levels; teachers don't teach the subject and students don't learn it. Some demur that voting systems are too complicated a subject for average citizens, yet the rules and terminology are way less complicated than those for professional football or baseball, with all the teams, players, and statistics, yet millions of Americans master those. In my experience, outside of a handful of specialist scholars and voting rights experts, most professors of political science don't even grasp it, routinely confusing terms and key concepts. To my astonishment, on one television show where I was a guest a nationally known professor of election law did not know the difference between the terms "proportional representation" and "parliamentary government," yet she inveighed against both like she was an authority.

Unfortunately, unlike other matters technological, when it comes to the area of democracy technology, including voting systems but also election administration and voting equipment, we are a backward nation, far behind other democracies. For instance, the entire country of Brazil now uses computer-based voting equipment for all local, state, and federal elections. It is a national system with plenty of safeguards in place. Voters see a list of candidates on the computer screen and type in the number of the candidate (such as 2, for the second candidate listed). Then the name, party, and *photo* of the candidate appear on the screen, so the voter is sure she's voting correctly (thereby preventing the overvotes and undervotes that plagued the Florida presidential election). The voter either can confirm or correct their vote, and move on to the next race. The United Kingdom conducted elections for the mayor of London—the highest vote for a single office in the U.K.—using high-speed optical scan voting machines that allowed voters to rank their first *and* second choices, and then counted the ballots in a way that simulated an "instant runoff" election to arrive at a majority winner in one vote. Meanwhile, New York City in 2001 spent more than $10 million and strained its administrative capacity to carry out a traditional two-round runoff for its mayoral election which spread out over months, many voters having to vote *three* times before finally electing a winer. This is not rocket science, yet the United States lags woefully behind.[2]

From ballot access laws to campaign finance to voter registration to training of poll workers and dozens of other electoral details, our electoral practices are a hodgepodge of confused regulation without national standards, uniformity, or rationale. Often they have been made up by inexperienced county or state officials at the behest of party leaders, with either little thought to unintended consequences or with conspicuous thought about ways to protect the two-party duopoly.

For instance, due to ineffective methods of purging its registered voter lists, the state of Alaska has more registered voters than voting-age people. Indiana has its registration lists jammed with hundreds of thousands of people who should not be on them, including the dead and many who have registered repeatedly. Indiana makes it very difficult to remove voters from the rolls, and one person might register six variations of their name; unless he or she got caught, the person could vote six times. Six other states have rolls with bogus names of 20 percent or higher, according to the *Los Angeles Times*.[3] A statewide voter registration database for each state—as opposed to decentralized local and county databases—can go a long way toward decreasing fraud and the numbers of duplicate voters, as well as ensuring accurate registration. Yet a recent survey by the Constitution Project of all 50 States revealed that only ten states have such unified statewide databases; 13 states have no registration database at all.

Poll watchers in Virginia inexplicably are prevented by law from telling a voter that she or he has made a mistake on their ballot that will disqualify their vote. In San Francisco, poll workers and their ballot boxes from several precincts during a December 2000 runoff election did not have transportation to the ballot-counting headquarters, and were driven there by partisans from one candidate's campaign. Most elections, instead of being staffed by professionals, rely on a cavalry of volunteers as poll workers, and because elections take place in the middle of a workday most of these volunteers are elderly people and retirees. While the seniors are certainly well-meaning and civically exemplary, too many also are easily confused and understandably slow-moving. Not surprisingly then, about 3 million voters nationwide said they were not able to vote in the 2000 presidential election because of registration problems, and another 1 million cited "long lines" or other polling place shortcomings.[4]

For no rhyme or reason, most state constitutions or local city charters currently do not permit sensible options for instant runoff voting, or fusion, or proportional representation. Federal election law currently does not permit states the option of trying proportional representation to elect their representatives to the U.S. House, even as the federal requirements for redistricting—which would be mitigated by the use of a proportional system—cost states millions of dollars and countless administration headaches every ten years, even as it locks down most voters into safe, non-competitive districts. Fortunately the U.S. Constitution is silent on these matters, and states and cities are free to experiment by upgrading charters and state constitutions as they choose. And there has been movement to amend federal law to permit states a proportional option.

New Mexico's state constitution inexplicably forbids a majority requirement necessitating two-round runoff elections or instant runoffs. If you ask New Mexico election officials and state leaders why they possibly would disallow a voting practice that produces winners with majority support, they will shrug and grunt things like "that's just the way it is" or "it's easier to administer" or "if it was good enough for the Founding Fathers, that's good enough for me." Party leaders will try to calculate the gains and losses for their party if a majority requirement is enacted, instead of thinking about what is good for the public. Inertia and status quo rule the day, and consequently, the mayor of Albuquerque won his election in 1997 with only 29 percent of the vote, in 2001 with only 31 percent.

California state officials have refused to allow political parties to use a None Of The Above (NOTA) option in their own party primaries. This silly rule is particularly harsh on third parties and leads to unnecessary "spoiler" campaigns, since without it third parties have no way to control their own ballot line or candidacies. Any private citizen, even a nutcase or one *opposed* to the party, can gather a handful of signatures and run as a candidate of that party, even if the minor party has chosen not to run in that particular race either because they lack resources or because they do not wish to play the role of "spoiler" in that race. When the Green Party of California tried to use NOTA to prevent an undesirable candidate who was running unopposed from winning a primary for a statewide office, California's Secretary of State and state court barred them from doing so.

Without NOTA or other considerations in party primaries, the inability of third parties to control their own ballot line can lead to ridiculous situations in a Winner Take All system. In Washington state, Republican operatives disguising their identities manipulated two Green Party members into running for two offices in close races, hoping the Green Party candidates would spoil the Democratic Party candidates. One of the races, for the state house from the 21st district, was the state's most closely watched race because the Democrats and Republicans were tied, forty-nine seats each, and that seat would determine which party controlled their House of Representatives. The stakes were huge, and so the Republican operatives went fishing for people to run as Greens, then organized a Green Party convention including renting the hotel room where it was held, donating money, and nominating the beguiled candidates. When the charade hit the media the GOP ended up with egg on its face, but the subterfuge revealed how easily the fragile Winner Take All system can be manipulated and gamed. Green Party leaders were understandably outraged. "Our First Amendment right to freedom of association is being destroyed when a candidate is put on the ballot who doesn't represent us," said a Green Party spokesperson. "There should be some sort of law that prevents an impostor being put up as a candidate."[5]

I already commented in Chapter 11 on the byzantine array of ballot access laws that have been rigged by the Democratic and Republican parties in most states to shut out third parties and independent candidates. These are just a small sample of the hundreds of ridiculous regulations and requirements erect-

ed in each of the fifty states that are backward, nonsensical, and have real consequences. There are no national standards whatsoever, simply a jumble of county and state rules enacted by officials who seemingly make it up as they go along
and cling to "the way we've always done it" so as to not upset their own bureaucratic applecart. In so many ways, the self-proclaimed "world's greatest democracy" has slowly become a cobweb-choked mausoleum.

Despite our obvious shortcomings, nevertheless there exists a long-standing
American arrogance that sees our political system as the Copernican center, the
jewel of democracy. Most Americans boorishly assume that the rest of the democratic world does democracy "just like us." But that view is, by any reasonable
estimation, extremely nearsighted. In the matter of voting systems, for instance,
the multiple varieties employed around the world are awe-inspiring, like a colorful palette of flowers in a vernal field. Fewer and fewer countries do it like the
United States. Even the nations of the former Soviet bloc, and of South Africa
too, as they came online as fledgling democracies, declined to borrow many of
our key political practices and methods, particularly our Winner Take All voting system or archaic methods like the Electoral College. Likewise, the newly
formed Scottish and Welsh legislatures specifically rejected our Winner Take
All methods, and New Zealanders recently discarded Winner Take All after
using it for 150 years. Like South Africa and the former Soviet nations, these
democracies instead chose forms of proportional representation.

Even our own national progenitor, the United Kingdom, from whom our
Framers adopted many of our eighteenth-century practices, is in the process of
shedding this old skin, having adopted recently more modern methods for
electing the London City Council (a German-style proportional representation
combined with single-seat districts), mayor of London (a form of instant runoff
voting), the aforementioned Scottish and Welsh legislatures (the German mixed
proportional system), and representatives to the European Parliament (proportional representation). When one has not been thoroughly dunked in the water-
logged mythologies of our system, when one can fly above the spray, the defects
of our antiquated eighteenth-century voting systems are too apparent to ignore.

The national myopia on this score is nothing short of appalling. Feckless
reformers and noted thinkers inveigh against all manner of political vices and
viceroys, yet they rarely mention voting systems, and when they do often they
get it wrong. Until the Florida debacle, supposedly informed television pundits,
award-winning columnists, charter commission consultants, academics, and
even the venerable *New York Times* and *Washington Post* regularly displayed an
abysmal level of confusion and even ignorance in matters of democracy technology, yet felt free to hold forth and opine like experts. The *New York Times* regularly has made great sport of lecturing the Italians, piously recommending that
they move away from their proportional representation system and toward
U.S.-style Winner Take All districts as a way of decreasing the number of politi-

cal parties and hence collapsing governments. When Italy began experimenting with using some single-seat districts mixed with their proportional system in the early 1990s, they discovered to their dismay that *more* political parties got elected under single-seat districts than under proportional representation. Italy's political system, in other words, began behaving more like India's and Canada's Winner Take All systems, not the United States'. Yet the *Times* was seemingly oblivious to this fact and brashly continued recommending more Winner Take All districts, until such a proposal was defeated by Italian voters in a national referendum in May 2000.[6]

The divinations of these "experts" would be good comic relief if they were merely those of a cranky neighbor whose miscues and malapropisms you could ignore overtop your adjoining fence. Instead these are members of the professional political class who act as the "gatekeepers of ideas." These are the sentinels of Winner Take All, viewing the world through their "Winner Take All eyes," deciding what will and will not be discussed, which ideas will live and which will be strangled in the crib. From the nation's Capitol to City Hall, these defenders of the status quo cite the Framers and quote the Founders like they were biblical prophets. They have elevated the eighteenth-century political institutions and democracy technology established by the Framers to a sacrosanct, untouchable level, even as the evidence mounts about their considerable deficiencies in the twenty-first century.

The American Blind Spot

Even following the meltdown of the UnElection 2000, the level of hubris remained at quasi-patriotic levels. During the six-week-long presidential crisis, pundits and TV talking heads fell all over themselves to reassure a bewildered, post-traumatic public that the system was stable, like damage-control specialists at the scene of a ten-car wreck. Following the December 12 Supreme Court installation of the president, one influential daily newspaper opined with a straight face: "Once again the Constitution, the collected wisdom of the Founders, has met the test of democracy."[7] While European and other international observers scratched their heads over a U.S. presidential election being decided by malfunctioning voting machines that disproportionately affected black, elderly, and poor voters, by a Republican-stacked Supreme Court halting the vote-counting on the flimsiest of grounds, and by an eighteenth-century voting procedure that failed to produce a majority winner in the popular vote or even in many states, a *Newsweek* columnist gushed about the "affirmation of the bedrock democratic principles that make the United States so formidable around the world."[8] The *New York Times* smugly declared that "any wise observer—domestic, foreign, or interplanetary—has to conclude that Americans' final verdict will be that theirs is a country in need of new voting machines, not a new electoral system."[9]

As I mentioned in Chapter 7, Lee and Oppenheimer in their groundbreaking study of the United States Senate expressed great bewilderment that their political scientist colleagues in previous decades and in recent years had spent so little time collecting data and analyzing the impacts of the representation subsidy for malapportioned low-population states in the U.S. Senate. "The most intensely debated issue at the Constitutional Convention—how to apportion representation among states—has received very little attention since. . . . Journalists, legal scholars, and political scientists have generally ignored the consequences of the Great Compromise and equal representation of states in the Senate."[10] So, while American political scientists have certainly been industrious and prolific over the years, when they have a blind spot, it can be a really large spot—as large as the United States Senate.

Unfortunately, the mechanics of voting systems has been another blind spot of American political scientists, and of journalists as well. The British are much further along in the study of their electoral practices—of studying its political *self*, so to speak—than we are. British political scientists and reformers, for example, for years have been gathering the data needed to study the impacts of their Winner Take All single-seat districts on competition, on representation, on political monopolies, on redistricting, and the like. They even have devised clever ways to count their actual ballots from national elections using different voting systems, modeling the electoral impacts when using single-seat districts compared to multiseat districts, plurality versus majority winners, proportional representation versus Winner Take All /First Past the Post, and even different types of proportional systems.

But here in the United States such efforts by political scientists are in their infancy. In fact, only recently have American political scientists even begun collecting the right data and sorting it into databases. Unbelievably, for most of our electoral history, right up until the 1990s, the electoral record of the self-proclaimed "world's leading democracy" was routinely lost or discarded; official election records in the fifty states were passed on to county offices where usually they were stuffed under desks, recycled, occasionally put into archives, or most often discarded.[11] A national study of voting equipment in the aftermath of the Florida meltdown conducted by the University of California–Berkeley's Institute of Governmental Studies concluded that "the national data are fraught with errors and problems" due to "different reporting standards and conflicting information" and the "erratic record-keeping of some counties."[12] In other words, at a time when genetic scientists have embarked on the mapping of the human genome, in the United States the political "science" of studying elections and the impacts of voting systems, or even voting equipment, has barely even begun collecting the data!

Given all the electoral studies generated year after year by political scientists at the finest universities like Harvard, Yale, Princeton, Stanford, Berkeley, and more, one may have assumed that the academic professionals were utilizing the best data available. Nothing could be further from the truth. It wasn't until the late-1990s that political scientists Gary King and Bradley Palmquist at Harvard University announced the release of a massive new data set on American politics called the Record of American Democracy (ROAD), which included election returns, socioeconomic summaries, and demographic measures of the American public starting with the year 1984.[13] As King and Palmquist commented upon the release of their ROAD database, this was the first data set to become generally available to the academic community that was "on a par in terms of quality and quantity with the data politicians and political strategists have been using for decades to target their campaign resources."

But the ROAD database reaches back only until 1984, and that's not a great many years. Much previous data have been lost. So, not only are our voting machines and election administration practices an abominable mess, as we learned during the Florida debacle, but so are our record-keeping, data collection, and analysis of the most fundamental aspects of our political system. In short, the election administration and political science professionals in the United States have completely dropped the ball on this score, and only in the wake of the Florida meltdown did these officials finally peel away the cobwebs from their eyes to get some idea of the scope of the problem—but they limited their interests mostly to voting equipment, leaving the fixing of our voting system to another day, another meltdown.

At least now some reliable data in the form of the ROAD database are finally available, and will be collected henceforth. Still, American political scientists are not even close to a sophisticated analysis of democracy technology like that displayed by their British and European counterparts. That's because most American political scientists, researchers, pundits, reporters, editors, and thinkers share this nationalist bias that the United States is the best, the first, the democratic paragon, rendering them insular, nonobjective and poorly versed in comparative political systems analysis. They are stuck seeing the world from inside the American box, and consequently are still tentative about asking the right questions.

For instance, certain statistical indicators are helpful for assessing the health of any democracy; they are like a doctor reading the vital signs of her patient, and I have been employing some of them throughout this book. Yet American political scientists and researchers do not keep track of these democratic vital signs on a regular basis, and the media does not report them. These indicators include the following.

- *Votes-to-Seats Index.* The votes-to-seats index builds on the theoretical work of political scientist Douglas Rae and measures what we called in Chapter 2 the "representation ripoff"—that is, the extent to which one party wins a greater percentage of seats than votes (overrepresentation) and the other party wins a smaller percentage of seats than votes (underrepresentation). It measures how well the intent of voters actually is reflected in the legislature. In Arkansas, for example, Democratic candidates for the U.S. House won only 45 percent of the statewide popular vote yet ended up with a whopping 75 percent of the House seats. These sorts of distortions occur in U.S. elections all the time, at local, state, and national levels, and have real impacts not only on representation but also on policy. But in contrast to their international colleagues, most American political scientists don't bother keeping track of the issue, and the media doesn't report it. Not surprisingly, therefore, the public is not much aware of it.

- **_Representation Index._** This index measures the percentage of voters in a state who voted for the winning candidate in an election. Every election, besides most voters not participating, even fewer voters actually help elect someone. In a Winner Take All system where only one side can win, millions of voters in the wrong districts vote for losers and waste their votes, turning them into what I have called "orphaned voters" or geographic minorities. Many orphaned voters vote for losers election after election, and eventually they get the message—there is no point in showing up on Election Day. So, besides the number of wasted votes, the Representation Index also measures the degree of futility of voting. In the 2000 U.S. House elections, the Representation Index was only 31.2 percent, meaning that fewer than a third of eligible voters had their vote count toward electing a House representative.

- **_Margin of Victory Index._** This is a measure of _how much_ candidates win by, which is a measure of competitiveness. It is important to know this because, as we saw in Chapter 5, there is a direct correlation between the competitiveness of many races and voter turnout, particularly for legislative elections. Generally speaking, the greater the margin of victory—the less competitive the race—the lower the voter turnout.

- **_Landslide Index._** Related to the margin of victory index, this index measures the percentage of all races won by at least 20 percent. This is a benchmark number because twenty-point victory margins are considered such a landslide that the other side did not have a chance of winning. It is an indicator of "safe" seats. Whenever you see a pattern of districts won by such margins, election after election, it generally means that so many partisan voters—Democrats or Republicans—reside in that district that you can easily predict who will win, regardless of inequities in campaign spending or other factors. Demography is destiny in landslide districts, and the sheer number of such districts gives you a measure of how _polarized_ a state or nation's politics is, and how badly gerrymandered the districts are. For the U.S. House, typically three-quarters of races are safe seats won by landslides.

- **Voter Turnout Index.** This is about the only democracy technology indicator that most researchers track on a semiregular basis. But finding voter turnout figures is not easy, particularly for local, state, and nonpresidential federal elections, since they are infrequently published by the Secretaries of State, election officials, or daily newspapers. Even when they do publish the figures, many researchers typically goof it up, regularly distorting the information by calculating *registered* voter turnout instead of *eligible* voter turnout. In other words, they neglect to include those adult citizens eligible to vote but who, for various reasons, have not registered (it's kind of like keeping track of unemployment without counting those discouraged workers who have given up looking for work). Eligible voter turnout is used by virtually every other democracy in the world because simply using the turnout of registered voters gives a skewed picture, artificially *increasing* voter turnout figures by 20 to 30 percent. I have asked various American researchers and reporters why they do this and have received vague and inconclusive responses. Given how embarrassingly low voter turnout is in the United States, the reasons have ranged from ignorance to a conscious attempt to artificially inflate voter turnout numbers.

- **Democracy Index.** This is a clever indicator devised by Rob Richie of the Center for Voting and Democracy which takes a state's average ranking in all the above key categories: average margin of victory (measuring overall competitiveness), landslide index (measuring number of safe seats), votes-to-seats distortion (measuring how well the intent of voters is reflected by results), voter turnout, and representation index (which measures the percentage of voters who had an effective vote, i.e., contributed to electing a representative). The Democracy Index is a relative one, aggregating all these categories to arrive at an estimate of the degree of democracy, comparing the states to each other. For instance, according to this methodology the four states with the highest democracy indicator in 2000 were Minnesota, Missouri, Wisconsin, and Connecticut; the four states with the lowest democracy indicator were Texas, Oklahoma, Louisiana, and Arizona.[14]

- **"Mirror" Index.** How well do our legislatures mirror the face of our population along numerous demographic lines, including race, gender, income, religion, trade/occupation, and more? In today's simple-minded Winner Take All climate, this is derisively labeled as "representation by affirmative action bean-counters," instead of one legitimate indicator among many of the representativeness of our political system. No doubt it is labeled thusly because the American political system so badly fails the test, hardly producing legislatures that mirror our population, as John Adams said it should over two centuries ago.

Like doctors of democracy, political scientists and journalists should be calculating these measurements and indicators immediately following every election for federal, state, and local races. That would give each state and our nation a measure of the health of our representative democracy. Measuring these indicators is like reading the oscilloscope monitoring the patient of American democracy, lying on the gurney. But other than the Center for Voting and Democracy's *Dubious Democracy* report for U.S. House elections and the Charlie Cook Political Report, which, like the Center for Voting and Democracy, uses a calculation similar to the Landslide Index to predict U.S. House races, these vital signs of our democracy are not measured to any consistent degree. There is practically no research or reporting done along these lines for state legislative or local elections. It is truly a gaping hole in scholarly research, a huge failure of American political scientists and journalists, and our understanding of our political system suffers greatly as a result.

Winner Take All analysis, M.I.A.

Obviously, trying to wade through the complex sociological, political, and economic forces that are creating the twin black holes of political depression and national division, and ushering in a fractious, voterless post-democracy, is a challenging task. But conspicuously missing from the various causes and etiologies cited by leading thinkers, reformers, and political scientists is the fundamental role of the Winner Take All system. To them, Winner Take All is operating silently in the background, of no more interest or note than their word processor's operating system. They take it for granted; it doesn't exist in their reckoning. It's not on their radar screen.

Numerous valuable books written by noted scholars and thinkers have weighed in on the subjects of American democracy, representative government and civil society, or campaign finance reform, campaign trends, voter turnout, and national division. We recognize these books because they have familiar names and provocative titles like *Bowling Alone, The Paradox of American Democracy,* two different books titled *Why Americans Don't Vote, Why Americans Stopped Voting, Why Americans Hate Politics, The Decline of Popular Politics, If the Gods Had Meant Us to Vote They'd Have Given Us Candidates, Everything You Think You Know About Politics . . . and Why You're Wrong, America: What Went Wrong?, Democracy At Risk, Campaign Talk, Civic Engagement in American Democracy, The Good Citizen, The Trouble With Government, The End of History, The New Majority, How to Overthrow the Government, Checkbook Democracy, Who Will Tell the People? The Rise of Political Consultants, The Postmodern Presidency, Spiral of Cynicism, By Invitation Only: The Rise of Exclusive Politics in the United States,* and many others, past and present. While most have contributed something valuable to our understanding of American politics, all of them are conspicuous in that they have completely ignored the impacts of Winner Take All, and voting systems in general.

Esteemed thinkers and intellectuals have utterly overlooked the mechanics of Winner Take All and democracy technology. For instance, Robert Putnam's fascinating *Bowling Alone*, while a treasure trove of statistics and charts advancing some much-needed focus on America's generational retreat from civic and political engagement, gave short shrift to the role our political institutions, especially their Winner Take All nature, are playing in our national depression and chronic division. Putnam treats these as just another symptom; I am suggesting that these are primary cause.

Leading reformers and reform organizations regularly inveigh against "the democracy gap," or against the infirmities of American democracy and representative government, yet the words "Winner Take All" rarely, if ever, cross their lips. National newspapers like the *New York Times, Washington Post,* and *Wall Street Journal* editorialize, opine, hold forth, and lecture, not only about and to American government and politicians but also to other democracies around the world, yet the words "Winner Take All" hardly ever so much as leak from their printing presses. Reams of articles from magazines on the left and the right—from *Mother Jones* to the *National Review,* from *American Prospect* to *American Spectator*—from writers and researchers all over the political map, routinely step up to the plate and take a big swing at analyzing American democracy and representative government, yet rarely do the mechanics of Winner Take All rate a mention.

The level of American myopia on this front is astonishing. It is the proverbial "elephant in the living room," around which everyone tiptoes and says approximately nothing. Instead of hard-hitting analysis that recognizes the pervasive and pandemic role that Winner Take All plays in our politics, and by extension in our economics, millennial thinking has become fashionable and downright eschatological. Fukuyama has declared the end of history, Mickey Kaus the end of equality, John Horgan the end of science, Manuel Castells the end of the millennium, Ilya Prigogine the end of certainty, Jeremy Rifkin the end of work, Bill McKibben the end of nature, and Neil Postman the end of education[15]—with everything smashing to such a cataclysmic close, what does it matter what happens in a mere presidential election, or if less than half, sometimes less than a tenth, of our citizens bother to vote, or the fault lines of national division have widened another crack? And how possibly could a *voting system* have anything to do with it, anyhow?

Oddly enough, one is much more inclined to find a mention of Winner Take All—and, consequently, more penetrating analysis on American politics—from *British* publications like *The Economist, The Independent,* and *The Guardian.* That's because, generally speaking, the British are much more informed about how their own Winner Take All system works, along with its defects and deficiencies, and perhaps are much less invested in America's opinion of itself and its eighteenth-century political institutions. Among mainstream American dailies, *USA Today* occasionally incorporates understanding of certain aspects of Winner Take All dynamics into editorials, particularly as related to redistricting and voting rights for racial minorities. Weekly publications like *The Nation* and *In These Times* in recent years have found relevance in analyzing our Winner Take All ways from time to time, as do a handful of syndicated columnists like William Raspberry, Tom Brazaitis, and Clarence Page. But for the most part, Winner Take All lurks silently and mischievously behind the American scene, unidentified and unrecognized.

The consequences of this national ignorance are severe. It's a bit like having your car break down on the side of the road, totally dead, and towing it to a mechanic who pronounces: "It's the headlights. You have to fix the headlights." You don't have to be a mechanical genius to know that the problem is certainly not the headlights. Our national understanding of our democracy technology, unfortunately, has been a lot like that myopic mechanic. In trying to grapple with impending post-democracy, with low voter turnout, with race-to-the-bottom campaigns, with regional balkanization and partisan polarization, with the daunting dilemmas of race and representation, and with the frequent failure of national policy, we look for problems in the headlights, the bumper, the hubcaps, the tires, the fenders, in numerous aspects of our political system, which, while important, are ancillary to the major problem. We look everywhere but under the hood—at the engine. The engine of any democracy is the voting system. And yet most American thinkers, researchers, reformers, pundits, and intellectual institutions neglect to lift up the hood, and so continue to overlook the fundamental impact of Winner Take All on our representative democracy.

The first important engineering principle of democracy technology is that *voting systems matter.* They are not neutral. Just like voting *machines* can differ in quality, as we saw in Florida's presidential election where punch card machines so badly botched the tabulation of votes, different voting systems also can give different performance levels related to our five pillars of representative democracy: representation, participation, campaigns and discourse, policy, and national unity. The fact of the matter is, some voting systems are better than others, depending on what you are trying to accomplish. And the eighteenth-century Winner Take All practices and institutions used for most elections in the United States are archaic and outdated for the demands of the twenty-first century.

18th-Century Technology in the 21st Century

Our Winner Take All democracy technology is malfunctioning right before our eyes, but we are continually misdiagnosing the breakdown. And we are paying a steep price with distorted policy, underrepresentation of certain voters and overrepresentation of others, plummeting voter participation and citizen involvement, superficial McCampaigns of mudslinging, sound bites, "crafted talk," and "simulated responsiveness," and exacerbation of internecine division that is threatening to disrupt our nation along partisan, regional, racial, and cultural lines.

At this particular historical juncture, as the sovereignty of governments is challenged by globalization, as the status of American workers erodes compared to their European counterparts, as the pace of technological change whirls at a dizzying velocity, as energy shortages, water supply, global warming, and nuclear waste disposal pose challenges for the human future, and as foreign policy produces explosive reactions and counterreactions like the September 11 tragedy with ramifications for domestic and international security, it becomes all the more important that American voting systems—in addition to our voting *machines*—act as efficiently as possible to produce an inclusive representative democracy that legislates sound national policy.

As populations increase and as consumption in this globalized world speeds up, putting ever more demands on the environment and resource allocation and demanding ever more efficiency in every nook and cranny, the ante is being raised, the price for ignorance and inefficiency is increased. This harsh reality is as true in the political domain as in the economic, trade, environmental, foreign policy, and domestic security domains—in fact, they are intricately connected. Appropriate twenty-first century policy—modern solutions to modern problems—hardly can pass safely through the gauntlet of our out-of-touch and unrepresentative Winner Take All legislatures without being contorted by the various gremlins and goblins that plague our political system.

It is imperative that our democracy technology act efficiently to allow new ideas to percolate into the public debate, and to allow new types of viable candidates to arise who can speak to and for the looming issues currently ignored in the Winner Take All milieu. It is urgent that these candidates begin to re-engage those who currently are overlooked, alienated, and unrepresented, those hundred million citizens eligible to vote but who regularly decline the invitation. And it's crucial that the democracy technology allow a majority of votes to translate into majoritarian policy, for without that vital feature government loses legitimacy, inch by inch, year by year. Without legitimacy, government loses its ability to bind a nation and its various peoples, until the body politic has rusted and rotted.

If democracy is about anything, it must be about *hope*—hope for a periodic resurgence and renewal, a revitalization resulting from the animal spirits of creativity unleashed by a political system that allows the popular genius to percolate to the surface. Yet our eighteenth-century democracy technology is antiquated and not up to that task in the twenty-first century. And that's why its continued use will hasten our spiraling into a fractious, voterless post-democracy, where a troubling future awaits.

CHAPTER FIFTEEN

"Winner Takes Nothing"

> Richard Nixon to John Erlichman: You gotta remember, the smartest thing the [Founders] did was to limit the voters in this country. Out of 3 ½ to 4 million people, 200,000 voted. And that was true for a helluva long time, and the republic would have never survived if all the dummies had voted along with the intelligent people.
>
> Now we've gone all the way and passed voting rights. We've got people voting down there, ah, we even got rid of the literacy tests now. So you got people voting now—blacks, whites, Mexicans and the rest—that shouldn't have anything to say about government; mainly because they don't have the brains to know.
>
> —FROM THE NIXON TAPES[1]

There's an old saying—"We don't know who discovered water, but we can be certain it wasn't a fish." That is to say, we don't always understand the nature of the sea in which we swim, since we are understandably steeped in the mythology and momentum of the time and place in which we live.

In the current context, it is not always easy to perceive our Winner Take All ways. Understandably, we look at the world through our "Winner Take All eyes," and we tend to think that the way we do it must be the best, the simplest, the rightest, the only way. But our way certainly isn't the only way; it's not even the only Winner Take All way.

The ancient Romans, for example, while they had a limited proto-democracy dominated by wealthy families, used a form of Winner Take All that in at least one way was more democratic than our own methods. The early Roman Republic had four primary political gatherings, and in one called the Centuriate Assembly all male citizens of military age, even the poorest, were enrolled into one of five voting groups based on economic class. Each property class voted as a unit on important issues, the poorest classes, like other citizens, having their say.[2] In the middle Roman Republic the poorer classes exclusively elected ten high-level leaders, called the tribunes of the plebeians, who could use their office to take up populist causes in opposition to the nobility. Although the Roman Republic overall was a very primitive Winner Take All democracy, one dominated by its wealthiest male citizens, still it is interesting that the Roman Republic explicitly granted a "representation quota" to its poorest citizens.

Even the lowest of classes had a political voice. Class was distinctly recognized, and formally incorporated, into their Winner Take All voting practices and institutions.[3]

Today, of course, the idea of such affirmative action along class lines would be ridiculed by the gatekeepers and defenders of Winner Take All. Instead, poor people pretty much have opted-out of our democracy, since there are no class quotas, no tribunes like the Gracchi to speak for their causes, and no hope that a viable political party might arise that can represent their interests. With the benefit of two thousand years of hindsight, we can see ways that the early Romans were pioneers of representative democracy—for instance, they initiated the secret ballot—and other ways that they were lacking in modern standards.[4] But can we see how our own practices are lacking?

I set out to demonstrate in this book how our current eighteenth-century Winner Take All practices and institutions have outlived their usefulness in the twenty-first century. In numerous ways, our nation is being impaired by our continued use of a geographic-based and two-choice political system, particularly when shaped by modern campaign techniques amid dramatically shifting racial, regional, cultural, and partisan demographics. I have promoted five standards, five sturdy tent poles, that hold erect the great tent of representative democracy—representation, voter participation, political discourse and campaigns, legislative policy, and national unity. Additionally, I have identified six Winner Take All gremlins—phantom representation, artificial majorities, the Winner Take All conundrum, swing voter serenade, the two-choice tango, and the redistricting roulette—and seven policy goblins that are mischievously subverting our political system. Let's review what we have discovered about how Winner Take All and its goblins and gremlins are affecting the Big Five.

Representation

The fact that a random lottery would make our legislatures far more representative of "the people" is a disturbing sign that something is woefully amiss with our current institutions and practices. As we have seen, Winner Take All, by design, tends to overrepresent majority constituencies and under-represent minority constituencies. We usually think "minority" means racial minority, but in the context of Winner Take All it really means "geographic minority," and more "orphaned" white Democratic and Republican voters lose out on representation than anyone else, due to the vagaries of Winner Take All. These voters, just like most racial and political minorities, are geographic minorities where *they* live and must be satisfied with what I have called "phantom representation."

Besides white orphaned Democrats and Republicans, racial minorities are vastly underrepresented in legislatures at every level of government, as are women, the working-class, political minorities, independents, and third parties.

The only constituency with sufficient representation is the 32 percent minority of white men who are grossly overrepresented and still, over two hundred years later, dominate all legislatures. Such "mirror representation"—the extent to which our legislatures mirror the diversity of our population—is a legitimate indicator, among several indicators, of the health of our democracy, and on that score the United States rates very low, both in absolute terms and when compared to nearly all other established democracies.

Rather than evolving our Winner Take All system to accommodate such diversity, instead we have wallpapered the gap with two peculiar versions of Winner Take All propaganda: (1) an elected official represents you even if they are opposed to your point of view and even if you in fact voted for someone else, what I have termed "phantom representation"; and (2) it does not matter the color of your representative's skin, or his or her gendered plumbing, or his or her class background, or even, oddly enough, his or her political opinions. All that apparently matters is—that you elect either a Democrat or Republican, and the rest supposedly will take care of itself. But as we become a multiracial society, with national diversity exploding at unprecedented levels—the Latino population increasing by 58 percent over the past decade, Asian Pacific Americans increasing by 41 percent—the zero-sum "if I win, you lose" nature of Winner Take All politics eventually will blow these archaic notions out of the water. Authentic representation *does* matter. In fact, in a fundamental yet flawed way, the Founders and Framers *founded* our nation on this principle.

Moreover, representation has become balkanized by geography—cities becoming Democratic Party strongholds and Republicans dominating rural areas and some suburbs. Entire regions of the country have become virtual sub-nations, with the West and the South solidly conservative and usually Republican constituting the sub-nation of Bushlandia, and the West Coast and the Northeast, particularly the thin thread of coastal regions, tilting toward the Democrats in the sub-nation of New Goreia. In these areas political monocultures have been created by overrepresentation—in some cases quite dramatic—of the majority party.

While U.S. democracy does not bestow an affirmative action "representative quota" based on economic class like the Romans did, and threatens to retreat from its three-decade opening to representation that is conscious of race, we *do* grant a huge representation subsidy to low-population and predominantly rural states in the U.S. Senate and Electoral College, as we have seen. At the current time, this representation subsidy disproportionately favors conservative representation, policy, and issues. That representation quota has overrepresented the Republican Party in the Senate in every election since 1958, primarily due to Republican success in low-population, conservative states in the West and South—in the sub-nation of Bushlandia. The Senate is perhaps the most unrepresentative body in the world outside Britain's House of Lords, with no elected blacks or Latinos and only 13 percent women. Naturally, this White Guy's Club has a dramatic impact on our five pillars of democracy.

For the presidency, our unique—increasingly, many say bizarre—way of electing our President was revealed to be an archaic eighteenth-century construct by the 2000 election. Without a majority requirement for the national popular vote, or even for the winners of each state's electoral votes, we ended with a winner who failed to earn the highest number of popular votes. Lacking a majority requirement, either nationally or state-by-state, the center-left vote split itself between Al Gore and Ralph Nader, and their popular majority fractured and was beaten by the largest plurality bloc of George W. Bush. Moreover, due to the "representation subsidy" or affirmative action quota granted to low-population, conservative states in the Electoral College, Republican candidates have a built-in bias that favors their election. In Election 2000, the small-state padding explained the difference between the Electoral College vote, which went to Bush by a lean 271–267 margin, and the national popular vote, which Gore won by over a half million votes.

Those who oppose affirmative action based on race because of its alleged unfairness also should oppose it based on low population. Any other position is hypocritical, just another special interest group protecting its turf.

Participation

Despite the pyrotechnics of the photo-finish 2000 presidential contest, most elections have been turned into pale farces of competition, and by extension of participation. We have seen an alarming increase in single-digit voter turnout levels all across the nation for various elections. Voter turnout for our national legislature regularly drops well below a majority, often barely a third, of eligible voters. Nine out of ten U.S. House races regularly are won by noncompetitive margins of at least 10 percentage points, and three-quarters by landslide margins of at least 20 percentage points. In recent years two out of five state legislative races have been uncontested by one of the two major parties. These races are so noncompetitive because of the lopsided partisan demographics in each district—not campaign finance inequities—that the party considers it a waste of resources to run a candidate. With numbers like these, most voters are bunkered down into safe-seat districts where they have little choice but to ratify the candidate (usually the incumbent) of the party that dominates their district. In other words, the frame of reference for most voters in our Winner Take All system is not of a two-party system at all, but of a *one*-party system.

Needless to say, this leads to wholly uninspiring elections, and not surprisingly research has demonstrated a strong correlation between voter turnout and competitiveness. For instance, two studies of U.S. House elections showed that voter turnout dropped dramatically by as much as 19 percentage points as

House races became less competitive. Another study found that voter turnout among California's Latino and black communities was far higher in those congressional districts redistricted to give candidates of color a fair chance at electing someone. Numerous other studies have found similar results, which makes perfect sense: if a voter feels that the act of voting is a waste of time, election after election, sooner or later they quit showing up. Moreover, various studies have demonstrated that the effect is handed down generationally: if one's parents did not vote, chances are greater that you won't vote, and neither will your children.

While it is true that these legislative districts are gerrymandered into their politically comatose state during the redistricting/"incumbent protection" process, it is also true that redistricting is the twin sibling of Winner Take All— you don't get one without the other. Even if the gaming incentives and ability of incumbents or party leaders to carve out their own personalized districts were curtailed by a more "public interest" redistricting process, many of the same effects still would occur because of the regional balkanization of partisan sympathies, that is, of liberals/Democrats dominating in cities and the sub-nation of New Goreia, and conservatives/Republicans dominating in rural areas and Bushlandia. With demographics like that, there are only so many ways to slice up the districts, and most of these will have limited impact on the lack of competition and low voter turnout. Even campaign finance reform will provide little relief, given the political terrain of Winner Take All that produces such lopsided partisan demographics and regional polarization, capped by gerrymandered districts.

National and state elections for our highest offices—president, governors, and the like—also are marked by declining participation as voters fail to turn out for the two-choice tango offered as standard fare. Targeted campaigns of poll-tested sound bites aimed at swing voters, swing districts, and swing states leave all other voters on the political sidelines, their issues and concerns unaddressed, wondering if the candidates are speaking to them. Not surprisingly, certain demographics of voters, such as the poor, low-income working class, youth, and racial minorities, are disproportionately nonparticipants in our dumbed-down elections.

People are awash in a sea of too many elections, and a declining pool of civic-minded voters continues to trudge off to the polls to do their dreary duty. What else is a good citizen to do? But the dirty little secret is that, today, for tens of millions of these citizens living in the vast numbers of noncompetitive districts and states, including "orphan" Democrats and Republicans who are a minority perspective in their districts as well as the supporters of third parties, minority candidates, and independents nearly everywhere, there are not a lot of viable choices when they step into the voting booth. Instead, there are lots of opportunities for wasting your vote on losers and third-party spoilers, or holding your nose and voting for the "lesser of two evils." Not surprisingly, voters have quit responding to the uninspiring electoral choices regularly manufactured by the Winner Take All system.

Political discourse and campaigns

One of the most marked changes to our Winner Take All politics in recent decades has been caused by new campaign technologies. As we have seen, the technologies and tactics used in commercial marketing, that is, polling, focus groups, dial meter focus groups, thirty-second TV spots, and more, are malignantly suited to Winner Take All's two-choice/two-candidate milieu. Without any third candidate intervening with conflicting messages, likely partisan supporters don't have any other electoral place to go and can be taken for granted, freeing candidates to concentrate on extreme targeting of undecided swing voters.

Highly sophisticated techniques conducted by winning-obsessed political consultants allow candidates to figure out which group of swing voters is crucial to winning a close race, and what campaign spin, TV images, "crafted talk," and "simulated responsiveness" will move these swing voters. Ironically, the swing voters, by definition, usually are those who are least interested, least informed, and least tuned in to politics, or alternatively the most zealous voters for a particular issue, like NRA supporters or Florida Cubans. These two categories of voters have disproportionate influence in our elections today. In a two-choice field, mudslinging and hack-attack sound bites become particularly effective means to drive swing voters away from your opponent and to mobilize your activist political base, and not surprisingly such negative campaigning dominates elections today. With the ideological space relatively wide open and undefined in a two-choice field, candidates and their consultants are free to game the system by reducing complex policy proposals into campaign slogans and sound bites, carving out positions vis-à-vis their lone opponent.

Consequently, in an era of declining participation, not only in the voting booth but also in the numbers of people paying attention *between* elections, Winner Take All's two-choice elections are devolving into an uncomfortable specter of the "canned campaign"—a cookie-cutter formula endlessly replicated every four years for national electoral consumption. Because of the impact of the new campaign technologies in a Winner Take All milieu, and given the regional balkanization and nationally dead-even status of the Democrats and Republicans, we can expect that political consultants and candidates will intensify their use of the modern campaign technologies to use centrist rhetoric and images in an attempt to hoodwink the crucial blocs of undecided swing voters about their policies, putting a gloss of "centrism" around their candidates, regardless of actual voting records or policies pursued. Indeed, in our two-choice, Winner Take All system, these campaign techniques have become the steroids of politics.

Moreover, because of the way candidates and parties now conduct campaigns, any semblance of real political exchange and discourse is being buried under the McCampaign jingles and sound bites. Indeed, we are losing political ideas. Under the mind-numbing influence of the new campaign technologies and the Winner Take All media, electoral politics in the United States has become like cotton candy for the political faculties. We are witnessing a whole-sale and widespread underdevelopment of the American voter, contributing to the atrophy of the national political consciousness. Voters are not challenged or stimulated to think about the great issues of our times because these issues mostly are left on the political sidelines. And the harsh terrain of Winner Take All's two-party bias does not allow the flowering of new parties or independent candidacies that can act as the laboratory for new ideas or give voters other viable choices. Tragically, at a time of rapid technological, ecological, foreign policy, and global change, when fresh, creative ideas for dealing with looming challenges and crises are at a premium, our nation is in the throes of an alarming loss of political ideas.

Legislative policy

Because Winner Take All is a geographic-based and two-choice system, it insti-gates certain dynamics that dramatically affect policy. The most obvious of these, the one that has been most analyzed and exposed in the media, is pork-barrel legislation, whereby legislators try to "bring home the bacon" for their districts in the form of federal subsidies. Tales of $600 toilet seats for the mili-tary and billions in military and transportation appropriations for favorite states and districts are legendary.

But the fact is that other aspects of our Winner Take All system affect policy, what I have called Winner Take All's policy goblins. These include safe-seat politicians who act as the pit bulls for their party, pursuing unpopular initiatives like the impeachment of a president. In the late 1990s, that dynamic worked in tandem with end-of-the-decade tussling over redistricting, when the two major parties pursued specific policies based on how they might affect the last two elec-tion cycles of the decade in 1998 and 2000, since the battle for control of state leg-islatures determined who would win the divine right to redistrict in 2001.

The gaming incentives of Winner Take All also drive the two parties to engage in bumper-sticker politics and "simulated responsiveness" for political positioning, as the two parties play off each other to craft policy initiatives on issues like Social Security, crime, gun control, tax cuts, military appropriations, education, and more, targeted at winning votes from crucial blocs of swing vot-ers. These sorts of pseudo-responsive policy initiatives can be particularly visi-ble leading up to and during election years. The regional polarization resulting from a geographic-based system also is affecting policy more and more as the region's fragment along partisan, racial, and cultural lines. For instance, policy for education and transportation between cities and suburbs has become a polit-ical football as Democrats and Republicans tilt for control of the Legislature, knowing with a high degree of certainty which areas they will win and which they will lose. Instead of coherent regional policy that works for the urban–sub-urban corridor, we end up with zero-sum policy pitting cities against suburbs.

Using modern mapping software and redistricting techniques like packing and cracking, a political party in control of redistricting can end up with an undeserved artificial majority or an exaggerated, overrepresented majority that allows it to pursue policies lacking support from the majority of voters. The "representation ripoffs" created by artificial or exaggerated legislative majorities have prevailed in various state legislatures and in the U.S. House and U.S. Senate, due to the distortions of our Winner Take All system. This effect has been particularly pronounced in the sub-nations of Bushlandia and New Goreia as one side is drastically overrepresented than the other side. This in turn creates a Political Power Ripoff, in some cases producing exaggerated, veto-proof majorities that can ram through radical policies without a popular mandate. The climate becomes one of a political monoculture, lacking the most basic levels of political discourse or pluralism, and the bitter partisan divide gets exacerbated by the political power and representation ripoffs as one side effectively wins more representation and political power than it deserves. Under Winner Take All, as we have seen and as various researchers have demonstrated, the majority does *not* necessarily rule.

In the U.S. House, one party or the other frequently has been ripped off by the vagaries of Winner Take All districts; between 1945 and 1980, congressional elections produced artificial majorities 17 percent of the time, where one party or the other received less than 50 percent of the national vote yet ended up with more than 50 percent of the U.S. House seats. In today's 107th Congress sits a Republican majority in the House that won only 48 percent of the national popular vote, about the same as the Democrats. But the Republican Party historically has been cheated out of seats due to such votes-to-seats distortions, losing as many as forty-three House seats in 1976, and an average of twenty-seven seats per congressional cycle from 1976 through 1988. More recently, it is the Democratic Party that has been on the short end of the stick. In the 2000 elections for the U.S. House, there were 371 U.S. House seats where both Democrats and Republicans fielded a candidate, and the Democrats won slightly more votes nationwide in those races, yet the Republicans won more of those seats, 191–179 (plus one independent).

In the U.S. Senate, the "representation subsidy" given to low-population states has had dramatic influences on policy, particularly on federal subsidies to states and on Senate leadership that is able to influence policy. The overrepresentation of the citizens of the least populous states means they receive more federal funds per capita than the citizens of the most populous states, and that the Senate will design policies in ways that distribute federal dollars disproportionately to the less populous states. One unanticipated consequence of the Great Compromise, then, is that citizens now are treated differently based on where they happen to reside. Moreover, due to the demands of campaign fundraising and constituency-serving for Senators from high-population states like

California, Michigan, Florida, and New York, which tend to see the most competitive Senate elections, Senators from the largest states no longer have the flexibility or time necessary to lead the Senate. Thus, the most influential positions in the Senate, those of the party and floor leaders and powerful committee chairs, which once were dominated by Senators from high-population states, have in recent years been occupied by Senators from low-population states like West Virginia, Kansas, Maine, South Dakota, Oklahoma, and Mississippi (similarly, many of the most powerful House leaders and committee chairs have been entrenched incumbents from safe districts—meaning that the most powerful members often face the least electoral testing).

Given the fact that this "representation quota" in the U.S. Senate mostly has benefited conservative, rural, white states, this adds additional dimensions to the impacts on policy. Because of the Senate's unique constitutional role in screening executive, lower court, and Supreme Court appointees and approving treaties, this thoroughly unrepresentative body has a powerful influence on all three branches of government, as well as on foreign policy. Over the years, conservative Senators from low-population, rural states representing a small fragment of the nation's population have flexed their representation quota to influence judicial appointments and foreign policy, as well as slow down or thwart numerous policy initiatives, including desegregation, campaign finance reform, healthcare reform, affirmative action, New Deal programs, gun control, and more. Large, corporate agri-businesses have been some of the biggest beneficiaries of the geographic basis for Senate malapportionment, pocketing billions in federal subsidies even as urban areas have faced cutbacks and political marginalization. The Political Power Ripoff of Winner Take All is tremendously exacerbated by this affirmative action quota for low-population states, which is hardwired into *both* the U.S. Senate and our peculiar Electoral College method of electing the president.

National division

The two-choice, geographic-based nature of Winner Take All is contributing to chronic partisan, regional, racial, and cultural division. As we have seen, representation as well as political power have become balkanized by geography— cities becoming Democratic Party strongholds, and Republicans dominating rural areas and to a lesser degree suburbs. As the *USA Today* map shows, entire regions of the country have become subnations, with an area larger than the European continent in the Western and Southern United States and Alaska solidly conservative and/or Republican (Bushlandia) and the Northeast and the West Coast, particularly the urban and narrow coastal areas, favoring the Democrats (New Goreia). In these regions, the zero-sum game of single-seat districts has created political monocultures where all but the winning side is reduced to political spectator status.

The bitter partisan divide gets exacerbated as one side effectively wins more representation and political power than it deserves, while the other side is frustrated and unfairly marginalized. When these Winner Take All dynamics cause citizens living in cities to lose some of their education or transportation funding at the hands of GOP legislatures, or frustrate the majority in South Carolina who wish to remove the Confederate flag from the capital grounds, or produce votes-to-seats distortions that cause the Congress to be more liberal than it should be, or more conservative, with consequences on policies passed, existing tensions are exacerbated. Moreover, while it is understood that in Winner Take All's two-choice field nasty, negative campaigning always will be a highly effective way to drive swing voters away from your opponent and mobilize your political base, this serves to further bruise relations, polarize voters, and fan the flames of internecine warfare.

In presidential elections, the regional balkanization has become so severe and hardwired into our state-by-state demographics that an astonishing 436 out of 538 Electoral College votes now are considered safe or mostly leaning toward one party or the other in a competitive presidential race. That leaves only 102 electoral votes—*less than 20 percent*—in nine states as toss-ups in a nationally competitive race, and we can predict that those areas will be campaign battlegrounds in 2004, with the most of the rest of the nation once again as bystanders. Based on these kinds of demographics, there are strong indications of another razor-thin race in the 2004 presidential election. We may have ringside seats to an ongoing and ugly political drama that once again rips apart the nation, courtesy of our defective Winner Take All method of electing the president.

Moreover, the regional balkanization creates some real zero-sum dilemmas for the Democratic and Republican Parties that will make it difficult for either of them to be act as a vehicle that can articulate, much less resolve, real conflicts of interest in society. For instance, to a substantial degree national politics still reflects the decades-old subtext of partisan competition being centered around appeals to culturally and racially conservative white voters, who still comprise the bulk of American voters. If anything, since Nixon's "Southern strategy" these trends have sorted themselves and deepened, Democrats now providing near-exclusive representation for the densely populated cities, the GOP for the vast territory of sparse rural areas; the Democrats are now the party preferred by the burgeoning population of racial minorities, while the GOP is the party of most whites, especially most white men.

Under these demographic pressures funneled through the pinhole of the clunky, antiquated Winner Take All system, and with regional, cultural, and racial balkanization exacerbated by representation ripoffs and political power ripoffs, and given the incentives of how you run and win elections with modern campaign technologies under Winner Take All, both political parties are tiptoeing as carefully as they can around the color line, strategizing as they go. Each side will continue to bunker down in their foxholes of Bushlandia and New Goreia, calculating ways to triangulate into pockets of white swing voters; and cross-partisanship and cross-fertilization of ideas will remain near impossible, except in campaign rhetoric around election time or when rallying around the flag following national tragedies like the September 11 attacks. With the two parties effectively acting as proxies on region, culture, and race, representing one side or the other of the divide, the conservative white vote and the multiracial burgeoning of our population are on a collision course.

The Way Forward

As was previously mentioned, choosing our representatives by lottery arguably would be superior to the methods we currently employ. While such a primitive practice obviously would have its downsides, it certainly would produce legislatures that are more "representative" than the predominantly white male country clubs that permanently occupy most legislatures, particularly at the federal level. The mere fact of that should be alarming to anyone who cares about our nation in the 21st century.

But I think we can do better than using lotteries for selecting our representative bodies. In fact, there is a rather straightforward path out of our Winner Take All dilemma. The first step on this path takes us to an unlikely place—to George W. Bush's old stomping grounds, the state of Texas. Specifically, Amarillo, Texas. In May 2000, Amarillo elected four members to its school board for the first time by a non–Winner Take All voting system known as cumulative voting (see the footnote for a description of how cumulative voting works).[5] Under Amarillo's previous at-large Winner Take All method, no blacks or Latinos had been elected to Amarillo's seven-member school board in more than two decades, despite Latinos and African Americans making up more than 20 percent of the city's population. Instituted to settle a voting rights lawsuit involving MALDEF (Mexican American Legal Defense and Education Fund), LULAC (League of United Latin American Citizens), and the NAACP, cumulative voting had an immediate impact: both a black candidate and a Latino candidate won seats with strong support in their communities, while white candidates won their fair share of seats, too. Previously orphaned voters all over the city suddenly had representation. Voter turnout increased more than three times over the previous school board election, and all parties involved in the voting rights settlement expressed satisfaction with the new system.[6]

That a generally conservative city of more than 150,000 people like Amarillo would adopt cumulative voting is only one example of how proportional and semi-proportional voting systems have become credible alternatives for decreasing the zero-sum game of Winner Take All politics. More than one hundred jurisdictions in the United States now have adopted such alternative voting systems to resolve voting rights lawsuits.[7] Cumulative voting and another non–Winner Take All system known as limited voting have been used in nearly two dozen localities in Alabama for a decade, as well as localities in Illinois, New Mexico, and South Dakota.[8] More than fifty localities have adopted cumulative voting in Texas alone, and in 1995, then-Texas governor George W. Bush signed legislation that allows school districts to adopt cumulative voting and limited voting.

The effects of these alternative voting systems have been studied for many years and are now well known. For instance, cumulative and limited voting have boosted turnout and increased black representation as much as or more than would have occurred if single-seat districts had been used.[9] Another study found that more women were elected in Alabama local elections using cumulative voting.[10] Peoria, Illinois, the quintessential city of "middle America," uses cumulative voting for its city council elections, and with blacks comprising only 20 percent of the city's population black candidates have won their fair share of seats in all three elections in which cumulative voting has been used.[11]

While proportional and semi-proportional voting systems usually are discussed in the United States in the context of racial representation, in fact they are being used by most of the established democracies in the world, even among nations with more racially homogenous populations. The reason is that these non–Winner Take All voting systems also offer significant advantages over Winner Take All in terms of the five tent poles of our representative democracy: representation, participation, campaigns and discourse, policy, and national unity.

For instance, instead of using the plodding single-seat districts, even so modest a change as combining three adjoining districts into one three-seat district elected by proportional representation (where the mathematics works out to just over 25 percent of like-minded voters electing one seat, see the footnote for a more detailed explanation)[12] will advance our five standards of representative democracy to an encouraging degree. A study of Southern states by the Center for Voting and Democracy showed that combining three adjoining one-seat U.S. House districts into one three-seat proportional district would more accurately reflect the demographics of the New South as it evolves in the new century.

A typical three-seat House district in the South, for instance, with a 25 percent victory threshold, likely would elect a black liberal Democrat, a white conservative Republican, and a relatively centrist Democrat or Republican (usually white). Congressional moderates, once a mainstay of national stability and now an endangered species, would suddenly have new life. Such a plan almost certainly would elect more women (of thirty-six Deep South seats, women only hold one). A black Republican or two might even get elected. The resulting cross-fertilization in Democratic and Republican caucuses certainly would lessen some of the ideological polarization and harsh partisan division that now infects the U.S.

House. Without gerrymandering a single district, such a "full representation" plan almost certainly would increase the number of African Americans elected to the U.S. House in states such as Virginia, North and South Carolina, Alabama, Mississippi, Arkansas, and Louisiana—as well as better represent far more orphaned white voters currently residing in the "wrong" districts and avoid costly redistricting lawsuits as well.

With such a full representation plan, moderate Rockefeller Republicans as well as conservative Republicans in the New England strongholds of New Goreia suddenly would be politically viable again. In the West, the formerly populist, pro-farmer, pro-labor New Deal-type Democrat, a Mike Mansfield or a Frank Church, which currently are overwhelmed by conservative Republicans, could give voice to the concerns of socially conservative but economic populist farmers and miners, as well as the new demographic of liberal high-tech workers who have fled with their companies from California. The Midwest—currently the battleground region—would see more stable coalitions in their state legislatures over time, rather than the destabilizing swings from Republican to Democrat and back again they currently are experiencing as each side claws for advantage. Cities like Chicago, San Francisco, Los Angeles, New York, and more would elect moderate Republicans to sit alongside the overflow of Democrats in their legislatures, giving those cities a genuine voice in the all-important legislative caucus of the Republican Party.

In addition, with a 25 percent victory threshold, independent candidates and third parties would have a fighting chance of electing a few of their own, bringing badly needed new ideas and voices into campaigns and policy decisions. The zero-sum game of Winner Take All campaigns would have been substantially transformed; if a candidate slams an opponent with hack-attack sound bites, disgusted voters would have another choice instead of being stuck with the "lesser of two evils" (although it must be recognized that 25 percent is still a high threshold for a third party to reach. Ross Perot only won 19 percent of the popular vote in 1992, and the German Green Party, currently a coalition partner in the German government's proportional representation system, has never won more than 10 percent of the popular vote).

As we saw in Chapter 2, three-seat districts using cumulative voting were used to elect Illinois' state house of representatives for 110 years until 1980, and many of these benefits were observed, causing a high-profile commission chaired by former Republican Gov. Jim Edgar and former Democratic congressman Abner Mikva to recommend its revival. But in our current system all of these potential benefits are missing in action, due to the use of single-seat, Winner Take All, geographic-based districts.

Full representation across the United States
A 25 percent threshold in three-seat districts would decrease the regional balkanization and political monocultures and would turn most elections into at least

a two-party competition instead of the one-party tinpot fiefdoms they have become. But even more benefits would be realized by lowering the victory threshold still further—to 10 percent, say, in ten-seat districts elected by proportional representation.[13] That is the "victory threshold" used by Cambridge, Massachusetts for its city council elections elected by a nonpartisan form of proportional representation system known as choice voting, and still at least twice as high as the winning threshold of approximately 5 percent used by most established democracies in the world. With a 10 percent victory threshold, voters would have more viable choices on Election Day, and the defects of the Winner Take All gremlins—the two-party tango, phantom representation, the swing voter serenade, redistricting roulette, the Winner Take All conundrum, and artificial majorities—would be mitigated further still.

Under the principle of proportional representation, all legislative seats are weighted equally, and whatever percentage of the popular vote a political party or nonpartisan grouping of like-minded voters wins, that's the percentage of seats they assume in the legislature. In an election for ten seats, a political party or nonpartisan perspective that wins 60 percent of the vote will win six out of ten seats; 30 percent of the vote will win three out of ten seats, and 10 percent will win one out of ten seats. There are different types of proportional representation voting systems, both partisan and nonpartisan, and the details of how each type works are important, but the Proportional Principle is illustrated by that example.

Compared to the Winner Take All Principle, where 51 percent of the vote wins 100 percent of the representation and 49 percent wins nothing in a two-candidate race (and 34 percent of the vote can win 100 percent of the representation in a three-candidate race), the Proportional Principle allows "groupings of like-minded voters to win representation in proportion to their voting strength." Fifty-one percent of the vote wins 51 percent of the representation, not more; 49 percent of the vote wins 49 percent of the representation, not less. Twenty percent of the popular vote wins 20 percent of the representation, instead of being shut out like you are in a Winner Take All system.

Under the Proportional Principle, more voters have what is called an *effective* vote that counts toward electing a winner. Voting for the "lesser of two evils" is unnecessary, since more voters win representation and have their point of view sitting at the legislative and policy-making tables. The Proportional Principle, as political scientists like Duverger, Lijphart, Dahl and Amy have pointed out, is virtually synonymous with a multiparty/multichoice democracy, where the various political perspectives and the voters that vote for them all win their fair share of representation. And because voting systems are the engine of the *entire* political system, this in turn transforms a host of dynamics that corrals the Winner Take All goblins and gremlins that usually undermine our five tent poles of representative democracy.

For instance, under the Proportional Principle virtually no one is excluded. There are far fewer "orphaned voters," and phantom representation is exorcised from the body politic. The problems of the two-choice tango, such as lack of choice for voters, gaming incentives, and extreme negative campaigning in a two-choice field, are substantially transformed because voters have more viable choices and may abandon the attacking or gaming candidate or party. The redistricting roulette is greatly diminished, since the drawing of multiseat districts has far fewer consequences than single-seat districts, and so partisan gerrymandering becomes obsolete. The swing voter serenade, which allows a tiny minority of voters to have awesome power, is commuted because with more voters having more viable choices to their political left or right, suddenly *most* voters are swing voters. So none can be treated preferentially, and none can be taken for granted.

The Proportional Principle produces "full representation," with a demonstrated ability to elect more women,[14] smaller parties, independents, racial minorities, and orphaned Democrats and Republicans living in the wrong districts. With more people having representation and a vote that counts, a lot of the hot air of the "if I win, you lose" zero-sum game and the Winner Take All conundrum is let out of the balloon. And with the share of legislative seats for each voting constituency more closely matching the number of votes won, *real* majorities are possible instead of artificial or overrepresented, exaggerated majorities. Representation becomes more of a power-sharing arrangement than a power-over arrangement; politics is conducted more on a basis of consensus-building and problem-solving, rather than on an adversarial battlefield plagued by political games and brinkmanship. As researchers like Huber and Powell have shown, these qualities have a quantitative and qualitative impact on producing policy that more accurately reflects the "will of the majority."

Cumulative voting, choice voting and limited voting, and other voting system types with names like open list, closed list, and mixed member are proportional and semiproportional voting systems that most closely fulfill the Proportional Principle. But they are not a panacea; there are downsides and quirky aspects to proportional and semiproportional systems as well. Kenneth Arrow won a Nobel Prize for proving there's no such thing as a perfect voting system. For instance, certain proportional systems are candidate-based, others are party-based, which has additional ramifications. Some proportional democracies use large multiseat districts—the size of their entire country—while others use smaller, moderately proportional three-to seven-seat districts. The various proportional methods used all over the world and for certain elections in the United States are not a monolith,[15] but all of them to a greater or lesser degree conform to the Proportional Principle: that "groupings of like-minded voters win representation in proportion to their voting strength." And from that principle other dynamics flow that positively impact our five great democratic standards:

representation, participation, campaigns and discourse, policy, and national unity. Space constraints prevent a fuller fleshing out of the considerable positives offered by widespread implementation of the Proportional Principle in U.S. elections.

The fork in the Road

Despite the potential offered by the evolution of our eighteenth-century Winner Take All practices, the American gatekeepers in the punditocracy, the media, the academy, and among reformers steadfastly overlook this course. As I have pointed out in other chapters, their degree of misinformation, misunderstanding, and outright disinterest in the area of voting systems is baffling as well as dismaying. Even as our Winner Take All democracy gasps for breath, some old Winner Take All war horses have faithfully circled the wagons and rallied the troops. These gatekeepers have clung to the hope that traditional methods will be useful still, and approach the subject in an uninformed and oddly dismissive manner. Even following the meltdown of UnElection 2000, they would countenance few new ideas or allow discussion that fell too far outside the orthodoxy.

For instance, many reporters and pundits, as well as political scientists (who should know better), when you mention the words "proportional representation" in one breath, will mention Italy or Israel in the next. For them, it is as knee-jerk a reaction as the sun rising. It is as if the sum total of their knowledge relies on stereotypes gleaned from these two nations. Whenever Italy and Israel are mentioned so quickly in the conversation, you know you are in the presence of one of the many Winner Take All gatekeepers or their uninformed accomplices. Not that Italy and Israel have not had their share of political difficulties, but reducing the vast field of study of proportional representation to the perceived troubles of Italy or Israel is no more legitimate than reducing the drawbacks of Winner Take All to the troubles of Algeria, Angola, or India, which also use Winner Take All.

Those who make great sport of bashing Italian and Israeli politics like to criticize proportional voting methods for being held hostage by minority parties that can precipitate the collapse of coalition governments. Yet, as we have seen, under our own Winner Take All system small slices of the most uninformed and uninterested spectrum of the electorate, or conversely of the most zealous parts of the electorate, can acquire vastly exaggerated power, determine which party wins a legislative majority or the presidency, and thereby hold hostage any semblance of sane policy. Despite the numerous drawbacks to our geographic-based, two-choice system, the Panglosses of political science and punditry persist in their blind and knee-jerk defenses of Winner Take All. And following the dictum that the "best defense is a good offense," they mount their defense often by making unjustified and insupportable charges regarding proportional systems.

The fact of the matter is, various proportional systems are used by *most* of the established democracies in the world today,[16] and virtually none of them experience the difficulties of Italy and Israel. Currently there are forty-one nations with at least 2 million inhabitants and high ratings from the human rights organization Freedom House, and of these forty-one nations only three (the United States, Canada, and Jamaica) do not use a form of proportional or semiproportional voting system to elect at least one of their national legislatures.[17] Most use a proportional system for their most powerful offices. In fact, the trend around the world is decidedly *away* from our Winner Take All system and toward these proportional alternatives. Even our own political progenitor, the United Kingdom, is in midstream of a most remarkable transformation of their old Winner Take All ways, recently adopting proportional representation for electing representatives to the European Parliament, the London City Council, and the Scottish and Wales regional assemblies, with some political observers predicting that the House of Commons is not far behind.

It is telling that, since their invention and systematic formulation by people like John Stuart Mill in the late nineteenth century, these other types of proportional voting systems overwhelmingly have been preferred by the world's newer democracies over the Winner Take All methods. Some voting systems certainly are better than others, depending on the needs of your democracy. Nothing in the U.S. Constitution requires single-seat districts for the U.S. House, the fifty state legislatures, or local government, although there is one federal law passed in 1967—ironically enough to support the now-besieged Voting Rights Act's efforts to elect more racial minorities—that mandates single-seat districts for U.S. House elections. By amending this federal law, states could begin tinkering with proportional systems for their congressional representatives, and state legislatures and city councils can do so now since they are not affected by that federal law.

Moreover, there also is no rule or law that says we cannot *combine* our single-seat districts with proportional representation, offering the benefits of both. Roughly speaking, single-seat district's geographic representation gives representation based on where you *live*, while proportional representation gives representation based on what you *think*. These are not mutually exclusive; indeed, they can be complementary, in theory and in practice, and incorporated into a proportional system known as "mixed member." Italian political scientist Roberto D'Alimonte has noted a remarkable convergence happening in many democracies of the world, with nations like Germany, Japan, New Zealand, Italy, and others successfully grafting together proportional and geographic representation in their "mixed member" legislatures, providing voters with a deeper democratic experience than we can possibly conjure here in the United States.

Our bicameral state legislatures provide an easy opening for such a mixed system. We could use geographic-based representation via Winner Take All districts in one house of the Legislature, and proportional representation where geographically dispersed "communities of interest" win representation based on what they think in the other. It is imperative that reformers and political scientists begin to think "outside the box" for creative solutions, begin to experiment a bit in the spirit of democratic tinkering like the Framers did. It is deeply ironic that corporations and entrepreneurs are extolled for innovation and modernization, even swashbuckling investment in the latest, greatest trend that amounts to the next dot-com bubble; free marketeers and their disciples celebrate Joseph Schumpeter's creed of "creative destruction" as the rationale for failing businesses and lost jobs, the necessary price to pay for a vital economy. Yet when it comes to our politics and democracy technology, we are hopelessly bogged down by tradition and defenders of the status quo, stuck to the fly paper of old ideas. Just as with the free market, there is no "one size fits all" plan when it comes to our political institutions. Each city and state will need to figure out the best method to evolve its antiquated Winner Take All ways, and the federal level will need to do the same.

A Democratic Vision for the Twenty-First Century

At this particular historical juncture, it is vitally important that American voting methods—in addition to our voting *machines*—act as creatively and efficiently as possible to produce an inclusive representative democracy that is not bedeviled by the Winner Take All gremlins and goblins. It is important that our democracy technology offer electoral opportunity to the millions of orphaned voters from all races and perspectives to finally cast a vote that counts, and win representation and a degree of influence that heretofore have eluded them. What's more, it's important that the democracy technology act efficiently to allow new ideas to percolate to the surface and enter into the public debate. And finally, it's crucial that the democracy technology allow a majority of votes to translate into majoritarian policy. But these requirements are *exactly* where the eighteenth-century Winner Take All system is most deficient.

Certainly reforming Winner Take All is not the end of the road. Other changes are needed to truly open up our democracy and allow the Founders' and Framers' political invention to fulfill its destiny. These include public financing of elections and curtailing soft money expenditures, which will reduce the impact of private donors on policymaking and party leaders (the Soft Money Kings and Queens and Captains of Cash), foster debate, and help to reverse the mind-numbing loss of political ideas; a beefed-up public broadcasting sector and government-subsidized daily newspapers that can counteract the profit-seeking motives and duopoly allegiance of the Winner Take All corporate media that undermines democratic pluralism and political debate (several European countries could serve as a model for this, including the British Broadcasting Company in the U.K. and Germany's public broadcasting sector);

streamlining and updating of electoral infrastructure and administration (voting machines, ballot design, recount procedures, etc.); and other electoral rules like Election Day voter registration,[18] a national voting holiday or weekend voting, and reasonable and fair ballot access laws.

In addition, the idea of increasing the size of the federal House of Representatives should be explored. The number of representatives has not changed since 1910, and the 435 Congress members now each represent over 600,000 constituents, three times as many as then. It is little-known that the original Bill of Rights proposed by the Framers included *twelve* amendments, and one that failed to pass would have established a ratio of "not less than one Representative for every fifty thousand persons." Alexander Hamilton and James Madison in *Federalist* No. 58 noted that the purpose of the Census, among other things, was to "augment the number of representatives," so clearly the size of the House and the expectation of growth was on the Framers' minds. The House generally expanded in size each decade since 1792, until 1910 when it froze.

Now, compared to the national legislatures of other democratic nations, ours is about the lowest per capita. Various estimates have established that regular growth since 1910 would have produced a House with about 588 members, still smaller than the national legislatures of either Germany or the United Kingdom.[19] In the U.K., for example, each Member of Parliament represents only about 70,000 residents, a manageable size closer to a city council district in many American cities that gives geographic district representation more meaning.[20] Purely from a consumers' point of view, today there are a lot more "customers" (i.e., constituents) for each "store clerk" (i.e., representative) to wait on, and the customer-constituent relationship is being short-changed by the inelasticity of The People's House over the last century. We have only one-third of the representation of our 1910 ancestors, and for a system that depends on geographic representation in an increasingly complex world, the sheer numbers undermine the very basis of its value.[21]

The overarching goal of all these reforms should be to open up our political system—a *perestroika*, so to speak—so that it is more responsive to the popular will, more representative, and fosters participation, national unity, informed public debate, majoritarian policy, and even civic enthusiasm. The goal should be the establishment of political institutions and practices that will promote a newfound sense of national pluralism. As we journey further into the twenty-first century, with our shifting racial demographic becoming the rising tide that lifts or sinks all boats, this is the only course that makes sense. In the longer term, that pluralism can only find expression via a multichoice/multiparty democracy founded on the bedrock of proportional representation. A pluralistic, mass society in the twenty-first century simply will not be well-served by the archaic, eighteenth-century Winner Take All political system with its strict reliance on exclusive geographic representation and a two-party duopoly.

But under the chronic nay-saying of the gatekeepers, reform always seems to have a ridiculously difficult road. Even a no-brainer like establishing Election Day as a holiday or on the weekends becomes hopelessly bogged down in cerebral red tape. Most modern democracies today vote on a holiday, a weekend, or over a series of days. There is nothing sacred or even constitutional about voting on the first Tuesday in November; most people have no recollection why it was established that way, how in 1845 President James Polk established the Tuesday voting tradition for the convenience of *farmers*. He set the day after the fall harvest, allowing Monday as a travel day to get to town so farmers could cast their ballots on Tuesday. A century and half later, most people don't live on farms, and Tuesday is a busy workday. The right to vote in a democracy is worth honoring and celebrating, instead of something to squeeze between errands, work, or at the end of a frantic workday if the commute home goes well. Yet even such a commonsense initiative as voting on a holiday, proposed by the high profile Carter–Ford commission in its July 2001 report regarding electoral administration, met with ridiculously stubborn resistance from the political class.

It is crucial that a national dialogue ensue about ways to bring our representative democracy, our pluralistic society, into the twenty-first century. And in that dialogue, the considerable deficiencies of our Winner Take All system must be front and center. For at the end of the day, the dynamics that exist in American politics today and that are contributing to post-democracy exist *because* of Winner Take All, not as a coincidence to it. Certainly it is inadequate for a pluralistic, free-trading, twenty-first century world that is no longer the sparsely populated agrarian society of our eighteenth-century wealthy and slave-holding founders. Instead, we live in a mass society of burgeoning diversity and complexity; our world is a hypertechnological, highly populated, and diverse one, hurtling toward yesterday's science fiction where an uncertain future awaits.

And right there at the eye of the maelstrom is the Winner Take All system and its disruptive gremlins and goblins. It's no coincidence that post-democracy should be happening now, at this historical juncture, with our political institutions and practices stuck in a two-choice, geographic-based political system from the eighteenth century. With the exception of local jurisdictions like Amarillo, Cambridge, Peoria, Hartford, and counties in Pennsylvania and Alabama and others scattered across the American landscape, the torch of bold democratic innovation has passed from the United States, stuck in its Winner Take All ways.

Toward "E Pluribus Unum"

Does the American Dream and way of life, extolled from shore to shore in the wake of the September 11 attacks, require an active and participatory democracy and an engaged citizenry? Or can our nation exist, as some like conservative columnist George Will and sociologist Michael Schudson have suggested, as merely a ratification democracy, a kind of "check-off" democracy, where most citizens only rise up at the ballot box when riled by offensive government policy, or repugnant personal behavior by a politician or party leaders, or an external threat?

This is a fundamental question that cuts to the heart of who and what will shape our society and what our society will look like in the future. Such a "ratification democracy" harkens back to the earliest days of the Roman Republic, which was dominated by wealthy elites but where major decisions were ratified by citizens who otherwise did not actively participate. Will such a bend in the road represent a step forward in our constantly evolving national destiny? Or will it amount to some version of Gaetano Mosca's elite ruling class, a post-democracy demonstrating once and for all that, indeed, at the end of the day, "the history of all societies has been, is, and will be, the history of dominant minorities?"[1]

I am reminded that President Abraham Lincoln ended his Gettysburg Address with the famous words, "that government of the people, by the people, and for the people shall not *perish* from the earth" (italics mine). Certainly Lincoln considered, on that brisk November day in 1863, as he reflected over a grim battlefield where brother had brutalized brother, that this bold experiment "conceived in liberty and dedicated to the proposition that all men are created equal" could not be taken for granted, that it could wither on the vine as much as flourish and ripen. Are we, the first of the twenty-first century progeny, resolute enough to reconsider with Lincoln his moment of doubt regarding the fragility of our political system?

Lincoln's "of, by, and for the people" is still a precious thing, still worth striving for, it seems to me. The fulfillment of the democratic Spirit of 1776 has been the most enduring legacy of the American revolutionaries, these last few hundred years having exhibited ceaseless heroic endeavor all over the globe to usher it forth, like a frail flower pushing up through the soil of calumny. Over the centuries millions of people have paid the ultimate sacrifice for their right to vote and practice democracy, and those of us benefiting today stand atop some mighty shoulders.

But we live in a time when the words "invention" and "success" have become intertwined and confused with entrepreneurial and corporate values. The greatest human invention ever, in my view, has been the practices, customs, and institutions of democracy. Everything else pales by comparison. Thomas Jefferson wrote the Declaration of Independence without a computer or the Internet; the Magna Carta was composed without automobiles or the telephone or a fax. Mary Wollstonecraft's *Declaration of the Rights of Women* was imagined without a PalmPilot or a Web page. And their ideas have spread across centuries, sometimes like wildfire, other times like slow and patient tree roots.

It has taken a relentless march to get here. The quest for democracy is hundreds of generations and over two thousand years deep, and we occupy only the topmost strata, a small plot of land at that. Our mudslide into post-democracy, if left unchecked, is more likely to unleash not Lincoln's government of, by, and for the people, but a government of, by, and for the few—that is, tyranny. But, ironically enough, *elected* tyranny, a historically unique phenomena where elections will be pale farces of participation, representation, and discourse, and super-wealthy private interests will dominate. In such a deformed democracy economics will dictate to politics and politics merely will provide the means to clear the boulders for those who control the economics, an enervating antipode of the old Soviet-style command economy where bureaucratic politics decreed to economics. It will complete a tragic interment of the Spirit of 1776, and already we are seeing the first signs of it in various American localities and landscapes. We should not relinquish the inspiring vision of a pluralistic democracy so easily, nor roll over and let it become a moribund remnant, a mere check-off democracy, one that is undernourished by the corporate media and the political duopoly and subordinated to unrestrained free market economics and the gremlins and goblins of Winner Take All.

But if Fukuyama is correct, that the march of history and ideology indeed has reached some "end of history" apotheosis in liberal democracy's balancing of equality and liberty, then certainly it also must be true that proportional voting systems—not Winner Take All—will provide the political engine of the new paradigm. The severe drawbacks of Winner Take All cannot be ignored much longer; they are threatening our national future. A disengaged public in a Winner Take All check-off democracy can be tricked too easily by the "crafted talk" and "simulated responsiveness" made so potent by modern campaign technologies in the hands of slick politicians and their pollster-geists and mad scientist consultants. Reflecting on the five sturdy poles that hold aloft the great tent of representative democracy—representation, participation, campaigns and discourse, policy, and national unity—Winner Take All breeds exclusion, alienation, ignorance, distortion, and adversarial division. While no voting system is perfect, given the alternative, proportional representation systems offer great hope for keeping these States united and evolving into the twenty-first century.

Government of, by, and for the people—not by emperors, not by a Politburo, not by preachers or mullahs, not by corporate CEOs or multinational media magnates and their proxies, nor by neo-aristocracy or kakistocracy, but "by the people." Two hundred years after our national birth-quake, that is still a vital animating force, still a revolutionary concept, albeit a fragile one. During this time of national anxiety, with minds that rarely seem to meet except in the most tragic of circumstances, and partisan, cultural, and racial lines that hardly cross, the potential offered by evolving our Winner Take All ways is a tantalizing prospect that demands our consideration. If we fail, around a future bend in the road awaits post-democracy.

ACKNOWLEDGMENTS

Democracy is an acquired taste, it seems. But the love of freedom is not, it is part of our autonomic physiology, as reflexive as a flower pushing up through the Spring soil. Few settle for their aspirations being fenced in, at least not for long, whether it's a teenager with wheels or citizens suffering under the heel of a despot. Books always have meant that kind of freedom to me, the freedom to let one's mind wander. But so many books on the shelf! And so many authors, so many literary trails to traverse—did the world really need one more, i.e. this book? I could not help but wonder, and constantly inquired of myself, what is the unique contribution this book has to offer? I think it is incumbent upon writers to grapple with that self-query. Hopefully my process has made the final product all the stronger.

This book grew out of a series of conversations with my colleague at the Center for Voting and Democracy, Rob Richie. In order to make the case for voting system reform, which in our minds is synonymous with democracy itself, we had to, as campaign finance reformer Janice Fine advised me several years earlier, "define what the problem is you are trying to solve." So, like "doctors of democracy" reading the vital signs of the American patient sprawled on the gurney, we set about diagnosing the problem. I cannot imagine a better co-prognosticator than Rob Richie. To my mind, Rob is one of the most insightful political analysts in the United States today. The Center's provocative "Monopoly Politics" and "Dubious Democracy" research and analysis, which have been imitated by everyone from the Charlie Cook Political Report to the New York Times, is his vision, his pioneering work, a display of political creativity and originality that is destined to reformat the American political landscape. Many of the ideas in this book either originated with Rob or in conversation with Rob; and the Center for Voting and Democracy, which we co-founded with Matthew Cossolotto, now 10 years old, could not have reached where it is without his untiring efforts and shrewd piloting. Rob, if the MacArthur people know what they are doing, yours is just around the corner.

I also want to acknowledge the encouraging and patient suggestions and e-mails of my other colleagues with the Center for Voting and Democracy (CVD), especially Eric Olson (who read portions of the manuscript), as well as Terry Bouricius, Caleb Kleppner, Dan Johnson-Weinberger, and Maritza Valenzuela. Each of you has inspired me in your own thoughtful way. Also I want to gratefully thank John B. Anderson, former Congressman and independent candidate, and now the President of CVD, for his years of inspiring service to the cause of democracy, and his gracious support over the years of my and Rob's work.

I also want to thank my longtime friend and intellectual hitchhiker, Jeffrey

Mitchell, a political geographer in New Mexico, who gave invaluable counsel on the chapters dealing with Anthony Downs and the impact of Winner Take All on policy. If I am still not down with Downs, it is through no fault of his. Jeff also gave important advice on the framing of the major themes, helping me to clarify my arguments.

Special gratitude also to Bill Greider, a journalistic giant of our times, for mentoring me along the way and for suggesting the "Fixing Elections" part of the title. Thanks to my good friend and good environmentalist, Emily McFarland, for invaluable feedback on parts of the manuscript, and to Steve Chessin from Californians for Electoral Reform who coined the insightful term "orphaned voters." Thanks to my editor at Routledge, Eric Nelson, who, according to his partner Renee is "the only person I know who likes what he does." It showed, in his enthusiasm, encouragement, and guidance for this project. For better or worse, Eric kept my "gloom and doom" side from hijacking the book and crash landing the narrative in a post-democracy corner of no return.

The final writing moments for this book were inspired by the historic passage on March 5, 2002 of San Francisco's Proposition A, by 55 percent of voters, which implemented a system of instant runoff voting for local elections. I was campaign manager for Proposition A, and I also was one of the leaders in the passage of San Francisco's Proposition O in 2000, which established public financing of elections for the city council. Accordingly, I would like to thank the many volunteers who walked precincts, mounted phone banks, donated money, and performed countless other tasks, in the bold pursuit of a still-radical idea -- democracy. Also I want to thank the many democracy activists out there who over the past ten years have worked with the Center and who stubbornly believe that American democracy still might one day live up to the potential of its own lofty rhetoric. It's been a great collaboration, I have learned valuable things from many of you. You are too many to name, but you know who you are. And I want to thank fellow reformers in the campaign finance and ballot access areas, organizations like Public Campaign, U.S. PIRG and Common Cause, we have shared a lot and learned a lot from each other, even when we haven't always agreed. A special thanks to Dragon NaturallySpeaking voice recognition software for keeping me in the saddle during the writing of this book. It works, it works!

Also, a tip of the Renaissance cap to Leonardo da Vinci, Michelangelo, Machiavelli, Galileo, and Dante. When I visited the Uffizi Gallery in Florence, Italy during one of my research trips for this book, I snapped photos of their life-size stone likenesses that lean over the piazza; I then taped these five photos on the four walls of my writing office, and during the course of my narrative ascent, particularly during moments of struggle, I channeled for clarity and guidance from this intellectual Guild, hoping they might apprentice me. If there's any glory to be had, it's partly theirs; the mistakes are all mine.

Finally, a special never-enough thanks to my parents, Pat and Jack Hill, for your love and support over the years; and my in-laws, Barb and Jim Colvin, for your intellectual- and creative-seeking, ongoing in your senior years, and Jim for your love of wordsmithery and the literary challenge, always a joy; and most of all, thank you with all my heart to my life-partner Lucy Colvin. For the past 18 years, you have been my guide, my scout, my co-pioneer, my fellow traveler, my intellectual and creative peer, my shaman and dear friend, my proofreader, a gift from the universe that I didn't even know I had coming to me. I must live under a lucky star. The universe works in strange and wonderful ways sometimes, if we are open to it, and that is the most life affirming spectacle of all.

NOTES

Prologue: The Landscape of Post-Democracy

1. In conducting the research for this book, I was surprised to discover how difficult it was to find statistics on voter turnout, especially for state and local races. Newspapers usually don't bother reporting the numbers, and Secretary of State web sites don't always calculate it or make it easy to figure out this most basic indicator of the health of our democracy. Voter turnout numbers for Dallas, San Antonio, Austin, and Charlotte come from the Web site of the Dallas County Elections, 1999 mayoral election results, www.dalcoelections.org/election99/index.html; from the Web site of the City of Austin, www.ci.austin.tx.us/election (although it appears that both Dallas and Austin list *registered* voter turnout instead of *eligible* voter turnout, making their actual turnouts lower than their listed figures); from Richard Berke, "Incumbent Big City Mayors Are Sitting Pretty," *New York Times,* November 2, 1997; from an Associated Press story, May 2, 1999; and from Henry Flores, professor of political science at St. Mary's University in San Antonio, in a paper prepared for the 1999 American Political Science Association entitled "Are Single-Member Districts More Competitive Than At-Large Elections?"

2. Patrick Crowley, "Voters May Be Scarce in N.Ky.," *Cincinnati Enquirer,* October 31, 1999.

3. Caleb Kleppner, "N.C. Could Avoid Costly Runoff Elections," *Raleigh News and Observer*, May 10, 2000.

4. *Standard-Times*, "Rain, Rain Go Away. Come Again Another Day," September 18, 1996, www.s-t.com/daily/09-96/09-18-96/b07lo092.htm.

5. *Eagle-Tribune* (Lawrence, MA) editorial, "Politicians Got What They Wanted Tuesday," September 22, 2000.

6. Amy Lee, Julio Ochoa, and Lisa Woods, "County Millages Pass, Oakland, Macomb Voters Support Area Schools' Upkeep," *Detroit News*, June 12, 2001. Voter turnout rates below 10 percent are common in Michigan school elections. In June 1995, Jackson County's North Adams school district recorded one of the lowest turnouts in Michigan history, with only five of the fifteen hundred eligible voters casting a ballot on an 18-mill property tax increase. See Lori Yaklin, "Consolidate School Elections with General Elections," August 15, 1999, located on the Web at www.educationreport.org/article.asp?ID=2232.

7. Figures obtained from the Web site of the Virginia State Board of Elections, www.sbe.state.va.us.

8. Douglas P. Shuit, "Lack of Interest Cancels Some Local Elections," *Los Angeles Times,* Sunday, February 21, 1999.

9. See "105.4 Million Voters Cast Ballots," Associated Press story written by John Heilprin, December 18, 2000. Voter turnout for the 2000 presidential election was 105,380,929 ballots cast, or 50.7 percent of those eligible, according to Curtis B. Gans, director of the Committee for the Study of the American Electorate. That figure was up slightly from 1996's 49 percent but was significantly lower than the 62.8 percent who voted in 1960, making the 2000 election among those with the lowest turnouts. Interestingly, among sixteen battleground states where the race was hotly contested, turnout increased by an average of 3.4 percent compared with a 1.6 percent increase in other states. Ten states—Arizona, Hawaii, Idaho, Kansas, Louisiana, Montana, New Jersey, Oklahoma, South Dakota, and Wyoming—none of them close—had lower turnout than in 1996. See Federal Elections Commission, "Voter Registration and Turnout—1996," www.fec.gov/pages/96to.htm.

10. Fifty-one million viewers watched the season finale of *Survivor*, according to *Newsweek* ("Reality TV's Real Survivor," Dec. 25, 2000, p. 77). Super Bowl 2000 was watched by over 43 million *households*, according to *USA Today*, which translates into roughly 120–130 million viewers. Al Gore, the winner of the 2000 presidential popular vote, had 50.9 million votes, which was the most votes for any presidential candidate since Ronald Reagan. See *USA Today* editorial, "Why the NFL Rules," Dec. 22, 2000.

11. The average voter turnout in House midterm elections from 1982 to 1994 was 37 percent; in presidential election years the House turnout was 48 percent—in both instances less than a majority of eligible voters (*Statistical Abstract of the United States*, 1998, p. 297). The turnout has been declining in the past decade, with 1998's midterm congressional elections having a turnout of less than 33 percent of eligible voters. In that year motor voter laws boosted registration roles by 5.5 million to include 64 percent of eligible voters, the highest since 1970. Yet still voter turnout declined to its lowest level since 1942, as 115 million Americans who were eligible to vote chose not to do so. See *The Political Standard,* "1998 Turnout, Lowest since World War II," newsletter of the Alliance for Better Campaigns, www.bettercampaigns.org.

12. David Cay Johnston, "Voting, America's Not Keen On. Coffee Is Another Matter," *New York Times*, November 10, 1996, p. E2. According to Johnston, an estimated 95 million people watched O. J. Simpson take his freeway ride, and 92.8 million cast ballots in the 1996 general elections.

13. "Voter Turnout for 1945 to 1997: A Global Report on Political Participation," published and distributed by the Institute for Democracy and Electoral Assistance, 1997, www.idea.int. "Created in 1995 by 14 countries, International IDEA promotes and advances sustainable democracy and improves and consolidates electoral processes world-wide."

14. Youth voter turnout figures are from Curtis Gans of the Committee for the Study of the American Electorate. Voter turnout of eighteen- to nineteen-year-olds in the 1994 midterm elections was 14.5 percent, which means voter turnout among this demographic dropped an astounding 41 percent between 1994 and 1998. The Voter News Service estimated that 38.6 percent of eighteen- to twenty-nine-year-olds made it to the polls in the 2000 election (see Wendy Sandoz, "GenY Voter Turnout Increased, Experts Say," Medill News Service, Wednesday, November 8, 2000). Typically, youth voter turnout drops by about 50 percent between a presidential election year and a nonpresidential (midterm) election year. According to a National Association of Secretaries of State study, youth electoral participation reveals a portrait of an increasingly disconnected and apathetic generation. Since the 1972 presidential election, when the voting age was lowered to eighteen, there has been almost a 20 percentage point decrease in voting among eighteen- to twenty-four-year-olds, with only 32 percent going to the polls in 1996, a presidential election year (see the press release from their Web site, www.nass.org, "State Secretaries Push Major Youth Voting Initiative, New Millennium Project: Why Young People Don't Vote").

15. One recent survey by UCLA's Higher Education Research Institute found a record-low interest in politics among new college freshmen in 2000, with 28.1 percent of respondents inclined to keep up with political affairs and 16.4 percent saying they discuss politics frequently. While that was only a slight decline from last year, nevertheless it was significant since "freshmen interest in politics traditionally increases during a presidential election year," instead of decreases, said survey director Linda Sax, a UCLA education professor. Historically, these results on political-engagement questions reflect a long steady decline, with highs in these two categories at 60.3 percent and 33.6 percent, reached in the late 1960s. Mary Beth Marklein, "Female Freshmen Doubt Tech Skills, College Survey Also Shows Record-Low Interest in Politics," *USA Today*, January 22, 2001. A 1999 Field poll found that, in 1983 35 percent of young adults ages eighteen to twenty-nine said they followed civic events most of the time, but only 23 percent said they did so in 1999. That decline was exhibited also in ages thirty to thirty-nine, where interest in government and politics drop from 44 percent to 27 percent in the same period. See Associated Press story, "Californians (Ho-Hum) Cool to Politics (Yawn)," published in *San Francisco Examiner*, April 30, 1999, p. A7.

16. By way of contrast, in certain European nations a less-than-majority turnout for national referendums automatically voids the election. Using that standard, virtually all American elections would be nullified.

17. Anthony Downs, *Economic Theory of Democracy* (New York: Harper & Row, 1957), p. 139.

18. See, for instance, Michael Barone, "The 49 Percent Nation," *National Journal*, June 8, 2001; David Brooks, "One Nation, Slightly Divisible," *The Atlantic Monthly*, December 2001, p. 53; *The Economist*, "One Nation, Fairly Divisible, Under God," January 18, 2001. For longer treatments of the estimation of national division, see Gertrude Himmelfarb, *One Nation, Two Cultures* (New York: Vintage Press, 2001) and Alan Wolfe, *One Nation, After All* (New York: Penguin, 1999).

19. Over two-thirds of Mississippi voters chose to retain the Confederate symbols on their state flag, in a racially split vote. The civil rights era still haunts Southern memories. "As Mississippians voted to keep the Confederate cross on their flag, jury selection was under way in Alabama for the trial of a white man accused in the 1963 bombing of Birmingham's Sixteenth Street Baptist Church, which killed four black girls. Several civil-rights cases have recently been reopened, including some in Mississippi. But the Confederate flag remains the main lightning rod of controversy. Last year, the National Association for the Advancement of Colored People (NAACP) led an economic boycott of South Carolina, bringing the eventual removal of a Confederate flag from the statehouse dome. Three months ago, Georgia's legislators opted to shrink [the size of] a Confederate symbol that had dominated that state's flag since 1956. Throughout Alabama, cities and counties have stopped flying the state's flag,

which bears a strong resemblance to the Confederate banner. In most of these cases, pressure from white business to change was as great as that from black politicians. Indeed, Mississippi's vote can also be seen as a rearguard action in the battle between rural white traditionalists and the proponents of a New South." *The Economist,* "Not as Simple as It Looks," April 19, 2001.

20. Instant runoff voting (IRV) simulates a series of runoff elections to produce a majority winner in a single election. At the polls, people vote for their favorite candidate, but they also may indicate their second, "runoff" choice and subsequent choices, ranking them 1, 2, 3. If a candidate receives a majority of first choices, she wins. If not, the candidate with the fewest votes is eliminated, and the "instant runoff" begins. Each voter's ballot counts for their top-ranked candidate still in the race. The eliminated candidate is no longer a "spoiler" because the votes of that candidate's supporters go to their runoff choice. Rounds of counting continue until there is a majority winner. IRV is used to elect the president of Ireland, the mayor of London, the Australian national legislature, and officers of various nongovernmental organizations like the American Political Science Association. For more information about instant runoff voting, see the Web site of the Center for Voting and Democracy, www.fairvote.org.

21. The "coup of one" comment came from a very sour outgoing Senate majority leader, Trent Lott. After losing the Senate leadership, Lott apparently agreed that something was broken about democracy in the Senate. In a final parting shot, an incendiary note that contradicted President Bush's call for a new bipartisan spirit, Sen. Lott wrote that Republicans must "wage war" because "we have a moral obligation to restore the integrity of our democracy, to restore by the democratic process what was changed in the shadows of the back rooms in Washington. . . . We must ensure that the decision by Senator Jeffords is accurately portrayed, now and for history. It was a 'coup of one' that subverted the will of the American votes who elected a Republican majority." Sen. Lott, who preferred to gloss over the untidy fact that Americans did not elect a Republican majority in the Senate—the Senate had been tied, 50–50, which is, after all, what allowed Senator Jeffords' resignation to overturn the Senate—then went on to confusedly assert that the *Democrats* should not now be treated as holding a majority. Democrats, he said, "hold a plurality, not majority in the Senate," and "their effective control of the Senate lacks the moral authority of a mandate from the voters." Despite Sen. Lott's confused tantrum, he had succinctly put his finger on a real problem—due to the Senate's bizarre internal rules, including the Winner Take All aspect of committee assignments, powers of committee chairs, dictatorship of a mere majority, and more, a "coup of one" was made possible. Richard L. Berke, "Lott Takes Parting Shot on Eve of Senate Power Shift," *New York Times,* June 3, 2001.

22. I am using the term "representative democracy" as a more descriptive term of what some call a republic or republican government. A republic is actually a subset of the larger genus of democracy, but unlike direct democracy exemplified by New England town meetings it is a form of democracy where public policy and decisions are made by democratically elected representatives. A republic or representative democracy is particularly more suited for larger populations and the mass society that we have become.

23. Gaetano Mosca, *The Ruling Class,* quoted in James H. Meisel, *The Myth of the Ruling Class* (Ann Arbor: University of Michigan Press, 1958) p. v.

24. In this book, I have adopted the distinction Robert Dahl makes between the terms Framers and Founders (or Founding Fathers) to distinguish between those who were at the Constitutional Convention, that is, those who actually participated in the *framing* of the Constitution, and those who were not. Among those who were *Founders* but not *Framers* included Thomas Jefferson, John Adams, Thomas Paine, and Samuel Adams.

25. Lester J. Cappon, ed. *The Adams-Jefferson Letters* (Chapel Hill and London: University of North Carolina Press, 1959) p. 572–73.

26. Alexis de Tocqueville, *Democracy in America* (New American Library, 1956), p. 104.

Chapter One: "A House Divided . . ."

1. According to *The Economist,* Gore won metro areas with more than 500,000 people by a huge margin of 71 percent to 26 percent, easily the largest gap since this figure has been tracked. See "One Nation, Fairly Divisible, under God," *The Economist,* January 18, 2001.

2. Jill Lawrence, "County vs. City, Spelled in Red and Blue," *USA Today,* November 9, 2000, p. 19A.

3. Source: Voter News Service, a consortium of the Associated Press and TV networks, published in *San Francisco Chronicle*, Nov. 9, 2000, p. A23.

4. Lawrence, "County vs. City," p. 19A.

5. Source: Voter News Service, published in *San Francisco Chronicle*, Nov. 9, 2000, p. A23.

6. Source: Voter News Service, a consortium of the Associated Press and TV networks, published in *San Francisco Chronicle*, Nov. 9, 2000, p. A23. Also, Thomas B. Edsall, "Bush Lost 9 to 1 among Blacks," *Washington Post*, Tuesday, December 12, 2000, p. A01. Also Cynthia Tucker, "The Browning of America," *San Francisco Chronicle*, Nov. 25, 2000.

7. *CBS News* National Exit Poll Analysis, "America the Conflicted," November 10, 2000.

8. Source: CNN exit polls, posted at www.cnn.com/ELECTION/2000/epolls/US/P000.html.

9. Bob Wing, "White Power in Election 2000," *ColorLines*, 4(1), Spring 2001, p. 7.

10. Lawrence, "County vs. City," p. 21A.

11. Alison Mitchell, "Two Parties Prepare for Biggest Battle Yet in Fight for Suburbs," *New York Times*, May 4, 1999.

12. The potato is one well-traveled tuber, having originated among native peoples in the Peruvian Andes, and then exported by the invading Spaniards to Europe, where it became a major crop. Before too long, the potato migrated back across the Atlantic to North America, where it hitched a ride on Conestoga wagons heading West.

13. Idaho's radical labor history includes labor unrest in 1892 that provoked martial law and an intervention of federal troops. Wobbly "Big Bill" Haywood and others later were charged with the assassination of the former governor.

14. Bob Bernick Jr., "Will Utah Demos Run No Legislative Candidates at All in 2000?" *Desert News*, March 27, 1998.

15. Ibid. Also see Michael Janofsky, "Utah GOP Endangers a Democrat," *New York Times*, November 23, 2001.

16. Representation in the U.S. Senate for these eleven Western states, including Alaska, currently is fifteen Republicans to seven Democrats: North and South Dakota each have two Democratic senators; Montana, Nevada, and Nebraska each have one. Electoral College votes for all eleven states, of course, went to George W. Bush.

17. U.S. Census Bureau, 1999 estimate.

18. Although it is rather jarring to view the exquisitely fine Western art that mythologizes, even romanticizes, the former Indian enemy, now vanquished, vilified, and largely banished to impoverished reservations. In these Western galleries, the alternatively heroic, or sad or plaintive, countenance of Native American subjects stares silently at the passersby, a discordant reminder of a painful and violent past that has left tracks into the present.

19. Given the current postures of the Democrats and Republicans on the national stage, with elected Republicans like former Klansman David Duke and with presidential nominees Bush and McCain bowing at the altar of the blatantly discriminatory Bob Jones University and defending South Carolina's flying the Confederate flag atop their state dome, it is easy to amnesiaize the role of the segregationist Democratic Party in the South. For instance, Democrat George Wallace, who was elected a judge of the Third Judicial Circuit of Alabama in 1953, in 1958 ran unsuccessfully for the governorship of Alabama, losing the Democratic nomination (which was tantamount to election) to a more radical segregationist candidate who had been endorsed by the Ku Klux Klan. Abandoning his moderate stance on integration, Wallace soon became known as the "fighting judge" owing to his defiance of the U.S. Commission on Civil Rights' investigation of discrimination in black voting rights. Wallace finally won the governorship of Alabama in 1962 on a Democratic Party platform emphasizing segregation and economic issues. Within his first year in office he kept his pledge "to stand in the schoolhouse door" by blocking the enrollment of black students at the University of Alabama (June 1963). Declaring that the federal government was usurping state authority in the field of education, he yielded only in the face of the federalized National Guard. Further confrontations at Tuskegee, Birmingham, Huntsville, and Mobile made him a nationwide symbol of intransigence toward racial integration in the schools. In 1968 Wallace was a vigorous but unsuccessful third-party candidate for the U.S. presidency, winning 13 percent of the vote and five Southern states as the nominee of the anti-liberal Amer-

ican Independent Party. He drew support mainly from white Southerners and blue-collar workers disenchanted with the Democratic Party's pro–civil rights policies.

20. Unbelievably, in Mississippi numerous *Democratic*-controlled legislatures over the years never ratified the Thirteenth Amendment abolishing slavery until March 21, 1995. In Georgia, where the Democrats control both houses and the governor's seat, nevertheless recently the Democrats still had to sneak through legislation to decrease the size of the state flag's Confederate emblem, in order to prevent defections from conservative members of their *own* party. Devised in secret by Democratic leaders, including Gov. Roy Barnes, the legislation moved rapidly from committee to the House floor, where it was approved and sent on to the less conservative Senate within six hours. Despite these ramrod tactics, still twenty-six conservative Democrats voted against the legislation. Rhonda Cook, "Georgia Flag Proposal Still Must Fly in State's Senate," *San Francisco Chronicle*/Cox News Service, Sunday, January 28, 2001, p. A9.

21. The two largest sources of group support for the Democratic Party in previous years were Southern whites and the working class. "Many have noted the significance of softening southern support for national Democratic candidates that began in the latter years of the New Deal period. Generally, the decay of the 'solid South' is associated with the shift there towards a two-party system, reflecting the politicization of latent divisions that eclipsed vestigial resentment against the Republican Party for its prosecution of the Civil War." See Richard C. Sauerzopf, "The Balkanization of America: Structure and Volatility in the Polis and Nation," p. 4, a paper presented at the annual meeting of the American Political Science Association, September 2000. Also see Everett Carl Ladd and Charles D. Hadley, *Transformations of the American Party System: Political Coalitions from the New Deal to the 1970s* (New York: W. W. Norton, 1975).

22. See "George Bush's Democrats," by Congressman Jesse Jackson Jr., *The Nation*, January 22, 2001.

23. B. Drummond Ayres Jr., "California G.O.P. Courts Schwarzenegger," *New York Times*, March 13, 2001.

24. To make matters worse, the California Republican Party is rather bitterly divided between its dominant ultra-conservative wing and its moderates. Mark Z. Barabak, "Schwarzenegger Won't Oppose Davis Next Year," *Los Angeles Times*, March 7, 2001.

25. Suzanne Dougherty, "Republican Mass. Appeal Weak as Filing Ends," *Congressional Quarterly*, Wednesday, June 14, 2000.

26. Ibid.

27. During the 1990s, there was a countertrend of moderate Republicans winning the mayors' seats of major cities (for example, Richard Riordan in Los Angeles and Rudolph Giuliani in New York City) and even the governorships of liberal states (like William Weld and Paul Cellucci in Massachusetts and Lincoln Almong in Rhode Island). But these candidates typically won on a socially liberal platform of pro-choice and pro–affirmative action, combined with a clever array of Quality of Life campaign promises that included everything from more cops and safer streets to street cleaning to urban environmental fixes. These moderate Republicans never could have been elected in Bushlandia. The vast number of elected officials in urban areas are Democrats and/or liberals, even as the "Republican mayor" trend seems to be abating in the decade of 2000, New York City's mayor-elect Michael Bloomberg notwithstanding.

28. Interestingly, blacks were the majority in some southern states after the Civil War—areas of Bushlandia—which of course has its own lesson: when hostility between races is combined with Winner Take All, zero-sum politics, one side may attack the political rights of the other side, erecting Jim Crow laws and other segregationist policies.

29. For a fascinating discussion of the Latinoization of huge swathes of the U.S. population, see Mike Davis' *Magical Urbanism, Latinos Reinvent the U.S. City* (Verso, 2000).

30. Daniel C. Desmione, "2000 Census Yields Unexpected Results," *Government Finance Review*, October 1, 2001, Vol. 17, No. 5, page 34.

31. Erica Werner, "Term 'Minority' Has Uncertain Future," Associated Press story published in *Asian Week*, May, 17, 2001.

32. See "One Nation, Fairly Divisible, under God," *The Economist*, January 18, 2001.

33. See the report "Minority Population Growth: 1995 to 2050" from the U.S. Department of Commerce, September 1999. The report clearly demonstrates the continuing trend in diversity in the U.S. popu-

lation; practically all states will be affected. Also see Melissa Nelson, "Latino Influx Main Issue in Arkansas GOP Runoff," *San Francisco Chronicle*, October 17, 2001, p. C12.

34. Ibid.

35. For instance, Alabama in 1990 passed a law that established English as the official language for state business, including English-only on driver's license exams.

36. Quoted in "One Nation, Fairly Divisible, under God, The Economist."

37. David O. Sears and Nicholas Valentino, "Race, Religion and Sectional Conflict in Contemporary Partisanship," August 27, 2001, p. 18–19, paper prepared for delivery at the annual meeting of the American Political Science Association, .San Francisco, September 1, 2001. The "blue states" taken by Al Gore also were much the same as those taken by the anti-slavery Republicans. In particular, according to this study, Texas, Alabama, and Mississippi stand out as strong James Buchanan (1856) and Bush (2000) supporters; Massachusetts, Rhode Island, and New York as strong Joehn Fremont/Republican (1856) and Gore (2000) supporters.

38. Quoted in an article by columnist Ronald Brownstein, "Battle over Impeachment Will Cost Country a Moment of Opportunity," *Los Angeles Times*, Monday, December 21, 1998.

39. To figure the disproportion between the popular vote and the number of legislative seats won by each party, it would be more accurate to add up the aggregate vote for Democrats and Republicans for all legislative races within a particular state, and then compare that aggregate vote to the percentages of legislative seats won. But since so many state legislative races are uncontested—41 percent in 2000—that has the effect of depressing turnout in the one-party races, distorting any statewide aggregate figures. Thus, the presidential vote becomes the better indicator of the numbers of actually voting (as opposed to registered) Democrats and Republicans in the state.

40. If anything, these figures probably *understate* the case, since Al Gore was disproportionately unpopular out West—his vote in Montana, say, was far less than that for relatively progressive Democratic candidates for the House and Senate. And in Massachusetts Republicans actually won the last three statewide races for governor, yet only have 14 percent of seats in Massachusetts' state House.

41. Some political commentators protest against viewing Republican and Democratic voters as partisan monoliths, pointing out that not all Republican voters are always head-over-heels sold on Republican candidates, or Democratic voters on Democratic candidates, which is certainly true. But when their only other viable choice is the other major party, many consider that going too far in the wrong direction and so they keep within the fold, voting the "lesser of two evils," albeit begrudgingly. Their politics are defined by voting *against* a particular candidate or party more than by being *for* anything, a kind of "negative consent" that increasingly defines American politics. Because of this dynamic, the voting patterns of most voters are increasingly consistent and predictable over time, as most political observers have come to realize.

42. Rhodes Cook, "No Contest, Why Most House Seats Remain Safe in This Year of Turmoil," *Washington Post*, October 4, 1998, p. C1.

43. Jackie Calmes, "Why Congress Hews to the Party Lines on Impeachment," *Wall Street Journal*, December 16, 1998, p. A1.

44. Cook, "No Contest," p. C1.

45. Sarah A. Binder, "Going Nowhere, a Gridlocked Congress?" *Brookings Review*, Winter 2000, Vol. 18, No. 1, p. 19.

46. Calmes, "Why Congress Hews to the Party Lines on Impeachment," p. A1.

47. Cited in David C. King, "The Polarization of American Political Parties and Mistrust of Government," Harvard University Working Paper, www.ksg.harvard.edu/prg/king/polar.htm. King's paper was included as a chapter in Joseph S. Nye, Philip D. Zelikow, and David C. King, editors, *Why People Don't Trust Government* (Cambridge, MA: Harvard University Press, 1997).

48. Sears and Valentino, "Race, Religion, And Sectional Conflict in Contemporary Partisanship," p. 29.

49. David Sears, J. Citrin and Richard Kosterman, "Jesse Jackson and the Southern White Electorate in 1984," in Robert Steed, Laurence Moreland and Todd Baker (eds.), *Blacks in Southern Politics* (New York: Praeger, 1987), pp. 209-225.

50. Many pundits have made this observation. For instance, Howard Kurtz of the *Washington Post* has written, "Scratch the surface of any issue in American politics and you'll find race. Housing. Schools. Hiring. Welfare. Law enforcement. Even the Internet has its digital divide, with many minorities on the have-not side. And, of course, voting—as dramatically demonstrated by the electoral breakdown in

Florida." Howard Kurtz, "Bush's Race Dilemma Dominates Coverage," *Washington Post*, Thursday, February 1, 2001.

51. See Sauerzopf, "The Balkanization of America," pp. 5, 41.

52. Bill Clinton even was perplexingly labeled the first "black president" by some African Americans, including author Toni Morrison. See Joseph H. Brown, "No Credit to Anybody's Race Is He," *Tampa Tribune*, March 19, 2001.

53. See Ruy Teixeira and Joel Rogers, *America's Forgotten Majority: Why the White Working Class Still Matters* (New York: Basic Books, 2000). Also see David Brooks, "One Nation, Slightly Divisible," *The Atlantic Monthly*, December 2001, p. 57.

54. David Brooks, "One Nation, Slightly Divisible," *The Atlantic Monthly*, December 2001, p. 64; Michael Barone, "The 49 Percent Nation," *National Journal*, June 8, 2001; Gertrude Himmelfarb, *One Nation, Two Cultures* (New York: Vintage Press, 2001); Alan Wolfe, *One Nation, After All* (New York: Penguin, 1999).

Chapter Two: Ex Uno Plures

1. A Caltech–MIT study later estimated that ballots from as many as 6 million voters nationwide—nearly 6 percent of the total—were never counted, due to either faulty voting machines, poorly designed ballots, polling place failures, or foul-ups with registration or absentee voting. Caltech president David Baltimore, who initiated the nonpartisan study, said, "It is remarkable that we in America put up with a system where as many as six out of every hundred voters are unable to get their vote counted. Twenty-first-century technology should be able to do much better than this." See Guy Gugliotta, "Study Finds Millions of Votes Lost," *Washington Post*, July 17, 2001, p. A1. Also see the press release from the Voting Technology Project, a comprehensive Caltech–MIT study initiated after the November election debacle, http://vote.caltech.edu, July 16, 2001.

2. See "A Day as a Banana Republic," *La Repubblica*, November 9, 2000. Also see Deborah Zabarenko, "US Officials Bristle at 'Banana Republic' Ridicule Abroad over Election," Reuters, November 9, 2000; CNN.com, "Europe Ponders U.S. Woes," November 9, 2000; "Europe Sees Lighter Side of U.S. Election," November 20, 2000, by Douglas Herbert, CNN.com; and a story by Andrew Chang of ABCNews.com, November 10, 2000. Zimbabwe's state-controlled newspaper *The Herald,* a Mugabe mouthpiece with a slanted history that knows "electoral intrigue" when it sees it, ran a headline that read, "Election Intrigue Not Monopoly of Third World."

   Said Jonathan Moyo, spokesman for Mugabe's government, "If this had happened in Zimbabwe, we would have been subjected to sanctions." Roger Cohen, "Electoral Collage: How the World Votes," New York Times Service, Friday, December 1, 2000. British bookmakers took a different tack to the U.S. vote: they let people bet on it. Two days after the election, with no clear winner in sight, the British on-line betting firm Blue Square had Bush as the favorite to win the election at 5–2—if you put down five British pounds you would get seven back, including your stake.

3. Instant runoff voting (IRV) simulates a series of runoff elections to produce a majority winner in a single election. At the polls, people vote for their favorite candidate, but they also may indicate their second, "runoff" choice and subsequent choices, ranking them 1, 2, 3 on their ballots. If a candidate receives a majority of first choices, she wins. If not, the candidate with the fewest votes is eliminated, and a runoff round of counting occurs. In this round your ballot counts for your top-ranked candidate still in the race. The eliminated candidate is no longer a "spoiler" because the votes of that candidate's supporters go to their runoff choice. Rounds of counting continue until there is a majority winner. IRV is used to elect the president of Ireland, the mayor of London, and the Australian national legislature. For more information about instant runoff voting see the Web site of the Center for Voting and Democracy, www.fairvote.org.

4. For the Democratic Party's presidential nomination, in every state primary each candidate wins a proportion of delegates that matches their proportion of the popular vote. Candidates accumulate delegates state-by-state until they reach the requisite number of delegates for nomination. The Republican Party also uses a proportional allocation in their presidential primaries for about a third of states and a Winner Take All allocation for the rest.

5. One objection that has been raised to a proportional allocation of electoral votes is that if a third-party candidate were to win a proportionate share of electoral votes it could prevent any candidate from winning a majority of electoral votes thereby throwing the election into the U.S. House of Representatives.

For instance, in 1992 when Ross Perot won 19 percent of the national popular vote, had he received approximately 19 percent of the electoral votes neither Bill Clinton nor George Bush would have garnered a majority of electoral votes. But this easily could be remedied by each state only awarding a proportionate share of electoral votes to the *top two finishers*. Such a method could be refined even further by using an instant runoff (allowing voters to rank their top choice and their "runoff" choice) to arrive at the top two finishers. Either of these methods would not suffer from the defects of the current method, and would considerably improve the democratic quotient of our presidential elections.

6. Daniel Lazare, "Senatorial Privilege," *The American Prospect*, September 24–October 2, 2000.

7. Whether the Electoral College favors large- or small-population states is a matter of some debate. Certainly in the 2001 election it favored the low-population states. See Harold Meyerson, "W. Stands for Wrongful," *LA Weekly*, December 8, 2000. Also see Jack Rakove, "Abolish the Electoral College—BUT DON'T HOLD YOUR BREATH," *San Francisco Chronicle*, Sunday, August 26, 2001, p. C3. Rakove is a history and political science professor at Stanford University and is the author of the Pulitzer Prize–winning *Original Meanings: Politics and Ideas in the Making of the Constitution*. Rakove writes that the Electoral College permits "a candidate to win a close election simply by carrying more states and capitalizing on the additional electoral votes the senatorial bump provides. That was as much the source of Bush's problematic victory as the machinations in Florida or the decision in Bush versus Gore."

8. Bob Wing, "White Power in Election 2000," *ColorLines,* 4(1), Spring 2001, p. 7.

9. Dewayne Wickham, "Blacks Rightly Ignore GOP," *USA Today*, November 9, 2000.

10. At least 2,000 felons whose voting rights had been automatically restored in other states were kept off the Florida rolls and, in many cases, denied the right to vote in the November 2000 election. This discrimination disproportionally affected African Americans—obviously more votes that would have been cast for Gore. See Robert E. Pierre, "Botched Name Purge Denied Some the Right to Vote," *Washington Post*, May 31, 2001, p. A1.

11. From the Democratic side of the aisle, Representative Patrick Kennedy, who was chair of the Democratic Congressional Campaign Committee (DCCC), stated in a *Providence Journal* interview about the 2000 presidential election: "We have written off the rural areas." These areas, of course, are charter areas of the sub-nation of Bushlandia. See *National Review*, "For the Record," July 12, 1999, p. 6.

12. Figures quoted in Bob Adams, "Choosing the President: Let Every Vote Count," *The National Voter*, published by the League of Women Voters, March/April 2001, p. 18; also an e-mail update from the Center for Voting and Democracy dated Nov. 22, 2000.

13. Thomas D. Elias, "Candidates Spend Next to Nothing in California," *Washington Times*, October 9, 2000. Specifically, the Gore campaign and the Democrats spent $6.5 million on advertising in Florida, against $3.2 million for the Bush campaign and the GOP. In Pennsylvania, Republican spending topped the Democrats by $7.7 million to $6.5 million. The two camps had spent a combined $11 million in Ohio and another $7.6 million in Michigan. They even spent $1.5 million in New Mexico and almost $6 million in Washington state. See also Peter Marks, "TV Spots Are Concentrated in Bush-Gore Battlegrounds," *New York Times*, September 19, 2000.

14. "Are Voluntary Standards Working? Candidate Discourse on Network Evening News Programs," a study by the Annenberg Public Policy Center of the University of Pennsylvania, www.appcpenn.org, December 20, 2000.

15. See "Electoral College Landscape: Clear Trends for 2004," a report published by the Center for Voting and Democracy, November 22, 2000, www.fairvote.org/map/pres2000.htm.

16. See Paul Rahe, "The Electoral College: A Defense," article published by the Oklahoma Council of Public Affairs, a public policy research and education organization, on the Web at www.ocpathink.org/Governance/TheElectoralCollegeDefense.html. A version of Professor Rahe's article was published in the *American Spectator* on November 14, 2001. Not long after the UnElection 2000 meltdown, this viewpoint was espoused by Professor Rahe and others, such as Norman Orenstein of the American Enterprise Institute. Also see the *New York Times* editorial dated December 19, 2000.

17. Dan Balz and Helen Dewar, "Analysis: Certification Brings Anything but Certainty," *Washington Post*, Sunday, November 26, 2000, p. A01. Some prominent Republicans, including the normally avuncular former presidential nominee Bob Dole, raised the possibility of a boycott of the inauguration if the

votes were counted and Gore was awarded Florida's electors. Always-pugnacious House Majority Whip Tom DeLay announced without evidence that the election was "nothing less than a theft in progress," and circulated a memo to congressional Republicans pointing out that the House and Senate could reject a state's electoral votes if they decided that the votes were tainted. See Eric Pianin and Juliet Eilperin, "Angry Hill Republicans Would Reject Gore Presidency," *Washington Post,* Monday, November 20, 2000, p. A8. The Marc Racicot anecdote was reported in Jonathan Schell, "Manufacturing a Crisis," *The Nation,* December 11, 2000. Implicit in these statements and others like them, both from GOP leaders and activists manning the parapets outside the hand counts, was the threat that if Bush didn't get his way in Florida, the Republican Party and their supporters were prepared to turn what so far had been a legal battle in one state into a true constitutional crisis.

18. Richard Winger, "Vote Study Has Surprises," *Ballot Access News,* May 1, 2001, p. 2, and "Errata," *Ballot Access News,* June 1, 2001, p. 3. In addition to 2000, 1998, and 1996, the other fours years are 1952, 1950, 1910, and 1914.

19. "One Nation, Fairly Divisible, under God," *The Economist,* January 18, 2001.

20. Jacob Weisberg from Slate.com, quoted by Howard Kurtz, "Gore Goes Out on a High Note," *Washington Post,* Thursday, December 14, 2000.

21. A partial list of corporations using cumulative voting include Hewlett-Packard, Walgreen's, Toys 'R' Us, Sun Microsystems, Aon, Abbott Labs, California Association of Homeowners Associations Incorporated, Industrie Canada, Pennzoil, Ingersoll-Rand, Lockheed-Martin, VWR Corporation, American Premier, and Allegheny Power System. Note that the American Business Association Model Business Corporation Act includes cumulative voting, and California and Ohio law still requires that unless stockholders specifically have voted not to have cumulative voting, the default is for corporations chartered in those states to include it. Outlaws Legal Service, under their section called Corporations II, says "Cumulative voting is mandatory in almost one-half of the states" (see www.outlawslegal.com/refer/corporations2.htm).

22. As we saw in the previous chapter, the contested cultural terrain splinters over issues of religion vs. secularism, the role of "big" government, abortion, gun control, gay rights, moral leadership qualities, public schools vs. school vouchers, and more.

23. "A Better Way of Voting," *The State,* Columbia, South Carolina, January 9, 2001.

24. Brad Werthen, *The State,* Columbia, South Carolina, January 23, 2000.

25. Martin Dyckman, "Districting Method May Explain Flag," *St. Petersburg Times,* January 25, 2000.

26. David Firestone, "46,000 March on South Carolina Capitol to Bring Down Confederate Flag," *New York Times,* January 18, 2000, p. A12.

27. Ibid., p. A12.

28. Sue Anne Pressley, "Flag War Isn't over at Carolina Statehouse," *Washington Post,* January 16, 2001, p. A03.

29. The "victory threshold" of representation for choice or cumulative voting is the same, and is derived by making all contested seats in a multiseat district equal to the same number of votes. The threshold is calculated by dividing the number of contested seats + 1 into 100 percent, and adding one more vote to that. Using this threshold, a three-seat district produces a victory threshold of 25 percent, plus one more vote.

$$\frac{100\% \text{ of total number of votes cast}}{\text{number of contested seats} + 1} = \frac{100\%}{3+1} = 25\% \text{ (+ 1 more vote)}$$

Qualitatively, this threshold, called the Droop threshold, is equal to the *minimum* number of votes a candidate needs to win such that, when all seats are filled, there are not enough votes left over to elect another candidate. See Edward Still, "Alternatives to Single-Member Districts," in Chandler Davidson, ed., *Minority Vote Dilution* (Washington, DC: Howard University Press, 1984).

30. See Christi Parsons, "New Legislature Reform Push," *Chicago Tribune,* July 8, 2001. Also see "Illinois Should Return to Cumulative Voting," report by the Mikva-Edgar panel called the Illinois Task Force on Political Representation and Alternative Electoral Systems, published by the Institute for Government and Public Affairs (IGPA) at the University of Illinois, July 9, 2001.

31. In fact, at one time the Speaker of the House in Illinois was a Democrat elected from heavily GOP DuPage County, due to cumulative voting in three-seat districts.

32. Rick Pearson, "Political Ideology," *Chicago Tribune*, April 29, 2001.

33. The quotes from Abner Mikva, John Porter, and Barbara Flynn Curie are from hours of videotaped interviews about Illinois's use of cumulative voting, conducted by the Center for Voting and Democracy.

34. "Better Politics From an Old Idea," *Chicago Tribune* editorial, May 30, 1995.

35. "Let's Bring Back Old Way of Voting," editorial in the *Chicago Sun-Times,* July 16, 2001. Cumulative voting was surreptitiously repealed in 1980 as a footnote to the populist Cutback Amendment, whose main feature was decreasing the number of state representatives and, wishfully, the cost of government. In Illinois, this populist movement was the culmination of the Reaganista tide, with its mantra of cutting back the size and cost of government. Unfortunately, the Cutback Amendment failed to shrink the cost of government even as it decreased the number of representatives and abolished cumulative voting in Illinois.

36. Indeed, until the 1840s, virtually all Congressional districts were multiseat, and most remained so into the 1860s, with many surviving thereafter. Below the congressional level, as late as the late 1950s, most state legislators were elected from multiseat districts. Single-seat districts weren't required for Congress until 1967. See Joel Rogers, John D. MacArthur Professor of Law, Political Science, and Sociology, University of Wisconsin-Madison, "Pull the Plug," unpublished paper.

Chapter Three: The Technology of Democracy

1. *World Almanac and Book of Facts, 1998* (Mahwah, NJ: K-III Reference Company, 1998), p. 379. Today, the U.S. population is less than one-quarter rural.

2. While originally American politics had no political parties—in fact, Washington and Madison warned against parties and factions—political parties quickly sprung up. By the election of 1800, Jefferson's Democratic-Republican Party and Adams' Federalist Party were going at it, full tilt. In fact, Madison's view changed dramatically, and more than anyone except Jefferson it was Madison who helped create the Democratic-Republican Party to defeat the Federalists. For an enlightening discussion of this, see Robert Dahl, *How Democratic is the American Constitution?* (New Haven, CT: Yale University Press, 2002).

3. As was noted earlier, in this book I have adopted the distinction Robert Dahl makes between the terms Framers and Founders (or Founding Fathers) to distinguish between those who were at the Constitutional Convention, that is, who actually participated in the *framing* of the Constitution, and those who were not. Among those who were *Founders* but not *Framers* included Thomas Jefferson, John Adams, Thomas Paine, and Samuel Adams.

4. *The Records of the Federal Convention of 1787*, ed. Max Farrand (New Haven, CT: Yale University Press, 1911-1937), pp. 44–45. Madison declared in *Federalist Papers* number 56: "Divide the largest state into ten or twelve districts and it will be found that there will be no peculiar local interests in either which will not be within the knowledge of the Representative of the district." Later in *Federalist* 56 Madison reasoned that "The Representatives of each state will . . . bring with them a considerable knowledge of its laws, and a local knowledge of their respective districts." In *Federalist* 57 Madison declared that "each Representative of the United States will be elected by five or six thousand citizens." Hamilton stated at the New York ratifying convention that "the natural and proper mode of holding elections will be to divide the state into districts in proportion to the number to be elected." Quoted in Lawrence F. Schmeckebier, *Congressional Apportionment* 131 (Washington, DC: Brookings Institution, 1941). From these arguments it appears that Madison and Hamilton both favored most U.S. House members being elected by districts rather than at-large.

5. As an example of how the sweep effect works, imagine there are five contested seats in a city or state elected by a Winner Take All at-large voting system. Under this system, a voter will have the same number of votes as there are contested seats, so in this example each voter will have five votes. Voters must use one vote per seat. The candidates with the most votes—called a "plurality"—win the seats. What happens in this type of election system is that all five of the seats in this example actually are contested as five *separate* races, all elected at the same time. And because every voter has the same number of votes as there are seats, each time the voters step up to vote the majority perspective has

more votes than any minority perspective and is able to out-vote the minority voters for each one of these seats. As a result, the majority perspective in such a voting system usually wins all the seats, producing a "sweep" effect. The important thing to note about the Winner Take All at-large voting system is that these lopsided results are a product of the mechanics of this democracy technology—where every voter has the same number of votes as there are contested seats, and must use one vote per seat. Whenever you have a situation like that, the majority perspective can out-vote the various minority perspectives, producing a sweep effect. For the most part electoral outcomes resulting from such a system are not a product of which candidates work harder, have more money to spend, or have more volunteers, and the like. It's purely a matter of the mechanics of the system and demographics—that is, which voting constituency has more voters. This type of voting system also is known as plurality at-large, block voting, or general ticket voting.

6. Rosemarie Zagarri, *The Politics of Size* (Ithaca, NY: Cornell University Press, 1987), p. 113.

7. Districts were used by Massachusetts, New York, North Carolina, South Carolina, and Virginia. At-large elections were used by Connecticut, Delaware, New Hampshire, New Jersey, Pennsylvania, and Rhode Island. See Zagarri, *The Politics of Size,* pp. 107-114, 154.

8. Ibid., pp. 126, 154-157

9. For a fascinating discussion of voting systems debate in the late eighteenth and early nineteenth centuries, see Nicolas Flores, "A History of One-Winner Districts for Congress," undergraduate political science thesis at Stanford University, published on the Web at www.fairvote.org/library/history/flores/index.html.

10. Typical of this view were the words of Sen. Isaac Bates of Massachusetts, who pointed out, "The general ticket (at-large) system disfranchises the minority in a State, however near it may approach a majority, and in however so many districts it would actually constitute a majority, and be entitled to a representation in Congress." *1842 Congressional Globe,* p. 793. Published by the Library of Congress, http://memory.loc.gov/ammem/amlaw/lwcg.html.

11. Said Jonathan Granoff, cochair of the American Bar Association's committee on arms control and disarmament, "What appears anomalous to me is that historically, the Republican Party has led in the area of arms control strengthening. The scuttling of arms control . . . is against the heritage of the Republican Party." Barbara Crossette, "Albright, at the U.N., Defend U.S. on Arms Plan," *New York Times,* April 25, 2000. Also see Helen Dewar and John Lancaster, "Helms Vows to Obstruct Arms Pacts," *Washington Post,* Thursday, April 27, 2000, p. A01.

12. Typical of this tendency to blame "bad politicians" rather than the political system was a recent conference organized by the Arsalyn Foundation, called "Bridging the Partisan Divide: Rediscovering Deliberation." The conference promotional material advertised a keynote speaker who had "conducted bipartisan retreats for members of the US House of Representatives in 1997 and 1999" and who was to speak "on the difference between debate and deliberation and conduct workshops with participants designed to teach them the art of civil and productive political deliberation." The conference also featured "workshops on managing political conflict." See www.arsalyn.org/TA.asp. Such a conference, while certainly well-meaning, rather naively assumes that congressional behavior as well as citizens' partisan behavior will benefit greatly from a crash-course on civil grooming and how to "talk nicely" to each other. While such kindergarten skills certainly are advisable, they will do little to restructure the strategic incentives of a two-choice Winner Take All political system to "go negative" as one party tries to carve out political space vis-à-vis their lone opponent.

13. Monopoly politics states include Alaska, Delaware, Hawaii, Idaho, Maine, Massachusetts, Montana, Nebraska, New Hampshire, North Dakota, Rhode Island, South Dakota, Vermont, and Wyoming. States that are one representative shy of a political monopoly are Arizona, Arkansas, Iowa, Kansas, Kentucky, Nevada, New Mexico, Oklahoma, Oregon, and West Virginia.

14. More than 38 percent of the Members of the 1998 U.S. House of Representatives were lawyers, and another 23 percent had primary occupations involved in real estate, insurance, or finance, a total of 61 percent. "Electing the People's House: 1998," a report by the Center for Voting and Democracy, www.fairvote.org.

15. Anthony Downs, *An Economic Theory of Democracy* (New York: Harper & Row, 1957).

16. Michael Gallagher, Michael Laver, and Peter Mair, *Representative Government in Modern Europe,* 2nd ed. (New York: McGraw-Hill, 1995), Table 7-1, p. 153.

17. James Travers, "Strutting toward Disaster," *Toronto Star,* Aug. 18, 2001.

18. Douglas Amy, *Real Choices, New Voices* (New York: Columbia University Press, 1993), p. 30.

19. Arend Lijphart, *Democracies: Patterns of Majoritarian and Consensus Government in Twenty-one Countries* (New Haven, CT: Yale University Press, 1984), p. 168.

20. The Center for Voting and Democracy is virtually the only organization in the United States, inside or outside academia, that regularly calculates these kinds of votes-to-seats distortion analysis. See the report "Dubious Democracy 2001" of the Center for Voting and Democracy on its Web site at www.fairvote.org/2001/index.html.

21. League of Women Voters of Washington Education Fund, "An Evaluation of Major Election Methods and Selected State Election Laws," Fall 2000, Committee Chair Janet Anderson, JanetRAnderson@msn.com.

22. Downs, *An Economic Theory of Democracy*, p. 85.

23. This electoral wisdom was imparted by Jennifer Laszlo, campaign consultant, quoted in Miles Benson, "Politicians Find U.S. Public Easy to Manipulate," Newhouse News Service, story published in the *San Francisco Examiner,* October 24, 1999, p. A12.

24. Conservative columnist Peggy Noonan, writing in the *Wall Street Journal,* gave credence to the Christian kitsch when she wrote that Ronald Reagan "would not have dismissed the story of the dolphins" but seen it as "possible evidence of the reasonable assumption that God's creatures had been commanded to protect one of God's children." Peggy Noonan, "Why Did They Do It?" *Wall Street Journal,* April 24, 2000, p. A38.

25. Deborah Sharp, "Little Havana Gives Boy Iconic Stature," *USA Today,* January 25, 2000.

26. Maurice Duverger, *Political Parties: Their Organization and Activity in the Modern State* (New York: John Wiley, 1954), p. 217.

27. Downs, *An Economic Theory of Democracy*. Downs' model predicted, among other things, that political parties in a Winner Take All system will have incentive to take policy positions that are as ambiguous and equivocal as possible, since such policy ambiguity allows for a wider range of interpretations and thus allows each policy stand to cover a greater number of voters. As a result, according to Downs, voters wind up making their electoral decisions on the basis of something other than the issues, such as the personality of candidates, traditional family voting patterns, and so on because voters *can never know enough* about each party's ambiguous policies to make a choice that will best serve their interests. This caused Downs himself to conclude that in a two-party system "rational behavior by political parties tends to *discourage* rational behavior by voters." Thus, hack-attack campaigning—going negative on one's opponent—becomes just another way to stay ambiguous and equivocal about position-taking.

28. Ceci Connolly, "Gore Goes on the Offensive in New Hampshire," *Washington Post,* December 11, 1999, p. A8.

29. The five third-party legislators from Vermont include one from the Libertarian Party and four from the Progressive Party. Moreover, the four Progressives all live within about a half-mile of each other in Burlington!

30. Richard Winger, "Georgia Lawsuit," *Ballot Access News,* June 1, 2001, p. 2.

31. Estimating the number of third parties in our nation's history is not easy. Third party specialist Darcy Richardson writes "including minor parties that existed in a single state, county, city, or town, my best estimate is that there have been over 1,250 third parties in American history." Third parties expert Professor Joel Rogers estimates that there have been about 1,100 third parties. Taking a more constrained view, Richard Winger of *Ballot Access News* says that 200 political parties have nominated a candidate for president in our nation's history.

Chapter Four: The People's House

1. Although it should be noted that some influential Founders did not completely trust "the people." In fact, many of the Founding Fathers didn't give a fig about the rights of the common citizenry, being as fearful of Shay's Rebellion, an insurgency in 1786 of poor farmers and debtors in western Massachusetts, as they were of kingly despotism. Typical of this viewpoint was John Jay, wealthy Founding Father, first Chief Justice of the Supreme Court, and President of the First Continental Congress. He believed that the upper classes "were the better kind of people, by which I mean the people who are

orderly and industrious." His theory of government was simple: "The people who own the country ought to govern it." Such a government, as ugly and contrarian as it might seem to modern sensibilities, is entirely in keeping with one strain of American thought and tradition. This suspicion of the "vox populi" became enshrined in the presidency and the Senate. Unlike the House, the founders insulated the Senate and presidency via indirect elections, the Senate initially elected by state legislatures until 1916, and the presidency to this day still elected by electors chosen by the state legislatures—not by popular vote, as was illustrated with an exclamation point by UnElection 2000.

2. See *We, the People: The Story of the United States Capitol* (Washington, DC: The United States Capitol Historical Society, 1991). p. 44.

3. In a game of musical chairs, a New Hampshire Senator ended up with Massachusetts Senator Daniel Webster's old desk. Webster's desk is occupied by a New Hampshire Senator because Ted Kennedy occupies his brother Robert's desk, and Robert represented the state of New York in the U.S. Senate.

4. Guy Fawkes was a British soldier and the best-known participant in the Gunpowder Plot (November 5, 1605) whose goal was to blow up the British Parliament building while King James I and his ministers met inside, in reprisal for increasing oppression of Catholics in England.

5. Following the 2000 elections, there were fifty-nine women (13.6 percent) and sixty racial minorities (thirty-seven blacks, nineteen Hispanics, and four Asians, 13.8 percent) elected to the U.S. House. Meanwhile, women comprise over a majority of our nation, and racial minorities over one-quarter, the latter a percentage about the same as South Africa's. Interestingly, of the ninety-six life-size statues perched in Statuary Hall and in the corridors all around the House chamber (two donated statues from each state symbolizing the political, military, and cultural history of the United States) only six are women—about as representative as the Congress. Sources include: Official List of Members of the House of Representatives of the United States Congress, December 20, 2000, Office of the Clerk, U.S. House of Representatives, www.clerkweb.house.gov/106/mbrcmtee/members/mbrsstate/Unoflmbr. htm; Center for American Women and Politics, www.rci.rutgers.edu/~cawp/ (January 2001); United States Senate, www.senate.gov (January 2001); "Latinos Grab Seats in State Houses Nationwide," November 2000, National Association of Latino Elected and Appointed Officials Education Fund, www.naleo.org/PressReleases/latinosgrab.htm; *National Asian Pacific American Political Almanac, 2000-01 Special Election Edition,* 9th ed. (Los Angeles: UCLA Asian American Studies Center, 2001); Center for Voting and Democracy, www.fairvote.org/vra/index.html.

6. See "Congress as America: Selected Occupations Comparison between Congress and the Voting Age Population in 1996," in *Electing the People's House: 1998,* a collection of statistical and written analyses published by the Center for Voting and Democracy on the Web (www.fairvote.org), first edition, August 1998.

7. John Adams, *Thoughts on Government,* 1776. Vol. 1, Chapter 4 (Chicago: University of Chicago Press, 1987), available on the Web at http://press-pubs.uchicago.edu/founders/documents/ v1ch4s5.html. This was a fairly common view among the Framers and Founders, expressed at the Constitutional Convention by James Wilson, who stated that "the legislature ought to be the most exact transcript of the whole society, the faithful echo of the voices of the people." See Hannah Pitkin, *The Concept of Representation* (Berkeley, CA: University of California Press, 1967), pp. 60-61. This view of "mirror representation" was pervasive among Congress members in the nineteenth century as well. During the 1842 debates over whether Congress should mandate single-seat districts over Winner Take All at-large elections, several Congressmen borrowed Adams' portrait analogy to advance their own theories of what Congress should look like. Rep. John Reynolds of Illinois thought that the House of Representatives was meant to be a "kind of facsimile and mirror of the [public]" since it was "the direct offspring of the people, and nearer the people than any other assembly of men." (*1842 Congressional Globe,* pp. 345-346). Rep. Atherton reasoned, "If there be any thing in the theory of representative government, it seems to follow conclusively that the people should have as thorough and extensive a representation as is possible" (p. 350). Senator Jacob Miller from New Jersey felt that if this law were passed, "The House of Representatives will become what the Framers of the Constitution intended it should be, a bright and honest mirror, reflecting all the lights and shades of the multifarious interests of this mighty people, as they lie spread out over this broad land" (*1842 Congressional Globe,* p. 790).

8. In the 2000 elections for the U.S. House, GOP candidates won only 48.2 percent of the popular vote, yet ended up with 51 percent of the representation. Moreover, there were 371 U.S. House seats where both Democrats and Republicans fielded a candidate, and the Democrats actually won slightly more votes than the Republicans nationwide in these races, yet because of the distortions of the geographic-based, single-seat districts, the Republicans won more of these seats, 191–179 (plus one independent). See *Dubious Democracy 2001,* a report by the Center for Voting and Democracy, located on the Web at www.fairvote.org/2001/index. html.

9. In 2000, only one-third of eligible voters voted for a winner, and eligible voter turnout was barely 47 percent. In 1998 barely one-fifth of eligible voters voted for a winner, and eligible voter turnout was only about 33 percent of eligible voters.

10. See Michael Schudson, "Voting: An Overrated Test of Good Citizenship?" *Washington Post,* Outlook section, Sunday, September 13, 1998, p. C03.

11. This point of view seems to be most conspicuous on the right. Another conservative columnist, Charles Krauthammer, has written, "Low voter turnout is a leading indicator of contentment." It seems hardly coincidental that the demographics of those who *do* actually vote are more inclined toward conservative opinions than those who do not vote. See Charles Krauthammer, "In Praise of Low Voter Turnout," *Time,* May 21, 1990.

12. Some good sources on voter turnout and related demographics include M. Margaret Conway, *Political Participation in the United States* (Washington, DC: Congressional Quarterly Press, 1991); Frances Fox Piven and Richard Cloward, *Why Americans Don't Vote* (New York: Pantheon, 1988); G. Bingham Powell, Jr., "American Voter Turnout in Comparative Perspective," *American Political Science Review,* 80 (March 1986); and Robert Putnam, *Bowling Alone* (New York: Simon & Schuster, 2000). And of course the dean of tracking voter turnout is Curtis Gans of the Committee for the Study of the American Electorate.

13. "Gun Deaths among Children and Teens Drop Sharply," press release from the National Center for Health Statistics, Center for Disease Control, U.S. Department of Health and Human Services, www.hhs.gov, July 24, 2000. Statistics are from 1998, children and adolescents under the age 20. Also see Phil Tajitsu Nash, "Looking Down the Barrel," *Asian Week,* October 12, 2000, p. 7.

14. At the time of the shootings and the congressional vote, national opinion polls uniformly had demonstrated for some time that Americans supported tighter gun control laws. According to the University of Chicago's nonpartisan National Opinion Research Center, in 1996 nearly 90 percent of the public believed that gun owners should be required to obtain licenses. Overwhelming majorities also favored restricting individual gun purchases to no more than one a month and requiring safety training for gun purchasers. Leading *law enforcement agencies* were outspoken in their support for gun control, and 72 percent of *gun owners* supported criminal background checks on gun buyers, while two-thirds supported mandatory registration. Despite this overwhelming tide of public opinion, Congress has been absolutely incapable of enacting policy that reflects the will of the majority. For instance, in 1996 it voted to repeal the assault weapons ban, even though the ban was favored by 71 percent of the public, according to a CBS News poll.

15. Melinda Henneberger, "Tom DeLay Holds No Gavel, but a Firm Grip on the Reins," *New York Times,* June 21, 1999. Also see Daniel Lazare, "Your Constitution Is Killing You," *Harper's,* October 1999, pp. 57–58.

16. "Armor-Piercing Ammo Being Sold as Surplus," *Chicago Tribune,* June 16, 1999.

17. One joke that circulated in Canada at the time went something like this: "What is a Canadian? Answer: a Canadian is an American with healthcare and no handgun."

18. When asked by police how he knew how to load and fire the pistol, the five-year-old replied that he had learned by "watching television." Associated Press story, "5-Year-Old Boy Fires Gun in Tiff with Friends," published in *San Francisco Chronicle,* March 4, 2000. Also see Associated Press story, "Six Children Are Wounded in Gunfire at National Zoo," published in *New York Times,* April 25, 2000.

19. John Wildermuth, "Rampages Elicit Little Outcry for Gun Control," *San Francisco Chronicle,* March 24, 2001. As a measure of how much gun-control proponents are in retreat, Jim and Sarah Brady's national group, Handgun Control Inc., is changing its name to one that is expected to be less confrontational than "handgun control." In March 2001 the organization spawned by the Million Mom

March for gun control fired thirty of its thirty-five employees and suspended plans to open new chapters.

20. One press release from Public Campaign offered the following details: "In the 1997–98 election cycle, political action committees and individuals advocating stricter gun control regulations gave $150,364 to federal candidates and parties. On top of that, they spent another $22,078 on TV commercials and other independent expenditures aimed at electing candidates favoring gun control. During that same period, the big money opposing gun control totaled $2,260,680 to federal candidates and parties, and another $2,319,557 in independent expenditures on behalf of candidates supportive of gun rights."

21. Robert Dreyfuss, "The NRA Wants You," *The Nation,* May 29, 2000.

22. Michael Powell, "Call to Arms," *Washington Post Magazine,* August 6, 2000, p. 25.

23. Ibid., p. 21.

24. For instance, the Illinois State Rifle Association, an NRA state affiliate, claims to have 10,000 active members complementing the NRA's 140,000 statewide members.

25. Dreyfuss, "The NRA Wants You."

26. "Gore Would Leave Gun Makers Suits to Cities," *New York Times* story published in the *San Francisco Examiner,* October 29, 2000, p. A5. Gore's retreat on gun control as Election Day neared was in marked contrast to the comments he made in the summer of 1999 when he joined President Clinton and other Democrats who attacked House Republicans on gun control and promised to make it an issue in the 2000 campaign.

27. John Mintz, "With a Poll-Tested Message, NRA Aims to Counter Labor Efforts in Midwest," *Washington Post,* October 5, 2000.

28. John Wildermuth, "Rampages Elicit Little Outcry for Gun Control."

29. A central theme of the NRA message is that the Second Amendment guarantees every law-abiding person the right to own a gun, but the U.S. Supreme Court has taken up the meaning of the amendment on only a single occasion, in a 1939 case that arose over the arrest of two Arkansas bootleggers. In that case, the High Court rejected the claim that an individual's right to bear arms is protected, ruling that the constitutional Framers sought to protect the states' right to raise militias, and the Second Amendment had "the obvious purpose to assure the continuation and render possible the effectiveness of such [state militia] forces." Ruled the court, unless a gun control law interferes with "the preservation or efficiency of a well-regulated militia, we cannot say that the Second Amendment guarantees the right to keep and bear such an instrument." Since that 1939 case, the courts have routinely rejected claims that the Second Amendment protects an individual's right to bear arms. Former Chief Justice Warren Burger has written that the Second Amendment was intended to ensure that states could maintain their militias and that "there is no support in the Constitution for the argument that federal and state governments are powerless to regulate the purchase of such firearms. Surely the Second Amendment does not remotely guarantee every person the constitutional right to have a 'Saturday Night Special' or a machine gun without any regulation whatsoever." David G. Savage, "A Right to Bear Arms? Courts Say Not Quite," *Los Angeles Times,* June 15, 1994.

30. Voter turnout from 1991 to 2000 in the democracies of Western Europe, United States, and Canada show the following average voter turnout rates for these countries (WTA indicates the use of a Winner Take All voting system, PR indicates the use of a proportional representation voting system, Mixed indicates the use of a combination of WTA and PR): Italy 90% Mixed, Iceland 89% PR, Sweden 84% PR, Belgium 84% PR, Australia 83% PR, Denmark 83% PR, Portugal 79% PR, Spain 79% PR, Austria 78% PR, Norway 76% PR, Netherlands 75% PR, Germany 72% Mixed, United Kingdom 72% WTA, Finland 71% PR, Ireland 71% PR, France 61% WTA, Canada 60% WTA, Luxembourg 60% PR, United States 45% WTA, Switzerland 38% PR. On average, with the exception of Switzerland, the proportional representation democracies have had far higher voter turnout rates than the Winner Take All democracies. Data are based on voting age population. Source: International Institute for Democracy and Electoral Assistance, www.idea.int.

31. Figure stated in Leslie Wayne, "Political Consultants Thrive in the Cash-Rich New Politics," *New York Times,* October 24, 2000.

Chapter Five: Behind Closed Doors

The epigraph for this chapter is Senator McDaniel quoted in John Hoeffel, "Six Incumbents Are a Week Away from Easy Election," *Winston-Salem Journal,* January 27, 1998.

1. Benjamin Sheffner, "Will 'Unholy Alliance' Be Back in 2001? Redistricting Could Team Republicans, Blacks Again," *Roll Call,* January 13, 1997, p. 13. Also see John B. Anderson and Rob Richie, "Let the Voters Decide Their Representation," *Legal Times,* February 23, 1998. The speaker of this prescient quote was Congresswoman Eddie Bernice Johnson, who had chaired Texas' Senate redistricting committee, during a civil rights gathering in 1997.

2. North Carolina state representative Robert Grady, quoted by the Associated Press, December 9, 1996. For other revealing quotes from the North Carolina redistricting practitioners, see "Admissions of Guilt: Redistricting and Non-Competitiveness," a report by the Center for Voting and Democracy published at www.fairvote.org/ reports/monopoly/guilt.html.

3. See, for instance, Mark Monmonier, *Bushmanders and Bullwinkles: How Politicians Manipulate Electronic Maps and Census Data to Win Elections* (Chicago: University of Chicago Press, 2001).

4. Pamela Karlan, Professor of Law, Stanford University, videotaped testimony at public hearings on "Race, Reapportionment and Redistricting," San Francisco, California, September 1997; followed by videotaped interview.

5. The origin of the term "gerrymander" has been oft-told, but it bears repeating: it was coined after the name of a Massachusetts governor, Eldridge Gerry, who in 1812 approved the efforts of the Jeffersonian-dominated legislature to create a famously contorted district that split Essex County in an effort to dilute the strength of the Federalists. Noting the resemblance of the new, oddly shaped district to a salamander, a local newspaper dubbed the creation a "gerrymander." Thus was produced the term of art that has passed down through the centuries.

6. Daniel M. Weintraub, "Brown Says Uncertainty of Jewish Vote Dictated Drawing of District," *Los Angeles Times*, September 20, 1991, p. A3. In response to Willie Brown, Stan Treitel, a representative of an Orthodox Jewish organization based in Hancock Park, called Brown's comment a "cheap shot," pointing out that Sen. Diane Watson, who is black, had represented the Hancock Park area since 1978. "Diane Watson is not Watsonstein," he said. The anecdote illustrates the divisions along ethnic and religious, in addition to racial, lines that can be exacerbated by redistricting.

7. Richard Simon, "Coveted Landmarks Add a Twist to Redistricting Task," *Los Angeles Times*, September 10, 1991, p. A1. When California state legislators redrew district boundaries in 1981, then-Assemblyman Mike Roos, a diehard baseball fan, asked that Dodger Stadium be drawn into his district. But he ran into a problem—Dodger Stadium was in the district of Assembly Reapportionment Committee Chairman Richard Alatorre, who was not about to give it up. Alatorre did offer Roos a consolation prize—the parking lot. This is just one crazy anecdote of many that shows how incumbent- and perk-driven the process can be.

8. This anecdote was related in Andrew Gelman and Gary King, "Enhancing Democracy through Legislative Redistricting," *American Political Science Review*, 88(3) (September 1994), p. 541.

9. Paul M. Green, "Legislative Redistricting in Illinois 1871–1982: A Study of Geo-Political Survival." In *Redistricting: An Exercise in Prophecy,* ed. Anna J. Merritt (Chicago: University of Illinois Institute of Government and Public Affairs, 1982); quoted in Gelman and King, "Enhancing Democracy through Legislative Redistricting," p. 541. Also see Rick Pearson, "Jim Ryan Takes Heat on Remap: Appointment of Democrats Irks Colleagues," *Chicago Tribune*, August 20, 2001.

10. John Gilligan, videotaped testimony at public hearings on "Race, Reapportionment and Redistricting," Minneapolis, Minnesota, November 1997; followed by videotaped interview.

11. Hanh Kim Quach and Dena Bunis, "All Bow to Redistrict Architect: Politics Secretive, Single-Minded Michael Berman Holds All the Crucial Cards," *Orange County Register*, August 26, 2001, p. 1.

12. Perhaps the most bizarre redistricting story of 2001: in St. Louis, acting Board of Alderman (city council) president James Shrewsbury ruled Alderwoman Irene Smith must yield the floor if she left for a restroom break during a filibuster of a unfavorable redistricting bill that would place her home and that of another Alderman into the same ward. So, Smith stood over a trash can while supporters gathered sheets and quilts around her, and allegedly relieved herself in the aldermanic chambers. Alderwoman Smith was summarily fined $500 for public urination. Yes indeed, the political insiders know that *a lot* is at stake in redistricting! Greg Freeman, "What Happened at Board of Aldermen Was Not Comic Relief," *St. Louis Post-Dispatch,* July 19, 2001.

13. "Packing" is a redistricting technique whereby those controlling the line-drawing create districts in which they "pack" as many as possible of their political opponents' voters into a few districts, sacrificing those districts but in effect "bleaching" opponents' voters out of the remaining districts, allowing the dominant party to win more seats. "Cracking" is where the party controlling the line-drawing splits their opponent's supporters into two or more districts, dividing them into two ineffective groupings without enough votes to elect anyone. By using techniques like these, those controlling the redistricting process can dramatically heighten their chances at winning the remaining districts and controlling the legislatures.

14. The results were similar for the 1998 House elections: ninety percent of races were won by comfortable victory margins greater than ten points, and 73 percent were won by landslide margins greater than twenty points, as 98 percent of incumbents won reelection, and the average margin of victory for incumbents was a whopping 43 percent. See *Electing the People's House: 1998, A Collection of Statistical and Written Analyses*, 1st ed. (Center for Voting and Democracy, August 1998), published on the Web at www.fairvote.org.

15. The year 2000 was not atypical. In 1998 there was no Democrat or Republican candidates in 41.1 percent of the state legislative races; in 1996, 32.7 percent; in 1994, 35.8 percent; in 1992, 32.8 percent. This information comes from a most useful little publication, *Ballot Access News*, a veritable font of election-related information published by the inestimable and dedicated Richard Winger, P.O. Box 470296, San Francisco, CA 94147, ban@igc.org. See *Ballot Access News*, "Dems, Reps Failed to Nominate in 2000," 16(9), (December 5, 2000), p. 2.

16. The states that had all U.S. House seats either uncontested or won by landslides are Louisiana, Alabama, Tennessee, Massachusetts, Alaska, Delaware, Hawaii, Idaho, Maine, Nebraska, Rhode Island, Vermont, Wyoming, and South Dakota. The states with all but one of their House seats uncontested or won by landslides are Virginia, Arizona, Wisconsin, Mississippi, Iowa, Oklahoma, South Carolina, Utah, West Virginia, and Maryland.

17. The Center for Voting and Democracy performs this highly provocative exercise —essentially handicapping the elections like horse races—every congressional election. They predict the winners in 85 to 90 percent of U.S. House races over a year in advance of the elections, without knowing anything about inequities in campaign finance (since that information is generally irrelevant to the predictions). In 1997, eighteen months prior to the 1998 elections, the Center predicted 340 congressional races with incumbents and twenty-one open seats where there was no incumbent. The results? They were right in 339 out of the 340 incumbent races, or 99.7 percent. In open seats they were right in nineteen out of twenty-one, or 90 percent. In 2000, the Center's accuracy rate once again was 99 percent.

18. Frank Luntz, "Voices of Victory, Part 1: Focus Group Research in American Politics," *The Polling Report*, May 16, 1994. Luntz has served as a consultant to the U.S. House Republican leadership, to the Dole presidential campaign, to New York Mayor Rudolph Giuliani, and to numerous candidates in the United States and abroad.

19. Monopoly politics states include Alaska, Delaware, Hawaii, Idaho, Maine, Massachusetts, Montana, Nebraska, New Hampshire, North Dakota, Rhode Island, South Dakota, Vermont, and Wyoming. States that are one representative shy of a political monopoly are Arizona, Arkansas, Iowa, Kansas, Kentucky, Nevada, New Mexico, Oklahoma, Oregon, Vermont, and West Virginia.

20. After Indiana lost a congressional seat in the 2000 Census, a Democratic-dominated commission redrew the congressional district boundaries so that two Republicans were forced to vie for the same seat in the 2002 primaries. Both were staunchly conservative Republicans and erstwhile allies, but once lumped in the same district a real catfight broke out, driven by the rawest of political impulses: survival. The intraparty feuding became so intense that Rep. Thomas Davis of Virginia, the chairman of the National Republican Congressional Committee, commented, "They don't help matters by going and carving each other up on a personal basis every day. [They] are gaming this in an inappropriate fashion." Well beyond Indiana, individual battles brewed in other states. "It's a very selfish enterprise," Mr. Davis said. "Everybody looks after themselves first, the party second. It's every man for himself." Richard L. Berke, "Democrats' New Map of Indiana Divides G.O.P.," *New York Times*, June 2, 2001.

21. John Wildermuth, "Lawmakers Use Creative License in Redistricting," *San Francisco Chronicle*, September 2, 2001, p. A6.

22. Will Pinkston, "New Computer Software Makes Redistricting Easier, Accessible," *Wall Street Journal*, April 24, 2001, p. B1.

23. Pamela Karlan, Professor of Law, Stanford University, videotaped testimony at public hearings on "Race, Reapportionment and Redistricting," San Francisco, California, September 1997; followed by videotaped interview.

24. Personal interview with Mr. Wice.

25. Gail Collins, "Other People's Election," *New York Times*, June 16, 2000.

26. See *Voter Participation and Victory Margins, 1994 Elections, U.S. House of Representatives,* and *Dubious Democracy 2001,* www.fairvote.org/2001/index.html, reports published by the Center for Voting and Democracy, www.fairvote.org.

27. See John Heilprin, "105.4 Million Voters Cast Ballots," Associated Press, December 18, 2000. Among sixteen battleground states, turnout increased in 2000 over 1996 by an average of 3.4 percent compared with a 1.6 percent increase in other states. Ten states—Arizona, Hawaii, Idaho, Kansas, Louisiana, Montana, New Jersey, Oklahoma, South Dakota, and Wyoming—had lower turnout than in 1996, and none of those presidential races were close. Five states—Missouri, Montana, North Carolina, North Dakota, and Wyoming—actually had competitive congressional or gubernatorial races in which voters cast more ballots than they did in the presidential contest. None of these states were close in the presidential race except for Missouri; there, the presidential race was outpolled by a macabrely riveting U.S. Senate race where incumbent Sen. John Ashcroft was beaten by a dead man who had been replaced by his widow. Also see the report released by Curtis Gans and the Committee for the Study of the American Electorate, reported in the *New York Times*, "Voter Turnout Rose in 2000, but No Lasting Impact Is Seen," August 31, 2001, p. A12.

28. James W. Endersby and Steven E. Galatas, "Electoral Competitiveness and Electoral Participation: Voter Participation in the 1998 German Bundestag Election," unpublished paper from the American Political Science Association national conference (See Table 1 on p. 22). As the authors note, Germany provides an excellent case for comparison because it has a combination of automatic voter registration, single-seat plurality district elections (combined with proportional representation elections), stronger political parties, and multiparty competition throughout the country.

29. The study was the first to provide empirical evidence in the debate over whether or not creating minority-opportunity districts leads to greater participation in the political process by minority groups. This effect was particularly strong among Latino voters; the report found that Latino registered voter turnout was 33 percentage points higher in Latino-opportunity districts than Latino turnout in majority-white districts. In districts where Latinos and blacks were more evenly matched, Latino turnout was 30 percentage points above rates in mostly white districts. And in multiethnic districts where Latinos played a more limited role, turnout was still 7 percentage points higher than in majority-white districts. The study noted that turnout among Latinos was particularly high in districts with Latino representatives as well as Latino majorities. See the report entitled, "The Effect of Minority Districts and Minority Representation on Political Participation in California," published by the Public Policy Institute of California, www.ppic.org, June 13, 2001.

30. Collins, "Other People's Elections."

31. Gelman and King, "Enhancing Democracy through Legislative Redistricting," p. 554.

32. Gelman and King's own article amply illustrates the jungle of researchers' opinions. After summarizing the raft of opinions into two schools of thought, one side holding that "gerrymanderers draw district lines in order to maximize only their party's seat advantage and have a large and lasting effect," and the other side arguing that "whatever gerrymanderers maximize, they have only a smaller transitory effect," Gelman and King then go on to say: "Paradoxically, we find that *both* sides in this debate are correct."!

33. Quotes were, respectively, by North Carolina state senator Leslie Winner (quoted by the Associated Press, December 9, 1996) and state representative Ed Mahan (quoted by the Associated Press, February 16, 1997). For other revealing quotes from the North Carolina redistricting practitioners, see "Admissions of Guilt: Redistricting and Non-Competitiveness," a report by the Center for Voting and Democracy published at www.fairvote.org/reports/monopoly/guilt.html.

34. Rep. Davis quoted in a *Washington Times* editorial, "Counting Americans . . . Redrawing the District Lines," January 21, 2001.

35. R.H. Melton, "U.S. House Trio Aims to Redraw the Lines; Incumbents' Seats Could Become Safer," *Washington Post*, Thursday, Feb. 15, 2001, p. B4.

36. In most states, the political party that completes the trifecta—winning control of both houses of the legislature and of the governor's seat—completely dominates the line-drawing in their state. That's because redistricting is treated just like any other legislative bill: it must be passed by both houses of the legislature and signed by the governor. If the minority party controls either house of the legislature or the governor's seat, that allows them a bit of a brake on the steamrolling by the dominant party.

37. Tim Curran and John Mercurio, "Parties Brace for Looming Remaps: Governors, State Legislators Hold Keys to Members' Fates," *Roll Call*, March 19, 1998.

Chapter Six: The Gravity of the Prize

1. Robert White, "Strategy Aims to Keep Foe's Voters at Home," *Fairfax Journal*, November 2, 1999, p. A1. Also see *USA Today* editorial, "No Contest, No Choice," Wednesday, November 3, 1999, p. 30A.

2. The GOP's Virginia strategy for state legislative races had its predecessor, possibly the one employed by Democrats in Florida in 1994. Florida Democrats did not run candidates against most of the GOP's Florida incumbents in the U.S. House in an effort to suppress Republican voter turnout and reelect Lawton Chiles as governor. This contributed to Chiles barely beating Jeb Bush. In 1998, both parties in Florida followed suit, with only five of Florida's twenty-three U.S. House races being contested.

3. In addition, California picked up one more congressional seat during the 2001 reapportionment that was drawn into the Democratic column, a Latino district in Los Angeles. And in an unabashed "incumbent protection plan," the Democratic line-drawers packed more Democratic voters into incumbents' districts, creating safe seats and locking-down voters into one-party fiefdoms.

4. Tim Curran and John Mercurio, "Parties Brace for Looming Remaps: Governors, State Legislators Hold Keys to Members' Fates," *Roll Call*, March 19, 1998. For instance, Mark Gersh, Washington director of the National Committee for an Effective Congress and a consultant to the Democratic Congressional Campaign Committee, is quoted as saying, "I would attribute about 60 percent of the gains Republicans made [in the House since 1990] to redistricting."

5. Control of a state legislature also dramatically affects the competitiveness of elections. A 1995 report entitled "The Mapmakers and Competitiveness" by the Center for Voting and Democracy assessed the impact of the 1991–1992 redistricting by comparing the 1992 and 1994 congressional elections with the 1990 elections. That study found that immediately following redistricting in the seventeen states where one party had a trifecta there was an average 7.5 percent increase in the number of competitive elections (elections won with less than 55 percent of the vote) from 1990 to 1994. But in states with split party control in the legislature, there was a 22 percent increase – nearly a threefold rise—in the number of competitive elections in the same years.

6. A report by Brigham Young University's Center for the Study of Elections and Democracy looked at soft money expenditures and issue advocacy in the 2000 election. That report concluded that the battle for control of the U.S. Congress was concentrated on relatively few races, but in those races candidates raised and spent record-setting amounts of money. The political parties—through soft money—and interest groups—through election issue advocacy, independent expenditures, and internal communications—effectively doubled the money spent on campaign communications in these contests. The report also concluded that closing the political party's soft money exemption from contribution limits will merely provide a tremendous incentive for individuals and groups to shift to issue advocacy and independent expenditures. Report quoted in *The Political Standard*, newsletter of the Alliance for Better Campaigns, 4(1) (March 2001), p. 2.

7. Alan Greenblatt, "The Mapmaking Mess," *Governing* (January 2001), p. 21.

8. Neil Irwin, "Elections for State Legislators Could Change Congress' Future," *Christian Science Monitor*, March 26, 2000.

9. Robert Tanner, "Close Race in State Legislatures," Associated Press, October 21, 2000.

10. Charles Babington, "Big Spending on Statehouse Races to Sway Redistricting," *Washington Post*, Monday, October 30, 2000, p. A2.

11. The following explication draws heavily from an analysis from a lengthy *Congressional Quarterly Weekly Report* written by Chuck Alston, called "Incumbents Share the Wealth, with Redistricting in Mind," May 25, 1991.

12. Quoted in Irwin, "Elections for State Legislators Could Change Congress' Future."

13. Chuck Alston, "Incumbents Share the Wealth, with Redistricting in Mind," *Congressional Quarterly Weekly Report*, May 25, 1991.

14. Source: Federal Election Commission, as reported by Holly Bailey, a "Party Spends Heavily in State Races to Influence Redistricting," *Capital Eye* (a publication of the Center for Responsive Politics), (12)1 (Spring 2000), p. 6.

15. Information on Pennsylvania is from the web site of the National Conference of State Legislatures, http://www.ncsl.org/ncsldb/elect98/profile.cfm?yearsel=2000&statesel=PA

16. Some of the notable highlights in Election 2000 included the GOP winning control of the house in Pennsylvania and completing their trifecta. Republicans also won the trifecta in Michigan, and the current congressional delegation of ten Democrats and six Republicans likely will reverse direction as a result. In South Carolina, for the first time in the 124 years since Reconstruction, the Republicans broke up the Democrats' majority in the Senate. On the Democratic plus side, Democrats took command of the Colorado Senate for the first time since 1962, breaking up the Republican trifecta and winning Democrats a say in the drawing of lines. The Democrats also fended off a Republican challenge in the Wisconsin Senate, holding onto their slight edge and preventing a Republican trifecta. Democrats cut into but did not substantially change the Republicans' national advantage in governorships, capturing eight of eleven gubernatorial contests, leaving Republicans in control of twenty-nine governors' mansions to the Democrats nineteen. See David Stout, "Democrats Win 8 of 11 Governor's Races," *New York Times*, November 8, 2000.

17. Tanner, "Close Race in State Legislatures."

18. Michael Barone, "The 49 Percent Nation," *National Journal*, June 8, 2001.

19. One of the biggest redistricting stories of the election was the passage of an initiative in Arizona that shifted the critical line-drawing process from the legislature to an independent commission. Including Arizona, six states used a commission for congressional redistricting in 2001, and state legislative redistricting in twelve states was conducted by a board or commission. In the rest of the states, legislatures are charged with the task.

20. Here's the breakdown on party control of state legislatures. Democrats (sixteen): Alabama, Arkansas, California, Connecticut, Georgia, Hawaii, Louisiana, Maryland, Massachusetts, Mississippi, New Mexico, North Carolina, Oklahoma, Rhode Island, Tennessee, and West Virginia. Republicans (eighteen): Alaska, Florida, Idaho, Iowa, Kansas, Michigan, Montana, New Hampshire, New Jersey, North Dakota, Ohio, Oregon, Pennsylvania, South Carolina, South Dakota, Utah, Virginia, and Wyoming. Split (fifteen): Arizona, Colorado, Delaware, Illinois, Indiana, Kentucky, Maine, Minnesota, Missouri, Nevada, New York, Texas, Vermont, Washington, and Wisconsin. Nonpartisan (one): Nebraska. The Republican trifecta states are Florida, Idaho, Kansas, Michigan, Montana, New Jersey, North Dakota, Ohio, Pennsylvania, South Dakota, Utah, Virginia, and Wyoming (but the states of Montana, North Dakota, South Dakota, and Wyoming only have one congressional district, so there is nothing to redistrict in those four states; and New Jersey uses a commission that this time favored Democrats.) The Democrat trifecta states are Alabama, California, Georgia, Hawaii, Maryland, Mississippi, North Carolina, and West Virginia. See "2000 Elections Bring Historic Balance to State Legislatures," press release of the National Conference of State Legislatures, November 15, 2000.

21. *Washington Times* editorial, "Counting Americans . . . Redrawing the District Lines," January 21, 2001.

22. Alan I. Abramowitz and Kyle L. Saunders, "Ideological Realignment and U.S. Congressional Elections," a paper prepared for delivery at the annual meeting of the American Political Science Association, September 2000, p. 3. Copyright 2000 by the American Political Science Association.

23. Frank Reeves and Peter J. Shelly, *Pittsburgh Post-Gazette*, June 1, 1998.

24. Other factors to consider when adding up the congressional scoreboard: Texas and Florida, both states with GOP trifectas—*and* expanding Democratic-friendly Hispanic populations—picked up two seats each, but other states with GOP state legislatures like Ohio, Pennsylvania, Wisconsin, and Oklahoma lost a total of five seats and electoral votes. Republicans in Pennsylvania, which lost two seats, redrew

the districts so that several Democratic incumbents had to run against each other, and the Democrats likely will lose three seats. States with Democratic legislatures showed gains (California, North Carolina, Georgia) and losses (Connecticut), and Indiana's one-seat loss will hurt the GOP since the lines were redrawn by a commission dominated by the Democrats, which lumped two Republican incumbents into the same district. Colorado, Arizona, and Nevada picked up a total of three new U.S. House seats and Electoral College votes as a result of reapportionment, and New York lost two seats, but in all these states neither party controlled redistricting so who wins and loses is not so obvious. Reapportioned states like Mississippi and Georgia, where Democrats hold a trifecta, might elect more Democrats as a result, but they will probably be conservative Democrats, many of them all but Republicans in name. See Tom Squitieri, "South, West Gains in House Continue," *USA Today*, December 29, 2000, p. 6A. Also see Michael Janofsky, "Redistricting Puts Fire into Legislative Races," *New York Times*, October 28, 2000.

25. See *Dubious Democracy 2001,* a report by the Center for Voting and Democracy, located on the Web at www.fairvote.org/2001/index.html.

26. France has maintained a merry dance with Winner Take All eccentricity for some time. France uses a two-round (runoff) system, and in 1993 a center-right coalition turned only 39 percent of the popular vote in the first round of elections into 80 percent of seats after the runoff. In their most recent elections, the Socialists dramatically overturned the center-right coalition, turning only 24 percent of the first-round vote into a majority of seats in the runoff with support from candidates from the Communist Party and Greens. Since 1977, India's Winner Take All system has lurched from one government to another with only a relatively minor swing in the popular vote. For instance, in 1984 the Congress Party won only 48 percent of the popular vote but ended up with 74 percent of seats in their national legislature. Five years later, it dropped a bit to 40 percent of the popular vote but lost over half of its legislative seats and with it, its majority control of the government. Two years later it dropped even further, to 37 percent of the vote, but oddly enough picked up enough legislative seats to win back control of the government. See the *International IDEA Handbook of Electoral System Design* (Stockholm, Sweden: International Institute for Democracy and Electoral Assistance, 1997), pp. 32–35.

27. It is interesting to note that Britain's Winner Take All system has produced dramatic swings in national policy, from nationalization to denationalization to renationalization to decentralization, depending on which party won power resulting from relatively small swings in the electorate and the distortions of their single-seat Winner Take All districts.

28. Greenblatt, "The Mapmaking Mess," p. 21.

29. For instance, redrawing the minority-opportunity districts helped boost the number of blacks in Congress to thirty-seven from seventeen, and Hispanics to nineteen from five.

30. George Will, "The Voting Rights Act at 30: Racial Gerrymandering Is One Reason Newt Gingrich Is Speaker," *Newsweek,* July 10, 1995. Also see David Lublin, *The Paradox of Representation: Racial Gerrymandering and Minority Interests in Congress* (Princeton, NJ: Princeton University Press, 1997).

31. These of course were the controversial Shaw rulings: *Shaw v. Reno*, 509 U.S. 630 (1993); *Holder v. Hall*, 512 U.S. 874 (1994); *Miller v. Johnson*, 115 S.Ct. 2475 (1995); *Vera v. Bush*, 116 S.Ct. 1941 (1996); *Shaw v. Hunt*, 116 S.Ct. 1894 (1996); and *Abrams v. Johnson*, 117 S.Ct. 1925 (1997).

32. Benjamin Sheffner, "Will 'Unholy Alliance' Be Back in 2001? Redistricting Could Team Republicans, Blacks Again," *Roll Call,* January 13, 1997, p. 13.

33. Associated Press, "Redistricting Brings Back Arguments," April 24, 2001.

34. Jeffrey Gold, "Tribunal Upholds N.J. Redistricting Plan," Associated Press story, May 2, 2001.

35. Associated Press, "Redistricting Brings Back Arguments."

36. Jackie Calmes and Greg Hitt, "Virginia Redistricting Plan Tests Bush Pledge of More Diverse GOP," *Wall Street Journal,* August 30, 2001.

37. Wayne Washington, "Hispanics Poised to Gain Clout in Redistricting Plan," *Boston Globe,* August 18, 2001, p. A1.

38. Pamela Karlan, Professor of Law, Stanford University, videotaped testimony at public hearings on "Race, Reapportionment and Redistricting," San Francisco, California, September 1997; followed by videotaped interview. Predicted J. Morgan Kousser, Caltech professor and author of a book on redistricting and race, "Redistricting in 2001 [and throughout the remainder of the decade] is going to be

the greatest bonanza for lawyers since the founding of the New Deal." See Greenblatt, "The Mapmaking Mess," pp. 21–22, January 2001.

39. Reaching the heights of absurdity, on November 27, 2000, the U.S. Supreme Court heard for the *fourth* time oral arguments in a lawsuit challenging Watt's district—only months before it would be redrawn during the 2001 redistricting. Greenblatt, "The Mapmaking Mess," p. 23.

40. Watt's district finally was upheld by the U.S. Supreme Court in April 2001, nearly ten years after it originally had been drawn, with the court deciding in its typically bumbling way that the most recent incarnation of Watt's district was, after all, a *political* gerrymander, not a racial gerrymander. In other words, it had been drawn to elect a Democrat, not a black representative; the former was constitutional, the latter was not. David Stout, "Court Upholds Congressional District," *New York Times*, April 18, 2001.

41. Greenblatt, "The Mapmaking Mess," p. 23.

42. Associated Press story, "Lawmakers Told Redistricting Could Be Legal Minefield," January 26, 2001.

43. Racial minorities are not the only "geographic minority" to find themselves shortchanged by the geographic majority during redistricting. In yet another fascinating redistricting wrinkle, students at the University of California–Berkeley organized and lobbied the Berkeley city council for a district that would be centered around the University, allowing the election of a student to the Berkeley city council. The students had thought that the progressive majority on the council, naturally enough, would support this. But in a replay of the Democratic Party's unpacking of minority-opportunity districts, the progressives on the council had other ideas. The clever progressives realized that if they packed the liberal-leaning students into one district, that would drain away their liberal votes from the surrounding districts, creating more conservative districts. Accordingly, the progressive majority, which had the privilege of redrawing the districts, ignored the students' wishes and split the student vote into two districts, including one moderate district that the progressives hoped to capture. This strategy was analogous to what the national Democrats did to racial minority opportunity districts in the 2001 redistricting—unpack them as a way of making the surrounding districts more Democratic. Again, this vividly illustrates one of the many paradoxes, the zero-sum nature, of redistricting—you can draw a district to empower a certain geographic minority group that feels shut out, whether students or racial minorities, but at the cost of draining their influence from surrounding districts, and possibly electing more representatives actually hostile to the minority group's broader interests. Charles Burress, "Bitter Fight for Berkeley Council Turf," *San Francisco Chronicle*, October 6, 2001.

44. Some judges, academics, and politicians, most of them white and/or Republicans, have argued that, to quote Justice Anthony Kennedy, "the assumption that . . . majority-white districts elect only white representatives, is false as an empirical matter." Unfortunately, such statements are a complete distortion of the overall picture. While it is true that several high-profile black politicians have been elected from majority-white electorates, it is also true that it happens infrequently. For instance, just to cite a few statistics, over a quarter of the U.S. population is black or Latino, but these groups are in the minority in every state and hold exactly zero out of a hundred U.S. Senate or fifty governor's seats. Until the close of the 1990s, no Latino had ever been elected to Congress in a majority-white district (See Susie Gonzalez, "Latino Leaders Foresee Power Shift," *San Antonio Express-News*, May 22, 1999), and no black had been elected from a white-majority district in the South. In the 6,667 House elections in white-majority districts between 1966 (the first election after the passage of the Voting Rights Act) and 1996 (including special elections), only thirty-five (0.52 percent) were won by blacks. Furthermore, a book called *Quiet Revolution in the South* showed that Southern cities with mixed election systems—with both plurality at-large and single-seat districts drawn to elect black representatives—provided an ideal test for the value of racial districts: in Southern cities whose black population was 30 to 50 percent, black candidates won 41 percent of the district seats but only 4 percent of the at-large ones. In cities with 10 to 30 percent black population, blacks won 23 percent of districted seats but only 2 percent of the at-large ones. In Alabama, Mississippi, and South Carolina, no black official has been elected to a city council by a plurality at-large scheme in any majority-white city. Thus, for most black voters in the South living in hundreds of majority-white legislative districts dotting the formerly Confederate landscape, it has been still the same old story—racially polarized voting in a Winner Take All system that renders their votes near meaningless. See Chandler Davidson and Bernard Grofman, eds., *Quiet Revolution in the South* (Princeton, NJ: Princeton University Press, 1994).

45. Videotaped interview at "Race, Reapportionment and Redistricting" conference, Minneapolis, Minnesota, November 1997.

46. Source: Federal Elections Commission report, *"Median Activity in Close House Races: House Districts where Winners Received 55% of the Vote or Less, 1992-2000,"* published on the Web at http://www.fec.gov/press/hseclose3000.htm.

47. One horizon to keep in mind is that a lot more soft money—money raised and spent by the political parties, rather than by the candidates themselves—is being spent in competitive races now, making it harder to know just how much money is spent on those races. For one special election in Virginia in the summer of 2001, approximately $5 million in soft money was spent on one race. Meanwhile, for races that are foregone conclusions, hardly any soft money from political parties gets spent.

48. "Sacramento for Sale," report by California PIRG, http://calpirg.org. Press release from the Center for Responsive Politics dated November 8, 2000, see www.opensecrets.org.

49. Janet Hook, "Handful of Seats Could Sway Battle over House," *Los Angeles Times,* January 17, 2000, p. A1.

50. Videotaped interview at "Race, Reapportionment and Redistricting" conference, Minneapolis, Minnesota, November 1997.

51. Mike Allen, "House GOP Goes Within for Money," *Washington Post*, Wednesday, June 14, 2000, p. A01.

52. Jim VandeHei and Tim Curran, "Parties Pushing for Early Money: DeLay Plans to Distribute $1M to 10 Members," *Roll Call*, Wednesday, June 16, 1999.

53. Louis Freedberg, "Pelosi Raises $3 Million for Democrats," *San Francisco Chronicle*, October 14, 2000, p. A1. For her efforts, Pelosi first was rewarded with the powerful post of ranking Democrat on the House Permanent Select Committee on Intelligence; later, she was elected by her Democratic House colleagues as the party's House whip, second in command, the first time in history a woman has held this powerful post.

54. Janet Hook, "A Kennedy Pursues Money Side of the Family Business," *Los Angeles Times,* July 3, 2000, p.1.

55. Source: Federal Elections Commission report, *"Median House Campaign Receipts by Type of Campaign: Median Activity of House Candidates: 1992-2000,"* published on the Web at http://www.fec.gov/press/hsemed3000.htm

56. In Maine's first publicly financed elections in 2000, for example, there was a 40 percent increase in contested primaries, and 118 of 392 legislative candidates ran with public financing. Sixty-two of these eventually won the seat, but most were from safe seats and would have won their races regardless of the origins of their funding (though at least two victories in Maine, that of Deborrah Simpson, a waitress and single mom who had never run for office, and sixty-eight-year-old Marilyn Canavan, can be attributed to public financing allowing an independent-minded candidate to knock off the anointed candidates of both parties). That translates into a dramatic increase in political dialogue where before there only had been monologue, a significant altering of Maine's primary landscape. See Jim Hightower, "Elections Coming Clean?" *The Hightower Lowdown*, December 22, 2000; and Nick Nyhart, press release written for Public Campaign, December 6, 2000.

57. While Bush and Gore nervously anticipated election results on November 8 in a bizarre waiting game that had no precedent, President Clinton issued this statement about "every vote counting" from the White House lawn. Jonathan Alter, pontificating in *Newsweek*, declared "for years to come, when the cynics start asking why anyone would bother to vote, the answer will be clear: because any one vote can make all the difference." See Jonathan Alter, "36 Days: The Fallout," *Newsweek*, Dec. 25, 2000, p. 56.

Chapter Seven: Worse Than Winner Take All

1. Douglas Waller, "Senator No," *Time*, May 29, 2000.

2. David S. Broder, "Jesse Helms, White Racist," *Washington Post*, August 29, 2001, p. A21.

3. Frances E. Lee and Bruce I. Oppenheimer, *Sizing Up the Senate* (Chicago: University of Chicago Press, 1999), p. 2.

4. Michael Lind, "75 Stars: How to Restore Democracy in the U.S. Senate (and End the Tyranny of Wyoming)," *Mother Jones,* January/February 1998, p. 46.

5. Daniel Lazare, "Senatorial Privilege," *The American Prospect*, September 24–October 2, 2000.

6. Robert Dahl, *A Democratic Critique of the American Constitution*, from the original manuscript, Chapter 3, p. 6, which has since been published under the title *How Deomcratic Is the American Constitution?* (New Haven, CT: Yale University Press, 2002).

7. Lee and Oppenheimer, *Sizing Up the Senate*.

8. Bruce Oppenheimer, "Hype Aside, All Senate Races Are Created Equal," *Christian Science Monitor*, December 30, 1999.

9. Lee and Oppenheimer, *Sizing Up the Senate*, p. 221.

10. Oppenheimer, "Hype Aside, All Senate Races Are Created Equal."

11. Lee and Oppenheimer, *Sizing Up the Senate*, pp. 4–5.

12. Lazare, "Senatorial Privilege."

13. Lee and Oppenheimer, *Sizing Up the Senate*, pp. 118–120.

14. Lind, "75 Stars," p. 47.

15. Alan Ehrenhalt, "Hijacking the Rulebook," *New York Times,* editorial section, Sunday, December 20, 1998; quoted in Greil Marcus, "The Man from Nowhere," *San Francisco Examiner Magazine*, May 28, 2000, p. 9.

16. John Lancaster, "Campaign Bill Unearths a Senate Relic: Debate," *Washington Post,* March 23, 2001, p. A1.

17. Lind, "75 Stars," p. 47.

18. Tom Geoghegan, "The Infernal Senate," *New Republic*, November 21, 1994, pp. 17–23.

19. Lind, "75 Stars," p. 47.

20. Dahl, *A Democratic Critique of the American Constitution*. This chapter owes a great debt to Dahl's original manuscript, which has since been published under the title *How Deomcratic Is the American Constitution?* (New Haven, CT: Yale University Press, 2002).

21. Ibid., from the original manuscript, Chapter 2, p. 6.

22. Ibid., from the original manuscript, Chapter 3, p. 9.

23. Lind, "75 Stars," p. 47.

24. Dahl, *A Democratic Critique of the American Constitution*, from the original manuscript, Chapter 2, p. 9.

25. Barry R. Weingast, "Political Stability and Civil War: Institutions, Commitment, and American Democracy," in Robert H. Bates, Avner Greif, Margaret Levi, Jean-Laurent Rosenthal, and Barry R. Weingast, eds., *Analytical Narratives* (Princeton, NJ: Princeton University Press, 1988), pp. 148–193.

26. Dahl, *A Democratic Critique of the American Constitution*, from the original manuscript, Chapter 3, p. 9.

27. Ibid., from the original manuscript, Chapter 2, p. 24.

28. Ibid., from the original manuscript, Chapter 4, p. 1.

29. From *Federalist* No. 68, written by Hamilton, quoted in Dahl, *A Democratic Critique of the American Constitution*, from the original manuscript, Chapter 4, p. 3.

30. Dahl, *A Democratic Critique of the American Constitution*, from the original manuscript, Chapter 4, p. 4.

31. Ibid., from the original manuscript, Chapter 2, p. 24.

32. Ibid., from the original manuscript, Chapter 4, pp. 5–6.

33. See the report "Overview: Plurality Wins in Major American Elections, 1992–1998," by the Center for Voting and Democracy, www.fairvote.org/plurality/collection1.htm. Interestingly, from 1992 to 1996 more U.S. Senate seats were won by plurality than had occurred since the 1930s. A relatively high number of governors were elected by plurality as well: of fifty sitting governors, twenty-two won a plurality victory in the 1990s, including fifteen (30%) in one of their general elections. Some governors won more than one election by plurality; Governor Christine Todd Whitman of New Jersey had three plurality victories in her two primary and two general election gubernatorial wins. Moreover, analyzing the election returns, it is clear that the winner of several important races would have changed with the use of a majority voting system, as used in most presidential races around the world.

34. See "Why Don't We Vote," essay contest at the Web site of the Center for Voting and Democracy, www.fairvote.org/contest.

35. Lazare, "Senatorial Privilege."
36. Lind, "75 Stars," p. 48.

Chapter Eight: Of Pollster-geists and Consultants

1. Quoted in Susan B. Glasser, "Hired Guns Fuel Fund-Raising Race," *Washington Post*, April 30, 2000, p. A1.
2. Although apparently not everyone observed the "rum custom." James Madison, it has been said, failed to win reelection to the Virginia legislature early in his political career because he refused to treat the voters with the customary rum punch. See Robert A. Dahl, *A Democratic Critique of the American Constitution*, (New Haven, CT: Yale University Press, 2002), from the original manuscript, Chapter 2, p. 19.
3. Michael Schudson, "A Look at . . . Political Disconnect. Voting: An Overrated Test of Good Citizenship?" *Washington Post*, September 13, 1998, p. C3. Also see Schudson's *The Good Citizen: A History of American Civic Life* (Cambridge, MA: Harvard University Press, 1999).
4. Michael Schudson, "A Look at . . . Political Disconnect," p. C3.
5. Doris Kearns Goodwin, "Every Four Years: Presidential Campaigns and the Press, 1896–2000," presented on the Web site of Newseum, www.newseum.org/everyfouryears/index.htm.
6. Jules Witcover, *No Way to Pick a President* (New York: Routledge, 2001); from the Introduction.
7. Goodwin, "Every Four Years: Presidential Campaigns and the Press, 1896–2000."
8. Douglas Frantz, "Plenty of Dirty Jobs in Politics and a New Breed of Diggers," *New York Times*, July 6, 1999, p. A1.
9. The *New York Times* article reports that the list of prominent politicians and political consultants who have employed private spies for so-called "opposition research" include President Clinton, Republican presidential consultant Ed Rollins, Senator Edward M. Kennedy, Rep. Henry J. Hyde (chair of the House Judiciary Committee), the former Mayor of New York David N. Dinkins, U.S. Senator Jon Corzine, and even aspirants for local city councils. The case of Democratic U.S. Senator Jon Corzine deserves special note. Corzine, a multimillionaire who self-financed his candidacy to the tune of $60 million and shattered all spending records for a single office with the exception of the presidential race, paid at least $200,000 to lawyer Stanley Arkin to have private investigators conduct an inquiry into Jim Florio, Corzine's opponent in the *Democratic* primary for U.S. Senate, and members of Florio's campaign staff. Florio expressed outrage at what he called an invasion of privacy. Nevertheless, Corzine won the primary and eventually the November election. David Kocieniewski, "Corzine Admits Paying Lawyer Who Had Private Investigators Check Out Florio," *New York Times*, May 31, 2000.
10. John F. Persinos, "Gotcha! Why Opposition Research Is Becoming More Important and How It Is Changing Campaigns," *Campaigns and Elections* (August 1994), p. 20. Also see Dennis W. Johnson, *No Place for Amateurs* (New York: Routledge, 2001), pp. 79–80. The Republican opposition research teams looking for dirt on Clinton dispatched operatives to Little Rock, where they amassed thirty file drawers of state papers, bought microfilms of the Little Rock and Pine Bluff newspapers for the past twenty years, and subscribed to every daily and weekly newspaper. Academics friendly to conservative causes obtained hundreds of hours of Clinton from C-SPAN, on the pretext that they needed the videotapes for scholarly research.
11. The *New York Times* researched and documented a case that perhaps best demonstrates the power of private investigators—the runoff for Houston mayor in 1991 between Bob Lanier, a millionaire businessman, and Sylvester Turner, a Harvard-educated lawyer and State Representative. Six days before the election, Houston's ABC affiliate broadcast a report questioning whether Mr. Turner had a role in an insurance scam in which a former law client had faked drowning. It said Mr. Turner had drawn up the man's will shortly before he disappeared and had been involved in efforts to collect his insurance money. Pollsters from the University of Houston interviewing voters the night the story was broadcast watched Mr. Turner's numbers plunge. Until then, the race had been close, but Mr. Turner never recovered and lost by an eight-point margin. Mr. Turner blamed Mr. Lanier for the report, an accusation that the campaign and the TV station vehemently denied. Mr. Turner later sued the station and its investigative reporter for libel, and in trial in 1996 the link between the Lanier campaign and the broadcaster was finally discovered. A private investigator on Mr. Lanier's campaign finance committee

had delivered a one-page summary of the accusations to the reporter and arranged for him to receive court files about the faked death, according to testimony. After the election, the investigator and a second detective who also played a role in providing the story to the TV station received a multimillion-dollar contract from the Lanier administration to collect overdue parking fines. Douglas Frantz, "Plenty of Dirty Jobs in Politics and a New Breed of Diggers," *New York Times*, July 6, 1999, p. A12.

12. For instance, the fight to ratify the Constitution in 1787–1788 was at times nasty and divisive. See William Riker, "Why Negative Campaigning Is Rational: The Rhetoric of the Ratification Campaigns of 1787–1788" paper delivered at the annual meeting of the American Political Science Association, Atlanta, August 1989, cited in Darrell M. West, *Air Wars: Television Advertising Election in Campaigns, 1952–1992* (Washington, DC: Congressional Quarterly, 1993), p. 47, n. 39.

13. Of course, Flynt confined his outrage to conservatives, an "eye for an eye" in the ongoing "Sex Wars." Flynt and his ilk never squawked about, for instance, when Democrats and liberal groups launched an attack against Republican Supreme Court nominee Robert Bork, to the point of investigating his video-rental records. See Dick Polman, "Americans Who Distrust the System Know More Than Clinton Is on Trial," *Philadelphia Inquirer*, December 27, 1998.

14. Mark Shields, "GOP Chastity Belt," *Washington Post,* January 13, 1999, p. A23. In Utah, the Attorney General sent affidavits to each of the Senators and House members requesting that they voluntarily sign an oath proclaiming their marital fidelity. All five legislators refused to sign, but then nonetheless publicly declared that they have been faithful in their marriages. Thus, the mere act of demanding that they sign on the line caused them to capitulate to the puritanical bullying.

15. Naftali Bendavid, "New Twist: Candidates Seek Dirt on Themselves," *Chicago Tribune* story published in the *San Francisco Examiner,* October 5, 1999, p. A1.

16. See Lorraine Adams, "The Script of Scandal," *Washington Post Magazine,* August 9, 1998, p. 12; and Michael Isikoff, *Uncovering Clinton: A Reporter's Story* (New York: Crown Publishers, 1999), pp. 32–33.

17. Bendavid, "New Twist," p. A14.

18. Quoted in Marshall Ganz, "Voters in the Crosshairs," *American Prospect,* December 1, 1994.

19. Robert Gunnison, "'Truth' And Political Advertising," *San Francisco Chronicle,* August 23, 1998.

20. David S. Broder, "Jerry Ford's Sense," *Washington Post,* June 16, 1999, p. A37.

21. Bill McAllister, "Consultants' Ethics: Politics Survey Finds Attitude of 'Don't Blame Us,'" *Washington Post,* June 18, 1998, p. C2.

22. Many years ago, when campaigns were relatively simple affairs, campaign managers and consultants learned the tricks of their trade as apprentices: they rolled up their sleeves and plunged into the nitty-gritty of actual campaigns. It was hard, gritty work, and you learned by doing. Today, universities offer advanced professional degrees in the "campaigning arts and sciences." Suffolk University in Boston offers a master's degree with course offerings on public opinion polling, speech writing, lobbying, and working in political campaigns, and places advertisements in respected political journals with headlines like "Elect to Make Politics Your Career" (see *The Nation*, and the advertisement placed in the October 16, 2000, issue). George Washington University now has an entire Graduate School of Political Management. At these "places of higher learning," the "political career-minded" can learn the basic Winner Take All tools needed to slice up the electorate into manageable bites and to target carefully crafted campaign spin to the right audiences—swing voters.

23. In 1976 evolutionary biologist Richard Dawkins formulated the notion of *memes* (rhymes with 'seems') as cultural ideas or "packets" that spread and reproduce themselves spontaneously, passed on from person to person almost like a "contagious idea." These memes function the same way genes and viruses do, propagating through communication networks and face-to-face contact between people. Derived from a Greek root meaning "to imitate," *meme* describes how ideas mimic the behavior of genes, propagating not from body to body, Dawkins wrote, but "by leaping from brain to brain." Meme is the root of the word "memetics," a field of study which postulates that the meme is the basic unit of cultural evolution. Other examples of memes include melodies, icons, fashion statements, phrases, scientific hypotheses, slang words, TV commercials, conspiracy theories, and the like. For more about memes, see Wired Magazine, "Idees Fortes," February 1998, and Richard Dawkins, *The Selfish Gene* (Oxford: Oxford University Press, 1990). A political meme, then, would be those behaviors and strategies which propagate because they *work*—they prove successful at winning campaigns and

quickly spread throughout the industry, embedding themselves into the broader political milieu.

24. Howard Kurtz, "Attack Ads Carpet TV," *Washington Post,* October 20, 1998, p. A1.

25. Ibid.

26. Daniel S. Greenberg, "Why Voters Should Just Say No to the Plague of Political Polling," *Chicago Tribune,* October 24, 1990, p. 19.

27. The sections of this chapter describing campaign technologies owe a great debt to former-political-consultant-turned-academic Dennis W. Johnson's *No Place for Amateurs.*

28. Bullet polls, according to Dennis Johnson, use automated voicemail systems that give the person answering the telephone a short record message: "In the election for senator next month, there are two candidates, George Shrub the Republican, and Alice Gore the Democrat. Press 1 if you are for George Shrub, press 2 if you are for Alice Gore." Bullet polls are relatively cheap, since automation replaces human beings, and they are "bulletlike" in speed, since answers can be tabulated and reported within hours. When human beings are used, the phone calling often is subcontracted to phone bank firms who specialize in advanced technologies that can produce instant information.

29. Johnson, *No Place for Amateurs,* p. 91.

30. Arianna Huffington, "News Polls Are In: 100% Shameless," syndicated columnist, www.OverthrowTheGov.com, February 12, 2001.

31. Paul Bedard, "Living, Dying by the Polls; Numbers Do Lie, Clinton Finds Out," *Washington Times,* April 30, 1993, p. A1; also see Johnson, *No Place for Amateurs,* p. 89.

32. Transcript, *60 Minutes,* CBS Television, December 13, 1998.

33. Frank Luntz, "Voices of Victory, Part II: The Makings of a Good Focus Group," *The Polling Report,* May 30, 1994. Luntz has served as a consultant to the U.S. House Republican leadership, to the Dole presidential campaign, to New York Mayor Rudolph Giuliani, and to numerous candidates in the United States and abroad.

34. Ibid.

35. "The focus group concept is about 50 years old," political consultant Frank Luntz has written, "and like many modern innovations, its roots date back to World War II. A group of sociologists were asked to investigate how the military's propaganda films were being received by their audiences. They learned that, with proper prodding, people can identify the exact reason certain scenes, lines, or phrases make them think or act in a certain way. The consumer culture was next to use focus group technology, turning to academically trained market researchers to determine everything from packaging and pricing to advertising and marketing." Politics was not long to follow. Frank Luntz, "Voices of Victory, Part I: Focus Group Research in American Politics," *The Polling Report,* May 16, 1994.

36. Johnson, *No Place for Amateurs.*

37. Frank Luntz, "Voices of Victory, Part I."

38. Frank Luntz, "Voices of Victory, Part II."

39. Johnson, *No Place for Amateurs,* pp. 104–105.

40. See Johnson, *No Place for Amateurs,* pp. 104–105. The Paramus focus groups have been widely cited, including in Roger Simon, *Roadshow: In America Anyone Can Become President, It's One of the Risks We Take* (New York: Farrar, Straus and Giroux, 1990), pp. 214–217; and Myron Levine, *Presidential Campaigns and Elections: Issues, Images and Partisanship* (Itasca, IL: Peacock Publishers, 1995), pp. 200–203.

41. Johnson, *No Place for Amateurs,* pp. 105–106. Also see Jacob Weissberg, "The Conformist: Republican Pollster Frank Luntz," *New York Magazine,* January 9, 1995, p. 16. Luntz was formally reprimanded by the American Association for Public Opinion Research (AAPOR) in 1997 for refusing to disclose the wording of poll questions and other details of his surveys conducted for the 1994 "Contract with America." The AAPOR, the nation's leading professional polling association, holds that researchers must disclose, or make available for public disclosure, the wording of questions and other methodological details. Luntz, not a member of the AAPOR, defended himself by saying he was only protecting the confidentiality of his client. *Campaign Insider,* April 30, 1997, p. 1.

42. Former spin-meister David Gergen, who practiced his craft for both Reagan and Clinton, later offered his *mea culpa* in his book *Eyewitness to Power* (New York: Simon and Schuster, 2000) for advancing "spin," which he admitted with deep regret "has become a polite way of saying lies."

43. Johnson, *No Place for Amateurs,* p. 109–111.

44. This story was recounted by Goodwin, "Every Four Years."
45. Miles Benson, "Politicians Find U.S. Public Easy to Manipulate," Newhouse News Service, story published in the *San Francisco Examiner,* October 24, 1999, p. A 12.
46. Steven E. Schier, "Why Campaigns Are Now Like Target Practice," *Washington Post,* Outlook section, October 24, 1999, p. B2.
47. Linda Leigh Kade, director of the Political Communication Center, quoted in Aron Epstein, "Technology Increasingly Mixes Up Political Candidates' Images, Reality," *Austin American-Statesman,* October 27, 1996, p. A17.
48. Richard Harwood, "All-Pro Politics," *Washington Post,* March 23, 1996, p. A15.
49. Johnson, *No Place for Amateurs,* p. 152, which quotes the American List Counsel catalogue, "The Only Mailing List Catalogue You Need," 1996.
50. Ad placed by Response Unlimited and the Rich List Company of Leslie Mandel Enterprises, *Campaigns and Elections,* January 1992, pp. 30–31, quoted in Johnson, *No Place for Amateurs,* p. 152.
51. Marshall Ganz, "Voters in the Crosshairs," *The American Prospect,* December 1, 1994.
52. Advertisement taken from their Web site at www.Geovoter.com. Also see Robert Dreyfuss, "The Turnout Imperative," *The American Prospect,* 9(39) (July 1–August 1, 1998).
53. Hal Malchow, "The Targeting Revolution in Political Direct Contact," *Campaigns and Elections,* June 1997, p. 36, quoted in Johnson, *No Place for Amateurs,* p. 154.
54. Dwight Morris, "Staving Off Gantt," *PoliticsNow,* www.politicsnow.com, September 23, 1996.
55. Johnson, *No Place for Amateurs,* pp. 164–165.
56. Dreyfuss, "The Turnout Imperative."
57. Ann Devroy, "Push Becomes Shove in Political Polling with Negative Phone-Bank Tactics," *Washington Post,* February 13, 1996, p. A9.
58. Peter Sinton, "Taking Polling to Another Level," *San Francisco Chronicle,* October 28, 2000, p. B1.
59. Lawrence R. Jacobs and Robert Y. Shapiro, *Politicians Don't Pander: Political Manipulation and the Loss of Democratic Responsiveness* (Chicago: University of Chicago Press, 2000).
60. Dreyfuss, "The Turnout Imperative."
61. Robert Cohen, "As-Yet Undecided Voters Will Probably Pick the President," Newhouse News Service story published in the *San Francisco Examiner,* October 31, 2000.
62. Wolfinger found that active precincts increased voter turnout in New Haven by as much as 10 percent. Ray Wolfinger's work cited in Ganz, "Voters in the Crosshairs."
63. Thomas Patterson, "Voters Cared about Outcome, but Didn't Care for the Process," commentary from the director of the Vanishing Voter Project, published in the *San Francisco Chronicle,* November 12, 2000.
64. Miles Benson, "Politicians Find U.S. Public Easy to Manipulate," Newhouse News Service, story published in the *San Francisco Examiner,* October 24, 1999, p. A 12.
65. Ganz, "Voters in the Crosshairs."
66. William Greider, "Stupefied Democracy," *The Nation,* December 4, 2000.
67. Arthur Miller, "American Playhouse: On Politics and the Art of Acting," *Harper's,* June 2001.

Chapter Nine: The Wizards behind the Curtain

1. Jonathan G. S. Koppell, "In Postmodern Politics, Style Is Substance," *Los Angeles Times,* October 30, 2000, p. B7.
2. Dennis W. Johnson, *No Place for Amateurs* (New York: Routledge, 2001), p. 110.
3. Koppell, "In Postmodern Politics, Style Is Substance," p. B7.
4. Steven E. Schier, "Why Campaigns Are Now Like Target Practice," *Washington Post,* Outlook section, October 24, 1999, p. B2.
5. Godfrey Sperling, "Election vs. Polls: There's a Difference," *Christian Science Monitor,* March 2, 1999.
6. Frank Luntz, "Voices of Victory, Part I: Focus Group Research in American Politics," *The Polling Report,* May 16, 1994.
7. Schier, "Why Campaigns Are Now Like Target Practice," p. B2.
8. Walter Shapiro, "Liberal Dose of History Shows Little Left of Old Party," *USA Today,* August 15, 2000, p. 11A.

9. Leon Panetta, Clinton's White House Chief of Staff, as well as Labor Secretary Robert Reich, constantly found themselves in battles with Clinton's consultant Dick Morris and pollster Mark Penn over how Clinton should frame certain issues. Both Panetta and Reich eventually resigned, and Panetta warned about the dangers when consultants cross the line between offering election advice to advising on policy. Consultants advise against risk, said Panetta, "but the real leaders have to take risks. And so, when you look at Congress and they aren't going to take on issues, whether its the budget, tobacco, campaign reform, a dozen other issues hanging out there, that's when the public is concerned that maybe this process is beginning to impact on the quality of leadership." John Jacobs, "How Consultants Are Driving Voters out of the Booth," *Sacramento Bee,* January 2, 2000.

10. Quoted in Howard Kurtz, "Making the Gingrich Connection," *Washington Post,* September 26, 2000.

11. John F. Harris and Ceci Connolly, "Gore Shaking Off Clinton's Strategy," *Washington Post,* August 24, 2000, p. A1.

12. Frank Rich, "Survival of the Fakest," *New York Times,* August 26, 2000.

13. Perhaps the essential difference between the two parties today was on display at their respective conventions: at the Democratic convention, the politerati and glitterati partied at the Hollywood star-studded Spago and Armani in Beverly Hills, while at the Republican convention in Philadelphia, instead of partying with celebs the GOP hosted fat-cat golf outings with right-wing Congressman Tom DeLay as the MC. Hollywood or irons and woods, take your pick.

14. Thomas Hargrove, "Bush Steals Weapon from Clinton Arsenal," *San Francisco Examiner,* July 31, 2000.

15. David Broder, "Analysis: Challenging Democrats on Their Turf," *Washington Post,* August 4, 2000, p. A1.

16. James Dao, "In Michigan, A Swing State, Bush Picks Words Carefully," *New York Times,* October 27, 2000.

17. The Republicans in Congress also attempted their own version of triangulation in the months leading up to election 2000. GOP legislative initiatives were focused on introducing bills designed to blunt political attacks by adopting popular Democratic issues and reframing them in Republican terms. On one issue after another, including minimum wage, gun control, managed care reform, and prescription drugs, GOP leaders aggressively sought to neutralize the Democrats' top legislative priorities before the November elections. But House Minority Leader Richard A. Gephardt (D-MO) accused Republicans of conducting a "David Copperfield Congress," in which they voice their support for popular issues without visible action. "I think they are heavy into illusion," he said. See Juliet Eilperin, "Election Realities Spur Drug Benefit Plan from House GOP," *Washington Post,* April 26, 2000, p. A1.

18. Alison Mitchell, "Treading on Rival's Turf, Bush Takes a Page from Clinton's Book," New York Times Service, published in the *International Herald Tribune,* April 19, 2000, p. 3.

19. As the *New York Times'* Frank Rich pointed out, Bush's Republican Party "opposes affirmative action even as he benefited from the affirmative action given to 'legacies' (the children of alumni) at Ivy League schools." Rich, "Survival of the Fakest."

20. As *Time* pointed out, the myth of Midland was wholly manipulated by Bush's mythmakers, using the favorite vehicle of the thirty-second TV spot. In actual fact the Midland of Bush's childhood was prosperous for a few white people and legally segregated. Even now, wrote *Time,* "it's easy to find pockets of good old-fashioned racism, even among old Bush family friends some of whom on a recent trip were loose with their language." For an interesting profile of the slick marketing of George W. Bush by his handlers, see James Carney and John F. Dickerson, "The Selling of George Bush," *Time,* July 24, 2000, p. 30.

21. As Brent Staples pointed out in the *New York Times,* the 2000 Republican convention in Philadelphia was whiter even than the Republican convention of 1912, when 6 percent of the delegates were black. Brent Staples, "The Republican Party's Exercise in Minstrelsy," *New York Times,* August 2, 2000.

22. Ibid.

23. Allison Mitchell, "Man in the News: The 43rd President—George Walker Bush," *New York Times,* December 14, 2000, p. A1.

24. Alison Mitchell, "Bowing to the Middle, Keeping to the Right," *New York Times,* August 5, 2000.

25. Jake Tapper, "How Dubyah Got His Groove Back," www.Salon.com, February 10, 2000.

26. James Carney and John F. Dickerson, "Behind the Rhetoric: Polling for the Perfect Pitch," *Time*, October 2, 2000.

27. Mary McGrory, "Loved It, Dubya," *Washington Post*, August 6, 2000, p. B1.

28. William Safire, "Forbes' Fortune Makes Him Bush's Immediate Worry; But McCain Is the Realistic Alternative," *New York Times*, October 21, 1999.

29. Terry Neal, "A Positive Plan for Convention," *Washington Post*, June 9, 2000.

30. Adam Clymer, "Campaigns' Strategies: Negative vs. Negative," *New York Times*, August 2, 2000.

31. Nancy Gibbs, "How the Bush Campaign Lost Its Edge," www.Time.com, September 11, 2000.

32. Dana Milbank, "The Evolved Panderer Is a Breed Apart," *Washington Post*, July 17, 2000, p. C1.

33. Tapper, "How Dubyah Got His Groove Back."

34. Kevin Merida, "A Politician's Perfect Example," *Washington Post*, October 10, 2000, p. C1.

35. As late as the day before the first anti-Gore ad appeared in September, keeping to the previous script, Bush had said on CNN, "I think you can win a campaign without personally attacking an opponent." By the next day, with his lead plummeted largely because female voters who had been flirting with a Bush vote had carpooled home to the Democrats, Bush dropped the "positive tone" like a lead zeppelin and mounted a relentless attack on Gore's character.

36. Jonathan Alter, "Bush Throws a Hail Mary Pass," *Newsweek*, September 11, 2000.

37. Carney and Dickerson, "Behind the Rhetoric."

38. Rich, "Survival of the Fakest." The ever-witty Rich, comparing the dreary presidential conventions to the TV season finale of *Survivor*, wrote: "Through a weird cultural reversal, America is now a place where there's more spontaneity and 'reality' in a prime-time network entertainment series than there is in the TV spectacles staged by our political parties over supposedly momentous issues of public policy." Observing that neither of the party's nominating conventions on their best nights drew close to half the audience of *Survivor*, Rich further commented that "the audience that cast its vote by Nielsen isn't stupid. It does prize authenticity over canned showmanship. And with John McCain long out of the race, authenticity isn't on the ballot. As that minority of Americans paying attention knows, the choice this year is between two distinctive brands of inauthenticity."

39. Arthur Miller, "American Playhouse, On Politics and the Art of Acting," *Harper's Magazine*, June 2001. *Harper's* printed the transcript of a speech given by Miller, who was invited by the National Endowment for the Humanities to deliver the 30th Jefferson Lecture in the Humanities, March 26, 2001. The Jefferson Lecture was established in 1972 as the highest honor the federal government bestows for distinguished intellectual and public achievement in the humanities.

40. Howard Kurtz, "Substance Surfaces on Campaign Trail," *Washington Post*, September 22, 2000.

41. Doris Kearns Goodwin, "Every Four Years: Presidential Campaigns and the Press, 1896–2000," presented on the Web site of Newseum, www.newseum.org/everyfouryears/index.htm.

42. The October 3 debate attracted a mere 47 million viewers, one of the smallest audiences in recent history. Nearly 10 million fewer people tuned in for the second and third debates, two of the smallest audiences since TV debates began in 1960. For comparison, the viewing audience for the October 1980 debate between Jimmy Carter and Ronald Reagan was 80.6 million.

43. Miller, "American Playhouse."

44. Interestingly, high-priced American political consultants have begun exporting their craft to other countries. The *New York Times Magazine* reported on the downward slide of Israeli politics since 1995 when Israel began using a Winner Take All method to directly elect its president. Political scientists argue endlessly about the pros and cons of parliamentary democracy versus presidential democracy, but certainly one of the downsides of the Winner Take All method is that it fosters endlessly negative campaigning—and such a posture is dangerous in the lethal brew of Israeli and Middle East politics. Not surprisingly, at the center of this transmogrification of Israeli campaigns was a cast of characters familiar to U.S. audiences—leading Democratic party consultants James Carville, Bob Shrum, and Stanley Greenberg all played central roles in crafting messages and developing ads for Labor Party candidate Ehud Barak, and Republican maestro Arthur Finkelstein plied his craft for Barak's opponent in 1999, prime minister Binyamin Netanyahu. These consultants exported to Israel their well-honed tactics of using negative campaigning and campaign technologies like the mass media, computer databases, polling, focus groups, photo ops, and marketing of their product—the candidate. See Adam Nagourney, "Sound Bites over Jerusalem," *New York Times Magazine*, April 25,

1999. But Israelis quickly tired of this tedious American game of mudslinging and after only three elections reverted back to their parliamentary system with its indirectly elected president. In the mid-1990s, Germany's Chancellor Gerhardt Schroeder and Britain's Tony Blair also employed U.S. consultants and modern media tactics to win their elections, and numerous commentators remarked on the resultant blandness and shallow sound bite nature of those campaigns. Mexico's presidential election in 2000 saw the PRI hire James Carville and PAN candidate and eventual winner Vicente Fox hire Dick Morris, both formerly Clinton consultants who became hired guns for opposite sides in Mexico (see Pilar Franco and Diego Cevallos, "Old Guard Called on to Rescue 'New PRI,'" InterPress Third World News Agency [IPS], May 3, 2000). Both Carville and Morris have advised other presidential candidates in Latin America, and Stanley Greenburg has advised in Austria (for an interesting article on the latter, see Roger Cohen, "Haiderism, Far from Moribund, Fuels Vienna's Election," New York Times Service, March 12, 2001). Italy's bungled political transformation to semi–Winner Take All received a rude awakening in their 2000 regional elections when the political campaigns turned uncharacteristically and relentlessly negative, à la the Americans. Nasty Winner Take All campaigns and the consultants who wage them, along with violent action movies, military armaments, McDonald's, and tobacco products, have become yet another one of America's most notorious exports about which the rest of the world is decidedly ambivalent. Yet apparently the techniques of Winner Take All campaigns are irresistible to candidates all over the world salivating to win.

Chapter Ten: The Winner Take All Media

1. Miller's vote combined with that of the Democratic Party's candidate amounted to 57 percent of the vote (17 percent plus 40 percent), yet the Republican candidate won this historically Democratic district with only 43 percent of the vote. In effect, the center-left vote had split itself, and Miller was accused of spoiling the race.
2. Information gathered from the national web site of the Libertarian Party, www.LP.org.
3. The Libertarian in the race, Jeff Jared, received about 65,000 votes, more than thirty-two times the spread between Cantwell and Gorton.
4. Cited in a report by the Electoral Reform Society called "State of American Democracy," 1999. See their Web site at www.electoral-reform.org.uk.
5. Mark Simon, "Feinstein Agrees to 2 Debates—Campbell Cries Foul," San Francisco Chronicle, October 14, 2000, p. A20.
6. Electoral Reform Society, "State of American Democracy."
7. Richard Cohen, "Bad-News Barons of the Media," Washington Post, September 28, 2000.
8. See the report, "Gouging Democracy: How The Television Industry Profiteered on Campaign 2000," a study by the Alliance for Better Campaigns (www.bettercampaigns.org), pp. 2–3. The study was based on a comparison of political advertising sales logs and rate cards at ten local television stations, an analysis of political advertising costs at all stations in the top seventy-five media markets in the country, and interviews with Democratic and Republican media buyers, television station ad sales managers and officials at the Federal Communications Commission.
9. "Gouging Democracy," p. 4.
10. Morgan, "A Made-for-TV Windfall," p. A1.
11. Quoted in The Political Standard, newsletter of the Alliance for Better Campaigns (www.bettercampaigns.org), 3(9) (December 2000), p. 2.
12. "Are Voluntary Standards Working? Candidate Discourse on Network Evening News Programs," a study by the Annenberg Public Policy Center of the University of Pennsylvania, www.appcpenn.org, December 20, 2000. Also see "Networks Skimped on Candidate, Issue Coverage during Campaign, Study Finds," The Political Standard, newsletter of the Alliance for Better Campaigns, 3(9) (December 2000), p. 1.
13. Gary Ruskin, "Disgusted by Politics on TV? Turn It Off," Fort Worth Star-Telegram, October 29, 2000.
14. Thomas Patterson, "Voters Cared about Outcome, but Didn't Care for the Process," San Francisco Chronicle, November 12, 2000.
15. Quoted in The Political Standard, newsletter of the Alliance for Better Campaigns, 3(9) (December 2000), p. 2.

16. Quoted in *The Political Standard,* newsletter of the Alliance for Better Campaigns, 3(7), (September 2000), p. 3.
17. "Gouging Democracy," p. 6.
18. Morgan, "A Made-for-TV Windfall," p. A1.
19. The explanation about the "Lowest Unit Charge" rates draws heavily from "Gouging Democracy."
20. "Gouging Democracy," p. 6.
21. Ibid., see the chart on p. 5.
22. Morgan, "A Made-for-TV Windfall," p. A1.
23. Cohen, "Bad-News Barons of the Media."
24. "Economic Self-Interest May Influence Newspapers' Free Air Time Editorials," *The Political Pulse,* newsletter of the Alliance for Better Campaigns (June 2000), p. 4; see also www.bettercampaigns.org.
25. Amazingly, one of the broadcasters who dedicated candidate-centered time was harassed and subjected to a lawsuit. A complaint was filed against Raleigh-based Capitol Broadcasting, claiming that the station's offer of dedicated time to gubernatorial candidates was an illegal corporate contribution to those campaigns. In the past, the Federal Election Commission has ruled that broadcasters' offers of free or dedicated time to candidates are not illegal contributions. Accordingly, this complaint was dismissed.
26. "Value of Public Airwaves Controlled by Broadcasters: $367 Billion, Analyst Says," *The Political Standard,* 4(3) (May 2001), p. 4; see also www.bettercampaigns.org.
27. Morgan, "A Made-for-TV Windfall."
28. It is instructive to recall the historical roots of the Winner Take All media. At the end of the nineteenth and beginning of the twentieth centuries, newspapers were predominantly mouthpieces of the wealthy ruling families that owned them. Names like the Ochs-Sulzbergers at the *New York Times*, the Otis-Chandlers at the *Los Angeles Times*, the DeYoungs at the *San Francisco Chronicle,* and William Randolph Hearst in New York, San Francisco and later all across the country, came to prominence during this period. In San Francisco, the rival *Chronicle* and *Call,* owned by adversarial local aristocracies, engaged in graft, bribery, even attempted murder, in an effort to create financial and real estate empires with the newspapers as their own propaganda mouthpieces that routinely savaged each other [for a fascinating discussion of the early wild-cat days of the San Francisco dailies and their ambitions for empire, see Gray Brechin's, *Imperial San Francisco* (Berkeley: University of California Press,1999), particularly the section called "The Thought Shapers"]. In this murky, rough-and-tumble world of the Great Free Press, William Randolph Hearst rose to be King of the Heap in the early twentieth century, eventually owning numerous dailies, magazines, wire services, radio stations, and newsreel and feature-film companies. Hearst, more than anyone else, pointed the way to the by-now familiar credo of modern media conglomerates: profitable and persuasive uses of communications technology, wrapped in the guise of entertainment and sensationalism. Much later, Henry Luce, whose media empire in the 1940s eventually included *Time, Fortune, Life,* and *Sports Illustrated,* like Hearst knew the value of news as a form of entertainment. His brand of "objectivity" revealed a staggering sense of proprietorship over what was to be considered "news." Journalists used to complain that the fiercely anti-Communist Luce totally rewrote dispatches from China in the 1940s to promote Nationalist leader Chiang Kai-shek. Luce joined with other media magnates to use their mouthpieces to turn a little-known Republican businessman, Wendell Willkie, into a "media star" of such magnitude that Wilkie pulled off a surprise coup by winning the Republican nomination for president. After the 1952 presidential campaign, in which Luce's *Time* magazine was blamed for attacking Democratic candidate Adlai Stevenson and glorifying Republican Dwight Eisenhower, Luce responded to his critics by unapologetically saying, "Stevenson was not right for the country . . . therefore it was *Time*'s duty to explain why the country needed Ike. Any other form of objectivity would have been unfair and uninvolved." Such directives defined the Luce brand of journalism, which sought to persuade at least as much as to inform. In Luce's hands the "free" press did not necessarily mean a "responsible" press.
29. Quoted in Doris Kearns Goodwin, "Every Four Years: Presidential Campaigns and the Press, 1896–2000," presented on the Web site of Newseum, www.newseum.org/everyfouryears/index.htm.
30. Mike McCurry, White House press secretary from 1995 to 1998, commenting on the vicious cycles of scandal said, "The reinforcing cycles of the Internet and cable television kept extending the shelf life of the story, turning it into a soap opera. We couldn't find the 'off' switch." *Newsweek* commented that

the great irony of the Clinton Administration was rooted in both the promise and the excess of the Information Age: Clinton successfully guided economic and regulatory policy in a direction that allowed the Internet and the New Economy to blossom, yet in the end the Internet's capacity for scandal-mongering contributed to his troubles. *Newsweek*, December 25, 2000/January 1, 2001, p. 60.

31. Sean M. Theriault and David W. Brady, "The Consequences of the Ideological Catfight," pages 1–2, 19–20, unpublished paper prepared for delivery at the 2000 annual meeting of the Western Political Science Association. Note that their results controlled for those factors that the political science literature suggests should lead to more coverage, such as powerful committee or party leadership positions.

32. Eric Brazil, "Micro-Radio No Small Battle," *San Francisco Examiner*, November 2, 2000, p. B1.

33. Dan Morgan, "A Made-for-TV Windfall," *Washington Post*, May 2, 2000, p. A1.

34. The *Wall Street Journal* reported in September 2000 that a yearlong study by the Federal Trade Commission (FTC) had concluded that the entertainment industry purposely marketed violent material to children and young adults. In what the *Journal* described as a "startling and remarkably detailed portrait of the entertainment industry's practices," the FTC report found that the music, movie, computer and video-game companies routinely promoted products that required parental warnings in venues where children were likely to see the ads. Moreover, they specifically targeted these ads "to children and teenagers for whom the firms admit such material may be inappropriate." For instance, the marketing plan for one violent film stated that "our goal was to find the elusive teen target audience and make sure everyone between the ages of 12–18 was exposed to the film." See Glenn R. Simpson and John Lippman, "Violence, Sex Marketed in Ads Targeting an Underage Audience, FTC Study Says," *Wall Street Journal*, September 11, 2000. Naturally, this provided great fodder for grandstanding politicians in an election year. But Sen. John McCain made a solid point when he said, "Defending these market practices does not defend art or free expression. It defends the bottom line of your corporations." Caroline Lochead, "Entertainment Leaders Spar with Senators," *San Francisco Chronicle*, September 14, 2000, p. A1.

35. The leading media analyst was Thomas Wolzien of the investment house Sanford C. Bernstein & Co. See "Value of Public Airwaves Controlled by Broadcasters: $367 Billion, Analyst Says," *The Political Standard*, 4(3) (May 2001), p. 4, published by the Alliance for Better Campaigns, www.bettercampaigns.org.

36. Robert H. Frank and Philip J. Cook, *The Winner Take All Society* (New York: The Free Press, 1995).

37. See Owen M. Fiss, *The Irony of Free Speech* (Cambridge, MA: Harvard University Press, 1996).

38. Ibid., p. A1.

39. The attempts to prevent media conglomerates from owning huge proportions of the nation's media resources and markets found an unaccustomed friend back in 1996 in arch-conservative Senator Jesse Helms. A little-known side note to the tragic story of the Telecommunications Act of 1996 is that Helms apparently was instrumental in preventing this bill from being worse than it turned out. According to one source, original drafts of the bill would have allowed a media conglomerate to own up to 50 percent of the nation's media. Helms, himself being a former executive of a local broadcasting company, Capitol Broadcasting in Durham, North Carolina, was sympathetic to the plight of "mom-and-pop" local broadcasters, which like family farmers were being swallowed up by corporate mergers and acquisitions. Helms, according to this source, understood that the Telecommunications Act was going to lead to the gobbling up of even more local broadcasters, and went to Senate Majority Leader Trent Lott and threatened to shut down the U.S. Senate if that 50 percent threshold wasn't reduced. Thus, the final Telecommunications Act came to include a much reduced but still-alarmingly high threshold of 35 percent.

40. Christopher Stern, "Media Companies Challenge FCC Ownership Rules," *Washington Post*, September 8, 2001, p. E1.

Chapter Eleven: Caught between a Poll and a Hard Focus Group

1. Arthur Miller, "American Playhouse, On Politics and the Art of Acting," *Harper's Magazine*, June 2001. Harper's printed the transcript of the speech given by Miller, who was invited by the National Endowment for the Humanities to deliver the 30th Jefferson Lecture in the Humanities, March 26, 2001.

2. John Wildermuth, "Less Fire This Time," *San Francisco Chronicle*, October 12, 2000.

3. Mary McGrory, "Voting 101: Ignored Youth Take a Pass," *San Francisco Examiner,* October 20, 2000, p. A-19.

4. Janny Scott, "Boom of 1990s Missed Many in Middle Class, Data Suggests," *New York Times,* August 13, 2001, p. A1.

5. "Household Debt and Delinquencies," a report of the Federal Reserve Bank of Cleveland, Research Department, published on the Web at www.clev.frb.org/research/Et97/0297/houdeb.htm.

6. A remarkable book, *Child Well-Being, Child Poverty and Child Policy in Modern Nations,* brought together economists, sociologists, and social policy analysts from America, Australia, and Europe, who have studied the extent of child poverty, its consequences for children, and the effectiveness of social policy in preventing child poverty. The approach of this volume is therefore multidisciplinary and international in scope. These researchers found, among other things, that a higher percentage of American children are growing up in poverty than those living in most European countries or Canada. Poverty-level jobs of their parents certainly lends itself to this disgraceful situation. The book puts American children living in poverty at 20.3 percent. This figure compares poorly with the following child-poverty rates in other nations: Sweden, 2.4 percent; Slovak Republic, 3.2 percent; Finland, 3.2 percent; Czech Republic, 3.4 percent; Norway, 3.9 percent; Luxembourg, 4.3 percent; Belgium, 5.1 percent; Austria, 5.3 percent; France, 5.6 percent; Switzerland, 6.4 percent; Netherlands, 7.0 percent; Germany, 8.7 percent; Hungary, 10.1 percent; Ireland, 12.4 percent; Spain, 12.4 percent; Poland, 12.7 percent; Canada, 14.7 percent; United Kingdom, 16.2 percent; and Italy, 19.5 percent. Among the major European countries, only Russia, at 23.2 percent has a higher percentage of children living in poverty than the United States. Within the U.S., both New York State, with 26.3 percent, and California, with 25.7 percent, have higher percentages of children living in poverty than Russia. See Koen Vleminckx and Timothy M Smeeding, *Child Well-Being, Child Poverty and Child Policy in Modern Nations* (Bristol, UK: The Policy Press, 2001).

7. Jeff Gates, *Democracy at Risk* (New York: Perseus Press, 2000).

8. See "Remarks by Chairman of the Board of Governors of the US Federal Reserve System, Mr. Alan Greenspan, at a symposium sponsored by the Federal Reserve Bank of Kansas City in Jackson Hole, Wyoming on August 28, 1998," Central Bank Articles and Speeches, *BIS Review,* July–September 1998, Bank for International Settlements, www.bis.org/review/r980904c.pdf. "The BIS is an international organization which fosters cooperation among central banks and other agencies in pursuit of monetary and financial stability."

9. Phil Bereano and Florian Kraus, "TransAtlantic Food Wars," *Seattle Times,* November 8, 1999.

10. Ibid.

11. The Web site of the Green Party of the United States (www.GreenPartyUS.org) says that the Green Party as of November 2001 had elected about 123 officeholders nationwide. Six Greens have been elected mayor in various California cities, including the mayor of Santa Monica, a city of 93,000 people. The Green Party also won its second majority on a city council in Sebastopol, California, and elected a Green to the San Francisco Board of Supervisors, two Greens to the Minneapolis City Council, one Green to New Haven's City Council, and reelected a Green City Councilor in Hartford, CT. In 2000, the Green Party more than doubled its number of candidates to 274, achieved ballot status in twenty-two states, and now has organized statewide chapters in thirty-five states. And of course, the Green Party and its presidential candidate, Ralph Nader, depending on who you talk to, either spoiled the election and helped elect George W. Bush (for instance, even one third of Nader's 97,488 votes in Florida or his 22,198 votes in New Hampshire would have tipped those states to Gore, either of which would have overturned the presidential election) or broke open the duopoly and showed how fragile our political system really is. Or both.

12. Mark Sandalow, "Politicians See No Need to Promote Urge to Conserve," *San Francisco Chronicle,* May 16, 2001, p. A1.

13. Joseph Kahn, "Core's Split on Energy Is Costly to Democrats," *New York Times,* August 3, 2001.

14. Sandalow, "Politicians See No Need to Promote Urge to Conserve," p. A1.

15. Amy Goldstein, "Ranks of Uninsured Americans Swelling," *Washington Post,* October 4, 1999, p. A1.

16. Ibid., p. A1.

17. Dale Russakoff, "Cut Out of Prosperity, Cutting Out at the Polls," *Washington Post,* October 24, 2000, p. A01,

18. Ibid., p. A01.

19. See Amy Hoak, "What Would It Take to Get Gen Y to Vote? Start by Listening," Medill News Service, October 16, 2000. Also see "Why Don't We Vote," essay contest at the Web site of the Center for Voting and Democracy, http://www.fairvote.org/contest/quotes.htm.

20. Lauren Sandler, "Political (De)Generation: MTV and America's Youth Vote," www.MediaChannel.org, October 27, 2000.

21. Youth voter turnout figures are from Curtis Gans of the Committee for the Study of the American Electorate. Voter turnout of eighteen- to nineteen-year-olds in the 1994 midterm elections was 14.5 percent, which means voter turnout among this demographic dropped an astounding 41 percent between 1994 and 1998. Voter News Service estimated that 38.6 percent of eighteen- to twenty-nine-year-olds made it to the polls in the 2000 election (see Wendy Sandoz, "GenY Voter Turnout Increased, Experts Say," Medill News Service, Wednesday, November 8, 2000). Typically, youth voter turnout drops by about 50 percent between a presidential election year and a nonpresidential (midterm) election year. According to a National Association of Secretaries of State study, youth electoral participation reveals a portrait of an increasingly disconnected and apathetic generation. Since the 1972 presidential election, when the voting age was lowered to eighteen, there has been almost a 20 percentage point decrease in voting among eighteen- to twenty-four-year-olds, with only 32 percent going to the polls in 1996, a presidential election year (see the press release from their Web site, www.nass.org, "State Secretaries Push Major Youth Voting Initiative, New Millennium Project: Why Young People Don't Vote").

22. Statistics for voter turnout by income brackets is from the Center for the Study of the American Electorate.

23. Sam Smith, "Why Third Parties Matter," The Progressive Review, www.prorev.com, November 1, 1999.

24. Ibid.

25. For a satirical glimpse of what such a candidate might look like, think of the movie Bulworth, starring Warren Beatty. Bulworth illustrated in a silly, spoofing way that even the most disenfranchised and disaffected inner-city voters might respond when they see a viable candidate singing their rap tune, in this case a half-crazed white guy dressed in faux-rap packaging a.k.a. U.S. Senator Jay Bulworth.

26. Mike Allen, "Minnesota's Ventura Tries to Lure a Maverick into the Presidential Race," New York Times, July 6, 1999, p. A17.

27. Maurice Duverger, Political Parties: Their Organization and Activity in the Modern State (New York: John Wiley, 1954), p. 217.

28. This information about ballot access laws was provided by Richard Winger, editor of Ballot Access News. Richard Winger is the foremost authority in the nation on the various and twisted legal maneuvers that Democrats and Republicans use to keep third-party and independent competition off the ballot. Richard has tirelessly worked to change unfair ballot access laws. For instance, the North Dakota law, which blatantly discriminated against third parties, was changed by Richard single-handedly by pressing the Secretary of State, who to his credit recognized the unreasonable nature of the law.

29. Richard Winger, "British Elections," Ballot Access News, June 1, 2001, p. 2.

30. Richard Winger, "Georgia Lawsuit," Ballot Access News, June 1, 2001, p. 2.

31. Eun-Kyung Kim, "Bleak Future for Third Parties," Associated Press, September 11, 2000.

32. Besides proportional representation, some of these "institutions of pluralism" include full public financing of elections, works councils elected at every job site, economic co-determination (boards of directors of large corporations are elected by stockholders AND employees), national referendums, and Children's Parliaments in schools (children and teen representatives are elected and convene to debate and propose legislation to their city councils). On the public broadcasting system, one can find children's channels, a varied menu of educational and cultural programs, and popular soap operas that purposefully integrate controversial issues like AIDS, immigration, gay relationships, impending elections and more into their scripts and characters. To reduce dependence on commercial television and to encourage newspaper reading, most European nations give special postal rates to newspapers and periodicals, and some subsidize newspapers, which has boosted national circulation figures. Henry Milner, Civic Literacy: How Informed Citizens Make Democracy Work (Hanover and London: University Press of New England, 2002), p. 108.

33. Uninformed critics of proportional representation voting systems like to stereotype it by saying that it leads to "dozens of small political parties" that cause collapsing governments. Yet the number of political parties is purely a function of the "victory threshold" used, which is chosen by those designing the electoral system. If you use a low victory threshold, where it only takes, say, 1 percent of the vote to win a legislative seat, you will likely see the "flowering effect" of numerous political parties. However, if you use a higher threshold like, for instance, the 5 percent threshold used by Germany, you will see what is called "moderate proportional representation," with approximately four to six political parties with any chance of winning seats, and two of these will be major parties (one liberal and one conservative) with two to four smaller parties that wax and wane in influence depending on the issues of the day. The victory threshold is established by the number of contested seats being elected from a multi-seat district, where all seats are set equal to the same numbers of votes. For example, if ten seats are being elected, each seat will be worth 10 percent of the vote. Winning 30 percent of the vote will gain three out of ten seats, 60 percent of the vote will gain six out of ten seats, and so on. What this suggests is that it is possible to *fine-tune* your democracy and decide how inclusive or exclusive you want it to be. If you want it to be extremely inclusive (and perhaps a bit fractious, with numerous parties that may not get along well) use a 1 percent threshold like Israel used for many years. If you want your democracy to be exclusive, with few parties and few choices for voters, use a U.S.- or British-style Winner Take All system, with victory thresholds of 60 percent or higher for most legislative races. But experience around the world suggests there is a happy medium, somewhere around Germany's 5 percent victory threshold.

34. From e-mail correspondence with Terry Bouricius, former Vermont state legislator elected from the Progressive Party.

Chapter Twelve: Winner Take All Policy

1. See Douglas H. Blair and Robert A. Pollak, "Rational Collective Choice," in *Readings in Public Sector Economics,* ed. Samuel Baker and Catherine Elliott (Lexington, MA: D.C. Heath and Company, 1990) p. 342. Blair and Pollak write, "the 'impossibility theorems' that began with Arrow's famous proposition define constraints on a society's choice of a rule for collective decision-making. The constraints are severe. Three widely shared objectives—collective rationality, decisiveness and equality of power—stand in irreconcilable conflict. If society foregoes collective rationality, thereby accepting the necessary arbitrariness and manipulability of irrational procedures, majority rule is likely to be the choice because it attains the remaining goals. If society insists on retaining a degree of collective rationality, it can achieve equality by adopting the rule of consensus, but only at the price of extreme indecisiveness. Society can increase decisiveness by concentrating veto power in progressively fewer hands; the most decisive rule, dictatorship, is also the least egalitarian."

2. Pam Karlan quoted in Robert Richie and Steven Hill, *Reflecting All of Us* (Boston: Beacon Press, 1999), p. 73.

3. Hotelling wrote in 1929, in a passage that still rings true today: "So general is this tendency that it appears in the most diverse fields of competitive activity, even quite apart from what is called economic life. In politics it is strikingly exemplified. The competition for votes between the Democratic and Republican parties does not lead to a clear drawing of issues, an adoption of two strongly contrasted positions between which the voter may choose. Instead, each party strives to make its platform as much like the other's as possible. . . . Each candidate 'pussyfoots,' replies ambiguously to questions, refuses to take a definite stand in any controversy for fear of losing votes. Real differences, if they ever exist, fade gradually with time though the issues may be just as important as ever. The Democratic party, once opposed to protective tariffs, moves gradually to a position almost, but not quite, identical with that of the Republicans. It need have no fear of fanatical free-traders, since they will still prefer it to the Republican party, and its advocacy of a continued high tariff will bring it the money and votes of some intermediate groups." Harold Hotelling, "Stability in Competition," *The Economic Journal,* 39(153) (March 1929), pp. 54–55.

4. Downs assumes that political parties are motivated by winning elections and that "to avoid defeat, the government must support the majority on every issue." Anthony Downs, *An Economic Theory of Democracy* (New York: Harper & Row, 1957), p. 55. Previously, Joseph Schumpeter had made similar claims in his classic work *Capitalism, Socialism and Democracy* (New York: Harper and Row, 1942).

5. As Downs put it, "We can turn Harold Hotelling's famous spatial market into a useful device for analyzing political ideologies. . . . This model confirms Hotelling's conclusion that the parties in a two-party system converge ideologically upon the center, and Smithies' addendum that fear of losing extremist voters keeps them from becoming identical." Downs, *An Economic Theory of Democracy,* pp. 115, 117, 140.

6. Anthony Downs, "An Economic Theory of Political Action in a Democracy," *Journal of Political Economy,* 65(2) (April 1957), p. 143.

7. Ibid., p. 143.

8. One writer opining for the libertarianesque online zine *Taipan* claims that Downs' *An Economic Theory of Democracy* is the most cited book in the discipline of political science. In the span of forty years, a book written by an economist is cited more often than any other "political" book (or article for that matter) written by a political scientist, more than Tocqueville's *Democracy in America,* Woodrow Wilson's *Congressional Government,* Charles Beard's *An Economic Interpretation of the Constitution,* even more than *The Federalist Papers.* See "Why People Don't Vote," http://taipanonline.com/archive/politics/politics-novote.html.

9. Lack of competition is even worse at the state legislative level, where 41 percent of over 7,000 state legislative seats were uncontested by one of the two major parties in both 1998 and 2000.

10. Elizabeth M. DeSouza, "When Tweedle-dee and Tweedle-dum Disagree: Position-Taking Strategies under Varying Electoral Conditions," unpublished paper prepared for delivery at the 2000 annual meeting of the Western Political Science Association, University of North Florida, pp. 1–3, 7, and 28.

11. Ibid., p. 6.

12. To catch a glimpse of the type of dross that has trickled down into mainstream culture and education, here is a passage from *Encyclopedia Britannica*: "Majority or plural methods of voting are most likely to be acceptable in relatively stable political cultures. In such cultures, fluctuations in electoral support, given to one party or another from one election to the next, reduce polarization and make for political centrism (my comment: *like in Angola, India and Algeria,* which use Winner Take All, one wonders?). Thus the 'winner take all' implications of the majority or plurality formulas are not experienced as unduly deprivational or restrictive." *Encyclopedia Britannica,* 2001 Deluxe CD-Rom Edition, article on "Elections: Systems of Counting Votes: Proportional Representation."

13. Paul Rahe, "The Electoral College: A Defense," article published by the Oklahoma Council of Public Affairs, a public policy research and education organization, on the Web at www.ocpathink.org/Governance/TheElectoralCollegeDefense.html. Rahe is the Jay P. Walker Professor of American History at the University of Tulsa. A version of Professor Rahe's article was published in the *American Spectator* on November 14, 2001.

14. See Justice O'Connor's concurring opinion, joined by Chief Justice Burger and Justice Rehnquist, in *Davis v. Bandemer,* 478 U. S. 109, 144-145 (1986), where she declared, "There can be little doubt that the emergence of a strong and stable two-party system in this country has contributed enormously to sound and effective government." Also see Scalia's dissenting opinion, joined by Chief Justice Rehnquist and Justices O'Connor and Kennedy, in *Rutan v. Republican Party of Illinois* (88-1872), 497 U.S. 62 (1990). In the latter, Scalia was opining on the patronage system, and in a loose tangent wrote about the differences between two political parties being moderated by Downsian-like incentives "as each has a relatively greater interest in appealing to a majority of the electorate and a relatively lesser interest in furthering philosophies or programs that are far from the mainstream. The stabilizing effects of such a [two party] system are obvious."

15. Robin Toner, "Willing Contenders at a Premium in Fierce Fight to Rule Congress," *New York Times,* January 3, 2000.

16. Alan I. Abramowitz and Kyle L. Saunders, "Ideological Realignment and U.S. Congressional Elections," a paper prepared for delivery at the annual meeting of the American Political Science Association, September 2000. Copyright 2000 by the American Political Science Association. Abramowitz and Saunders analyzed data from the 1972–1996 American National Election Studies in their efforts to identify major shifts in the behavior of the electorate over time.

17. Other empirical evidence has found that the Democratic and Republican parties, both their elected leaders and their party rank and file, rather than converging ideologically for the past two decades, actually have grown apart ideologically and less centrist. For instance, research has found that party activists have become more extreme than average Americans, and significantly less likely to compromise (they might say "betray") core beliefs. They are ideological purists, making them less likely to shift policy positions to attract the median voter. The preferences and motivations of party loyalists are of significance because almost all elected politicians are drawn from their ranks. Since the mid-1970s, some of the strongest partisans have been showing up in the United States Congress. Bills that read more like ideological litmus tests have become increasingly common—both among Democratic leadership throughout the 1970s and 1980s and under Republican leadership in the mid-1990s. See David C. King, "The Polarization of American Political Parties and Mistrust of Government," Harvard University Working Paper, www.ksg.harvard.edu/prg/king/polar.htm. King's paper was included as a chapter in Joseph S. Nye, Philip D. Zelikow, and David C. King, eds., *Why People Don't Trust Government* (Cambridge, MA: Harvard University Press, 1997).

18. Sarah A. Binder, "Going Nowhere, a Gridlocked Congress?" *Brookings Review*, Winter 2000, Vol. 18, No. 1, p. 19. Binder, a congressional scholar at the Brookings Institution, has charted the recent disappearance of centrists, estimating a decline from about one-quarter of all members in 1980 to 10 percent in 1996.

19. Abramowitz and Saunders, "Ideological Realignment and U.S. Congressional Elections."

20. Donald Stokes in 1963 challenged the linear/one-dimensional spatial arrangement of the model, writing that "most spatial interpretations of party competition have a very poor fit with the evidence about how large-scale electorates and party leaders actually respond to politics. . . . The 'space' in which American parties contend for ideological support is very unlike a single ideological dimension." To illustrate, Stokes noted that voters often position themselves differently with respect to domestic and foreign policy issues, making it difficult for politicians who attempt to identify themselves only along a single liberal-conservative axis. Donald E. Stokes, "Spatial Models of Party Competition," *American Political Science Review*, 57(2) (June 1963), p. 368.

21. Downs, *An Economic Theory of Democracy*, p. 68. As previously noted, Downs assumes that political parties are motivated by winning elections, that "to avoid defeat, the government must support the majority on every issue" (p. 55), and that "a majority of the legislature is always equivalent to a majority of those voting" (footnote, p. 144).

22. Lawrence R. Jacobs and Robert Y. Shapiro, *Politicians Don't Pander: Political Manipulation and the Loss of Democratic Responsiveness* (Chicago: University of Chicago Press, 2000). For useful reviews of this interesting work, see Daniel Yankelovich, "Guise and Pols," *American Prospect*, September 25, 2000, p. 75; and Richard Morin, *Washington Post*, March 19, 2000.

23. Jacobs and Shapiro, *Politicians Don't Pander*, quoted from the preface.

24. David C. King, "The Polarization of American Political Parties and Mistrust of Government," Harvard University Working Paper, www.ksg.harvard.edu/prg/king/polar.htm. King's paper was included as a chapter in Joseph S. Nye, Philip D. Zelikow and David C. King, editors, *Why People Don't Trust Government* (Harvard University Press: Cambridge MA, 1997).

25. See Alison Mitchell, "Bush's Tax Cut Tactics Show Hardball Beating Conciliation," *New York Times*, March 9, 2001.

26. John D. Huber and G. Bingham Powell, Jr., "Congruence between Citizens and Policymakers in Two Visions of Liberal Democracy," *World Politics*, 46 (April 1994), pp. 291–326. Under the Majority Control vision Huber and Powell placed the democracies of Australia, Great Britain, and New Zealand (the latter has since become a mixed system). Under the Proportionate Influence vision category Huber and Powell placed the democracies of Belgium, Denmark, Italy, and Netherlands, which all used what has been called "extreme" proportional representation; under the mixed category was Germany, which uses a combination of U.S.-style Winner Take All single-seat districts and proportional representation, and France, Ireland, Spain, and Sweden, each of which had either some notable majoritarian properties or proportional influence properties, but also some features that the authors figured diminished the fit.

27. G. Bingham Powell Jr., *Elections as Instruments of Democracy: Majoritarian and Proportional Visions* (New Haven, CT: Yale University Press, October 2000).

Chapter Thirteen: The Roller-Coaster Policy Ride of Winner Take All

1. All of the Republican House impeachment managers except one hailed from some of the safest Republican districts in the country—a prime reason they were selected to be House managers in the first place. Four ran unopposed in 1998, and only three of them won with less than 63 percent of the vote. Only one of them, Rep. James Rogan in California, was considered vulnerable, and indeed Rogan was the only impeachment manager to lose reelection in 2000. Nicholas Confessore, "Targeting House Managers?" *American Prospect*, May 8, 2000, p. 8.

2. In theoretical terms, this political reality of safe-seat politicians taking bold ideological positions disputes the traditional "centrist convergence model" of two-party systems promulgated by neo-Downsians and others.

3. Charles Madigan, "'Safe' Politicians Driving Impeachment," *The Missoulian*, October 29, 1998.

4. From 1994 to 1998, 141 U.S. House primaries and eighteen U.S. Senate primaries resulted in winners who did not gain a majority of the vote. For example, in 1998, one new House member won his party's primary with only 23 percent of the vote; in 1994 a House member won his party primary with less than 20 percent.

5. "Don't Repeal Runoff Primary," *St. Petersburg Times*, March 31, 2001.

6. Jill Lawrence, "County vs. City, Spelled in Red and Blue," *USA Today*, November 9, 2000, p. 19A.

7. As far as the concerns about the integrity of the office being sullied by presidential lying, who can remember any Republican qualms over their president, Ronald Reagan, who sat on the witness stand and invoked his "I can't remember" chorus forty-seven times to questions regarding his illegal funding of Nicaraguan mercenaries and other shady dealings? The sudden Republican conversion to truth-telling appeared, like so much of today's politics, an opportunistic ruse.

8. Polls varied, but at least 62 percent of the public disagreed with the House's impeachment of President Clinton. After House members voted 228–206 to charge the president with perjury concerning his relationship with a White House intern, 65 percent of the public stated it was better for the country that he finish his term. And 72 percent of the public stated they approved of the way Clinton was handling his job. Adam Nagourney with Michael R. Kagan, "Public Support for the President, and for Closure, Emerges Unshaken," *New York Times,* December 21, 1998.

9. See, for example, Edward Walsh, "House Impeachment Leaders Are Managing Just Fine," *Washington Post*, May 22, 2001, p. A19.

10. Jeffrey Kluger, "Space Pork," *Time*, July 24, 2000, pp. 24–26.

11. Robert Novak, "Spending Unlimited . . .", *Washington Post*, Thursday, June 24, 1999, p. A27.

12. Cal Thomas, "Those Spendthrift Republicans," syndicated column published on the opinion page of the *New London Day,* December 2000.

13. Jeanne Cummings and David Rogers, "As House Passes Budget, Clinton Savors a Win," *Wall Street Journal*, November 19, 1999, p. A22.

14. Thomas, "Those Spendthrift Republicans."

15. Most of this episode draws heavily from William D. Hartung, "Ready for What? The New Politics of Pentagon Spending," *World Policy Journal*, Spring 1999.

16. Alison Mitchell, "Clinton, Avoiding Party Split, Signs Military Fund Bill," *New York Times*, October 26, 1999, p. A19.

17. For instance, ignoring the Navy's wishes, two Republican members of the House Armed Services Committee pushed to reopen a closed assembly line of soon-to-be-obsolete Tomahawk cruise missiles that would benefit a company in one of the lawmaker's districts. Associated Press wire story, "Support for Missiles the Navy Doesn't Want," July 8, 1999. During one round of negotiations, the Republicans even added $1 million for the Army to conduct research on socks. Chronicle News Services, "House Approves $290 Billion Defense Budget," *San Francisco Chronicle*, July 20, 2000, p. A10; Associated Press story, "Congress Passes Pentagon Spending Hike of $20 Billion," *San Francisco Examiner*, July 28, 2000, p. B10.

18. Mitchell, "Clinton, Avoiding Party Split, Signs Military Fund Bill," p. A1.

19. David Abel, "GAO Slams Pentagon Fraud, Waste, Abuse," *Defense Week*, February 1, 1999.

20. Associated Press, "Official Acknowledges Pentagon Books a Mess," Saturday, March 4, 2000; Tim Weiner, "Pentagon Misused Millions in Funds, House Panel Says," *New York Times*, July 21, 1999, p. A1.

21. Abel, "GAO Slams Pentagon Fraud, Waste, Abuse."

22. Astonishingly, the second largest and most capable air force in the world, besides the current U.S. Air Force, is sitting in *mothballs* at the U.S. government's "boneyard" at Davis Air Force Base in Arizona, in the form of fighter jets, transports, and attack aircraft that have been retired prematurely to make room for the new improved models. Hartung, "Ready for What?" p. 19. The world's top military spenders in 1997 were the United States at $276 billion; China, $75 billion; Russia and France, $42 billion; Japan, $41 billion; Britain, $35 billion; and Germany, $33 billion. Barry Schweid, "U.S. Leads All Nations as Weapons Spending Rises, State Dept. Says," Associated Press story in the *San Francisco Chronicle*, August 22, 2000, p. A7.

23. Much of this anecdote was reported by Daniel J. Murphy, "Social Security's Trust Deficit," *Investor's Business Daily*, May 4, 1999, p. A1.

24. See Howard Kurtz, "Attack Ads Carpet TV," *Washington Post,* October 20, 1998, p. A1. According to Kurtz, the Clinton campaign had charged that the Republicans tried to cut $270 million from Medicare, but that was in fact a distortion of a GOP plan to slow the rate of growth in the medical insurance program.

25. See Edmund L. Andrews, "Germany Clears Way for Pension Reform," New York Times Service, published in the *International Herald Tribune,* May 12, 2001; and *The Economist,* "Germany's Pension Reform," May 10, 2001.

26. Richard W. Stevenson, "Seeking Common Ground on Federal Tax Cut," *New York Times,* July 25, 1999.

27. Miles Benson, "Politicians Find U.S. Public Easy to Manipulate," Newhouse News Service, story published in the *San Francisco Examiner,* October 24, 1999, p. A. 12.

28. See Alison Mitchell, "Hastert Triumphs, but Faces a Long High-Stakes Negotiation," *New York Times,* July 22, 1999; and Alison Mitchell, "A Speaker under Pressure Beseeches the Membership," *New York Times,* July 20, 1999. Also see James Dao, "Shift on Tax-Cut Bill: Gain or Loss for Moderates?" *New York Times,* July 24, 1999, p. A9.

29. The compromise was an agreement that the largest component of the tax cut would take effect only if regular progress had been made in bringing down the national debt. It turned out that the compromise was nothing more than a hastily arranged and poorly understood gimmick. It created a "trigger" for the tax cuts that made little sense. In the light of day, when outside tax experts on both sides of the tax-cut debate had a chance to read the final measure with its triggering mechanism, they pronounced it absurd. "It's just a dumb idea," said one Republican economist, a Treasury official in the Reagan Administration and a devotee of deep tax reductions. David E. Rosenbaum, "'Gimmick' Eased Passage of Tax Bill," *New York Times,* July 23, 1999.

30. Rosenbaum, "'Gimmick' Eased Passage of Tax Bill."

31. Anthony King, "Running Scared," *The Atlantic Monthly,* January 1997, p. 49.

32. Ibid., p. 48.

33. The *Denver Post* reported on February 15, 2001, that "both the U.S. Surgeon General and the National Academy of Sciences have issued reports saying that DARE's approach is ineffective. . . . One six-year study by the University of Illinois found that the program's effects wore off by senior year of high school; in fact, it detected some increased use of drugs by suburban high schoolers who had taken the program. A 10-year study by the University of Kentucky found the program had no effect on students by the time they were 20." Meanwhile, a new study by Columbia University's Center on Addiction and Substance Abuse reports that parents are the key to kids avoiding drugs. The *Chicago Tribune* reported Feb. 24, 2001, that "Children who live with attentive parents stand a better chance of never using drugs than do those with 'hands-off' parents," according to the Center's sixth annual report on attitudes of US teens on drug use, peer pressure, and parental involvement.

34. Eric Schmitt, "House OKs Tax-Cut, Minimum-Wage Bill," *New York Times,* Friday, March 10, 2000.

35. Michael Grunwald, "A Quiet Crisis in Housing Prices," *Washington Post,* Monday, March 6, 2000, p. A6.

36. Ibid., p. A6.

37. Not that Democrats have been perfectly respondent to urban needs. While cities can suffer under Republicans who don't depend on urban voters, they also can suffer under complacent Democrats who feel they can take their urban constituency's political support for granted.

38. "Losing Patience," editorial in the *Minneapolis Star-Tribune*, June 16, 2001, p. A22.
39. Elizabeth Becker, "Treaties May Curb Farmers' Subsidies," *New York Times*, August 31, 2001, p. A1.
40. Michael Grunwald, "Pork Barrel Prevalent Despite GOP Vows," *Washington Post*, August 3, 1999, p. A1.
41. Gail Collins, "Politics of Real Pork," *New York Times*, January 18, 2000.
42. "Rethink the Farms," *Washington Post* editorial, October 1, 2001, p. A20.
43. For instance, one Toyota advertisement in 1999 said, "Democrats say Toyota Camry is the #1 selling car in America, two years in any row. Republicans say Toyota Camry is the #1 selling car in America, two years in any row. Scary, huh?" Popular singer Sheryl Crow had one song containing the lyrics, "Allegations, interrogations, investigations, then more taxation. National pastime is aggravation. . . . All you politicians do is fight." "Subway" by Sheryl Crow, *The Globe Sessions*, 1998.
44. Wendy Koch, "Legislators Leave Some Issues Dangling till Next Year," *USA Today*, November 22, 1999, p. 13A.
45. *USA Today*, "Poor-Quality Tests Threaten School-Reform Efforts," editorial, December 28, 2001, p. 13A. According to *USA Today*, standardized tests have been plagued by administration mistakes and bungled test scores. For instance, Maryland school officials delayed releasing statewide testing results when they noticed "wild swings" and fluctuating test scores that defied logical explanation. In 1999, scroing errors on tests in New York City mistakenly forced 8000 students to attend summer school and another 3500 to be mistakenly held back a grade. And in Arizona, thousands of students were affected by inaccurate math and reading scores on the state exam. State testing directors who work with the publishers of these standardized tests say the quality problems stem from a lack of competent test experts who can adequately handle jobs such as test design, printing and scoring.
46. William M. Welch, "Lawmakers Back at Each Other's Throats," *USA Today*, December 28, 2001, p. 2A.

Chapter Fourteen: The Gatekeepers of Winner Take All

1. Guy Gugliotta, "Study Finds Millions of Votes Lost," *Washington Post*, July 17, 2001, p. A1. Also see the press release from the Voting Technology Project, a comprehensive Caltech–MIT study initiated after the November election debacle, http://vote.caltech.edu, July 16, 2001. "This study shows that the voting problem is much worse than we expected," said Caltech president David Baltimore, who initiated the nonpartisan study. "It is remarkable that we in America put up with a system where as many as six out of every hundred voters are unable to get their vote counted. Twenty-first-century technology should be able to do much better than this," Baltimore said.
2. To see a Brazilian ballot, visit www.tse.gov.br/eleicoes/eleicoes2000/Urna/index.htm and click on "Veja como se vota na Urna Eletrônica" to cast a simulated vote for several offices. The Brazilian national election site is www.tse.gov.br.
3. Los Angeles Times Staff Writers, "A 'Modern' Democracy That Can't Count Votes," *Los Angeles Times*, December 11, 2000. Posted at www.latimes.com.
4. Gugliotta, "Study Finds Millions of Votes Lost," p. A1.
5. Reid Forgrave, "Candidate Who Says He Was Tricked Gets His Name off Ballot," *Seattle Times*, August 11, 2001, p. B1. Also see Neil Modie, "Greens Say Republicans Crashed Their Party," *Seattle Post-Intelligencer*, August 7, 2001, p. A1.
6. See Steven Hill, "Taming the Electoral Beast," *Italy Daily/International Herald Tribune*, May 18, 2000, p. 2. As one Italian political scientist commented: "The argument that Italy is evidence that proportional representation carries instability may be rejected by arguing that, being unstable in Italy was not cured, but even enhanced, by Winner Take All." A slightly more enlightened editorial view than the *New York Times'* comes from one of London's leading daily newspapers, *The Independent*, which wrote in 1999 that "opponents of proportional representation have often cited Italy as an example to show the dangers of a proportional system. But the Italians have built an economy as successful as [Britain's]. Italy's postwar political mess was not the fault of proportional representation; it was the product of the determination of the Western Allies to block the Italian Communist Party from ever being in power." *The Independent*, editorial, "The Italians Can Teach Us Something about Referendums," April 20, 1999.
7. "Gore's Time Ran Out; Democracy Wins," *Chicago Sun-Times* editorial, December 13, 2000.

8. Jonathan Alter, "36 Days: The Fallout," *Newsweek*, Dec. 25, 2000, p. 55.

9. *New York Times*, editorial, December 3, 2000.

10. Frances E. Lee and Bruce I. Oppenheimer, *Sizing Up the Senate* (Chicago: University of Chicago Press, 1999), pp. 4–5.

11. Gary King and Bradley Palmquist, "The Record of American Democracy, 1984 to 1990." Prefatory statement received by e-mail publicly announcing the availability of a new aggregate data set on American politics called Record of American Democracy (ROAD), September 1997.

12. Henry E. Brady, Justin Buchler, Matt Jarvis, and Matt McNulty, "Counting the Votes: The Performance of Voting Technology in the United States," report from the Department of Political Science, Survey Research Center, and Institute of Governmental Studies, University of California, Berkeley, September 2001, pp. 1, 5, and 47.

13. King and Palmquist, "The Record of American Democracy, 1984 to 1990."

14. To see examples of these various indices, visit the Web site of the Center for Voting and Democracy and its report, *Dubious Democracy 2001*, published on the Web at www.fairvote.org/2001/index.html.

15. In the final decade of the twentieth century, eschatology—the study of the "end of things"—became one of publishing's growth industries. Among the more notable "End of . . ." titles to appear in bookstores were *The End of Nature* (Bill McKibben), *End of Millennium* (Manuel Castells), *The End of Education* (Neil Postman), *The End of History* (Francis Fukuyama), *The End of Equality* (Mickey Kaus), *The End of Work* (Jeremy Rifkin), and *The End of Science* (John Horgan). Ilya Prigogine, a chaos theorist, gave lectures on "the end of certainty" that were lapped up by, according to one observer, "sycophantic disciples." For an amusing reflection on this eschatological scatology, see Scott Rosenberg's "Been There, Discovered It," at www.Salon.com.

Chapter Fifteen: "Winner Takes Nothing"

1. James Warren, "Some Vintage Nixon Saves the Day," *Chicago Tribune*, August 19, 2001.

2. William G. Sinnigen and Arthur E. R. Boak, *A History of Rome to A.D. 565* (New York: Macmillan Publishing Co., 1977), pp. 71–72. However, the voting in the Centuriate Assembly was weighted in such a way as to allow the wealthier elements always to outvote the poorest.

3. Sinnigen and Boak, *A History of Rome to A.D. 565*, pp. 68, 70, and 78.

4. For instance, Roman senators' fear of unbridled popular legislative power played a role in the passage of a peculiar law about 150 B.C. which provided that a magistrate could be prevented from passing a bill on religious grounds by another magistrate claiming to have witnessed unfavorable omens, in a procedure called *obnuntiatio*. Imagine such a procedure in the hands of Republicans or Democrats.

5. In cumulative voting, voters cast as many votes as there are contested seats in a multi-seat district (single-seat districts are not used). But unlike Winner Take All systems, voters are not limited to giving only one vote to a candidate. Instead, they can put multiple votes on one or more candidates running in the multiseat district. Cumulative voting uses the same victory threshold as the proportional representation system known as choice voting, such that if four seats are being elected any candidate or political party winning 20 percent of the vote will win one seat, 40 percent will win two seats, and so on. Cumulative voting was used to elect the Illinois state legislature from 1870 to 1980, and in recent years it has been used to resolve voting rights cases for city council elections in Amarillo (TX) and Peoria (IL), for county commission elections in Chilton County (AL), and for school board elections in Sisseton (SD) and more than fifty other jurisdictions. Example: in a race to elect four candidates, voters cast one vote for each of four candidates, all four votes for one candidate or a combination in between. Candidates win by a simple plurality of votes, but any candidate reaching the victory threshold of 20 percent is guaranteed to win one seat.

6. Robyn Followwill, "Cumulative Voting," *Amarillo Globe-News*, (August 1, 1999).

7. "Alternative electoral systems" like cumulative voting, limited voting, and choice voting (also known as preference voting or the "single transferable vote") are designed to provide more opportunity for the electoral viability of geographic minorities than the traditional, Winner Take All method, even though they do not involve the use of single-seat districts. Each such system features elections held jurisdiction-wide ("multiseat"), without carving the jurisdiction into subdistricts. See Edward Still, "Alternatives to Single-Member Districts," *Minority Vote Dilution*, ed. C. Davidson (Washington, DC: Howard University Press, 1984).

8. Richard L. Engstrom, "Modified Multi-Seat Election Systems as Remedies for Minority Vote Dilution," *Stetson Law Review*, 21 (1992), pp. 743, 750; Richard Engstrom, Delbert A. Taebel, and Richard L. Cole, "Cumulative Voting as a Remedy for Minority Vote Dilution: The Case of Alamogordo," *Journal of Law and Politics*, 5 (Spring 1989), pp. 469–497; Richard Engstrom and Charles Barrilleaux, "Native Americans and Cumulative Voting: The Sisseton-Wahpeton Sioux," *Social Science Quarterly*, 72 (1991), pp. 388, 391–392; Robert Brischetto and Richard Engstrom, "Cumulative Voting and Latino Representation: Exit Surveys in Fifteen Texas Communities," *Social Science Quarterly*, 78 (1997), p. 4.

9. David Brockington, Todd Donovan, Shaun Bowler, and Robert Brischetto, "Minority Representation under Limited and Cumulative Voting," *Journal of Politics*, 60 (November 1998), pp. 1108–1125.

10. Jerome Gray, *Winning Fair Representation in At-Large Elections: Cumulative Voting and Limited Voting in Alabama Local Elections* (Washington, DC: Southern Regional Council and Center for Voting and Democracy, 1999).

11. Peoria actually uses a mixed system since a voting rights settlement in 1988, combining cumulative voting with single-seat districts. The districts seats are subject to redistricting. Richard H. Pildes and Kristen A. Donoghue, "Cumulative Voting in the United States," *University of Chicago Legal Forum* (1995), pp. 241–313.

12. The "victory threshold" of representation for proportional voting systems is based on all contested seats in a multiseat district being made equal to the same number of votes. The threshold can be determined by one of two formulas. The first, called the Hare threshold, is determined by dividing the number of contested seats into 100 percent. For three seats, that would be 100 percent ÷ 3 = 33.3 percent. The second, called the Droop threshold, is determined by dividing the number of contested seats + 1 into 100 percent, and adding one more vote to that. Using this threshold, three seats produces a victory threshold of 25 percent, plus one more vote.

$$\frac{100\% \text{ of total number of votes cast}}{\text{number of contested seats} + 1} = \frac{100\%}{3+1} = 25\% \ (+ \ 1 \text{ more vote})$$

Qualitatively, the Droop threshold is equal to the least number of votes a candidate needs to win such that, when all seats are filled, there are not enough votes left over to elect another candidate.

13. Using the Hare calculation, the victory threshold would be 100 percent ÷ 10 = 10 percent of the popular vote needed to win one seat, 20 percent to win two seats, 60 percent to win six seats, and so on.

14. For instance, while representation for women in the U.S. House is still stuck at a paltry 13 percent, nearly ten years after the "Year of the Woman," the top ten nations for women's representation are all proportional representation democracies, with rates up to three times higher: Sweden, 43 percent; Finland, 37 percent; Denmark, 37 percent; Netherlands, 36 percent; Norway, 36 percent; Iceland, 35 percent; Germany, 31 percent; Austria, 26 percent; South Africa, 25 percent; and Belgium, 23 percent. Of particular note is Germany, which uses a mixed system combining U.S.-style single-seat districts with a proportional system, and where women tend to win *three* times as many seats in the national legislature under the proportional election than under the Winner Take All election. Other democracies that use a similar mixed system, such as New Zealand and Italy, also tend to elect two to three times the number of women under the proportional elections as under the Winner Take All elections.

15. Besides the previously cited jurisdictions using cumulative voting, limited voting is used for county commissions in Pennsylvania, for City Council in Hartford, CT, and Philadelphia, and for various local races in Alabama. Choice voting, also known as single transferable vote and preference voting, is used for City Council and school board elections in Cambridge, Massachusetts, and for community school board elections in New York City. Cumulative voting also is used by numerous corporations to elect their Board of Directors, including Hewlett-Packard, Walgreen's, Toys 'R' Us, Sun Microsystems, Aon, Abbott Labs, Industrie Canada, Pennzoil, Ingersoll-Rand, Lockheed-Martin, VWR Corporation, American Premier, and Allegheny Power System; and choice voting is used by the Academy Awards to select the five finalists in each major category, by universities like Stanford University and University of California–Berkeley to elect their student government, and by Price Waterhouse, the global accounting firm, to elect their national and international boards of directors.

16. The Institute for Democracy and Electoral Assistance (IDEA) defines "established democracies" as those states with a population of more than a quarter of a million which have held continuing free elections for over twenty years. Of those democracies twenty-one out of thirty-six nations (59 percent) use proportional systems. See the *International IDEA Handbook of Electoral System Design* (Stockholm, Sweden: International Institute for Democracy and Electoral Assistance, 1997), p. 21.

17. This list is compiled by political scientist Mark Rush. See the table on the Web site of the Center for Voting and Democracy, www.fairvote.org/library/geog/Europe/systems.htm.

18. Election Day voter registration is used effectively in six states—Maine, Minnesota, Wisconsin, New Hampshire, Wyoming, and Idaho. Those states have some of the highest voter turnouts in the nation, and include large metropolitan areas such as Minneapolis–St. Paul. Also, North Dakota has no voter registration at all, a voter just shows up at the polls with identification and evidence of address.

19. Political scientists Rein Taagepera and Matthew Shugart analyzed apportionment systems around the world and found that the size of the largest legislative body of a national legislature today tends to be the cube root of the voting age population. Using that calculation, the size of the U.S. House would be 588 members today. Although that formula tracks the size of the House fairly well between 1790 and 1910, in 1910 the House stopped growing. Margo Anderson, "Growth in U.S. Population Calls for Larger House of Representatives," *Population Today*, 28(3) (April 2000), p. 4. Anderson is a professor of American history at the University of Wisconsin-Milwaukee.

20. Compared to other nations, legislative districts for many states, counties, and cities in the United States contain ridiculously high numbers of residents. State senate districts in California, for example, have approximately 800,000 residents. City Council districts in the cities of Houston, Phoenix, San Diego, and Los Angeles all have approximately 150,000 residents or more, with Los Angeles the highest at 240,000 residents per city council district. Incredulously, the five districts for the county government of Los Angeles County each have a whopping 2 million residents, an astronomical number that renders any notions of "geographic" representation into an absurd joke.

21. Anderson, "Growth in U.S. Population Calls for Larger House of Representatives," p. 1.

Epilogue: Toward "E Pluribus Unum"

1. Gaetano Mosca, *The Ruling Class*, quoted in James H. Meisel, *The Myth of the Ruling Class* (Ann Arbor: University of Michigan Press, 1958), p. v.

BIBLIOGRAPHY / RESOURCES

Amy, Douglas J. *Behind the Ballot Box: A Citizen's Guide to Voting Systems*. Westport. CT: Praeger Publishing, 2000.

Amy, Douglas J. *Real Choices/New Voices: How Proportional Representation Elections Could Revitalize American Democracy* (second edition). New York: Columbia University Press, 2002.

Barber, Kathleen. *A Right to Representation: Proportional Election Systems for the Twenty-first Century*. Columbus: Ohio State University Press, 2000.

Cole, K.C. *The Universe and the Teacup: The Mathematics of Truth and Beauty*. New York: Harcourt & Brace, 1998.

Dahl, Robert. *How Democratic Is the American Constitution?* New Haven: Yale University Press, 2002.

Douglas J, Amy. *Real Choices/New Voices: How Proportional Representation Elections Could Revitalize American Democracy (Second edition)*. New York: Columbia University Press, 2002.

Downs, Anthony. *The Economic Theory of Democracy*. New York: Harper and Row, 1957.

Guinier, Lani. *Lift Every Voice, Turning A Civil Rights Setback Into A New Vision Of Social Justice*. New York: Simon & Schuster, 1998.

Hayduk, Ronald and Kevin Mattson (editors). *Democracy's Moment: Reforming the American Political System for the 21st Century*. Lanham, MD: Rowman and Littlefield, 2002.

Keyssar, Alexander. *The Right to Vote: The Contested History of Democracy in the United States*. New York: Basic Books, 2000.

Lijphart, Arend. *Patterns of Democracy: Government Forms and Performance in Thirty-Six Countries*. New Haven: Yale University Press, 1999.

Milner, Henry (editor). *Making Every Vote Count: Reassessing Canada's Electoral System*. Peterborough, Ont., Canada ; Orchard Park, N.Y. : Broadview Press, 1999.

Monmonier, Mark S. *Bushmanders & Bullwinkles: How Politicians Manipulate Electronic Maps and Census Data to Win Elections*. Chicago: University of Chicago Press, 2001.

Powell, Jr., G. Bingham. *Elections as Instruments of Democracy*. New Haven: Yale University Press, 2000.

Reynolds, Andrew and Ben Reilly *The International IDEA Handbook of Electoral System Design*. Sweden: Broderna Carlssons Boktryckeri AB, 1997.

Richie, Robert and Steven Hill. *Whose Vote Counts?* Boston: Beacon Press, 2001.

Rule, Wilma and Joseph F. Zimmerman (editors). *United States Electoral Systems: Their Impact on Women and Minorities*, New York: Praeger, 1993.

Rush, Mark E. and Richard L. Engstrom. *Fair and Effective Representation*, Lanham, MD: Rowman & Littlefield, 2001.

Sifry, Micah. *Spoiling for a Fight: Third Party Politics in America*. New York: Routledge Press, 2002.

Taagepera, Rein and Matthew Soberg Shugart. *Seats & Votes: The Effects & Determinants of Electoral Systems*. New Haven: Yale University Press, 1989.

Zimmerman, Joseph F. and Wilma Rule (editors). *The U.S. House of Representatives: Reform or Rebuild?* Westport, CT: Praeger Press, 2000.

Web sites

Center for Voting and Democracy, www.fairvote.org

Proportional Representation Library, www.mtholyoke.edu/acad/polit/damy/prlib.htm

International Institute for Democracy and Electoral Assistance (IDEA), www.idea.int

Demos, www.demos-usa.org

Common Cause, www.commoncause.org

US PIRG, www.uspirg.org

INDEX

ABC, 183, 192–93, 197, 329n. 11
Abramowitz, Alan, 230, 231, 341n. 16
accountability, 88, 228
Adams, John, xv, 65, 273, 307n. 24, 314n. 3, 317n. 7
Adams, Samuel, 307n. 24, 314n. 3
Adams, Senator Brock, 121
advertising, 150, 189 (see also television ads; media)
affirmative action, 4, 18, 66, 102, 104, 107, 125, 127, 136, 153, 167, 204, 279–81, 286, 332n. 19; Electoral College, 25–26, 29, 128–29, 260, 280; for conservatives, 25–26, 125–29; for low-population states, 119–37, 280, 286
African Americans, 4, 5, 9, 12, 17, 18, 26, 33, 45, 46, 65, 102, 104, 120–21, 131, 136, 153, 159, 281–82, 288–90, 310n. 52, 312n. 10, 322n. 29, 325n. 29, 326n. 44
agribusiness, 258–60, 286
agricultural policy, 223, 258–60
Alabama, 8, 216, 290, 297, 306n. 19, 308n. 19, 309n. 33, 310n. 37, 326n. 44, 346n. 15
Alaska, 8, 266, 286, 308n. 16
Algeria, 33, 293
Alliance for Better Campaigns, 190, 192, 193, 334n. 8
allocation: disproportionate, 123; electoral, 37; proportional, 5, 29, 311nn. 4
Alter, Jonathan, 174, 327n. 57
American: children, 205, 210, 212, 247, 337n. 6; Farm Bureau Federation, 260; Independent Party, 13, 308n. 19; Revolution, 46; workers, 204–206, 262
American politics, viii, xi, xvi, 5, 12, 17, 19, 38, 40, 45, 52–53, 59, 64, 78, 117, 142, 150, 186, 195, 199, 202, 211, 215, 218, 227, 232, 271, 273–75, 284, 287, 297; and television, 142–43, 150 (see also advertising; media; television ads)
American society: diversity of, 12–13, 41–42, 280, 309n. 33; racial makeup of, 12–13, 32
Amy, Douglas, 54, 111
Anderson, John, 186, 187
Angola, 293
Annenberg Public Policy Center, 189–90
Archer, Bill, 243
Arctic National Wildlife Refuge, 208
Argentina, 129
Arizona, 8, 12, 20, 26, 115, 273, 305n. 9, 323nn. 19
Arkansas, 8, 13, 51, 73, 272, 290
Arkansas Education TV v. Forbes, 183
Armey, Representative Dick, 67, 87, 115, 241
Arrow, Kenneth, 224, 292

Ashcroft, Senator John, 321n. 27
Asian Americans, 12, 280
Asians, 4, 12, 19, 46, 102, 136, 317n. 5
Atwater, Lee, 153
Australia, 24, 92, 307n. 20, 311n. 3, 341n. 26

baffleds, 52–53
Baird, Representative Brian, 74
Baker, Russell, 142
ballot(s), 21–22, 216, 270; absentee, 30; access laws, ix, 216–17, 218, 265, 267, 296, 338n. 28; design of, 22, 296, 311n. 1; initiatives, 146, 155; recounts of, 296; secret, 141, 279; system, 22, 267
Baltimore, David, 311n. 1, 344n. 1
Barak, Ehud, 334n. 44
Barnes, Governor Roy, 309n. 20
Barone, Michael, 20, 30, 99
Bates, Senator Isaacs, 315n. 10
Bellow, Saul, 177
Benjamin, Medea, 183–84, 185
Bereano, Phil, 207
Berlusconi, Silvio, 200
Berman, Michael, 82
Bernstein, Carl, 144
Billmire, Richard, 144–45
Binder, Sarah, 16
Blair, Tony, 48, 101, 236, 334n. 44
Bloomberg, Mayor Michael, 18, 309n. 27
Bonior, Representative David, 208
Bradley, Bill, 56, 192, 209
Braun, Senator Carol Moseley, 121
Brazaitis, Tom, 276
Brazil, 12, 129, 265
Brennan, Justice William, 188
Britain, 24, 48–49, 50, 92, 130, 217, 265, 295, 296, 317n. 4, 341n. 26; Conservative Party, 49; democracy in, 132, 135; elections in, 48, 89, 217, 268, 294, 311n. 3, 325n. 27; House of Commons, 48, 294; House of Lords, 122, 280–81; Labor Party, 48–49, 101
Broder, David, 119
Brooks, David, 19
Brown, Willie, 80
Buchanan, James, 310n. 37
Buchanan, Pat, 18, 19, 23, 24
budget: appropriations, 242–44; balanced, 125, 214, 243; deficit, 262; military, 244–45, 247, 342n. 17; surpluses, 248, 251, 253, 262
Burton, Phil, 80
Burton, Representative Dan, 144, 241